A Taste of the Past

A Taste of the Past

The Daily Life and Cooking of a Nineteenth-Century Hungarian Jewish Homemaker

ANDRÁS KOERNER

with illustrations by the author

University Press of New England • HANOVER AND LONDON

University Press of New England, 37 Lafayette St., Lebanon, NH 03766
© 2004 by András Koerner
All rights reserved
Printed in the United States of American
5 4 3 2 1

LIBRARY OF CONGRESS CATALOGING-IN-PUBLICATION DATA
Koerner, András.
  A taste of the past : the daily life and cooking of a nineteenth-century Hungarian-Jewish homemaker / András Koerner. — 1st ed.
    p. cm.
  Includes bibliographical references and index.
  ISBN 1–58465–209–8 (cloth : alk. paper)
   1. Cookery, Hungarian. 2. Cookery, Jewish. I. Title.
TX723.5.H8 K64 2004
641.5'676'09439 – dc22   2003016336

To the memory of my mother,
who told me most of these stories,
and to Max, my grandson,
who I hope one day will enjoy them.

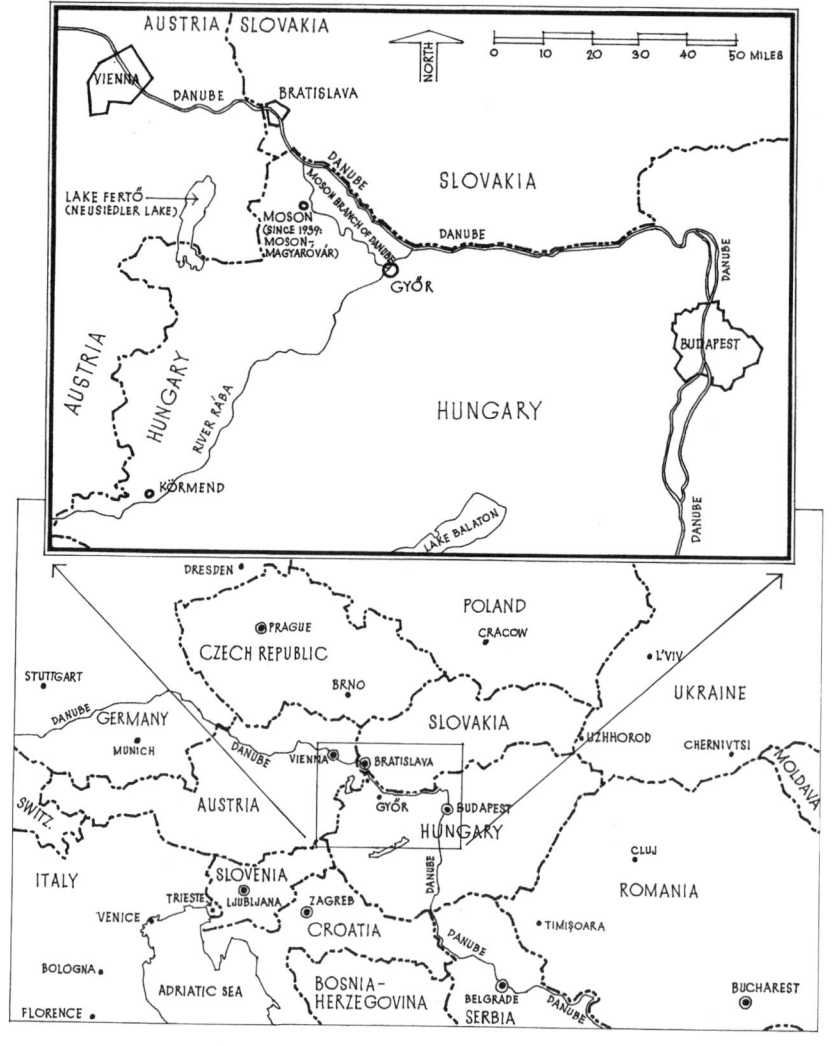

Map of the region described in the text.

CONTENTS

PREFACE — xi

PART ONE (1851–1876)

The House in Győr — 1

The Education of Therese Baruch — 3

Cultural ambitions: poetry and letter writing / Should women pursue a profession? / National identity / Charity / Social life / Christian friends / Conflicts with parents concerning Christian friends / Intermarriage and conversion of a Jewish friend / Love / Pressure from parents to get married / Marriage

PART TWO (1876–1926)

The House in Moson — 31

A Journey to the Past — 35

A Typical Day at Riza Néni's — 47

MORNINGS AT RIZA NÉNI'S — 47

Flatbread for snack, 62 / *Corn cake*, 67 / Putting Up Fruits and Vegetables, 68 / The Kitchen and the Pantry at Riza Néni's, 71 / Dietary Laws in Transition, 76

LUNCHES AT RIZA NÉNI'S 77

Green pea soup with egg dumplings, 83 / *Boiled beef*, 86 / *Beef-vegetable soup*, 88 / *Ginger-flavored soup biscuits*, 89 / *Liver dumplings for soup*, 91 / *Braised chicken with game sauce*, 93 / *Almond-studded meatballs in sweet-and-sour sauce*, 96 / *Gooseberry sauce for boiled beef*, 98 / *Braised beef with vegetable sauce*, 99 / *Braised veal cutlets in onion-lemon sauce*, 101 / *Braised veal tongue "Bohemian" style*, 104 / *Noodles with toasted farina*, 107 / *Cabbage dumplings*, 108 / *Farina-potato dumplings*, 111 / *Potato dumplings*, 113 / *Kohlrabi*, 116 / *Green pea purée*, 119 / *Green beans*, 120 / *Fermented dill pickles*, 123 / *Almond-meringue noodles*, 126 / *Farina dessert dumplings*, 128 / *Potato dessert dumplings*, 130 / *Plum-filled bread dumplings*, 133 / *Napkin dessert dumpling with vanilla sauce*, 136 / *Yeast crêpes*, 139 / *Baked apricot foam*, 143 / *Rice and apple pudding with wine sauce*, 145

AFTERNOONS AT RIZA NÉNI'S 148

Farmer cheese biscuits, 152 / *Bread pudding in noodle dough*, 155 / *Jam or almond turnovers*, 159 / *Apple-filled noodle dough "wheels"*, 163 / *Fruit cake*, 166 / *Sour cherry cake*, 169 / *Poppy seed squares*, 172 / *Walnut squares*, 176 / *Almond macaroons*, 179 / *Sponge dough discs*, 182 / *Evening flowers*, 184 / *Hazelnut slices*, 185 / *Meringue-coated almond sandwich cookies*, 187 / Rainy Afternoons at Riza Néni's, 190

DINNERS AT RIZA NÉNI'S 195

Diced pickle and carrot sausage, 196 / *Chopped calves' liver*, 198 / *Pickled herring*, 200 / *Anchovy eggs*, 204 / Evenings at Riza Néni's, 206

The Holidays at Riza Néni's 211

SABBATH AT RIZA NÉNI'S 211

Butter challah, 215 / *Poached carp in vinegary broth with horseradish*, 220 / *Pike in sour aspic*, 225 / *Chicken or squab stuffed under the skin*, 229 / *Chestnut torte*, 232 / Saturday Mornings and Lunches, 237 / *Cholent*, 239 / *Stuffed goose neck (halsli) and cholent dumpling (ganef)*, 244 / *Bread kugel with raisins and diced apples*, 247 / *Apple kugel*, 251 / *Apple torte*, 255 / *Meringue torte with almond cookie dough base*, 257 / *Lemon-almond torte*, 261 / *Potato torte*, 265 / Saturday Afternoons and Evenings, 268 / *Spice torte*, 270 / *Spice strudel*, 274

ROSH HASHANAH AND YOM KIPPUR AT RIZA NÉNI'S 279
Honey cookies, 285 / *Rich gugelhupf*, 288 / *Chocolate gugelhupf*, 291

SUKKOT AT RIZA NÉNI'S 296
Wine cake, 299

CHANUKAH AT RIZA NÉNI'S 303
Pastry fritters, 305 / *Candied apple fritters*, 309

PURIM AT RIZA NÉNI'S 312
Fish with walnut-vegetable sauce, 315 / *Potato noodles with poppy seeds*, 318 / *Kindli*, 320 / *Fládni*, 325 / *Cookies as in Brno*, 330 / *Nut hoop*, 333

PESACH AT RIZA NÉNI'S 335
Matzo balls, 344 / *Apple-matzo kugel*, 347 / *Matzo kugel*, 350 / *Matzo fritters*, 353 / *Riza néni's matzo fritters*, 354 / *Lujza néni's matzo fritters*, 355 / *Jam-filled potato-matzo dumplings*, 357 / *Potato flour torte*, 360 / *Macaroon torte*, 362 / *Chocolate-almond cookies*, 366 / *Hazelnut macaroons*, 369 / *Meringue-almond clusters*, 370 / *Almond-chocolate kisses*, 372 / *Walnut meringue kisses*, 374

PART THREE (1926–1938)

Last Years in Budapest 377

The End of Riza Néni's World 379

APPENDIX A: *Family Tree* — 387
APPENDIX B: *List of All the Recipes in Riza Néni's Collection* — 388
GLOSSARY — 395
BIBLIOGRAPHY — 403
ACKNOWLEDGMENTS — 407
SUBJECT INDEX — 409
INDEX OF RECIPES AND FOODS — 415

PREFACE

THE SUBJECT of this book is life, the lives of Jews about one hundred years ago in Moson, a small town in western Hungary—but my motivation for writing it had much to do with death. Not with the death of my great-grandmother, the central figure of my work, but rather with the demise of the Jewish community of Moson where she had lived. Decades ago, when I first visited this town and counted the names on the memorial to the victims of the Holocaust, I realized that more than two-thirds of the Jewish population had perished in that upheaval. Staring at the hundreds of names on the four black marble plaques on the wall, I felt envious of my ancestors who had been nurtured by an intact community in which changes occurred gradually and ties to the past had not been broken.

My desire to restore this link to the past was the reason for trying to gather every bit of information I could find about the life of the Jews of Moson. When it occurred to me to write a book using some of this material, I wasn't interested in writing my great-grandmother's biography (which her ordinary life wouldn't have warranted), nor a family history, nor even a usual cookbook. Instead, I hoped that by patiently piecing together the details of her everyday life, household, and cooking, I could somehow bring her and the community she was part of back to life. I felt that even an illusion of continuity was better than resignation to the reality of the schism caused by the Holocaust.

The harmonious coexistence of Gentiles and Jews in Moson during the late nineteenth and early twentieth century depicted in this book would give a misleading picture without mentioning that—as in so many other places—this was not to last. By the 1930s there were increasing signs of antisemitism and in 1944 the overwhelming majority of Christians did nothing to help their Jewish neighbors when they were first collected into the ghetto and then deported. Though the government in Budapest gave the orders—at the request of the Germans who had been occupying

Hungary since March 1944—the actual execution of these horrors was left to the local authorities, mainly the police and the gendarmes.

When I started work on this book, like most authors, I was curious to see books similar to mine. I found plenty of memoirs, some of them with brief descriptions of a household, and many cookbooks of historical Jewish recipes, but no book that describes the cooking of a nineteenth-century Jewish woman as integral to a comprehensive description of her household and way of living. I was most surprised because this idea seemed so obvious to me that I was sure many other authors had tried it. I hope that after reading this book you will agree with me that recipes become more meaningful if they are presented in the context of the daily life of the individual who cooked them.

I based the description of my great-grandmother's household almost completely on the oral history I had conducted with my mother in the last years of her life. She had been raised by my great-grandmother and was able to vividly describe her household to me. When, in preparation for this book, I reread the transcripts of the tapes I had made with my mother, I realized that—detailed as her story was—at a few places it needed additional material for depth and context. I used recollections of contemporaries and material from written sources to supplement her account, but as it has remained essentially her story, I decided not to interrupt the text with footnotes documenting these additions.

Though my mother told me disproportionately less about Purim and Sukkot than about the other festivals, I couldn't bear leaving these holidays and the recipes that go with them out of my book. Therefore, I expanded her narrative with period accounts of the local Purim ball and the Simchat Torah celebrations and in a few instances with invented anecdotes, such as the story of decorating my great-grandmother's gazebo for Sukkot.

In my desire to make you feel at home in this household so different from our way of living, I opted against using the few rather stiff archival photos available and decided to illustrate the story with my drawings. The drawings are based—wherever possible—on factual data, such as the furniture plan my mother prepared of my great-grandmother's apartment, surviving family artifacts, old photos, photos of existing buildings, and archival research. Where such information was not available, I studied books about the applied arts of the period to be able to reconstruct the scenes.

Luckily, my great-grandmother's 1869 collection of recipes has survived and made it possible to include updated versions of her recipes, frequently the very same dishes my mother had recalled eating at her house. By offering these recipes, I hope to tempt you to try some of these wonderful dishes and desserts—another way of getting close to this distant world.

She may have even started the collection a few years before 1869, because the travel itinerary scribbled in the back of the copybook proves only that she must have been using it by that date. The other end of the time spectrum can be defined by her endearing habit of specifying quantities of some ingredients, such as chocolate or vanilla, by their price in kreuzer, a unit of small change that was in circulation only until 1892. She must have gathered most of the one hundred and thirty recipes in her collection in the nineteenth century, since only in the last few recipes did she stop measuring vanilla in kreuzers.

In updating her recipes, I made substitutions for ingredients that are either hard to find in the United States or would be unappealing to the modern cook. These days, few people would have the time to hunt for rendered goose fat or wish to make their sweet Sabbath pudding with chopped beef fat. I used chicken fat, margarine, oil, or butter to replace these ingredients. I also made small adjustments, such as sometimes cutting back on the number of egg yolks, to make the recipes more appropriate for our health-conscious age, if this could be done with no detriment to the original. Instead of museum pieces, I wanted to make enjoyable and practical versions for today's cook. But in spite of these small changes, the updated versions remain true to the style and character of the original recipes, and I am confident my great-grandmother would have no trouble recognizing them. To make the reader aware of changes to the original, I mention them in my introductions to the recipes. Most of the recipes' English titles are new, because the originals rarely described the recipes well. Following the English titles, however, I included my great-grandmother's original German or Hungarian titles—old-fashioned language, idiosyncratic spelling, and all.

I hope that as you read about the details of daily life in my great-grandmother's household the illustrations will seem to come to life: as though you were present in her kitchen, watching this elderly woman, dressed in a floor-length black dress, getting ready to serve lunch for her family. Your eyes will dwell on the strangely shaped cast-iron legs of her nineteenth-century wood-burning range—showing a faun's face affixed to his hoofed leg—and you will notice the incongruous presence of a bathtub and bath stove behind the range. As you imagine hearing the murmur of the simmering dish on the range and catching a whiff of its sweet-and-sour smell, my great-grandmother will wave to you to step closer and taste the almond-studded meatballs she is preparing—a taste of the past.

PART ONE

The House in Győr

1851–1876

The Education of Therese Baruch

THE TRAIN WAS RUNNING through a flat and rather dull-looking part of western Hungary toward Győr, an industrial town about halfway between Budapest and Vienna. Staring at the uninspiring countryside, I wondered whether I would be able find in this town the house where my great-grandmother was born. Was the house still standing after almost a hundred and fifty years? I was traveling from Budapest, where I had recently arrived from my home in New York, and was taking a day off from my visit to relatives. Looking out the train window, watching the landscape run backward, my thoughts also moved in reverse as I recalled the moment ten years earlier in my mother's living room in Budapest that marked the beginning of my obsession with my great-grandmother, a person about whom I had known very little before that day. Now, years after my mother's death, it felt good recalling that distant moment, the beginning of my quest.

At that time, I had put my little tape recorder on the table in my mother's living room in Budapest and had asked her to tell me the story of her life. She had begun by telling me about her grandmother's household in Moson, a small town near the Austrian border. Mother was born in this town and spent her first six years there because her parents, who moved to Budapest when she was not quite one year old, left her with her grandparents until she was ready to go to school in Budapest. I became intrigued by my mother's description of how her conservative and religious grandmother, who had been born in 1851 and had run her household as if life had stopped in the nineteenth century, had remained close to her children and grandchildren, who had become increasingly secularized.

I felt captivated and wanted to hear more about her. Luckily, despite the gap of almost three-quarters of a century, my mother had an amazing ability to remember minute details of her grandparents' daily life, down to the location of every piece of furniture in their large house. Listening to her, a picture of this long-dead woman started to emerge in my mind. I was there with my great-grandmother as she prepared lunch for the family according to the rules of kashrut, although she knew that her beloved son, who ate kosher food at home, was not above eating pork elsewhere. Had she sent me to her pantry to fetch a few eggs she needed for cooking, I could have found them as easily as if I had grown up in her household. I started to feel that I knew her and found myself longing to taste her delicious pike in sour aspic, a dish my mother had been raving about.

Now, as the train sped toward Győr, I reached into my bag to make sure that I had with me the paper I had brought from New York with the address of my great-grandmother's house. Mother hadn't been able to remember the address of her ancestral home in Győr, but years after her death I found the address in the Family History Center of the Mormon Church, across from Lincoln Center, where the Church keeps an amazingly rich collection of microfilmed old census records, registers, and other documents from around the world.

After putting the slip with the address back into my bag, my thoughts again wandered back to the past years, years that now seemed like one long preparation for this trip. I recalled my surprise and excitement when my aunt, who had been living for some forty years in New York, told me that in her closet she had cartons of documents, photos, and personal items belonging to my great-grandmother. Going through the cartons, I was amazed to find, among other artifacts of my great-grandmother's life, her nineteenth-century haggadah, prayer book, and several copybooks in her handwriting. I was thrilled when I realized that one copybook contained drafts of eighty-five letters my great-grandmother had written in the three years prior to her marriage in 1876, letters that provided a continuous narrative of her life during this period, covering exactly that period in her life about which my mother could offer only scant information. In another copybook I found a collection of about a hundred and thirty recipes. A date scribbled in the back of this copybook showed that my great-grandmother had already been using her recipe collection in 1869, when as an eighteen-year-old young woman she had still been living with her parents in Győr.

I recalled rushing home with this box of treasures and spending days trying to decipher the old-fashioned handwriting in the copybooks. I could still remember my excitement as I had tasted my great-grandmother's rice-apple pudding, the first dish I had made from her recipe collection. What a joy it was to be able to treat my daughters to meals composed entirely of dishes their distant ancestor had cooked some hundred and thirty years ago! What a joy it was, too, to be able to tell them about her letters and talk to them about how this woman had spent her days!

Reading my great-grandmother's letters and studying her recipes reinforced the impression I had gained from my mother's stories of my great-grandmother as a woman who constantly seemed to look both forward and backward, accepting change but wishing to preserve tradition. My feeling that she was typical of so many Jews of her time who faced the dilemmas posed to them by Jewish assimilation heightened my initial interest in her as an ancestor. I started to see forces of history lurking behind the frequently quirky details of her ordinary life.

Now, in the train, I glanced at my watch. I had about half an hour before I would arrive in Győr, and so I continued going through the things I had put into my travel bag in Budapest. I made sure that I had with me a slip with the address of the local Jewish community organization, where I hoped to get assistance for my visit to the synagogue and the cemetery. I opened my Hungarian guidebook and re-read the section about Győr. It contained lots of interesting historical information about the town but nothing about the history of the Jewish community. I had read all this before and there was really no need to go through it again, except as a way to keep me busy and help me to control my anxiety about whether or not I would find the building that witnessed my great-grandmother's life in this town.

When the conductor came into the car to announce the approaching station, I put on my coat and grabbed my bag, eager to get off. I hardly knew Győr where, with the exception of one memorable visit in 1956, I had only spent a few hours on my way to other places. Even that 1956 visit was short, only one night, and certainly not conducive to sightseeing. At that time I had arrived with a police escort after I had been caught trying to sneak across the Austrian border following the failed Hungarian revolution. Then the authorities had forced me, and dozens of others similarly caught at the border, to spend a night in a detention center in Győr. Years later I had more success leaving Hungary, and by now I have lived in the United States longer than in the country of my birth.

When I got off the train I bought a map of the town and set out to find Híd utca (Bridge Street), the address of my great-grandmother's house. With its present population of approximately 130,000 people, Győr, the major industrial center of western Hungary, is considered a fairly large town in Hungary. On my way from the train station, I enjoyed looking at the eighteenth-century Baroque church and the nice old houses. Most of the houses in the historic center were built in the eighteenth and nineteenth centuries, although the origins of the town go back much further than that. Following my map, I crossed a bridge over the River Rába. In my great-grandmother's time, that far side of the river was a separate town, called Győrsziget (Győr-island), and only later became part of its larger sister town.

Híd utca was only a few steps from the river. Looking down the curving street I had the strange feeling of being transported into the past. The unbroken line of beautiful old two-story houses on both sides of the street looked virtually identical to what my great-grandmother must have seen there, and I had no trouble finding Number 12, a freshly renovated corner building. Although quite narrow on the street side, because the longer façade faced the cross street, the house was actually one of the largest on the street. Mother, who as a child around 1915 or 1920 had visited this building, described it to me but couldn't remember the address. By that time my great-grandmother's oldest brother ran the family store, which took up much of the first floor and sold ribbons, embroidery, laces, and sewing accessories. After more than eighty years in business, the store finally closed in the 1920s, when he, its last owner, died.

The entrance doors to my ancestors' building had been altered in the renovation and I looked in vain for their original blue-glass door handles. Mother had always called the store the "store with the blue-glass door handles," which was how the store was referred to in her family. The family apartment was above the store and was large enough to accommodate the many children in the family and the grandmother who lived with them.

Great-grandmother's father, Eduard Baruch, had started the store in the 1840s. Although he was born in Győr, his family came from a much smaller town. His wife, the daughter of highly religious merchants, was also born in a small town in western Hungary. Compared to those small towns, Győr must have seemed like a cosmopolitan urban center. It had recovered from its occupation by Napoleon's army in 1809 and was now rapidly developing into a lively industrial center. Capitalism and industrialization started rather late in Hungary, but Győr was, together with Budapest and a few other towns, in the forefront of this process. The proximity of both Vienna and Budapest helped make the cultural life lively. Of the about twenty thousand people who lived there in 1869, about 11 percent were Jewish. But in the much smaller Győrsziget, where the Baruch family lived, Jews represented more than 30 percent of the population. Many other towns in Hungary had similarly large Jewish population, though in 1890 only 4.7 percent of the general population in Hungary was Jewish. Notwithstanding their urban concentration, the Jewish population was dispersed, not separated into isolated communities.

The 1860s and the following decades, the time when my great-grandmother became a young woman, got married, and raised her children, were a time of accelerating change in the history of Hungarian Jews. In 1867, at long last, they received almost complete equality under the law. A Jewish Congress was convened in 1868 to review the state's relationship to Jewish schools and religious organizations. The majority of the delegates at the Congress belonged to the *neológ* movement, which was most popular in urban areas, especially in the central and western parts of the country. It wanted to reconcile religious traditions with reforms, such as establishing modern institutions for training rabbis, omitting the traditional screens separating women's balconies from the rest of the synagogue, or allowing weddings and organ music in the synagogue. They agreed with the state's goal for the Congress: that the Jewish community should establish an administrative structure ranging from parishes to a central office in Budapest. Delegates representing Orthodox Judaism, which constituted the majority among Hungarian Jews but was in minority at the Congress, refused to accept the concept of a central authority and insisted on complete autonomy. Finally, the resolutions were passed without their participation. A third group, the so-called *status quo ante*, didn't want to join either of the other two and wished to preserve pre-Congress conditions. Thus the result of the Congress was increased tensions and structural disunity in the Jewish community. No wonder that there hasn't been another Jewish Congress since then.

My great-grandmother's family belonged to the neológ movement; one uncle was a delegate to the 1868–1869 Jewish Congress and voted with the majority to approve the organizational reforms. While her parents, aunts, and uncles were all religious Jews, they wished to participate in the modern economy and become an accepted part of Hungarian society.

In Hungary, where the old nobility and the gentry still maintained feudal habits, it was primarily the Jews who were knowledgeable in commerce and money matters. As a result, they became central to the late-starting rise of Hungarian capitalism. Decades later, demagogues would use this fact to incite renewed antisemitism, but for now, this was still a period of relative tranquillity and optimism among Jews.

My ancestors' store was a modest but typical example of Jews becoming part of modern urban economy. Eduard Baruch recalled his early years of business and family in a speech he wrote in old age: "My wife soon became an exceptional business woman. She worked with enthusiasm and tireless energy from morning to evening. Soon she became a mother and over the years our family grew to eight children. We had to endure many trials during this time, but through all of them she devoted herself to her family and our business as a faithful and religious wife." He added proudly, and a bit oddly, "I must say, we haven't had a single fight since we met each other, not even to this day."

This speech, just like all my great-grandmother's recipes and letters, was written in German, which didn't surprise me because I recalled my mother telling me that this had been my great-grandmother's and her family's preferred language. In this they were typical of a large percentage of Jews in western Hungary and Budapest. While most of them, including my great-grandmother, also spoke Hungarian, German was their language of choice. Most of the Yiddish-speaking Jews lived in the northern and northeastern part of the country.

The family, like most Jewish families in town, was religious. In the speech just quoted, Eduard Baruch also spoke proudly of having been a lifelong member of local Jewish cultural and community organizations, where he was elected to honorary posts. I know from other documents that for years he was the comptroller of the Jewish community and between 1855 and 1862 its president. The old synagogue of Győrsziget was only a few steps from his house, but the new synagogue built in 1870 for the recently merged Győr and Győrsziget Jewish communities was close, too. I decided I would also make the ten-minute walk from their former house to this temple. It looked familiar to me from afar, and now

I realized that the five big domes towering over the trees, which I had seen on my way to the house, belonged to it. The immensity of the structure only became clear to me, however, as I approached it. The entrance to the grandiose nineteenth-century temple was through a spacious courtyard that was open on one side to the street and surrounded on the other three sides by the temple and the flanking two-story structures of the former Jewish school and community organizations. This synagogue was built to serve the neológ Jews, who by that time constituted the majority of the Jewish population in Győr and had a large following in Győrsziget, too. The synagogue was on the Győr side but near the bridge leading to Győrsziget, and thus convenient to both communities.

Standing in the courtyard of the synagogue complex, I could hear the sound of somebody practicing a violin sonata coming from a window on the first floor of one of the side wings. When I stepped closer to the entrance, I could see from the nameplate that a music school now occupied some of these structures. Unfortunately, it wasn't possible for me to enter the crumbling synagogue, which is no longer in use, but even from the outside, the imposing old buildings surrounding the courtyard were testimony to the size and wealth of the former Jewish community in Győr. When I went inside to find the offices of the local Jewish community that were somewhere in the building, a young man showed me the way to the office, a small room in the building the Jewish community once completely occupied. I explained to the woman in the shabbily furnished office why I had come to Győr and asked her if she knew where I could find records of the nineteenth-century Jewish community. Unfortunately, she said, the only records she was aware of were the burial records that were with the caretaker of the Jewish cemetery.

I decided to put off my visit to the cemetery until the afternoon and go back, now, before the threatening rain arrived, to take another look at my great-grandparents' house. As I remembered from my mother's stories, the family's haberdashery was a flourishing business, and by the time my great-grandmother Therese, or Riza as she was called in the family, was born in 1851, the family was already sufficiently well-off to have two live-in servants: a young woman who cooked and cleaned and a young man who helped with other chores. The children also helped out in the family store and around the household. As was typical for young middle-class women of her time, Therese and her sisters learned to play the piano, sing, knit, embroider, and, last but not least, cook. Judging from the instructions she wrote for the recipes in the collection that she started as a teenager in this house, it seems probable that at that young age she was already a reasonably accomplished cook.

Her copybook of letters shows that she was an equally accomplished writer, and her letters paint a vivid picture of a typical young urban middle-class Jewish woman's daily life in the 1870s. But even more interesting, they describe for us her opinions on social issues and contemporary ideas. The increasing assimilation in the Jewish community is well documented by her many references to the social interaction between Jews and Gentiles.

As I stood in front of the house where my great-grandmother had grown up, and where she had written all those letters, I could almost see her coming out the front door, pulling the blue-glass door handle behind her, and hurrying to drop her letters in the mailbox just in time for the mail man to pick them up. After returning home she probably opened again the pretty marble-patterned cover of her copybook and reread the drafts of the letters she had spent the better part of the morning writing. When she came to a part she particularly liked, she smiled proudly at some witty phrase or elegant metaphor. I, always a reluctant letter-writer, stood on the sidewalk opposite her house, oblivious to passersby and the drizzling rain, and thought about her letters, in which her passions and involvement seem so palpable in spite of the old-fashioned, formal style. With all their occasional naiveté, the letters contain the hopes, dreams, and social aspirations of a strong personality, this woman whom I have never met but who seems so alive to me.

When I returned to New York I decided to reread my great-grandmother's letters. I had read these letters before, but now the images I returned with from my visit breathed new life into them. Reading her opinions on important social issues of her age, many of them unresolved to this day, as well as the more mundane events of her daily life elicited my thoughts: it was almost like having a conversation with her.

While my great-grandmother Riza, like many Jewish and Gentile women of her time, class, and economic situation, never went beyond grade school, she was eager to appear culturally literate. In addition to the copybooks containing her letters and recipes, I have yet another of her copybooks, in which she copied the words of German art songs and opera arias, as well as some sentimental German poems that are so trite they sound like parodies.

Letter writing was the only way Riza could keep in touch with her sisters, cousins, and the other members of her extended family who lived in other towns of Hungary. She also corresponded with her two brothers, who had immigrated to the United States around 1870, a few years prior to the period covered by the letters.

    Although letter writing was a necessity in those days, it was also a creative outlet for young middle-class women, an opportunity for them to show, and show off, their erudition, literary style, and social skills. Letter writing was something of a hobby for my great-grandmother Riza, too, at least in the years before her marriage. She tried hard to write in what she considered to be an elegant and sophisticated style and she admired her better-educated friends who she thought wrote well. About one of them she wrote: "As our friend Novák informed me, he has already poured out his heart to you in writing and now wishes good luck to the continuation of your new correspondence. I like to go through his old letters and read them again and again, because, if one understands his writing style really well, one can learn a lot from it. So get on with your correspondence my dear Julia. As usual, we will be called bluestockings, which only means that we don't shy away from something better." This Károly Novák was one of her Catholic friends. He was the secretary (a position similar to a program director) of the *Casino*, which—contrary to the connotation of its name in English—was not a gambling place but a social club. It is easy to smile today at Riza's stilted and flowery style. Although she could be amusingly pretentious in her letters, this was all part of her effort to live up to her ideal image of a young, sophisticated, middle-class woman. Her attempts to emulate the culture of the secular middle class set her apart from her parents and were indicative of larger changes in Hungarian Jewish society in the second half of the nineteenth century.

Riza's secular education, merely four years in grade school, was limited by the middle-class concept of domesticity. Even if her parents had wanted to keep her longer in school, it would have been difficult, because the local Jewish school had only four grades for girls in those years. In the late 1850s, when she studied there, most of the subjects were still taught in German, although at least the rudiments of Hungarian were taught, too. Only in the 1860s did Hungarian begin to replace German as the primary language of this school. It tells us a lot about what society expected of women, that in the 1850s needlework was still considered the most important subject in the girl's school. As for religious education, according to Jewish tradition it was primarily a male domain. Many traditional Jewish families sent their sons to yeshivas, schools for higher learning in Judaism. Even those young men who didn't study in yeshivas in order to become Judaic scholars received more religious education from their rabbis than young women did. Formal religious education for Jewish girls was typically restricted to the study of Hebrew, the prayers, and the few religious tasks reserved for women, such as lighting the Sabbath candles.

Young Jewish women of the urban middle class usually received language and music instruction at home. More and more, Jewish families were adopting the standards of their Gentile neighbors in this regard, as well as in other matters, and Riza's family was no exception. She was tutored at home in piano and French. I have no reason to doubt the recollection of my mother, who as a child had to play four-hand piano with her grandmother, that Riza was a competent amateur pianist. However, I have doubts about the extent of Riza's knowledge of French. She loved to insert an occasional French word here or there into the German text of her letters for good effect, but the result was not as elegant as she must have intended it to be, because she frequently misspelled the French words.

Middle-class Jewish society discouraged women from working outside their homes for a living out of fear that this would make them neglect their duties at home, where they were expected to take care of the household and oversee the children's education. However, women frequently assisted their husbands or parents in running the family business. As I mentioned earlier, Riza's father spoke about how tirelessly his wife worked in the family store and what "an exceptional business woman" she was. Riza also helped in her parents' store and, occasionally, in the businesses of other family members. In one letter, for example, she writes about visiting one of her married sisters, who lived in another town, to help her run their store in the absence of her husband.

Her creative ambitions were pretty much limited to improving her skills in letter writing. She didn't mind being called a bluestocking for this, but she was reluctant to pursue her vaguely expressed interest in poetry out of her concern that she would face the disapproval of society. "Although my education didn't go beyond what is usual for the daughter of ordinary middle-class parents," she wrote, "I had a desire to delve into poetry. But I would have been considered a bluestocking had I pursued this. Even in my fantasies I never tried to reach beyond the goal that lies so totally out of reach. Had I done so, I would only have felt the unhappiness of seeing unfulfilled plans dissolve in the air like soap bubbles. Man is called upon to get a higher education because he can profit from it. Women, who shed their femininity in their pursuit to become like men, will see that emancipation is only a seductive melody in their ears that they have followed to the point of no return while striving to be celebrated and appreciated for their intellect. But what happens later? When they get older, men can continue advancing in their fields while the women's chosen careers stall as their weakness becomes noticeable, and they belatedly mourn their missed avocation. Do not think that I speak in generalities! What I have written is only applicable to young women similar to me and not to those who were raised since early childhood to be independent and to find their own livelihoods. Women like me have been raised to be ordinary housewives. Isn't it God's special gift to assign a guardian spirit to a young girl that programs her for an education commensurate with her social standing? One doesn't strive for something higher than what is within reach. However, should one be so lucky as to attain that higher goal, then being modest in all areas of life becomes easy."

Riza was in many ways straddling different worlds. Although raised in a conservative Jewish household, she was intrigued by the forces of assimilation, and even if she didn't wholeheartedly embrace them, at least she accepted them as something inevitable. In a similar way she looked both backward and forward when it came to a choice of national identity. She considered herself Hungarian, and she spoke Hungarian if she had to, but she felt more comfortable speaking German, the language she was raised with and the language of her German-speaking ancestors who had moved from Bohemia to western Hungary in the eighteenth century. When she wrote about her "Hungarian temper," she did this in German. As she wrote in a half-teasing, half-serious letter to Ludwig Hirsch, a friend in Vienna: "How easily someone like you can laugh at the ideas of another person, given that you don't have to bear the shackles of womanhood. But I will engrave your advice in my mind and, whenever possible, will try to switch from the quick temper of a Hungarian woman to the quiet and steady one of a jovial German."

Actually, Riza's conservative preference for the German language, which she kept up well into the twentieth century, was not typical, because most of the assimilated Hungarian Jews, even many of the Orthodox, were much more willing to embrace the Hungarian language and culture. Hungarians were a minority in nineteenth-century Hungary; of the roughly thirteen and a half million people who lived there in 1867, only six million were Hungarian. In the multiethnic and multidenominational country, national identity was not based on race, ethnicity, or religion, but on the dominance of Hungarian culture. Of the various minorities, such as the Germans, Croatians, Serbians, Slovaks, and Romanians, who lived in Hungary at the time, the Jews were the most willing to adopt the Hungarian language and culture. Hungarian nationalism, in the nineteenth century still a rather positive force, was based on a belief in Hungarian cultural superiority. As the historian Vera Ránki has noted, it was almost like a bargain: Hungarian Jews who adopted the Hungarian language and culture became Hungarian nationalists, and in turn the Hungarians accepted them as useful agents of magyarization and capitalist modernization. Antisemitic movements were relatively limited and not state-supported in nineteenth-century Hungary, and antisemitism played a smaller role there than in neighboring Austria.

Perhaps the most hilarious, or tragicomic, if you wish, proofs of my great-grandmother's Hungarian nationalism are two photos of her young daughter, my future grandmother, dressed in Hungarian national costumes. In the first photo, taken in 1894, the "Hungarian theme" is still relatively restrained. She is wearing a stylized folk costume decorated with a striped ribbon featuring the colors of the Hungarian red, white, and green national flag. But it seems that by the time the next photo was taken, in 1901, Riza was swept up in the nationalist fever of the "Millennium," the 1896 celebration of the thousandth anniversary of the arrival of

Magyar tribes from the east to the Carpathian basin, the present-day Hungary. At this celebration in Budapest, Emperor Franz Joseph wore a Hungarian hussar uniform, and stylized versions of folk costumes and the costumes of seventeenth- or eighteenth-century noblemen became all the rage. My great-grandmother didn't want to be left out, and she clearly felt that being Jewish and preferring to speak German should be no obstacle to showing what a proud Hungarian she was. Therefore, she decided to dress her daughter as the mythical personification, the guardian spirit, of Hungary. But instead of the intended solemnity the effect is quite ridiculous and unintentionally humorous. The staff of the Hungarian flag is weirdly sticking out of her hair, and she is wearing military epaulettes and a sword to go with her role as the guardian of the nation. The Hungarian crown and national shield—featuring the double cross, the symbol of Christian Hungary—are embroidered on a banner hanging from her neck, and she is draped in what looks like a huge striped flag. I am sure my great-grandmother found it perfectly natural that her daughter should wear the double cross; for her it was a symbol of Hungary, not a Christian symbol. I am also sure the costume was a great success among the locals in the small town where Riza and her family lived. How much more Hungarian could one get? I wonder if my grandmother thought of this picture in 1944, when Hungarian followers of the Nazis confined her to the Budapest ghetto. I was there with her but she didn't mention it.

Just as my great-grandmother Riza's father was active in the Jewish community's charitable organizations, she was also eager to help the needy. As she wrote in December 1873: "It will be rather lively here in Győr, and you seem worried that our entertainment might be paid for with money that should go to the poor. Should we lower ourselves so much? Aren't there some people left who could spare a little money for us? In fact, we women have been very successful fundraisers. Even without the help of the gentlemen we managed to raise twice as much money as expected. For Sunday we organized a little dinner party in the Casino. We are sixty-six women: nine of us will handle the tobacco shop, six the flower shop, five the pastry shop, and forty-six will assist the waitresses. Most of us will wear short white dresses with black aprons and daisy handbags to carry the money. A white ribbon on our left shoulder will show the table number. With this sort of magic we will be able to help the needy. I would like to know how many in the elite will be able to resist the high ticket prices we are charging."

But while Riza's father was doing charity work within Jewish organizations, the Casino, where the fancy charity dinner she describes was held, was a club with mostly Christian members. The secretary of this club was the same Mr. Novák whose writing skill she so admired. It is not clear from the letter whether the other women in the group were Jewish, although my guess would be that most of them were not. The letters also don't say whether Riza and her friends had been supporting needy Jews or Gentiles—probably both. But the difference between the two generations of the Baruch family is striking.

Riza frequently wrote enthusiastically about balls: clearly, she loved dancing and partying. I still have several little ornaments that she received from admirers at balls. According to my mother, these ornaments were called cotillions, named probably after the dance. They are made of embossed, color-lithographed paper cutouts surrounded by lace and ribbons. It was customary for young men to give cotillions to ladies when they asked them for a dance. One of the cotillions shows a lute in the middle of a fancy flower wreath. A ribbon is threaded through the lute and the letters on it spell "souvenir." Another such cotillion features the picture of a pretty young lady bearing an uncanny resemblance to photos of the young Riza, except that the woman depicted on the cotillion has blond hair and a cross hangs from her necklace.

Riza's love of dancing and partying, according to the letters, occasionally provoked the anger of her strict, traditional father. As she wrote in December 1873: "Although it is not carnival season yet, I have already been to three parties. At the first one, which was given by my sister Lujza, one couldn't overlook, in spite of the best entertainment, the bad organization. More successful was the second party. A small group of about twenty couples gathered Thursday in the salon of the Hotel Lamm. As required by the organizers, we all arrived at 8:30 in the evening and were greeted on the front steps. We entered the hall dancing, and aside from the rest period, which was more pleasant than such breaks usually are, we didn't slow down for one minute during this terrific ball. Like a sudden angry storm out of the clear blue sky came my dear father at four in the morning to fetch me. He was angry, and I left unhappy because the night was cut so short. Now there are no more parties for this year. But no, it just occurs to me, soon Christmas will be here."

From Riza's reference to expected invitations in the Christmas season, it is already clear that the daughter of this traditional, religious Jewish family found it just as natural to socialize with Christians as with people of her own religion. Other letters also show that while most of her friends were Jewish, several of them were not. Nowhere in her letters is there any hint of a mentality to maintain strict separation from the surrounding Gentile society or of antisemitism experienced in her social contacts. Indeed, there seemed to be a rather relaxed relationship between people of different religious beliefs at this time and place. This was not necessarily the case for Jews in all towns and across all social strata in late nineteenth-century Hungary, but, as far as I know, neither was this atypical. In the few decades following the law passed in 1867 emancipating Hungarian Jews, Jews enjoyed a period of relative social peace and religious tolerance. Nevertheless, the situation was far from ideal—for example, one of the last major blood-libel show-trials, where Jews were accused of killing Christians in order to use their blood, was held in Hungary in 1882. Still, the situation was better in the last quarter of the nineteenth century than it had been before, and certainly it was better than the waves of antisemitism following the failed Communist revolution in 1919, not to mention the years before and during World War II.

Therese Baruch was religious, and she tended to make a point in her letters of emphasizing the difference between herself and her Christian friends, but this usually amounted to nothing more than gentle teasing about the subject. She wrote in a rather flirtatious letter to Mr. Schmidt, a Catholic friend: "Beware of the consequences because I am not always this good-natured or this ready to forgive you. You haven't yet found the opportunity to take steps toward reconciliation, but if you confess, as a good Catholic should do, at least you will have one sin fewer." When this Mr. Schmidt sent her belated New Year's greetings in January 1875, a few days after the New Year, she answered: "Not being Christian, I wasn't expecting any holiday greetings. But I was all the more overwhelmed by the extraordinary kindness with which you thought to make up for what you had missed. The repentant ones are dearer to the angels than those who have never wavered, and as I am the opposite of an angel . . ."—and so on in the ornate style that she liked so much.

In another letter Riza mentions that she was one of only two Jews to participate in an amateur theater group: "In order to raise money for the poor suffering people, we are performing the operetta *The Dormitory*. I am a member of the chorus in this show. As a result, I was given the main role in the following production, which will be the comedy *The Last Letter*. But to learn all that much by heart, and in Hungarian to boot, strains my limited memory and comprehension rather badly. I have trouble identifying myself with the role of an elderly and power-hungry woman, and the only thing that makes this task easier is that Mr. Rappach will play the role of my servant, so at least I will not be the only Jew in the performance." This also shows that she felt uneasy about the task of learning the role in Hungarian. German, the language of her letters and the language she used at home with her family, would obviously have been easier for her.

Although Riza's parents led more conservative social lives than she did, they were nonetheless on friendly terms with her Gentile friends. For example, her letters mention that one friend was a houseguest of the Baruch family. But at the same time, Riza's parents were concerned that their daughter might get into uncomfortable situations and might feel out of place at the Gentiles' parties. She refers to this by writing: "On a whim I accepted at least one invitation to the lawyers' ball [later she accepted their invitation quite a few more times, because she seemed to like this circle of fun-loving, partying young lawyers] in spite of my mother storming into my room with the prediction: 'You will be left sitting there, like all Jewish girls who risk visiting a ball given by Christians.'"

Riza's relationship to the dominant Christian community was complex. Although most of her friends were Jewish, she also had Gentile friends. But she had rather mixed feelings when a Catholic friend, the same Mr. Novák who is already familiar to us from other letters, and who between 1870 and 1873 was the organist of the newly built neológ synagogue in Győr, decided to marry one of her best Jewish friends, Mina Pollák. Apparently Mr. Novák had been courting Miss Pollák for a long time but couldn't make up his mind. When he finally reached a decision and confessed this to Riza, who appears to have been his confidante, she was delighted. As she wrote to Mina Pollák's sister, who lived in southern Hungary, far from Győr: "Mr. Novák himself aired the secret to me and inner happiness radiated from his soulful eyes. I was delighted to be the first person with whom he shared this news of light in the darkness. If I am not mistaken, Mr. Novák is not quite unknown to you, my dear Julia. Already at the time when you were here, he occupied the distinguished position of the secretary of the Casino. But you might not be familiar with the abilities that a demanding world requires from him. Dear Julia! My heart beats with joy, as I am more convinced than ever that there is such a thing as divine intervention. The merits of our good Mina will be richly repaid when a man, who is ready for sacrifices and doesn't weigh love against money, but considers it to be a holy and incorruptible feeling, will marry her. To this end he will joyfully convert to Judaism, because only the thought of reaching little Mina fills his soul."

Behind all this flowery language is the news that Mr. Novák decided to become a Jew. This surprised me a great deal, because not only was this, as far as I knew, practically unheard of in Hungary before the 1890s, to the best of my knowledge it was actually illegal. A quick check in reference books confirmed this. Before 1894, when civil marriages were first permitted, a Jew and a non-Jewish person could not marry. Conversion was the only solution to this dilemma. But as Christians were not allowed to convert to Judaism, this was always resolved by the conversion of the Jewish person.

Riza then continues her letter to the uninformed Julia Pollák, by writing, "The dear Mina will be able to move into her new home happy and free of worries. She will not be torn away from her family, because a faithful sister and a husband who values feminine feelings will support her. Our Mina and your dear parents have already given their 'yes,' and the overjoyed Mr. Novák is speeding up the steps he is taking toward conversion as much as possible, because each passing day seems like a year for him now."

It is clear from subsequent letters that Julia Pollák wasn't happy about her sister's choice of husband and even less happy that the whole matter had been kept secret from her. It would not surprise me if she became even more unhappy when she learned the further developments, because about two months later Riza wrote to her cousin, Julia Pollák's husband: "In the two moons since I have known about Mina's christening, I haven't told anybody of this. I thought I was the only person to know, but what a disappointment! As it turned out, the whole family learned of it and on top of that from strangers, naturally. We only wanted to hide this from your parents, who have been silently suffering, trying to understand the events. I hide my face behind a mask, because nobody knows their pain better than I do. By following their own interests, the Polláks are selling out their souls and religion. And there is more to it. What I had been trying to heal for a long time with great effort has now split apart. Soon I will curse the day our dear Julia became a member of our family, because she will have to innocently suffer, even more than now, for the thoughtlessness of her sister." As I see it, both Mr. Novák and Mina Pollák honestly tried to resolve a difficult problem, and Mina only decided to convert to Christianity when it became obvious that Novák could not become a Jew. Riza, however, clearly saw things differently.

In the following weeks somebody must have explained to her the dilemma confronting her friends. In any case, her anger had blown over, because a month later she wrote to one of her friends: "Little Mina celebrated her wedding feast on the first night of Christmas. We were all there together, including the three gentlemen whom you know from Vienna and three others who are probably unfamiliar to you. It was quite a jolly party thanks to Mr. Schwarmeier, who is a comic singer and an excellent piano player. There were speeches, and we danced until 1:30 A.M., when everybody departed in the merriest of moods." All's well that ends well.

Great-grandmother Riza had an on-again, off-again relationship with Ludwig Pollák, Mina and Julia Pollák's brother, for more than seven years. Almost half of the letters are about this relationship. Of course I only know Riza's version of what happened, but it seems that his other relationships wrecked any marriage plan. Of the many lady friends we hear about, one stands out: "I have known about your relationship with a Christian woman in Vienna for two years, but I respected you too much to allow any jealousy to show." But in spite of the periodic crises, she must have been in love with him, because she was clearly unable to end the relationship. Each furious, accusatory letter was soon followed by a peaceful one, as if nothing had happened.

In the meantime Riza was in her mid-twenties, an age when most women in nineteenth-century Hungary, including her four sisters, were already married, and when she began to feel a perhaps not so subtle pressure from friends and family: "You can imagine how I live under such a pressure. My dear parents consider it to be their duty to care for me and support me. And if I don't find a husband I fear that the first push from them will loosen my tongue, because I am convinced there is a fight for everything." I am sure that notwithstanding her claims to the contrary, she also felt it was time to get married.

For whatever reason, the continuous flow of letters doesn't prepare us for the news of Riza's engagement. My guess is that when her cousin, who was thirteen years older, perhaps unexpectedly proposed marriage to her, she must have felt that there was no point waiting any longer, and quickly agreed. Now she used all her powers of persuasion to try to convince Ludwig Pollák, with whom she hadn't had any contact for almost a year, to come to her engagement party. He sent his good wishes but decided not to come. The ice had been broken, however, and he agreed to attend the wedding. "True friendship needs to be tested, and you gave proof of it by promising to be present at my wedding. The news of your arrival made me so happy that I immediately reported it to my fiancé, who, contrary to your concern, wasn't at all jealous. He knows me and realizes that mistrust would hurt me terribly. I neither give nor require accounting for the past, and with God's help the future will be untroubled."

After the wedding in October 1876, in the Győr synagogue, Riza and her husband, my great-grandfather, decided to move to Moson, a small town about twenty miles west of Győr, near the Austrian border. Both were familiar with Moson, which they had visited frequently over the past few years. My great-grandfather's younger brother and Riza's older sister had been living there since their marriage three years earlier and he was making a living as an insurance agent. Moson was a center of agricultural trade in the region, in particular of grain trade, and there were several grain merchants in the town, most of whom were Jewish. Grain trade was one of the traditional occupations of Jews both here and in the nearby Vienna. There were 464 Jews living in Moson in 1880, about 10 percent of the population. The first Jews settled there in the late eighteenth century and throughout the second half of the nineteenth century, the period I am describing, the relationship between the Jews and largely Catholic Gentiles of the town was excellent. In the 1850s, the early years of the local Jewish community, the priest of the town's Catholic church was entrusted by the Jewish community, in a highly unusual gesture, with keeping the

Jewish birth, marriage, and death records. The priest must have been pleased with this task, because he wrote the following fascinating note—of course in German—in the book of Jewish records: "As I dearly value and respect the honor of receiving their beautiful and noble trust, I am pleased to undertake the keeping of the records of the Moson Jewish community." This sounds as close to an idyllic coexistence as one can get. The idyll didn't last forever, but that is another story.

The newlywed couple and their relatives in Moson decided to buy a house there, which they would share. I am sure that my great-grandmother continued to write occasional letters in her new home, although as far as I know she didn't keep copies of them. I am also sure that she kept that copybook of letters from the years before her marriage for more than sentimental reasons—she was also proud of them. During the years before her marriage, she poured her considerable energies into trying to educate herself, and her carefully worded letters were an important part of that effort. She seems to have been genuinely interested in culture, yet I suspect that she had other motives, too. She thought that by becoming "cultured," she would improve her chances of marrying well. Whether she did this consciously or instinctively by responding to the expectations of the middle-class society in which she lived makes little difference. Now, running her own household, planning her meals, and raising her children became the focus of her energies.

PART TWO

The House in Moson

1876–1926

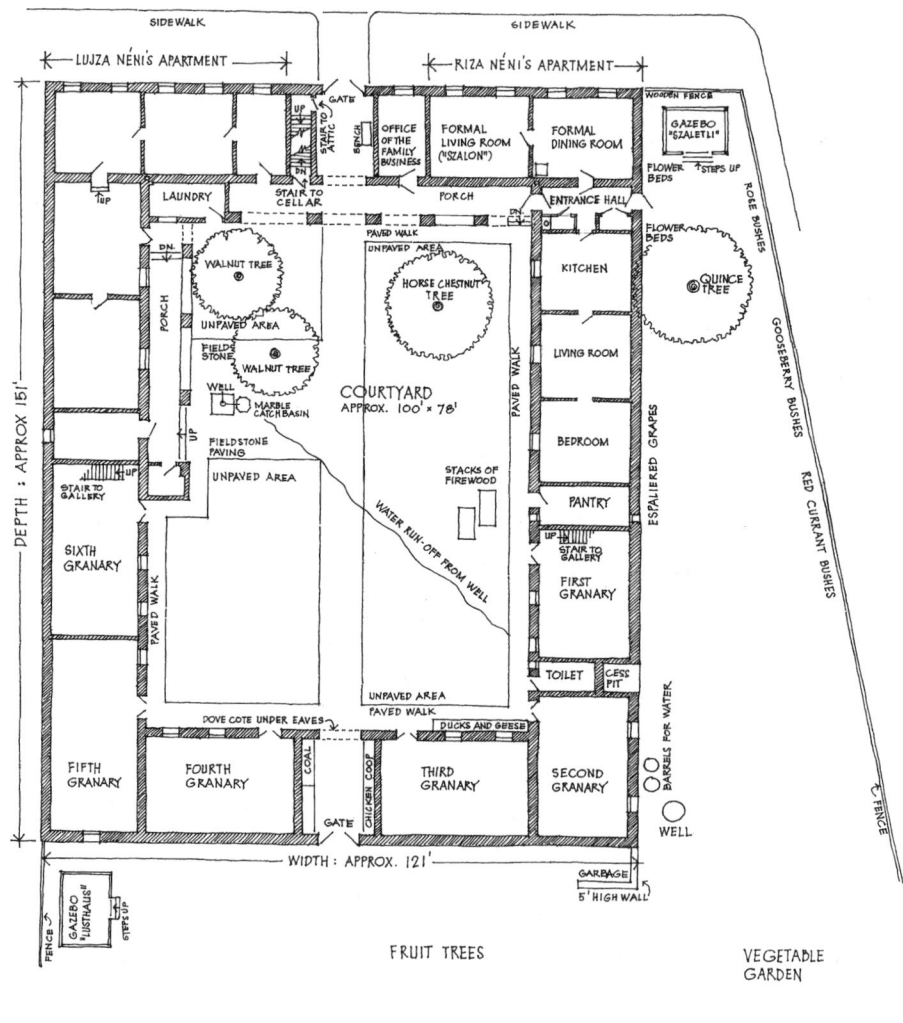

The floor plan of my great-grandparents' house in Moson.

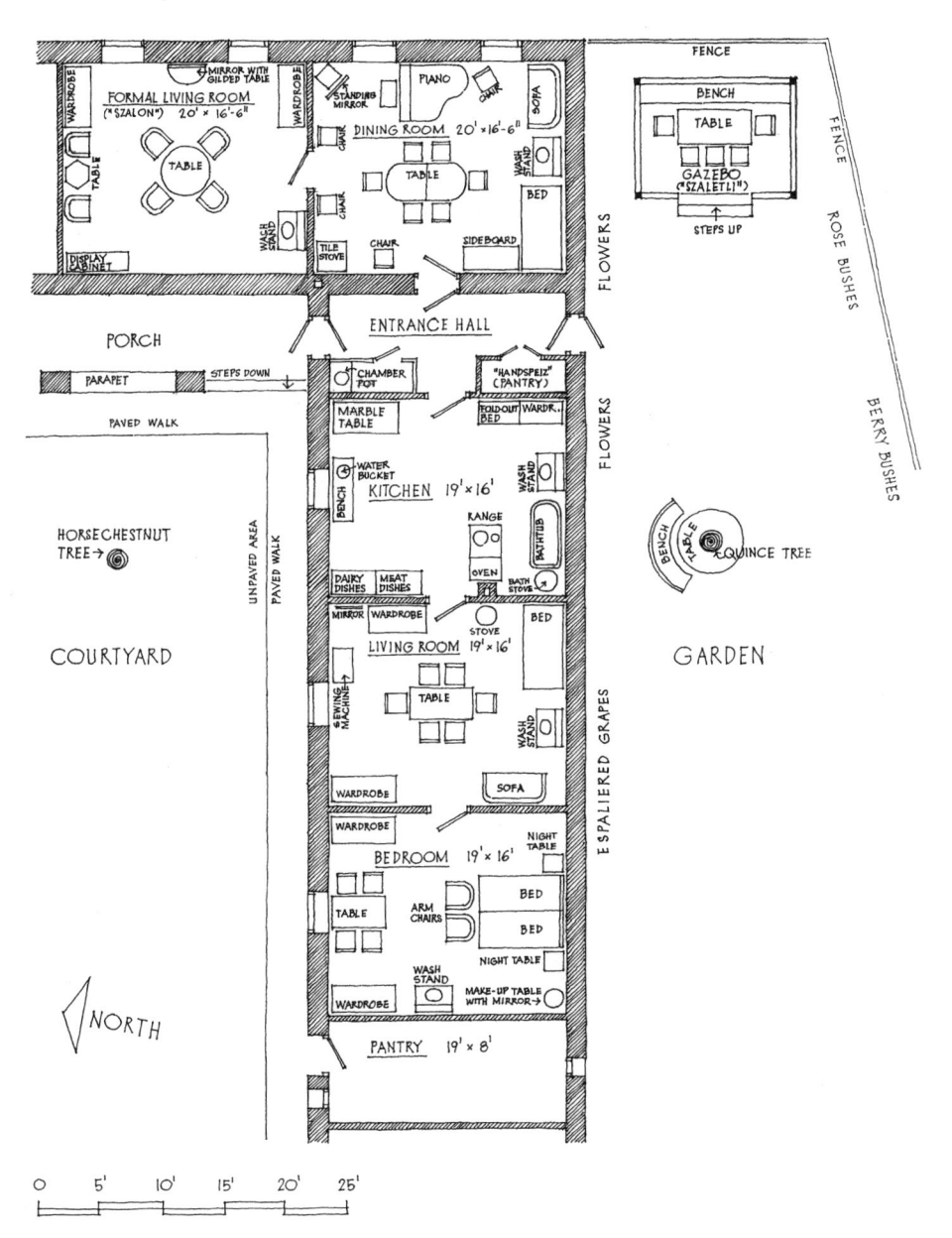

My great-grandparents' apartment in their house in Moson.

A Journey to the Past

IN OCTOBER 1988, my mother asked me if we could stop in Moson on our way to Austria so she could visit her grandparents' house one last time. She could no longer make the trip by herself because by that time she had trouble walking, even with a cane. My brother drove us from Budapest to Moson. Although it was my mother's idea, I also looked forward to stopping in this small town. I had seen the house in Moson during a visit many years before, but this was different. After taping my mother's reminiscences about her life in that house, I had many questions to ask her and was hoping that being there would coax more stories out of her.

The closer we got to Moson, the place of my mother's birth, the more her thoughts wandered back to this town, which for her after a life full of such upheavals as antisemitic laws, war, concentration camp, and communism represented the peace and security of a childhood idyll, a time when she could enjoy the comfort of continuity. Although she was not religious, as she was talking about life at her grandmother's I could sense in her voice the longing for the traditions of her ancestors, longing for a time when the communities that nurtured those traditions were still intact. In the many hours I spent recording the recollections of her life it became clear to me that through all the tensions of uncertainty in her later life, the memories of this place remained an unshakable reference point, a source of strength for my mother. While her memories about Győr were a bit hazy, they were amazingly detailed and specific about daily life at her grandmother's house in Moson. Her face flushed with excitement as she reminisced about her life there, and it was clear how much she was looking forward to this visit and how much it meant to her.

Approaching town, she appeared happy when she noticed the familiar image of a branch of the Danube visible through the trees on our right and told us stories about the time when as a child she had spent long summer afternoons swimming in the river. Now, the river glistened behind the trees in the beautiful October sun. We were driving on the main highway connecting Budapest with Vienna. Moson is built around this highway, which constitutes its main street. Soon we could see the nice one- and two-story houses of the town, mostly built in the nineteenth century, to the left and right of the highway. I observed how oddly this disproportionately wide main street, its width established in the nineteenth century according to the requirements of the highway that extended beyond the town, dwarfed the small houses along its sides. There was little traffic and the town looked pretty in the crisp morning light. Mother pointed out for us buildings along the way, steadfastly referring to the street as "Fő utca" (Main Street), instead of Lenin Street, the name painted on the street signs. She showed us the large granary on the right and explained that it used to belong to the archduke. A little later she called our attention to a beautiful two-story building, which used to be the foremost inn of the town and where the concerts and formal balls had been held in the elegant ballroom on the second floor. Beyond this inn was the *korzó*, which was what the town folks called that stretch of the street where people went for evening walks and where my teenaged mother and her slightly older sister paraded with their admirers.

Instead of stopping at her grandparents' house, we decided to first visit Miklós Löwin, an old acquaintance of hers and one of the few remaining Jews in Moson, who took care of the old Jewish cemetery in his spare time. We wanted to make sure that we would have access to the cemetery after our visit to the house. When we asked him if he would like to come along with us to my great-grandmother's house, he was glad to do so.

To my surprise, in spite of her difficulty walking, my mother suggested that we walk part of the way on Fő utca from Mr. Löwin's house to her grandparents' house. After sitting for hours in the car, it felt wonderful to walk a little in the beautiful fall weather. Mother explained that about half their neighbors at the western end of the town, where she grew up, were Jewish. "If you continue on Fő utca and turn right at the chapel," she said, "you come to Ostermayer Street, which was also heavily Jewish, especially the beginning of the street. Way back it was even called 'Jewish Street.' The synagogue was also nearby." At that point Mr. Löwin, who knew the persecution of the Moson Jews from personal experience, interjected, "—and the Deutsch house too, which served as the ghetto in 1944 for the Moson Jews before they were taken to Auschwitz."

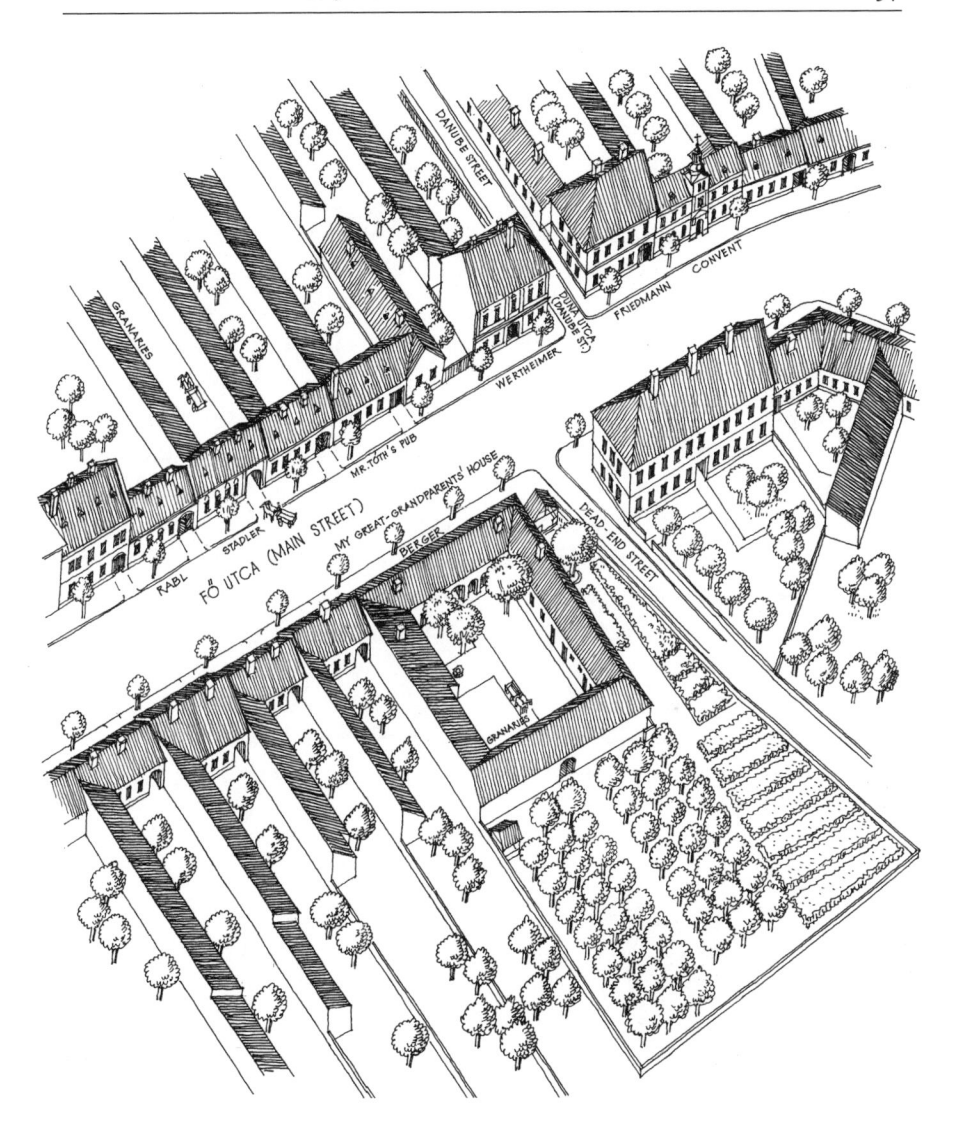

"Look," said my mother, pointing to a house on the other side of the street, "that's where I used to go in the morning to buy milk. And that one-story house next to it belonged to the Stadler family. Carl Flesch, the world-famous violinist, was the brother of Mrs. Stadler, but he left Moson as a child because his parents sent him to study in Vienna. Mr. Stadler was one of the several Jewish grain merchants in town. The Stadlers, who were good friends, liked to come over after dinner to sit and chat with my grandparents in front of our house. We were also on good terms with the Catholic Tóth family who had a pub next to the Stadler house. They loved me very much, and as a child I liked to go over to help a little around the pub. That elegant, old two-story house a bit down the street used to belong to the rich Jewish Wertheimer family, and the Orthodox Jewish Friedmanns, also wealthy grain merchants, owned that other big house next to the side street. Do you see that beautiful two-story house next door, with the cross over its central tower?" my mother asked. "It used to be a convent. My mother was among the first kids to study in the kindergarten that opened in this building in the 1890s and was run by the nuns. A wealthy Catholic bachelor bequeathed the building for the convent and the money for the kindergarten with the proviso that it must accept children of any religion. He also left money for the Hebrew Ladies' Society of Moson. You see, Jews and Gentiles didn't keep so separate in those years in Moson. The tensions came much later."

When we got to the former home of her grandparents, my mother was

The house was built around this big unpaved courtyard.

happy to see that the house she knew and loved so much had been nicely renovated. This must have occurred when it was converted to its present use, an old-age home. The façade of the large house looked virtually the same as in her childhood, only a new and ugly building stood on the site of their former garden.

The date 1786, probably the year of construction, was carved on the keystone of the stone arch over the entrance. Mother explained to us that Riza *néni* (Auntie Riza) as all her grandchildren called her, moved there from Győr after her marriage in 1876. (It is difficult to accurately translate "néni," perhaps "auntie" is the closest. In Hungary, young people call any older woman, relative or unrelated, "néni.") Her husband, Bernhard Berger, and his younger brother Sándor decided to become business partners. Sándor had started the family insurance business in 1872, when he became the regional representative of Assicurazione Generali, a very large insurance company with offices throughout the Austro-Hungarian Monarchy, selling crop, fire, house, and life insurance to farmers in the region. He had been living in Moson for a few years when he married Riza néni's older sister, Lujza. As if this wasn't enough, the two Berger brothers were first cousins to Lujza and Riza. Mother wryly commented that considering how frequently first cousins in her family had intermarried, it was surprising that more of their descendants weren't crazy. The Berger brothers and their wives decided to share the old one-story farmhouse they bought; it was huge, about a hundred and twenty feet long on the street side and even longer in the other direction.

Mother led us through the wide, vaulted entrance-passage designed to allow carriages to drive into the large square courtyard. Though as my mother said, the building looked unchanged from the street, she was sad to see that from the courtyard side only the nice porch with its spacious arches remained as she remembered. The side wings of the house and the former granaries in the back had been replaced by new buildings.

The house was built around this unpaved courtyard, which was so big that it could have passed for a town square. The front of the yard, shaded by walnut and horse-chestnut trees, was the center of life for the two families. The living quarters were on the street-side of the house, and six large granaries occupied the rear and part of the side wings. The farmers drove their carriages loaded with grain to the space they rented in the granaries, and this provided additional income for the families.

An L-shaped garden surrounded the house on two sides. Mother showed us where a passage, which also served as the entrance hall to her grandparents' apartment, used to provide access from the courtyard to the garden. There was also another way to the garden—through a gate in the wide passage in the rear of the courtyard. But by the time my mother lived there, this huge, heavy gate, designed specifically for carriages, was no longer used because it was too inconvenient for casual access.

"Hardly anybody sat in the garden," my mother explained, "We only sat there once in a while, either under the quince tree or in the *szaletli*, a gazebo near our kitchen. I liked to step from the bench at the side of the szaletli to the top of the backrest, then grab a tie beam over my head, and pull myself up into the roof structure. There, I sat on a beam, hugging the king post for balance, and looked over the wooden fence to see who was coming on the street, and when I recognized somebody, I reported this back to Riza néni."

The two families occupied almost symmetrical apartments to the left and right of the street entrance, and the family business took up one room on Riza néni's side of the house. The two families bought identical furniture; even the upholstery had the same pattern. But the shared house was the cause of perpetual friction between the sisters. They usually bickered over their common garden and attic. The arguments flew back and forth: "You picked so many pears, there are hardly any left for us." Or "You didn't leave enough room for us in the attic."

Mother pointed to a place in the middle of the courtyard where the well and its fancy pink marble catch basin used to be. "When I was a child in Moson," she told us, "our house had no running water or sewer connection, and the well was our only source of water. We put the bucket on a board set over the stone catch basin and pulled on a pole hanging from the well post to pump the water. The water that spilled over from the bucket ran into the basin and through a hole at its bottom to the ground. There it ran, like a little creek, diagonally across the sloping unpaved courtyard.

"Clean water had to be carried in buckets into our house, and the dirty water carried out. The house had no bathroom and our weekly baths were taken in the kitchen. Hot water was so valuable that we took turns to bathe in the same tub of hot water. For daily use, pitchers of water were set next to the washbasins. Each room in the house had such a washbasin, not only for hygiene but also because washing hands before meals and in the morning was a religious rule. Theoretically, we were not allowed to walk more than two yards after getting up in the morning without performing the ritual of pouring water over our hands. Though it was part of the house, the only way we could get to the toilet, even in winter, was through the courtyard. There was another small, closet-size restroom, called *szobavécé*

(room toilet), off the entrance hall, which had a chamber pot set into a bench. But we used this only when we were too sick to go out to the courtyard, though once in a while my elderly grandparents also used it when they were well. At night all of us used chamber pots in our rooms."

According to my mother, in the 1910s none of the surrounding houses had indoor plumbing or running water. Her grandparents' house stood close to the edge of the town, and only those houses nearer to the center were connected to the sewer. The house was connected to electric power in 1912, but petroleum lamps were still kept in all the rooms because electric service was unreliable.

Even discounting the lack of bathrooms, the house could have been a strong contender in a competition for the least practical room layout. As was typical for eighteenth-century farmhouses, one room led to the next; therefore most of the rooms were not separately accessible. Mother remembered that to get to her grandparents' bedroom, she first had to go through the kitchen and the living room.

Doing laundry, my mother explained, was also quite a chore. It was done in a little annex built in the corner of the courtyard on Lujza néni's side of the house. They first soaked the clothes overnight in a large, round, wooden tub in a mixture of water and lye made of wood ashes. Then they boiled the clothes in a big cauldron that was heated by a wood-burning stove. In winter, the servant girls boiled the laundry in the annex, in warm weather they carried the cauldron to the courtyard on laundry days, and in the fall they cooked the plum butter in this oddly multipurpose cauldron, too.

"Look," my mother continued, pointing to the rear wall of the courtyard, "that was where the cages for geese and ducks stood. The mother hens were above them in cages made of woven wood slats. It was always my duty to take the eggs out from under the hens, because they liked to sit on the eggs meant for eating. My God, how they could pinch; they didn't want to let me remove the eggs. The chicken coops were under the passage that led to the garden, and the pigeon house hung under the eaves above the arch of this passage. During winter, when the granaries had no grain in them, the chickens, ducks, and geese were kept in the first granary."

As we stood there, it was difficult to recognize in my mother's time-ravaged, sagging features the child I recalled from old photographs. Only the intense gaze of her eyes, which seemed to record everything, remained the same. But in her description of her grandparents' life from a distance of almost seventy-five years, she was again the child with the dark, serious look, who can be seen in a photograph from 1914, standing next to her grandparents a few steps from the place where she was standing now.

In the photo, which must have been taken on a warm spring day, she is holding a peony that she probably picked from the garden, and she is leaning against Bernhard, her grandfather. He must have been cold, the cold that results from old age, because he is wearing a wool coat and a hat, while Riza néni, his wife, and the two granddaughters are wearing only light dresses. Riza néni, who was a very good-looking woman in her youth and only sixty-two at the time of this picture, is overweight and her neck is disfigured by goiter.

While I thought of this old picture, my mother went on talking enthusiastically, eager to tell us the details of her daily life with her grandparents. I could see from Mr. Löwin's face that he would have been just as happy with a slightly less elaborate description, but he tried hard to appear interested. My brother made fewer pretenses; he looked rather bored and frequently glanced at his watch. He was anxious to get going, because we still had to visit the cemetery, eat some lunch, and make it to Vienna before nightfall.

Luckily, most of the things my mother told us that morning she had already described on the tapes I had been making with her for the past four years. Of course, it was nicer to hear her stories at the place where they all happened, but I had to agree with my brother, it was time to mosey on. So I continue my mother's description of a typical day at Riza néni's based on her taped reminiscences.

A Typical Day at Riza Néni's

MORNINGS AT RIZA NÉNI'S

EVERY DAY, as my mother explained, Riza néni was up at seven in the morning, because she had to help Paula, her live-in servant, prepare breakfast for her husband and Frigyes *bácsi*, her bachelor son who lived at home. (Even in old age, my mother always referred to Frigyes as "bácsi," the way young people call older men in Hungary.) Middle-aged, heavyset Paula had been with the family for decades. She was a young woman, a "Swabian" (the German-speaking minority in Hungary) farm girl from Levél, a nearby village, when she started working for them. She was the nicest person one can imagine, and everybody in the family loved her. Although Paula was a Catholic, after all the years with Riza néni, she knew the Jewish customs and dietary laws as well as any born Jew.

The first thing my great-grandfather did after getting up, even before eating breakfast, was to pray at one of the courtyard-facing windows. Great-grandfather, who was born in 1838, was a small, thin man. When my mother knew him he was already in his late seventies and a little senile. He no longer worked in the family business, which by that time was run by Frigyes bácsi, his eldest son. Sándor bácsi, my great-grandfather's younger brother and business partner, the person who started the business, was also too old to pay much attention to it. Although he was a bit feeble, my great-grandfather still got around, and he was the main guardian of traditional Jewish life in the family.

As my mother remembered: "I loved to watch him as he stood at the window, draped the tallith—the prayer shawl—around his shoulders, wrapped the leather strap of a little black tefillin box around his left arm, strapped another tefillin around his forehead, and prayed. But I have to confess to you, I don't know what the tefillin signifies. Before breakfast, and two more times during the day, my grandfather soaked his leg because he had an ulcer on it that didn't want to heal. Then Riza néni spread some stinky brown ointment over it and bandaged it. I can still see him sitting there shaking his head and quietly asking Riza néni as she was bandaging him: 'Rizl, mein Schatz, was ist aus Bernhard geworden?' (Riza, my darling, what has become of Bernhard?) It was heartbreaking."

The other grown-ups also got up around seven, about an hour before the grandchildren, because Frigyes bácsi started work early in the office of the family business. Every Thursday, the day of the weekly market, the grown-ups rose even earlier; the whole house was *meshuggeh* (crazy) then. This was the time when the farmers from the larger Moson area brought their livestock and produce to the market and used the opportunity to come to my great-grandparents for insurance matters. On such days my great-grandmother helped in the office as well, and once in a while my mother also helped fill out forms.

    After getting up, the grandchildren had to pour water from a big pitcher into the washbasin, which stood in the room where they slept, and wash themselves. When it was not in use, a fold-down lid covered the washbasin, which was recessed in the top of a cabinet. Underneath, doors concealed a bucket used for carrying water from the courtyard and a pitcher for bringing hot water from the kitchen. The children tried to get washed up as quickly and superficially as possible. Sometimes, though, Riza néni stood next to them, and if she found their efforts unsatisfactory, she scrubbed them herself. The children always left an awful mess around the washbasin, which they had to clean up later after breakfast. By then, it was no longer so early.

Both the children and the adults ate breakfast in the room next to the kitchen, which they used as an informal living and dining room. Breakfasts had a special magic at Riza néni's: the joy of awakening to a new day. Even before entering the room the children could smell the aroma of coffee floating toward them from the kitchen. The rectangular table in the middle of the room was nicely set. Paula was greeting them with a big smile from the kitchen door. As they sat down they glanced out the window to admire the horse-chestnut tree in the courtyard lit by the morning sun.

Riza néni usually kept them company at the table. In those years the children always spoke German with her, the language usually spoken in my great-grandparents' house. She was a short, stocky woman whose thick brown hair was the only thing that reminded the children of the beautiful young woman they knew from old photos. Her hair never turned gray, but

remained brown until the day she died. She always wore one of those old-fashioned long, black dresses, typically with a light, knee-length jacket echoing the fashion some thirty years earlier, and kept her money in a pouch under her long skirt. As my mother recalled, "I will never forget the sight of her reaching under her skirt for money. Upside-down 'TB' [for Therese Berger] monograms were embroidered on her long knitted socks; I guess she wanted to be able to read her initials when she looked down." But in spite of her old-fashioned outfits and customs, she was a modern woman. Many old people cannot accept the changing ways of the world, but she was different. She tried to understand her children and grandchildren and to accept their lifestyles, even if they were different from her essentially traditional world-view. She had a great sense of humor and knew how to find the right tone with the kids. They all adored her.

Breakfast was quite simple at Riza néni's. They drank coffee with milk, once in a rare while cocoa, but never tea. Usually, they ate bread with butter, homemade preserves, or honey, only rarely a slice of *gugelhupf* (see recipes on pages 288 and 291). Early in the morning, Paula brought milk from Mr. Rabl, a Catholic man who lived on the other side of Main Street and sold milk from his farm, but sometimes, if my mother managed to get up early, she went for the milk. After breakfast she had to help clean off the table and carry the dishes to the kitchen next door.

Every Thursday Riza néni went to the market and took my mother with her to help carry her basket. The market was held on Thursdays and Saturdays, not too far from my great-grandparents' house, on the other side of Main Street. People came from the entire region to buy and sell at the bustling market. The farmers, mainly "Swabians" from nearby villages, stood along the edge of the sidewalk selling produce from baskets next to them and livestock from the back of the horse-drawn carriages behind them.

Every few weeks, after the family had eaten a goose, Riza néni bought a live goose at the market to replace it. Three times a day Paula went with Ilka, the servant of Riza néni's sister, to the passage in the back of the courtyard to force-feed the geese. There they sat on shallow crates, gossiping while they each shoved a goose under their legs to hold it down, forced its bill open with their left hand, and stuffed corn mush into it with the right. Then they massaged the bulge of food down the neck of the bird. It wasn't easy to hold the frisky young geese, because they tried to jump out to escape this undignified treatment. The servants also fed the young geese a copper coin, which stayed in their stomachs and made their livers even larger. The grandchildren received this shiny coin when the goose got slaughtered. The children were also happy when they were allowed to taste the warm and soft corn mush that the servants cooked every few days for the geese from corn, salt, and a little fat. In my great-grandmother's household they never fattened more than two geese at a time and they killed one only every other week, because in addition to goose the family had chicken, duck, pigeon, and store-bought meat to eat. But aside from meat, they raised most of the food they ate.

In the morning Riza néni told Paula what to cook for lunch and dinner that day. Sometimes my great-grandmother flipped through her red-marble-paper-covered copybook of recipes to get inspiration or to look up some less common dish, but usually there was no need for this because, after so many years of cooking for the family, Paula knew exactly how to prepare the usual repertory of dishes.

They had something different for lunch and dinner every day; it took weeks before Paula might cook the same dish again. I was quite surprised to hear from my mother that she had rarely eaten *pörkölt* at Riza néni's. Pörkölt is a meat stew seasoned with paprika, perhaps the most common way of cooking meat in Hungary today. Looking through Riza néni's recipe collection confirmed my mother's observation that pörkölt used to be less ubiquitous. The collection included no recipe for pörkölt and paprika rarely appeared in the recipes as seasoning. Paprika is by far the most frequently used seasoning in Hungary today, but it only became popular in the early nineteenth century. In this respect, Riza néni's cooking style reflected the taste of a bygone era that was still quite close to her. While she hardly used paprika, consistent with her conservative taste in cooking, she loved to season her dishes with ginger. From the Middle Ages to the nineteenth century, dried ginger had been one of the most common spices in Hungary. But by Riza néni's time it was somewhat passé, and these days it seldom appears in local cooking.

This story about the pörkölt proves that sometimes a surprising omission in a book can be just as revealing as what is included. Looking through Riza néni's copybook of recipes I was similarly intrigued by the absence of dishes made with tomatoes. Aside from the occasional pörkölt, the only tomato dish my mother recalled eating at her grandmother's was stuffed green peppers. This is all the more remarkable because tomatoes are almost as common in Hungarian or Austrian cooking as they are in Italian or French cooking. The tomato—originally from Peru—was imported into Spain in the sixteenth century. Though it appeared in Hungary not much later, it was considered an ornamental plant and became popular in cooking only at the beginning of the nineteenth century. In Hungarian Jewish cuisine—typical of Ashkenazi Jewish cooking—tomatoes were rarely used, and certainly not in the traditional dishes, such as cholent, kugel, and so forth, but only in dishes adopted relatively late from Gentile cooking. The Sephardim, however, most of whom lived in a warmer climate than the Ashkenazim, used plenty of tomatoes.

But the Sephardim were a tiny minority among Hungarian Jews and had little influence on the local Ashkenazi-style cooking. A review of nineteenth-century Hungarian Jewish cookbooks confirms the infrequent use of tomato in local Jewish cooking of the period. A cookbook published in 1873, for example, included only one dish using tomato and two versions of tomato sauce among its 875 recipes. Though I am not aware of such beliefs among Hungarian Jews, Ashkenazi Jews in some other countries came up with a strange explanation for their avoidance of tomato, making it a virtual taboo. As John Cooper writes in his book *Eat and Be Satisfied*, "Tomatoes were not considered kosher by many Jews in Eastern Europe, as they were thought to contain blood. When Kim Chernin's [the author of *In My Mother's House*] mother first tasted a tomato upon immigrating [from Russia] to the United States her apprehensions caused her to vomit." Why these Ashkenazi Jews singled out the red tomato, but had no doubts about the other red vegetables or fruits, is a mystery to me.

Riza néni always used the vegetables and fruit that happened to be in season in her garden; she rarely had to buy vegetables or fruit at the market or from Mrs. Horváth, her neighbor who had a large orchard next to the Danube. Each season had something new in store for my great-grandmother's family, but the arrival of spring was something special. Soon after the first daffodils bloomed and the first tender leaves appeared on the trees in their garden, they could admire the flowers on the apricot trees and a little later on the apple and pear trees as well. The berry bushes filled out with leaves. The gooseberry bushes flowered, then wilted, and slowly the bases of the flowers began to swell until eventually they turned into berries. What could compare with the joy of greeting the first asparagus in April and the first peas in May, or with the excitement of tasting the first raspberries and strawberries in late spring?

If Riza néni needed meat for lunch or dinner, she took the shopping basket and went to Mr. Schlesinger, the kosher butcher, who had a shop on the corner of Duna Street diagonally across the street from her. Farther down on that side of Main Street, past Vilmos Rév Street, there was another kosher butcher shop, but she rarely went there because Mr. Schlesinger's shop was more convenient for her. Mother liked to accompany Riza néni to the butcher because he usually gave her a slice of roast to munch on. Riza néni knew all the customers at the butcher, and it was another occasion for the women to gossip a little.

If Riza néni decided to have chicken or any other fowl for lunch, in the morning Paula caught the bird, bound its feet, put it in a wicker shopping basket, and gave it to my mother to take it to the *shochet*, the Jewish ritual slaughterer. The shochet, who was also the assistant cantor, had a little wooden cabin behind the one-story building containing his apartment and that of the *shammas* (synagogue beadle) in the courtyard of the synagogue. My mother knocked on a window of his apartment, the shochet came out, and while they walked to the shack he inquired about the health of my great-grandparents. At the shack he first used his nail to check the sharpness of his blade, which by religious requirement had to be perfectly sharp and free of any nicks to avoid torturing the animal. Then for a second he let the bird loose to see if it could move, because it was forbidden to kill a sick animal. Now, while my mother waited outside the shack, he clasped the wings of the animal, bent its neck back, plucked some of feathers from the neck, said a brief blessing, and slit the throat of the bird with one quick, decisive movement. It was a virtuoso performance. Then he hung it for a few minutes from one of the hooks on the wall to drain its blood, which was carried by a trough at the foot of the wall to a pit in the courtyard. After my mother had brought the chicken home, Paula took it out to the garbage pit behind my great-grandparents' house, where she cleaned it with amazing speed. When she plucked geese, she carefully kept the down for later use in pillows and quilts.

To kosher the poultry, Paula cleaned out its insides, cut open or removed parts that could contain too much blood, cut up the bird if she planned to cook it in pieces, soaked the pieces for about half an hour. Then she placed them on a big round basket, which was held in a slanted position by two legs at one end, and salted them. After waiting for an hour for

The shochet's cabin.

the salt to draw out the remaining blood, she shook off the salt, rinsed each piece three times, and briefly soaked them again. Finally, she rinsed off the salt from the basket, placed the meat pieces on it, poured another bucket of water over them, and let them drain on the basket.

In the mornings my mother had to help with house cleaning. Paula swept the rooms and my mother helped dust. She had to take the garbage out to the garbage pit behind the house, and, when she was a little bigger, she had to help shovel grain in the granaries to aerate it. "I was not too keen on shoveling grain," she recalled, "but I loved to be in those cavernous cool granaries. A wooden stair led up to the gallery in the first granary. There you could walk on the gallery connecting the granaries all the way to Lujza néni's side of the house and come down in the sixth granary. Small windows set high in the wall on the courtyard side provided ventilation and light. We grandchildren loved to play around in those huge heaps of grain. We slid down the stair railings and jumped off halfway down into the grain underneath us. It was great fun! You can imagine how the grain skidded in all directions."

At times the grandchildren had to help Paula pick fruits or vegetables in the garden, carry them to the kitchen, and peel them. Except for gathering what she needed for cooking, Paula didn't work in the garden; there was a man who came periodically to do the tilling, planting, weeding, and whatever else had to be done in the garden. Even if they were not asked to help, the grandchildren liked to hang about the kitchen while Paula was getting lunch ready. Paula understood the children's yearnings to be the cook's helper, and gave them some simple tasks, such as peeling onions, podding peas, pitting cherries, or stirring the roux. The children were more hindrance than help, but she had infinite patience with them.

Frequently, the family had a ten o'clock snack, although there was hardly enough time between breakfast and lunch to get hungry. They didn't eat this snack together at the table like they ate lunch or dinner. Usually Frigyes bácsi made a sandwich for himself in the office, where he kept some sausages and bacon. The snack served to the other members of the family could be a sandwich, hard-cooked eggs, or *pénecl*, as great-grandmother called the fried bread, using a word derived from the Yiddish for "slice." She didn't speak Yiddish, but this was the name for this snack in Jewish families. To make it, Paula heated goose fat in a wide pan, fried slices of bread in it until they were crisp and golden brown, and sprinkled them with salt. Other options were fruit or *prósza*, a sweet corn cake (see recipe on page 67), which Paula made of cornmeal with goose fat and raisins; it was wonderfully light and the grandchildren adored it.

Lángos, a type of flatbread, was another favorite snack. Paula made it on the days when she made bread, and she used a piece of the bread dough for this snack, whose name means "with flame." As my mother recalled, at Riza néni's, the lángos had been baked instead of fried in hot fat as is common in Hungary today.

All the grandchildren loved to eat lángos, but watching Paula make bread dough was almost as much fun as eating it. Paula made bread twice a week, and the preparations began the previous evening. First she made a starter by taking dried bits of dough preserved from previous batches of bread and soaking them in a little lukewarm water, to which she added a bit of sugar. Then she took a large wooden trough, which was carved from half a tree trunk, and put it on a special stand shaped to fit the trough's round bottom. She sieved flour into it, made a well in the center of this heap, poured in the starter, and with a wooden spoon stirred a little flour into the liquid. She covered the trough with a kitchen towel and left it in

a warm place in the kitchen. In the middle of the night, she got up to see if the starter had risen and, when necessary, would start kneading the dough. If Paula was lucky, the starter needed more time and she could catch a little more sleep. But even if she could go back to sleep, she couldn't rest long because she had to get up very early to add some sieved boiled potatoes, caraway seeds, and lukewarm salty water to the risen starter in the trough and to begin to knead. The wooden stand squeaked as Paula used all her considerable weight and strength to push and knead the dough in the trough. With the skill brought on by years of practice, Paula kept kneading and slapping the dough for a long time, until finally it stopped sticking to the sides of the trough and turned into a satiny smooth ball. After allowing the dough to rise, Paula cut off a small part for the lángos, formed a loaf from the bigger part, put it into a special round basket, which she had previously lined with a kitchen towel and sprinkled with flour, and left the dough to rise again. She then put the smaller pice of dough for the lángos into a bowl to rise, and, after it rose, rolled it out and transferred it to a baking sheet.

After the bread dough had risen, Paula carefully folded the edges of the kitchen towel in the basket to cover the dough and gave the basket—weighing about eight pounds—to my mother to take to Mr. Flesch, the baker, who had a shop near the beginning of Ostermayer Street. Mr. Flesch, whose nose seemed to try in vain to compete in size with his considerable belly, stuck an identifying number on the bread dough and gave my mother a ticket, plus a cookie for noshing. She quickly stuffed them into her pocket and hurried home because she wanted to be there when Paula took the lángos out of the oven. Shortly before noon, she returned to the baker to pick up the big round loaf of bread and on the way home broke off bits from the fresh, crisp, warm crust to munch.

Flatbread for Snack
Lángos

Everyday Hungarian cooking in the last fifty years has shown an increased awareness of foreign cuisines but the variety of traditional dishes has decreased. A relatively limited number of traditional dishes are repeated again and again, while many regional specialties and interesting variations of the more standard repertory have been forgotten. Of course, cooking is part of a living culture, and it shouldn't be surprising when new dishes replace some old ones. Still, I think it is worthwhile to study the history of cooking to revive some of the interesting but forgotten dishes.

Lángos is a good example of how interesting dishes disappear and food preparation gets codified. As my mother noted, lángos is known today in Hungary as a snack made of deep-fried bread dough or potato dough, sometimes made with some chopped cabbage mixed into the dough. But it is always fried. I must confess to not knowing that a baked variety used to be common until I heard about Riza néni's lángos and found some similar variations in old cookbooks.

Originally, lángos was a byproduct of homemade bread. Just like Riza néni, people used some of their bread dough to make this snack. These days, when homemade bread has become less common, making lángos is no longer tied to bread making. Lángos, which is somewhat similar to the Italian *focaccia*, belongs to the family of flatbreads. Both lángos and focaccia used to be baked on the hearth, and this is reflected in their names: we can see the flame (*láng* in Hungarian) of the hearth in *lángos* and *focus* (Latin for hearth) in the Italian word *focaccia*. Lángos can be served as a snack or appetizer or with a large salad as a light lunch. I will suggest a few traditional variations, but you can also invent new ones. Just like pizza or focaccia, it is easy to come up with personal variations. You can divide the dough on the baking sheet into two or three strips and use a different topping on each strip for variety. Unbleached all-purpose flour can be substituted for the bread and rye flour. The texture and flavor of the lángos will be different, a little blander, but nevertheless nice. By the way, you can use the same dough for making bread.

Unlike the vast majority of recipes in this book, this and the following recipe were not included in my great-grandmother's collection. My mother remembered eating them frequently at Riza néni's, however, and in order to include examples of snacks served at my great-grandmother's, I reconstructed them based on my mother's descriptions and contemporaneous recipes. Most people today rarely make bread at home, and so I decided to use yeast in my recipe instead of starter made of leftover dough from a previous batch of bread. But I used less yeast than usual and used the long-proofed (slow rising) method to make the dough, because it gave similar results to the type of dough Paula had made. If you feel that you have less time than Riza néni's servant, however, you might decide to let the bread rise faster at room temperature.

YIELD:	18 small pieces
TOTAL TIME:	about 1 hour 10 minutes, plus 11 hours for rising
INGREDIENTS:	1 small (about 6 ounces) russet (Idaho) potato
	½ cup barely warm (105°–110°) water
	1 teaspoon (about ½ envelope) active dry yeast
	1 teaspoon sugar
	¾ cup rye flour
	2¾ cups bread flour (the exact quantity depends on the moisture in the flour and potato)
	1½ teaspoons kosher salt
	1 tablespoon caraway seeds, bruised in a mortar
	2 tablespoons canola oil, or rendered chicken, goose, or duck fat
	⅓–½ cup barely warm water
	1 teaspoon canola oil (to coat the baking pan)
	1 teaspoon coarse kosher or sea salt (to sprinkle on top)
	1 teaspoon caraway seeds (to sprinkle on top)
	2 tablespoons rendered chicken, goose, or duck fat
SPECIAL EQUIPMENT:	potato ricer
	food processor, at least 7-cup capacity
	baking sheet (12" x 18")

1. Boil the potato in its skin until tender when tested with a fork or paring knife, about 35 minutes; peel it, cut it into 3 or 4 pieces, while it is still hot put it through the ricer, spread it on a baking sheet or large plate, and let it cool to lukewarm. Place ½ cup barely warm (not hot) water in the bowl of the food processor and stir yeast and sugar into the water. Let it stand at room temperature for about 10 minutes, until little bubbles appear on the surface.

2. Use the plastic dough blade in a 7-cup processor and the metal blade in a larger one. Place 2 kinds of flour, salt, caraway seeds, oil or fat, and potato in the bowl of the processor. Turn on the processor and pour in ⅓ cup water. Process for 20 seconds; wait 3 minutes, and process for

about another 20 seconds, until the dough sticks together, cleans the inside of the bowl, and forms a ball. If the bowl is very full you will have to scrape down the sides of the bowl after the initial processing. If you see that the dough doesn't want to come together because it is too dry, with the motor running add more water—1 tablespoon at a time—and briefly process after each addition to see if that does it.

3. Turn the dough out onto a floured work surface and knead it for about 5 minutes, adding more flour as needed for a smooth, elastic dough that is not sticky and springs back when pressed with your finger. Knead by pressing down into the dough with your hands, pushing forward, folding the dough back on itself, giving it a quarter turn, and repeating the same sequence.

4. Transfer the dough into a large clean bowl and cover the bowl tightly with plastic wrap or a well-fitting lid. Place the bowl in the refrigerator and allow the dough to slowly rise for about 8 hours or overnight, until it has doubled its bulk. Alternatively, let the dough rise for about 3 hours at room temperature.

5. Punch down the risen dough in the bowl by bringing the outer edges of the dough toward its center and pressing down to push out the air; cover it again and allow it to rise at room temperature for about 3 hours to double in bulk.

6. Set a rack at the lower third of the oven and preheat the oven to 425°F. Lightly coat a baking sheet with a little canola oil.

7. Place the dough on the floured work surface. Punch it down again, knead it for a few seconds, and roll it out with a floured rolling pin to about 12" × 17" in size. Transfer the dough onto the baking sheet and stretch it to fit. Pierce the dough at frequent intervals with a fork, brush it with a little water, and sprinkle it evenly with caraway seeds and coarse salt. With a dough scraper or knife, cut the dough sheet into 3 strips lengthwise and into 6 sections in the other direction.

8. Bake it in the preheated oven for about 20 minutes, until light golden brown. I prefer to eat the pieces of lángos warm, but you can also serve

them at room temperature. They are irresistibly delicious when fresh out of the oven, but the ½"-thick lángos dries out quickly, so it is best to keep cooled-down leftovers in a plastic bag where they will keep for a day or so. To revive slightly stale pieces, brush both their sides with cold water and place them for a few minutes directly on a rack in a 350°F oven.

VARIATIONS:

1. Cut the dough into 8 or 10 equal pieces and stretch each piece to a ½"-thick oval. Heat 1" vegetable oil in a wide pan over medium heat until the oil is about 370°F. Fry as many pieces at a time as your pan can accommodate in one layer, and turn them over in the hot oil to make sure they brown evenly on both sides. Drain them on a wire rack set over a plate or paper towels. Rub them with peeled garlic and sprinkle them with salt. Serve them hot.

2. Mix chopped *griebenes* (chicken crackling) and freshly ground pepper into the dough. (See page 111 for instructions on how to make cracklings.)

3. Rub the rough bottom of the lángos with a peeled clove of garlic.

4. To make wonderfully tasty cabbage lángos, core ½ of a small, 1½-pound cabbage and shred it very finely with the shredding disc of a food processor. Transfer it to a bowl, mix it with 1 tablespoon salt, and let it stand for about 15 minutes. Rinse out the salt and squeeze the water from the cabbage. Heat a little oil in a large skillet, add the cabbage, mix, cover, and cook over medium-low heat for 5 minutes. Season it with freshly ground pepper and let it cool to lukewarm. Add ¾ to 1 cup of the cooked shredded cabbage together with the other ingredients when you mix the dough. Use less water in the dough, about ¼ cup or so, because the cabbage also contains some moisture. You can always add a little more water if the dough doesn't want to come together. Cabbage lángos stays moist longer than the basic one, but this matters only if you can resist gobbling up all of them the first day. I couldn't.

5. Instead of cabbage, add chopped dill to the dough.

6. Spread sour cream over the fully baked lángos. If you want to comply with Jewish dietary laws, you must use lángos made with oil or butter for this.

Corn Cake
Prósza

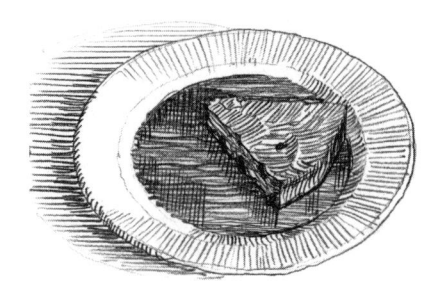

Pouring hot milk or water into a mixture of cornmeal and sugar, and adding melted butter or fat, sometimes also eggs to this, was the way the earliest versions of prósza were made. But this rather dense cake couldn't have been the "wonderfully light" prósza my mother recalled eating at Riza néni's. Probably, Paula made a yeast-leavened version that became popular around the turn of the century. I decided to substitute baking powder for yeast to make preparing this simple coffee cake even faster and easier.

YIELD: 6–8 servings

TOTAL TIME: about 40 minutes

INGREDIENTS:
- 1 teaspoon unsalted butter or canola oil (to grease the form)
- 1¼ cups stone-ground fine (not coarse) yellow corn meal
- 2 tablespoons sugar
- ¼ teaspoon kosher salt
- ¾ teaspoon double-acting baking powder
- ⅓ cup golden raisins
- ¾ cup milk or water
- 2 tablespoons melted unsalted butter or canola oil (Riza néni used rendered goose fat)
- 1 large egg, lightly beaten

SPECIAL EQUIPMENT:
7" tart form with removable bottom or 7" spring form
baking sheet

1. Center a rack in the oven and preheat the oven to 375°F. Grease a form.

2. In a large bowl, mix well corn meal, sugar, salt, baking powder, and raisins. Add melted butter or oil to milk or water and stir this and the egg into the dry ingredients. Pour the batter into the form and place it on a baking sheet.

3. Bake it in the preheated oven for 30 minutes. Let it cool a little in the form on a cake rack. Transfer the approximately 1"-high cake to a plate, cut it into slices, and serve it while it is still warm. I like to eat it with a little raspberry or other fruit syrup, or with compote.

Putting Up Fruits and Vegetables at Riza Néni's

Every few weeks during summer the sweet smell of cooking fruit would waft from my great-grandmother's kitchen. Putting up fruits and vegetables for the long months of winter was an important task in those years when nobody used commercially canned products. During winter, when the only available fruit was apples and the only vegetables were cabbage or root vegetables, they yearned for the taste of fruit and green vegetables, such as peas or beans. It was as if the balmy days of summer had been preserved in those canning jars. Opening one of those jars had the power of instantaneously evoking for them the summer, the sharp morning light in their garden where Paula or my mother had picked the fruit, and the wonderful aroma of the fruit cooking in a large pot on the stove.

During winter the jars of preserves and vegetables on the shelves of Riza néni's pantry had been gradually replaced by empty jars, and by early spring only a few full jars helped recall the previous summer. Then in late spring the shelves slowly began to fill up again. First came the jars of various berry preserves and bottles of raspberry syrup. Then cherries, apricots, green beans, peas, and by the end of summer one had to look hard to find an empty jar on the shelves. The neat rows of canned fruit and vegetables on the shelves of her pantry were my great-grandmother's pride and joy. Sterilizing the jars, selecting and cooking the fruit, and filling the jars had to be done with meticulous care. On such days Riza néni was always in the kitchen to help and to supervise Paula.

On the day before canning my mother had to help pick the fruit in the garden. Fruits my great-grandmother didn't grow in her garden, such as cherries or plums, she bought from Teréz Horváth. She was a rather well off Catholic widow who had, in addition to a huge orchard near the Danube, a public steam bath in an annex to her house, and a lumberyard in Duna Street.

My great-grandparents had a huge quince tree in their garden; my mother's swing hung from one of the branches, and there was a table and bench around its trunk. From its fruit, Riza néni put up cooked wedges in syrup and made preserves and quince paste, which was the grandchildren's favorite. She made this by pressing the cooked fruit through a sieve, cooking the purée with sugar until it got very thick, pouring it into a long, narrow cake form, and finally allowing the unmolded quince paste to dry. At other times she poured the thick, cooked purée onto a board, pressed almonds into the paste and, after letting the paste harden for about a week, cut it with a cookie cutter so that each piece had an almond in it. The quince paste would have kept in the pantry for years had the children not eaten it up sooner.

Canning always meant bustle and excitement, but nothing could compare with the commotion of making plum butter in late summer. They needed a lot of it because they liked to eat it on bread and Riza néni used it in baking. Though not quite as hard as quince paste the dark blue, almost black, plum butter was so thick you could cut it with a knife. In the morning of the plum-butter–cooking day Paula and Ilka, Lujza néni's servant, carried the big cauldron from the laundry room to the courtyard. For the occasion, Riza néni and Lujza néni, the two perpetually quarreling sisters, decided to make peace and join forces. The stove under the cauldron was fired up and the washed prune plums put in for a short time to separate the pits from the fruit. Then Paula and Ilka took the fruit out, sieved it to separate the pits, and returned the fruit to the cauldron to cook. They used no sugar or preservatives in making plum butter, only patience and muscle power, as it had to be cooked and stirred for at least a day and constantly watched so that it didn't burn on the bottom of the pot. Paula and Ilka took turns stirring the furiously splattering hot plum butter in the pot, and the children had to help, too. The fruit purée had to be cooked until it was so thick that it wouldn't drop from an inverted spoon. Usually it was late evening by the time they could pour the hot purée into large ceramic jars, which they covered and sealed the next day when the plum butter was cold.

Perhaps the most unusual types of canned fruit my great-grandmother made were the whole sour cherries or prune plums preserved in spiced vinegar. These they ate as side dishes with meat. To make them, my great-grandmother punctured each fruit with a needle, put it in a jar with cinnamon and cloves, and poured a hot mixture of vinegar and water over the fruit. The next day she poured off the liquid and repeated the procedure. After repeating this the third time, she put the jar in a sunny place to ripen for a week or two.

The Kitchen and the Pantry at Riza Néni's

Riza néni and her family entered the apartment from the covered arcade in the courtyard through a hallway, which they called the "small entrance hall," although it wasn't small at all. The formal dining room was on the street side of this hallway and the kitchen on the opposite side. Next to the kitchen door was the *Handspeiz*, a closet-like pantry. There, my great-grandmother kept the more expensive ingredients, such as chocolate, cocoa, raisins, and cone sugar. Refined sugar, which was very expensive in those days, was frequently sold in cone-shaped blocks. Riza néni used a hammer or the heavy brass pestle to break off lumps from the cone sugar, and her dessert recipes usually specified how finely these lumps had to be pounded in the mortar. For my mother and the other grandchildren this closet-like pantry was like a secret chamber, because it was kept locked. As my mother fondly recalled, "With all its goodies it was the secret chamber of our dreams."

The other provisions were kept in a separate room that opened from the courtyard. This pantry was quite far from the kitchen. If Riza néni or Paula wanted to go there from the kitchen she had to pass through the hallway to the courtyard and walk toward the granaries. The pantry had a tiny window facing the courtyard and another one facing the garden. Huge enameled mixing bowls in the room held barley and all kinds of other grain. They kept eggs in the same bowl with the barley because, according to Riza néni, eggs kept well that way.

The enameled steel pot of *schmaltz* was also there. Schmaltz at Riza néni's always meant rendered goose fat, never chicken fat. She used goose fat for much of her cooking, so it is not surprising that she needed a big pot for it. The eighteen inches high, enameled steel pot had two handles on its sides and its hinged lid had a strap for a padlock. Though Riza néni never locked it because she locked the pantry door, similar pots were usually kept locked in Hungarian Gentile households, where they were used for storing lard. People wanted to guard the valuable rendered fat, and the lockable lid reflected this. Riza néni also used the schmaltz pot for conserving roast meat, which kept in it for weeks, provided it was completely buried in the fat.

In addition to food, all kinds of no-longer-used old things were kept in the pantry, including some old-fashioned capes that hung in a wardrobe. Coachmen in the family business had worn them back when Frigyes bácsi had traveled by coach from village to village to sell insurance, but by my mother's time this was no longer done. The family no longer had coaches, much less coachmen, but for some reason my great-grandparents kept those capes. The wardrobe with the capes was the only piece of Biedermeier furniture at Riza néni's; all other furniture was in the historic revival styles fashionable in 1876, when she had bought them new to furnish her apartment. The 1840s wardrobe, which would be a sought-after piece in any antique shop today, must have seemed old junk to her, not yet distant enough to be considered antique. It shows how little she thought of it that she not only banished it to the pantry but also, as the ultimate insult, had its original French-polished inlaid walnut veneer painted white.

Next to the wardrobe stood a chest of drawers full of old hats. They kept everything at my great-grandmother's; they never threw anything out! My mother and Lili, her sister, were only allowed to go into the locked pantry when they were a little older. It was a great place to play: they took the hats out of the drawers to try them on, checked out those big mixing bowls, and stuck their hands into everything to see what was there.

The kitchen itself was large, about nineteen by sixteen feet. Its big, four-legged, wood-fired metal stove had two burners and an oven. Riza néni had bought this Viennese *Sparherd* (economy stove) about forty years earlier and saw no reason to replace it with a more modern one. Every morning Paula got on her knees in front of the stove to empty the ashes from the drawers under the two fireboxes—one for the burners and another one for the oven—and to set the fire for the day. She didn't throw out the ashes but kept them for the laundry, which she soaked in a mixture of ashes and water. The burners of the stove had concentric cast iron rings, and the number of rings removed could regulate the heat under the pot. The oven sat like a big box on top of the stove next to the burners, not under them as is usual today. Plates or dishes waiting to be served could be kept warm on top of the oven, which had a low railing around it for protection.

The bathtub stood behind the stove in the corner of the kitchen next to another stove, a tall cylindrical one used just for heating bath water. Once a week Paula lifted off the heavy lid of this stove, filled up the drum with water carried from the well in the courtyard, and everybody took a bath. That is, everybody except for Paula, who bathed in the laundry tub in the laundryroom and used the washstand in the kitchen for daily hygiene. She slept in the kitchen, where she had a small wardrobe and a fold-out bed. The bathtub in the kitchen, when not in use, was covered by a board, which they used as another work surface.

The large kitchen table, which had a thick, red marble top, stood in

Paula bathed in the laundry tub.

one corner on the window side of the room. On a shelf above the table, the heavy, cast brass mortars and the copper bowls glistened next to the cast iron scale with its two brass trays and a wooden box containing the brass weights. Paula set the bucket filled with water for cooking on a bench in front of the window. The separate cupboards for the meat and dairy dishes stood in the other corner.

The cooking pots were made of enameled steel or cast iron; the baking pans, of tinned steel. If the enamel of the pots got chipped and the steel started to rust, the pot was patched by a roving tinsmith who came to my great-grandmother's house. Every few weeks a knife grinder also came by to ask if she had any knives to sharpen.

They hadn't, of course, a refrigerator in the kitchen; they hadn't even an icebox there. Meat and other perishables were kept in a locked part of the cellar, which was under Lujza néni's side of the house. The cellar, which stayed cool even in hot weather, was Riza néni's refrigerator, and the meat kept there for a day or so. She rarely used ice for chilling food, because the ice had to be bought. During winter she kept onions, potatoes, root vegetables, and cabbages in wooden crates in the cellar.

Dietary Laws in Transition

Riza néni kept kosher. She kept dairy and meat separate and had separate sets of dishes for them. Sometimes, though, she bent the rules a bit. She claimed, for example, that if she wiped off the red marble top of the kitchen table it could be used for dairy, and that if she washed it off again it could be used for meat. But she never cooked dairy products and meat at the same time on the stove, and she placed a metal plate over the burners when she used them for dairy dishes.

If by accident some dairy product touched a knife designated for *fleischig* (meat) cooking and thus the knife became *treyf* (not kosher, forbidden), it had to be stuck into the ground in the courtyard. Riza néni would keep it there for a few days, claiming the knife became all right again because the earth "sucked the milk out of it." This was not something unique to my great-grandmother, but a widespread Jewish custom.

My great-grandmother and especially my great-grandfather were religious. Naturally, they bought beef and veal at a kosher butcher. At the same time, my great-grandmother knew that her three sons hadn't kept kosher when they served in the army during World War I. In addition to paying no attention to dietary rules, her sons hardly observed the holidays; and they bought pork sausages from Ördögh (ironically the name means "devil" in Hungarian), the local Christian butcher. In deference to my great-grandfather, his sons never brought sausages or bacon into the family's apartment because they didn't want to eat such things in front of their father. They kept their sausages in one of the large granaries and ate them there. In this respect Riza néni was a very flexible person. While she kept kosher, she accepted that her children didn't. When Riza néni came for a day to visit her daughter in Budapest, she knew that her daughter didn't have a separate set of dishes for dairy products and that she occasionally cooked pork, but she thought: "Now I am at her place; I'll eat her food." Great-grandfather, on the other hand, never visited his daughter in Budapest, perhaps because he was too old, or perhaps because he knew that he couldn't eat at her house.

✠ LUNCHES AT RIZA NÉNI'S ✠

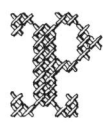

PAULA COOKED LUNCH, the main meal in Hungary, but Riza néni told her what to cook. My great-grandmother taught Paula to cook when she started working for them, but Riza néni baked the cakes and oversaw the canning and preserving. Most of the food preparation was done by hand or using only a few simple manual devices, such as meat, nut, and poppy seed grinders.

Some of Riza néni's recipes give charming and evocative descriptions of lunch preparations. Instead of the usual way of describing the time needed for various cooking steps, such as "cook this for thirty minutes," they tell at what time in the morning the cooking tasks should begin in order to have lunch ready by noon. Her recipe for green beans, for example, goes like this: "Wash and cut enough green beans for 6 people. Heat ⅓ cup rendered beef fat, add 2 finely chopped onions and let them brown. Then at 9:30 add the green beans and cook covered until 11. At that time you should dust them with ⅝ cup flour and allow this to cook until 11:30, stirring diligently. Add ⅝ cup vinegar, 1¼ cups water, enough ginger to fit on the tip of a knife, part of a cinnamon stick, and salt. Let it all cook well." As this shows, the green beans were "ready" by noon, although after two and a half hours of cooking they must have been terribly overcooked. Traditional Jewish cooking, just like Hungarian cooking in this respect, has many wonderful features, but crisp, lightly cooked vegetables are not among them.

Lunch was exactly at noon, when the church bells rang. It was served in the family's informal living room next to the kitchen. The formal dining room and the formal living room, called the *szalon*, were used only on holidays or when there were visitors. The formal living room didn't even have a stove, so in winter it couldn't be used at all. In the summertime, if the weather was good, the family ate in the *szaletli*, the large covered wooden gazebo in the garden.

Shortly before noon Riza néni tasted the dishes cooking on the stove to see if the seasoning needed to be adjusted; then she called my mother in from the courtyard or the garden where she was playing and told her to wash up and help set the table for lunch. They used a simple set of sturdy plates for everyday meals. Riza néni only pulled out her elegant

Riza néni tasted the dishes cooking on the stove.

hand-painted, blue-patterned china if she had guests or for holidays. But the everyday china was also nice: the plates had pretty flowers painted along the rim. My mother carried the breadbasket from the kitchen to the table, and Riza néni gave her a small pitcher of wine to set on the table for Frigyes bácsi, who liked to drink a little wine with his meals.

The whole family had lunch at the same time. Unless Frigyes bácsi was away on a business trip, he always showed up a few minutes before noon to join his parents for lunch. He teasingly said as he entered the kitchen: "Was für ein fabelhaftes Geruch! Was ist das, Schweinebraten?" (What a fabulous smell! What is it, roast pork?) To which Riza néni answered in mock horror: "Aber geh, Frigyes, mach nicht immer blöde Witze." (Come on, Frigyes, don't make always silly jokes.) Great-grandfather also came in from the porch where he liked to sit, and asked: "Rizl, Schätzle, was gibt's zum Essen?" (Riza darling, what's there to eat?)

Before sitting down to the table, all of them went to the washbasin, which stood between the bed and the sofa in the informal living room, for the ritual handwashing. They poured water over their right hand from a strange-looking metal cup that had two handles next to each other, then switched the cup to the rinsed hand and rinsed the other hand while saying the appropriate *broche*, blessing. They also had to perform this ritual first thing in the morning, to remove the "uncleanness" of the night, and before any meal, even a snack. According to my mother, the reason for the two handles was that one handle was designated for the "dirty" and the other for the "clean" hand—at least that was how my great-grandfather had explained it to her.

While Riza néni helped her husband tuck a big napkin in his shirt collar, Paula brought the steaming soup bowl from the kitchen and set it in the middle of the table. Paula didn't eat with them, but ate in the kitchen after they finished lunch. Great-grandmother served Frigyes bácsi first, since he was the family's wage earner at the time. Years earlier, my great-grandfather had been the first to be served, but by now he was a little senile and Frigyes bácsi ran the family business. Great-grandfather offered a short blessing over the bread and then they were allowed to eat. Great-grandfather's hands were quite unsteady: sometimes he spilled the soup from his spoon, and sometimes he dropped a piece of food by accident. My God, he was old. But he would never forget to say the blessing before and after the meal.

Every day they started the meal with soup; one could perhaps imagine lunch consisting of only soup, but not lunch without soup. Riza néni had an astonishingly large repertoire of soups: hot and cold soups, hearty and light soups, savory and sweet soups, and even caraway seed soup to cure stomach ache. She rarely served chicken soup during the week because it was reserved for the Sabbath. Occasionally, she started lunch with beef soup, served with one of her many soup garnishes, such as ginger-flavored soup biscuits or liver dumplings (see recipes on page 89 and 91), but most of the soups were vegetable soups made from vegetables from her garden. Although borscht is considered in the United States to be a traditional Jewish dish, my mother couldn't remember ever eating

Riza néni helped her husband tuck a napkin in his shirt collar.

it at Riza néni's. Jews in Poland, Russia, and the Ukraine adopted borscht from local Gentile cooking. In Hungary, where beet soup is not common, borscht is not part of traditional Jewish cuisine and most nineteenth- or early twentieth-century Hungarian Jewish cookbooks don't include it.

Mother liked to watch Paula cook, and Paula showed her how to make soup by thickening the water or stock in which the vegetables have been cooking with roux, which she allowed my mother to stir. She also showed her how to make soup by first sautéing the vegetables and chopped onion in fat, then sprinkling this with a little flour, allowing the flour to cook for a few minutes, and then adding water or stock. This was the way Paula made her wonderful kohlrabi soup in late spring, when the kohlrabi was still tender, and the sautéing of the kohlrabi with a little sugar was the trick that gave this soup its intense flavor my mother raved about even after seventy years.

The main dish was usually meat or poultry, but sometimes Riza néni served some offal or innards, such as veal tongue in "Bohemian"-style sweet-and-sour sauce (see recipe on page 104) or calf lung. She also made vegetable dishes such as layered or stuffed cabbage, green pepper, or kohlrabi. The flavorful combination of vegetables and ground or chopped meat in these dishes could stretch a little meat to make a satisfying main course.

Potatoes, rice, or dumplings accompanied the meat dishes. There were so many kinds of dumplings that my great-grandmother could have made a different dumpling every day for weeks on end. There were potato dumplings, farina-potato dumplings (see recipes on pages 113 and 111), bread dumplings, and napkin dumplings, but my mother especially loved Riza néni's cabbage dumplings (see recipe on page 108), usually served as a side dish or occasionally as a light main course for dinner. Frequently, they had freshly picked vegetables from the garden along with the meat. Riza néni might serve fresh peas, for example, which she puréed (see recipe on page 119), made with a cream sauce, or, in a dish called *risibisi*, combined with rice. One of my mother's favorite vegetable dishes was sweet-and-sour summer squash with dill, which was eaten as a refreshingly tart cold dish in warm weather and as a hot vegetable dish in winter. Paula used the traditional wood-framed steel cutter to cut the squash into long, narrow strands. To be able to serve this dish in winter Riza néni made canned squash, preserving the cut strands of the squash in vinegar.

During the week they rarely ate cake after the main dish at lunch; usually they had cake only on Fridays and Saturdays. It wasn't because my great-grandparents were trying to save money, it was simply the custom. Instead, they ate a simple home-style dessert. Occasionally, such a warm, sweet noodle-dish or dessert dumplings would replace the meat and vegetable course after the soup. For example, they would have *derelye* (similar to large jam-filled raviolis), which were sometimes made with regular noodle dough, at other times with potato dough. Or Riza néni would serve warm potato noodles with ground poppy seeds (see recipe on page 318) or walnuts sprinkled over them. My mother's favorite among all those warm noodle dishes was not a sweet but a savory dish in which boiled noodles were mixed with cooked toasted farina (see recipe on page 107).

The noodles were never store-bought, but freshly made on the kitchen marble table by Paula. She would take them out to the sunny courtyard to dry on a white linen–covered table. Mother was in charge of guarding the noodles against the chickens who during the day roamed free in the courtyard and unfortunately seemed to like noodles or at least the elevated, sunny spot of the tabletop.

When Paula made plum or apricot dumplings (see recipe on page 130), made of potato dough stuffed with the pitted fruit and rolled in toasted bread crumbs, the children had dumpling-eating contests, usually won by Lili, my mother's older sister. She could eat as many as fifteen, while my mother could usually manage only eight or ten.

Then there were the strudels! Paula made the dough on the kitchen table, which she moved to the middle of the kitchen and covered with a tablecloth. After putting the ball of dough on the floured tablecloth, she rolled it out, then walked around the table, stretching the dough with the back of her hand until it was paper-thin. She tore off the thicker edge of the dough, let the thin dough dry for a few minutes, then filled it and used the tablecloth to help roll up the strudel. She used either a sweet filling, like apple, poppy seed, or cottage cheese, or a savory filling, such as cabbage, potato, ground meat, or for a dairy meal salted cottage cheese with chopped dill mixed into it.

Green Pea Soup with Egg Dumplings
Grüne Erbsen Suppe

Riza néni must have liked fresh peas because she included more recipes for peas in her collection than for any other vegetable. She raised her own peas, but if she had not, she could have bought inexpensive fresh peas at the market. Much later, in the 1940s and 1950s, my mother frequently cooked fresh peas for us in Budapest. I wasn't much help in the kitchen, but I didn't mind shelling peas because of the joy of tasting them fresh out of the pod. For me, they were better than any candy.

Today fresh shelling peas (English peas) are almost impossible to find in an average supermarket in the United States and are usually available only at farmers' markets. Even there they tend to be expensive; and one needs about two pounds of peas in the pod for four soup servings. Unfortunately, this once-common and inexpensive vegetable has become a rare luxury item. If you can find and afford fresh peas by all means take advantage of them, but test them before buying by tasting the peas from two or three randomly picked pods. The pods should be crisp and juicy, and the peas small, sweet, and tender. If the peas are large and starchy, with dry-looking pods, change your menu plans or use frozen peas. Although the texture of frozen peas is not as good as that of the young fresh ones, in my opinion their flavor is not inferior. The problem in preparing Riza néni's version of the traditional Austro-Hungarian pea soup from frozen peas is figuring out how to coax out the flavor from the peas. Frozen peas are always parboiled and usually salted in the processing plant. Since they are parboiled, they need only about five minutes cooking time as compared to about fifteen minutes for the fresh ones, and this is not enough time to transmit their flavor to the cooking liquid. As if this were not enough of a handicap, when the soup is prepared from fresh peas, the empty pods, after they have been shelled, are first cooked in the liquid that will later be used for cooking the shelled peas, further contributing to the flavor of the soup. Unfortunately, frozen peas have no pods. After several unsuccessful attempts, however, I figured out a way to reproduce with frozen peas the wonderful flavor of pea soup I remember from my childhood. The trick is to carefully defrost and dry the peas, then to quickly sauté them with slightly caramelized sugar, and, finally, to flavor the cooking liquid with a small quantity of puréed soup. The small amount of sugar will not make the soup sweet, but it will enhance the flavor of the peas. Except for the inevitable defrosting, all these extra steps add only three or four minutes to the preparation time and the result is well worth the extra effort.

The best kind of frozen peas for this soup are the so-called baby sweet peas, which are between the size of the "tiny" and the regular peas. The baby peas are almost as tender as the tiny peas and can withstand the little additional cooking time necessary for this dish. I used peas from a one-pound bag of the Birds Eye brand of baby peas, but other brands are probably just as good.

In this and several other recipes, I substituted canola oil, margarine, or butter for the fat specified by Riza néni. By "fat" she usually meant rendered goose fat; when she wanted to use beef fat she always said so specifically.

YIELD:	4 servings
TOTAL TIME:	about 45 minutes, a little longer if you use fresh peas
DUMPLING INGREDIENTS:	⅔ cup unbleached all-purpose flour
	¼ teaspoon kosher salt
	¼ teaspoon freshly ground black pepper
	1 large egg, lightly beaten
	2 teaspoons canola oil

1½–2½ tablespoons water

SOUP
INGREDIENTS:
- 2 cups frozen baby peas (about ⅔ of a 1-pound bag of frozen peas) or fresh shelling peas
- 2 tablespoons canola oil, unsalted butter, or a mixture of the two
- 1½ teaspoons sugar
- 2 tablespoons chopped fresh flat-leaf parsley (optional; it wasn't part of the original recipe)
- 2 tablespoons unbleached all-purpose flour
- 2 cups unsalted homemade or low-salt canned chicken broth
- 3 cups water
- ½ teaspoon very finely chopped fresh ginger (or ¼ teaspoon ground ginger, as in the original recipe)
- ¼ teaspoon freshly ground black pepper
- ½ teaspoon kosher salt (a little more if your broth is completely salt-free)

SPECIAL
EQUIPMENT:
- 12" or larger skillet
- blender or hand-held blender

1. If you are using frozen peas, spread them in a large skillet and let them defrost at room temperature for about ½ hour. Pour about 2 quarts water into a medium saucepan or pot, add about ½ tablespoon salt, and bring it to a boil.

2. Meanwhile, prepare the dumplings. In a medium bowl, mix flour, salt, and pepper. Add egg, oil, and 1½ tablespoons water. Mix it with a fork to get a soft and smooth dough. Add more water by the teaspoon, as necessary. In fairly low humidity, I needed to add 2 more teaspoons of water; in humid weather I would need less, in very dry weather more. Let the dough rest for 10 minutes.

3. Transfer the soft dough into a sturdy plastic bag, such as a Ziploc bag, cut a tiny hole in one corner of the bag, hold the bag over the boiling water, and squeeze the dough through the hole. Use a knife to cut the

dough into about ¼" pieces and let them drop into the water. Clean the knife by dipping it into the water. Cook the dumplings for about 5 minutes. Drain them in a strainer, rinse them briefly under cold running water, place them in a bowl, and put it aside until you prepare the soup.

4. Heat the skillet with the defrosted damp peas for 1 minute. Remove the skillet from the heat but leave the peas in it to finish drying.

5. Heat oil or butter in a large saucepan. Adjust the heat to medium, sprinkle sugar into the hot fat and let it brown slightly. Don't allow the sugar to clump into one hard piece of caramel. Add the peas and stir to coat them with sugar and oil. After about 30 seconds, stir in 1 tablespoon of the chopped parsley and sprinkle the peas with flour. Stir to distribute the flour evenly on the peas. Cook for 2 minutes, then add a little of the chicken broth and stir. Gradually add the remaining broth, then the water, ginger, ground pepper, and salt, stopping several times to stir. Bring it to a boil and remove it from the heat. The peas should be cooked by now; they should be tender but not mushy. If you are making the soup from fresh-shelled peas you will have to cook them for about another 10 minutes. Taste the soup and adjust the seasoning.

6. Remove ½ cup of the soup, including a fair share of peas, and purée it in a blender or the cup of a hand-held blender. Return the puréed soup into the saucepan. Add the cooked dumplings and the remaining tablespoon of chopped parsley to the soup. Serve immediately.

Boiled Beef

This recipe for boiled beef and the following one for beef-vegetable soup are not from Riza néni's collection, although she frequently made these staples of the local cuisine. I include them here to complement Riza néni's recipes for soup garnishes (see recipe for ginger-flavored soup biscuits on page 89 and for liver dumplings on page 91) and gooseberry sauce (see recipe on page 98) that couldn't be served on their own. This is a simpler recipe for boiled beef than one finds in most Austrian and Hungarian cookbooks, but it gives good results. It is primarily a recipe for boiled beef; the soup is a bonus. If one wanted maximum flavor in the soup and cared less for the flavor of the meat, one would place the meat together with the vegetables in cold water at the beginning.

Boiled beef has been one of the most popular dishes in Austria and to a slightly lesser degree in Hungary. Its popularity among the Jewish middle class of Moson is documented by the recollections of Carl Flesch (1873–1944), the famous Moson-born violinist, of his physician father, an exact contemporary of my great-grandfather: "Altogether, in fact, [my father's] mode of life was of Spartan simplicity. To the end of his days, he forced his entire household to eat, lunch after lunch, soup and boiled beef with vegetables; only on Sabbath did we get the traditional roast goose." Boiled beef happens to be one of my favorite dishes. I love its flavor, which is both delicate and intensely beefy at the same time, but I admit I would also be frustrated if I were forced to eat boiled beef every day.

YIELD: 4 servings

TOTAL TIME: about 2 hours 45 minutes, including 2½ hours cooking time

INGREDIENTS:
6 cups water
1 onion, peeled and sliced (add the onion peel, too, for a richer colored soup)
1 carrot, peeled and sliced
½ parsnip, peeled and sliced
1 celery stalk, cleaned and sliced
2 stalks of flat-leaf parsley
1½ teaspoons kosher salt
3–4 black peppercorns, coarsely crushed on a cutting board with the bottom of a heavy skillet
1 clove
1 or 2 pounds beef bones (optional)
1½ pounds of beef brisket, not too closely trimmed

SPECIAL EQUIPMENT: 3-quart or larger saucepan

1. Pour water into a saucepan, add optional bones, and bring it to a boil. Add beef, make sure that the water covers it, and return the water to a boil. Skim off the scum that rises to the surface. Add vegetables and seasonings, bring it again to a boil, cover, lower the heat, and simmer, barely bubbling, for about 2½ hours or until the meat is tender.

2. Remove the meat to a carving board, let it stand for 10 minutes, trim and discard all the fat, and slice the meat against the grain. Serve immediately or keep in a 200°F oven for up to 30 minutes in enough cooking liquid to barely cover the slices. Serve it with gooseberry, horseradish, or chive sauce, or with a little beef soup and good crusty bread.

Beef-Vegetable Soup

YIELD:	4 servings
TOTAL TIME:	about 25 minutes
INGREDIENTS:	broth from the previous recipe for boiled beef
	1 or 2 carrots, peeled and sliced ½" thick
	1 parsnip, peeled and sliced ½" thick
	1 small leek, cleaned and sliced ¼" thick (optional)
SPECIAL EQUIPMENT:	none

1. Strain the broth and discard the vegetables, which will be overcooked. Let it cool and skim off the fat. Taste the broth and boil it down a little if you think it is too thin.

2. Add peeled, sliced carrot, parsnip, cleaned and sliced leeks, or whatever other appropriate soup vegetable you have in your refrigerator. Bring the soup to a boil, cover, lower heat, and simmer for 20 minutes.

If you decide to include mushrooms among the vegetables, add them about 5 minutes before the dish is ready. Taste the soup and add a little salt and freshly ground pepper, if you wish.

3. Serve it with ginger-flavored soup biscuits (see the following recipe), liver dumplings (see recipe on page 91), or by itself sprinkled with chopped parsley.

Ginger-flavored Soup Biscuits
Semmelfanzeln für Suppe

This is quite an unusual soup garnish. It is in the Austro-Hungarian cooking tradition, but different from other Austrian or Hungarian recipes I know. I love the texture and the nice ginger flavor of these biscuits in beef-vegetable soup (see recipe on page 88) or other meat soups. Sprinkle chopped parsley around the biscuit slices in the soup and you will have an interesting, elegant, yet easily prepared dish.

Though Riza néni used ground ginger to make these biscuits—she couldn't buy fresh ginger in Moson—I used fresh ginger in this and several other savory recipes calling for ginger because, given the choice, I prefer its taste to ground ginger in such recipes. If you don't have fresh ginger on hand and wish to bask in the glory of super-authenticity, you can always substitute half the amount of ground ginger for the fresh one.

YIELD: 4 servings

TOTAL TIME: about 45 minutes

INGREDIENTS:
- 1 teaspoon canola oil or rendered poultry fat (to grease the pan)
- 1 tablespoon dry bread crumbs, made from stale white bread in the food processor (to coat the pan)
- 1 whole large egg
- 1 large egg white
- 2 slices white bread (about 2 ounces), cut into ½" cubes, dried for 5–7 minutes on a baking sheet in a 400°F oven, soaked for 1 minute in enough water to cover, and squeezed out
- 1 tablespoon canola oil or rendered poultry fat
- ⅔ cup unbleached all-purpose flour
- 2 teaspoons very finely chopped fresh ginger
- 1 teaspoon sweet paprika, preferably Hungarian
- ½ teaspoon kosher salt

SPECIAL EQUIPMENT: 3½" × 8½" (2½" × 7½" at the bottom) loaf pan or a baking pan of about the same area

1. Preheat oven to 400°F. Grease the loaf pan or baking pan with oil or poultry fat, add bread crumbs, and tilt the form to coat it with crumbs.

2. Place the eggs in a large bowl, whisk them, and add all the other ingredients. Mix thoroughly with a fork to make a thick, sticky dough. Transfer the dough to the loaf or baking pan and with the back of a moistened spoon spread it in an approximately 1"-thick layer. If you have time for it, let it rest for about 10 minutes. Place it on a baking sheet and bake it in the preheated oven for about 25 minutes.

3. Turn it out onto a cooling rack to cool for at least 5 minutes. The dough, which has puffed-up in the oven, will slightly deflate during cooling. Using a serrated knife, cut it into ½"-thick slices and use about 4 slices for each serving. Add the slices to the soup only in the last minute before serving.

Liver Dumplings for Soup
Leberknedel für Suppe

Riza néni's version of this ubiquitous Austro-Hungarian soup garnish differs in two subtle ways from the usual preparation: it doesn't include sautéed chopped onion, and she adds ginger to the usual seasonings. One can use either calves' or beef liver for the dumplings. I opted for calves' liver, which I prefer, and after cutting off the small quantity of liver required for the dumplings, I used the remaining part of the liver to make a separate main course. Come to think of it, the dumplings could also make a nice main course if you served them with, for example, good sauerkraut and some onion or chive sauce. In this case, double the recipe. Or serve them, as originally intended, in soup using the broth from the boiled beef recipe.

YIELD: 16–18 walnut-sized dumplings for 4 servings

TOTAL TIME: about 55 minutes

INGREDIENTS:
- ¼ pound calves' or beef liver cut into about ½"-thick slices
- 1 large egg
- 1 large egg white
- 1–3 tablespoons canola oil or rendered chicken, goose, or duck fat
- 1½ slices of slightly stale white bread cut into ¼" cubes, placed in a small bowl, briefly soaked in water to cover, and squeezed out
- 1½ tablespoons finely chopped fresh flat-leaf parsley
- ¼ teaspoon kosher salt
- ¼ teaspoon freshly ground black pepper
- ½ teaspoon very finely chopped ginger (or ¼ teaspoon ground ginger)
- ½–⅔ cup bread crumbs

SPECIAL
EQUIPMENT: blender or hand-held blender (only necessary if you kosher the liver)

1. Wipe the liver with a paper towel and cut out all veins, skin, and connective tissue. Jewish dietary laws require a special koshering process for liver. If you keep kosher, first prepare the liver in the following manner before proceeding with the recipe: Preheat broiler. Sprinkle the liver with salt. Place it on aluminum foil, turn up the edges of the foil to contain the juices, and broil the liver about 4" from the heating element for about 3 minutes on each side or until it changes color and no trace of pink remains. Rinse the koshered liver, pat it dry with a paper towel, cut it into ¼" cubes, place them in a blender or the cup of a hand-held blender, add 3 tablespoons oil or fat, and process the liver into a smooth purée.

2. If you decided not to kosher the liver, scrape very thin slices from the edge of the raw liver with a sharp knife held on the bias. Chop it to become a smooth pulp. If you wish it to be super smooth, press it through a sieve or a food mill.

3. Place the puréed koshered or the scraped and pulped raw liver in a bowl; mix in the eggs, soaked bread cubes, seasonings, and ½ cup of the bread crumbs. If you didn't kosher the liver, add 1 tablespoon oil or fat. Thoroughly blend the ingredients to get a soft and smooth, not chunky, mixture that can be formed into dumplings. If it is too runny, add a little more bread crumbs. Allow the mixture to rest for at least 15 minutes for the bread crumbs to absorb the moisture.

4. Boil 5 or 6 cups of beef broth (from recipe on page 86), beef-vegetable soup (see recipe on page 88), or water in a fairly wide saucepan or pot. Form walnut-sized small dumplings by rolling a teaspoon of mixture between your moistened palms. You should have 16 to 18 dumplings. Cook them in 2 batches under partial cover in the barely simmering liquid for 10 to 12 minutes. Keep cooked dumplings on a plate and reheat in the soup only those you wish to serve immediately.

Braised Chicken with Game Sauce
Hühner wild bereitet

In this recipe, one of my favorites in this book, root vegetables are first cooked in a small amount of water with aromatic spices and herbs, then this flavorful vegetable broth is thickened with flour to make a sauce for the braised chicken. Although I couldn't find this wonderfully tasty dish mentioned in any cookbook, this doesn't mean that it is Riza néni's creation. As is typical with handwritten recipe collections, Riza néni got her recipes from friends, family, or published sources. If some of her recipes seem unusual to us today, it is because they have been forgotten in the hundred and thirty years since she got them.

In her recipe, she didn't call for browning the chicken pieces before braising them, but in my adaptation I decided to follow the usual method of browning them first, because I felt that this improved the flavor of the dish. She had cut the chicken into quarters; I thought that the usual stewing pieces would be more practical. Another small change was that I cooked the dark meat longer than the white meat. Although I adhered to her list of vegetables and their method of cooking, I increased the amount of vegetables in the recipe, because I felt that this made the sauce more intensely flavored and could take the place of a vegetable side dish.

YIELD: 4 servings

TOTAL TIME: about 55 minutes

INGREDIENTS:
- 1 chicken (4–4.5 pounds) cut into 8 pieces (2 drumsticks, 2 thighs, 2 breasts cut in half, leaving each wing attached to a breast half)
- ½ teaspoon kosher salt
- ¼ teaspoon freshly ground black pepper
- 1½ tablespoons canola oil
- 1 medium onion, peeled and finely chopped
- 1 small carrot, peeled and finely diced (optional; it was not in the original recipe)

½ cup white wine or water
1 medium carrot, peeled
1 medium parsnip, peeled
1 small celery root (6 to 8 oz.), peeled
3 bay leaves
8 cloves
3–4 twigs of flat-leaf parsley
½ teaspoon black peppercorn, coarsely crushed on a cutting board with the bottom of a heavy skillet
1 teaspoon very finely chopped fresh ginger (or ½ teaspoon ground ginger)
½ teaspoon kosher salt
1¼ cups of water
2 tablespoons all-purpose flour
1 large egg yolk
2–3 tablespoons lemon juice
½ teaspoon sugar
2 tablespoons chopped fresh flat-leaf parsley

SPECIAL EQUIPMENT:
12" sauté pan with a tight-fitting lid
cheesecloth
hand-held blender or food mill (optional)

1. Rub chicken pieces with salt and pepper. Heat oil in a large pan over medium-high heat until the oil starts to smoke; immediately add chicken pieces skin down, and sauté them, for 2 minutes on each side, until nicely browned. If your pan isn't large enough, brown a few pieces at a time. Don't overcrowd the pan or the pieces will not brown properly. Remove the pieces to a plate. Adjust heat to medium, add onions, and sauté them for 1 minute. Add diced carrot to the onion and continue sautéing for another minute. Add chicken leg pieces and wine or water, bring to a boil, adjust heat to low, cover, and simmer for 13 minutes. Add breast pieces, cover again, and simmer all the pieces for another 15 minutes.

2. While the chicken is cooking, cut carrot, parsnip, and celery root into ¼" × ¼" × 2½" sticks. Put the cut-up vegetables into a medium

saucepan. Tie bay leaves, cloves, and sprigs of parsley in a piece of cheesecloth and add this to the saucepan. Add crushed pepper, chopped ginger, salt, and water. Bring it to a boil, cover, reduce heat to low-medium, and simmer for 7 minutes or until vegetables are almost done. The vegetables should be slightly underdone because they will cook a little more in the oven.

3. Pour the liquid off the vegetables into a measuring cup. You should have 1 cup vegetable broth. Adjust quantity if necessary by adding a little water or pouring out a little of the liquid. Discard the cheesecloth-wrapped herbs and spices. Heat the oven to 175°F. Cover the saucepan of vegetables and place it in the oven.

4. Evenly dust the chicken pieces with 1 tablespoon flour, then turn them over and dust them on the other side with the second tablespoon flour. Roll the pieces in the braising liquid. Add the vegetable broth and bring it to a boil. Lower heat, and simmer for 2 minutes. If you wish to save calories, you can remove the skin from the chicken pieces at this point.

5. Pour the approximately 2 cups of sauce into a bowl or measuring cup, and after it has cooled, skim off the fat. Riza néni didn't purée her sauce but if you prefer it smooth, as I do, use a hand-held blender or a food mill to purée the bits of onion and carrot in the sauce. Lightly beat the egg yolk in a small bowl or cup and add it to the cooled sauce. Add lemon juice and sugar. Add the sauce to the chicken pieces in the sauté pan, warm the chicken and the sauce over medium heat without bringing it to a boil, stir, and turn off the heat. Taste and, if necessary, adjust the seasoning.

6. Place the vegetables and chicken pieces on serving plates and ladle sauce over them. Sprinkle some chopped parsley over them and serve them with small boiled potatoes, bread dumplings, or, most appropriately, with Riza néni's cabbage dumplings (see recipe on page 108). Then relax, enjoy this fabulously tasty dish, and raise your glass of wine—a Riesling or a Sauvignon Blanc perhaps—to the memory of Riza néni and the other Moson Jews.

Almond-studded Meatballs in Sweet-and-Sour Sauce

Fleischherzl oder Zunge

This is an interesting and unusual variation of a slightly more familiar dish of sweet-and-sour beef or veal tongue, which Riza néni offered as an alternative to the basic recipe. Almost half of the meat dishes in her collection are characterized by the combination of sweet and sour flavors. This is no mere accident or arbitrary personal taste. As one can see from Jewish cookbooks, her fondness for such dishes is consistent with the frequent use of sweet-and-sour flavors in Ashkenazi Jewish cooking. In addition to the few uniquely Jewish dishes and the role of some foods in the celebration of the holidays, such taste preferences provide another common element in the tremendous diversity of regional Jewish cooking.

YIELD: 4 servings (20–24 meatballs in total)

TOTAL TIME: about 40 minutes

INGREDIENTS:
- 1 pound ground, preferably coarsely ground, beef chuck
- 1 small onion, peeled and grated or very finely chopped
- 2 slices of stale white bread cut into ½" cubes, soaked for about 1 minute in water to cover and squeezed out
- 1 large egg
- ½ teaspoon kosher salt
- ½ teaspoon sweet paprika
- ¼ cup slivered almonds, cut in half
- ¾ cup canola oil (or enough to fill a 10" skillet about ¼" high)
- 1 tablespoon canola oil

	1 tablespoon all-purpose flour
	1¼ cup water
	3 tablespoons lemon juice (or 1½ tablespoons vinegar, as in the original recipe)
	2–3 teaspoons fine threads of lemon zest, made with a zester (optional, wasn't in the original recipe)
	⅓ cup golden raisins
	½ cup slivered almonds
	1 small cinnamon stick, broken to pieces (or ½ teaspoon ground cinnamon)
	2 tablespoons sugar
SPECIAL EQUIPMENT:	10" skillet or sauté pan

1. In a bowl, mix ground beef with onion, soaked bread, egg, salt, and paprika. Divide the meatball mixture into 4 approximately equal parts and make 5 or 6 little meatballs from each. You will end up with 20 to 24 balls, each about 1¼" diameter. Stick a few slivered almonds into each meatball, but you can omit this if you are in a hurry.

2. Pour about ¼" oil into the skillet or sauté pan. Heat the oil and fry the meatballs in 2 or 3 batches. Fry them for 3 or 4 minutes and turn them every minute to make sure that they brown on all sides. Place the finished meatballs on a paper-towel-covered plate and keep them in a 175°F oven until you finish the sauce.

3. Discard the frying oil, wipe out the skillet or sauté pan and heat 1 tablespoon oil in it. Stir in flour and while continuing to stir cook it over medium heat for about 2 minutes to make a light-golden roux. Mix water and lemon juice in a cup, add a little of this liquid to the roux and stir to dissolve any lumps. Gradually dilute it with the remaining liquid, stirring constantly. Add all the remaining ingredients, bring it to a boil, reduce heat, and simmer gently for 10 minutes.

4. Place 5 or 6 meatballs on a heap of boiled rice and ladle some sauce over them. Serve them immediately.

Gooseberry Sauce for Boiled Beef
Agras Sauce

In the nineteenth century, fruit sauces and cooked fruit were frequently served with meat dishes. But already the first Hungarian cookbook, a handwritten collection from the sixteenth century, included a recipe for beef with gooseberry sauce. Perhaps Riza néni selected this sauce for her collection because it coincided with the traditional Jewish taste for sweet or sweet-and-sour dishes.

YIELD:	4 servings
TOTAL TIME:	about 40 minutes
INGREDIENTS:	1 cup gooseberries, fresh or canned (I used some of the drained berries from a jar of Polish gooseberries in light syrup. You can find such Polish or Hungarian canned gooseberries in stores that stock imported food.)
	1 cup water
	¾ tablespoon canola oil
	¾ tablespoon all-purpose flour
	¾ tablespoon sugar
	¼ teaspoon kosher salt
	½ cinnamon stick (or ¼ teaspoon ground cinnamon)
SPECIAL EQUIPMENT:	food mill fitted with a fine screen

1. Place gooseberries and water in a saucepan and bring them to a boil. Cover and simmer for 20 minutes or until the gooseberries are very soft and start to fall apart. If you use fresh berries, they will have to be cooked longer. Press the cooked berries and the cooking liquid through a food mill fitted with a fine screen into a bowl.

2. In a large, heavy-bottomed saucepan, heat oil (Riza néni would have used rendered goose fat), stir in flour, and cook it, stirring occasionally, for 2 minutes. It should be a light-brown roux. Add about ⅓ of the fruit pulp and stir it until smooth. Add the remaining ingredients, bring it to a boil, and simmer for 5 or 10 minutes. The sauce should be medium thick; add a little water if it is too thick. Discard the cinnamon stick.

3. Serve this sauce with meat dishes. I particularly like it with boiled beef (see recipe on page 86) that has been cut into approximately ½" × ½" × 2½" sticks (my preference) or ½" slices. Cook the boiled beef for a few minutes in the sauce to integrate the flavors. I would serve it with boiled ribbon pasta, such as fettuccine, or with small boiled potatoes. Sprinkle chopped parsley over it. This dish can be reheated but stir frequently to keep the fairly thick sauce from burning.

Braised Beef with Vegetable Sauce
Gedünstetes Fleisch

The combination of the flavorful puréed vegetables and the strong beefy flavor of the pot roast makes this one of my favorites dishes.

Of the nine recipes for meat dishes in Riza néni's collection, four are for braised preparations. This is probably no coincidence. In the nineteenth century, beef, as well as poultry, was less tender, although more tasty than today. Meat was more expensive, so people tended to use the flavorful cheaper cuts, which are usually tougher. The slow, moist cooking process of braising was ideally suited to this kind of meat.

But beyond these factors, there are special reasons for the frequent use of braised beef dishes in Jewish cooking. The hindquarters of the cow contain the most tender cuts, such as the tenderloin or the porterhouse steak, but this part of the animal usually cannot be sold as kosher meat because it is too hard to remove the forbidden sciatic nerve. In addition, meat gets more tender if it is allowed to mature for a period ranging from a few days to two weeks after slaughtering. But there is little time for this with kosher meat because it must be koshered, that is, soaked, salted, and washed, not more than seventy-two hours after slaughtering.

Although the original recipe didn't call for it, I decided to follow the usual method of browning the meat before braising it, because I believe this improves the flavor of the dish. The meat will shrink substantially during braising.

YIELD:	4 servings
TOTAL TIME:	about 3 hours
INGREDIENTS:	1 tablespoon canola oil
	1½ pounds brisket of beef (or top or bottom round)
	¼ teaspoon kosher salt
	1 large onion (about 6 ounces), peeled and sliced
	1 carrot, peeled and sliced
	1 parsnip, peeled and sliced (optional; it was not in the original recipe)
	1 tablespoon lemon juice (or ½ tablespoon distilled white vinegar, as in the original recipe)
	1½ teaspoons kosher salt
	2 cups water
	1 teaspoon black peppercorns
	4 bay leaves
	2 tablespoons chopped fresh flat-leaf parsley
SPECIAL EQUIPMENT:	large, heavy braising pan with a tight-fitting lid
	cheesecloth
	hand-held blender

1. Cut off all visible fat and rub the meat with salt. Heat the oil in a heavy pan (an enameled cast iron braising pan is ideal) that is big enough to accommodate the meat. Brown the meat over medium-high heat for about 2 minutes on each side. Remove the meat to a plate. Add sliced onions and sauté them for 2 minutes in the remaining juices in the pan. Add carrot, optional parsnip, lemon juice, salt, and water. Tie bay leaves and peppercorns in a piece of cheesecloth

and add them to the pan. Return the meat to the pan, bring the liquid to a boil, and cover.

2. Either bake it in a 300°F oven for 2½ to 3 hours or cook it on the stovetop over very low heat, barely simmering, for about 2½ hours or until tender. Check after about 2 hours, because different cuts of meat require slightly different cooking times. Meat should be tender but not grainy or overdone.

3. Remove the meat to a plate and allow the vegetables and liquid to cool. Skim off the fat (there shouldn't be much) and discard the cheesecloth bag of bay leaves and pepper. Tilt the pan to move all the vegetables and liquid to one side and purée them with a hand-held blender. Start at slow speed or you will end up with sauce on your kitchen ceiling. Taste the sauce and adjust the seasoning. Put the meat back into the pan, bring the sauce to a boil, lower heat, and simmer for about 5 minutes.

4. Take the meat out again, let it rest for a few minutes and slice it across the fibers. Serve it with small boiled potatoes, bread dumplings, or Riza néni's cabbage dumplings (see recipe on page 108). Ladle some sauce over the sliced meat and the dumplings. Sprinkle them with chopped parsley.

Braised Veal Cutlets in Onion-Lemon Sauce
Kalbschnitzel braun gedünstet

I find Riza néni's German title for this recipe puzzling. She calls it "Veal cutlet braised to get brown" and the recipe describes braising the cutlets on a bed of sliced onions and carrots until they are brown. She doesn't call for the prior sautéing of the cutlets, which would be the usual way of browning them. From reading her recipe, I couldn't imagine why the cutlets would brown during the slow, moist cooking in the covered pan. Testing the recipe confirmed my suspicion. Out of curiosity, I also tested a version where I briefly sautéed the cutlets before braising them on the vegetables. The meat got slightly brown but was in no way superior to the simpler version where it was braised without browning.

Looking in nineteenth-century Hungarian cookbooks, I found a few similarly named recipes. Most of them were for veal, usually cutlets or rib chops, and all described by and large the same idea of preparation: first braising the meat on a bed of vegetables, then temporarily removing the meat from the pan and making a sauce of browned flour diluted with stock. Similar to Riza néni's recipe, the sauce was always flavored with lemon juice, at times with lemon peel, too. This explains the source of her title, but not why the meat in her recipe would get brown.

Even if the meat doesn't look the way she describes it, I decided to include this recipe because it is an interesting, tasty dish that can be prepared in hardly more than an hour with very little effort.

Veal cutlets are quite expensive, but the overall cost will not be exorbitant, because two cutlets, about a quarter pound of meat, are enough for one serving. The flavorful and quite filling sauce of puréed vegetables complements the large but thin slices of meat and helps making this a satisfying main course. The sauce is similar to the vegetable sauce Riza néni used in her recipe for braised beef, the previous recipe in this collection, but it is a little more tart to balance the sweetness of the onions. It is a terrific combination of flavors. I suggest serving it over boiled rice, boiled small red potatoes, or noodles.

YIELD: 4 servings

TOTAL TIME: about 1 hour 10 minutes

INGREDIENTS:
8 veal cutlets, about 3" × 6" × ⅜" each, about 1 pound total
½ teaspoon kosher salt
2 tablespoons canola oil
2 medium onions, about 8 ounces total, peeled and thinly sliced

1 carrot, peeled and sliced
2 tablespoons all-purpose flour
1 cup unsalted homemade or canned low-salt chicken broth
3 teaspoons grated zest of lemon
3 tablespoons lemon juice
2 tablespoons chopped fresh flat-leaf parsley

SPECIAL
EQUIPMENT: large (about 10" diameter) heavy pan with a tight-fitting lid
blender, hand-held blender, or a food processor

1. Sprinkle the cutlets with ¼ teaspoon of the salt. Heat the oil in a large sturdy braising pan. Add the sliced onions and sauté them for about 1 minute. Add the carrots and lay the cutlets on top of the bed of vegetables, distributing them evenly. Cover the pan, adjust the heat to low and cook for 20 minutes.

2. Remove the cutlets to a plate. Raise the heat to medium, sprinkle the flour over the vegetables, stir to coat them evenly, and cook uncovered for 3 minutes. Gradually pour in the broth, stopping frequently to stir. Bring the liquid to a boil, return the cutlets to the pan, cover the pan, reduce the heat to low, and cook for about 30 minutes, until tender.

3. Remove the cutlets again to a plate and purée the vegetables in a blender, a food processor, or in the pan with a hand-held blender. This last method is the simplest, but make sure you tilt the pan so that the head of the blender can be completely immersed in the sauce.

4. Add the remaining ¼ teaspoon salt, the lemon zest and juice. Taste the sauce and adjust the seasonings. Put the cutlets back into the pan, bring it to a boil, cover, adjust the heat to low, and cook for another 5 minutes. Serve it sprinkled with chopped parsley.

Braised Veal Tongue, "Bohemian" Style
Böhmische Zunge

The original recipe didn't specify whether to use beef or veal, but I am sure it was meant for fresh beef tongue, because it described one large piece of tongue that, as with all of her recipes, should have been enough for about six or eight servings. But families and appetites tend to be smaller today; therefore I substituted fresh veal tongue, which is also more tender and faster to cook than beef. Riza néni's original recipe suggested calves' foot as an optional ingredient to contribute to the taste and gelatinous texture of the sauce. I decided to omit this because it is not absolutely essential to the recipe and the chances of finding calves' foot in a supermarket are slim.

Riza néni's recipe for braised veal tongue is an example of a dish enjoyed year-round by Jews and Gentiles alike. Although it has been popular among Eastern and Central European Jews, similar recipes can be found in non-Jewish cookbooks not only of the region but also in France. Jews frequently prepared this dish for Sukkot, probably because they associated the wine in the sauce with harvest time; but they also prepared it at other times of the year.

In this respect this recipe is typical of a large category of dishes in Jewish cuisine. These dishes are not exclusively Jewish, but they are prepared by Jews for certain holidays and to some degree have become part of the tradition of that holiday. The relationship between these dishes and the holidays, however, is less close than, say, between cholent and Sabbath or matzo kugel and Pesach, typical of foods intended almost exclusively for specific holidays.

To make matters even more complicated, a dish we usually associate with a certain holiday might occasionally be prepared for another. For example, the book *Old Jewish Dishes* by Zorica Herbst-Krausz includes *kindli*, a pastry that Riza néni only made for Purim, among traditional desserts not only for Purim, but for Sukkot as well. The same book describes a tongue recipe similar to this one as typical for Purim but doesn't include it among its recipes for Sukkot. Jewish cooking is part of a living culture and while one can discern trends in it, there are always plenty of exceptions.

YIELD:	2 generous or 3 skimpy servings
TOTAL TIME:	about 3 hours
INGREDIENTS:	1.3–1.6 pounds fresh veal tongue
	1–2 tablespoons kosher salt (1½ teaspoons per quart of water)
	2 tablespoons canola oil
	1 medium onion, peeled and sliced
	1 large carrot, cleaned and sliced
	1 tablespoon all-purpose flour
	1 cup red wine
	1 cup beef broth (unsalted homemade or low-salt canned broth) or the water in which the tongue has cooked
	5 cloves
	¾ teaspoon kosher salt (½ teaspoon if you used salted cooking water instead of broth for the sauce)
	¼ cup dark or golden raisins
	¼ cup slivered almonds
	2 tablespoons chopped fresh flat-leaf parsley
SPECIAL EQUIPMENT:	braising pan or heavy pan with a tight-fitting lid (I used a 10"-long enameled cast-iron oval cocotte)
	blender or hand-held blender

1. Buy 1 small tongue for 2 servings or a larger one for 3 servings. Double the recipe for 4 servings. You can usually find fresh tongue in some ethnic neighborhoods or in stores with a well-stocked meat department, such as New York City's Citarella. You can also try to order it from your local butcher. If you have time for it, soak the tongue overnight in cold water in the refrigerator, but this is not essential. Trim the fat from the tongue; the fat is usually on the bottom side toward the back. Put the tongue into a pan with enough water to cover by about 2", add salt, bring it to a boil, lower heat, and simmer for 1 hour. Remove the tongue and hold it briefly under cold running water to cool slightly. Reserve 1 cup of the cooking water if you don't

have beef broth, although broth is preferable. Working on a platter or a board with a perimeter groove to catch the juices running out, remove the skin of the tongue in the following way: hold a paring knife by its blade, make a skin-deep incision along the perimeter, and with the help of the knife pull off the skin. If the skin doesn't want to come off, you will have to peel it by sliding the knife under the skin and cutting against the tough skin. After peeling off some of the skin, try pulling off the rest; sometimes it works.

2. Heat oil in a heavy-bottomed braising pan that will be big enough for the tongue. Add onion and cook over medium heat for 2 minutes, add carrots and cook for 1 more minute. Sprinkle flour over the vegetables, stir, and cook for 2 minutes. Add wine, broth (or reserved cooking water), cloves, salt, and the tongue. Bring it to a boil, cover, lower heat, and gently simmer (rapid boiling would toughen the tongue) for about 1½ hours or until it is tender. Turn it every 30 minutes. The tongue is done when a pointed knife can easily pierce it.

3. Remove the tongue to a cutting board. Purée the sauce and vegetables in a blender or in the pan with a hand-held blender, tilting the pan so that the head of the blender is completely immersed in the sauce. Add raisins and almonds; cook them with the sauce for a few minutes. Taste it and adjust the seasoning. Though it was not part of her recipe, many analogous recipes include sugar and I decided to add 1 tablespoon of it.

4. Riza néni presented the whole tongue on a serving platter with slivered almonds stuck into the tongue and sauce around it. You can follow her example or carve it in the kitchen, as I have done, and cook the slices a few minutes longer in the sauce so that the flavor of the sauce can permeate them even better. Regardless where you do it, slice the tongue on the bias, approximately parallel with its sloping top, trying to make ⅜"-thick slices of about the same size. If you decided to slice it in the kitchen, place the slices in the pan, bring the sauce to a boil, lower heat, and simmer for 5 minutes.

5. Serve it with cabbage dumplings (see recipe on page 108), bread dumplings, boiled noodles, potatoes, or rice. Sprinkle it on the serving plate with chopped parsley.

Noodles with Toasted Farina
Grízes metélt

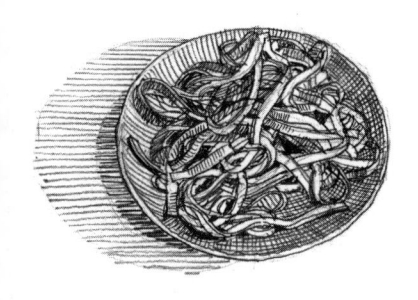

To my taste, there are few dishes as satisfying as this very simple one. It offers a combination of great flavor, cheap ingredients, and quick and easy preparation that is hard to beat. I like to add freshly ground pepper, although this is not quite authentic.

Instead of farina, the original recipe used semolina, called *gríz* or *dara* in Hungary, a kind of coarsely ground high-gluten wheat. It is available in our country in some Italian and Middle Eastern groceries but can be hard to find, and of course not everybody has such ethnic groceries nearby. Finely ground semolina flour used for making pasta is easier to come by but its texture is inappropriate. Farina, typically used in the United States as a hot breakfast cereal, becomes uniformly soft and dense when cooked while coarse semolina retains more texture. But all in all, substituting farina for coarse semolina in this and other recipes seemed to me the most practical compromise and I tested them with the commonly available "two minute" quick-cooking kind.

YIELD:	4 servings
TOTAL TIME:	about 30 minutes
INGREDIENTS:	½ pound dry fettucine
	3 tablespoons canola oil or unsalted butter
	½ cup farina or coarse semolina
	¾ cup hot water
	¼ teaspoon kosher salt
SPECIAL EQUIPMENT:	10" skillet

1. In a large, wide pot, bring about 3 quarts of water to a boil, add about ¾ tablespoon salt and the dry pasta, and cook it for about 12 minutes. If you decided to use fresh instead of dry pasta, make fairly stiff noodle dough from 1½ cups unbleached all-purpose flour, 2 large eggs, and 1–3 tablespoons water. Allow the rolled-out sheets of dough to dry slightly for about 10 minutes on a kitchen towel, then cut them into ⅓"-wide noodles. The customary width of noodles used in Hungary for this dish is a little wider than fettucine, therefore the ⅓" noodles would be even more authentic than the usual fettucine. Homemade fresh noodles need much less cooking time than store-bought dry pasta. Drain the cooked noodles and transfer them into a large bowl.

2. While the noodles are cooking, heat oil or butter over medium heat in a heavy-bottomed 10" skillet (it is more difficult to brown the farina evenly in a smaller skillet) and add the farina. Brown the farina to an even golden brown color while stirring constantly, about 3 minutes; don't over-brown. Add hot water and salt. Stir, cover, remove skillet from heat, and let it rest under cover for a few minutes until the farina absorbs the water. Mix it with the drained noodles and serve it hot.

Cabbage Dumplings

Káposztás gombóc

This is Riza néni's version of a now largely forgotten nineteenth-century Austrian recipe. Supposedly, Emperor Franz Joseph liked to eat a similar dish as a main course accompanied by cucumber salad. Geographically the Emperor and Riza néni were not so far from each other: Moson is only about forty miles from Vienna. In social standing, however, they were light-years apart, but this didn't keep them from liking essentially the same dish.

Kidding aside, this points to an intriguing fact in the social history of eating: in spite of huge differences in the lifestyle of the different social classes, in both Austria and Hungary there was a great deal that was common to their diets. Many of the same dishes were popular among farmers, the urban middle class, and the upper class.

All dumplings, savory or dessert, are fairly fast and easy to make, but people who try them the first time frequently run into trouble because they don't know the consistency and "feel" of the dough and therefore cannot make the small necessary adjustments to the recipe. The moisture content of potatoes, flour, and farina, which are typical ingredients in dumplings, can vary depending on the season and the weather. Most of the time the quantities in the recipes will give you perfect results, but once in a while you must add a little more flour or farina to get the perfect dough. Don't be discouraged by the long recipes for the various dumplings in this book, it takes much less time to make them than to accurately describe what the dough should feel like.

YIELD:	6 servings (20 dumplings total)
TOTAL TIME:	about 1 hour 15 minutes
INGREDIENTS:	1 very small (about 1 pound) or ½ of a medium-sized cabbage
	2 tablespoons kosher salt
	2 slices of stale white bread, cut into ½" cubes, soaked in water to cover for 1–2 minutes and squeezed out
	1 large egg, lightly beaten
	1 tablespoon canola oil or unsalted margarine
	1½ cups unbleached all-purpose flour
SPECIAL EQUIPMENT:	food processor

1. Halve the cabbage, cut out and discard the white core, then cut the cabbage into pieces that fit the large feeding tube of the food processor.

Use the shredding disc and apply almost no pressure on the pusher of the feeding tube to very finely shred cabbage. In a large bowl, mix the cabbage with salt, place a small plate upside down on it, and place a large can or other similar weight over the plate. Let the cabbage rest for at least 30 minutes, pour off the juices, put the cabbage into a strainer and rinse out most of the salt under running water. Squeeze out the cabbage and put it into a large bowl.

2. Add the soaked bread and all the remaining ingredients to the cabbage in the bowl. Knead it by hand in the bowl and don't be discouraged if in the beginning it looks as if it will never stick together. After a few minutes of kneading it will form a ball. If the dough is too sticky, knead in a little more flour. Clean your hands by sprinkling a little flour over them and rubbing them together over the bowl. If there is time for it, let the dough rest for 15 to 30 minutes. Boil plenty of lightly salted water in a large pot. Place the dough on the lightly floured work surface and with floured hands form it into a roll of about 1½" to 2" diameter. Cut the roll into 5 parts and make four 1½" balls of each part. You should have 20 dumplings.

3. If you have time to do it, it is a good idea to first cook 1 trial dumpling to test the exact cooking time, but if you are short of time you can omit this step. Place the dumplings in boiling water and move them around a little with a wooden spoon to keep them from sticking to the bottom. Do not overcrowd the dumplings; rather, cook them in batches. Let the water come back to a boil, lower the heat, partially cover the pot, and let the dumplings simmer for about 12 minutes. Use a perforated spoon to remove the dumplings to a colander and briefly rinse them under cold running water. Keep the cooked dumplings loosely covered on a plate in a 175°F oven, but don't keep them there for more then 20 minutes.

4. Serve the dumplings as a side dish, or take your cue from Emperor Franz Joseph and serve them with cucumber salad as a light luncheon dish. They are also terrific with arugula leaves, which I would arrange, as shown in the drawing, around the dumplings to form a "nest."

Note: Uncooked leftover dough will keep for one day in the refrigerator, but lay a piece of plastic wrap on the dough to keep it from drying out. It will take one or two minutes longer to cook the dumplings made from the cold dough.

VARIATION:

Make cracklings by heating 1 tablespoon oil or previously rendered chicken fat in a skillet covered with a splatter-guard or in an uncovered and fairly deep (to contain the splatter) pan, adding chicken skin cut into ½" squares and slowly sautéing them over medium heat, stirring occasionally, until the fat is rendered and the skin is golden brown. Remove the cracklings with a skimmer, drain them on a paper towel, and sprinkle them with a little salt. Briefly brown the cooked dumplings in some of the rendered chicken fat. Serve the dumplings with the cracklings sprinkled over them.

Farina-Potato Dumplings
Gries Knödel

Dumplings have long been served in Austria and Hungary with meat dishes, such as the various braised chicken or meat recipes in this book, to whose thick and rich sauces they are the ideal accompaniments. They can be also served as light luncheon or supper dishes, perhaps with a salad or some homemade sausage. The bewildering variety of dumplings eaten in this part of Europe can be divided into three categories: savory dumplings, then a category that I like to call double-duty dumplings, because they have both savory and fruit- or jam-filled dessert versions, and finally those that are served only as desserts.

Riza néni, like most homemakers in the region, was proud of her extensive repertory of dumplings. In addition to the usual potato and bread dumplings, both of the double-duty kind, her collection included recipes for such less common specialties as these savory farina-potato dumplings or her cabbage dumplings.

YIELD:	about 30 dumplings, enough for 4 lunch servings or 8 servings as a side dish
TOTAL TIME:	about 2 hours 30 minutes (but much of this is waiting time)
INGREDIENTS:	2 large or 3 medium russet (Idaho) potatoes (about 1¼ pounds) ¾ cup farina (I tested the recipe with the most commonly available quick-cooking farina) or coarse semolina (see page 107 about semolina) 1 large egg 1 tablespoon rendered chicken fat or canola oil ½ teaspoon kosher salt
SPECIAL EQUIPMENT:	potato ricer or a food mill

1. Scrub potatoes and place them in their jackets in a medium saucepan with enough cold water to cover by about 1". Bring water to a boil over medium heat, lower heat and simmer for 30–40 minutes, until the potatoes are tender when tested with a fork or the point of a paring knife. Don't allow the potatoes to burst. Drain them and as soon as they are cool enough for you to hold them with a folded kitchen towel, pull their skin off with a paring knife. Cut them into 1" slices and while still warm put them through a potato ricer or a food mill set over a baking sheet. Spread the potatoes on the baking sheet and allow them to cool and dry for about 1 hour.

2. Mix and knead the dough on the baking sheet where the potatoes dried or in a large bowl. Add farina, egg, oil, and salt to the potatoes. Knead them for about 4 minutes or until the dough is well blended and no longer sticky. Cover it with plastic wrap and let it rest for about 30 minutes for the farina to absorb the moisture.

3. While the dough is resting, boil about 4 quarts of lightly salted water in a wide, about 10"-diameter, pot. Preheat oven to 175°F.

4. With a tablespoon, cut a small piece from the dough and roll it between your hands into a 1¼"–1½" diameter dumpling. Repeat this until you have used up all the dough and made about 30 dumplings.

5. Drop about 15 dumplings evenly distributed into the boiling water, adjust the heat to a gentle simmer and carefully move the dumplings with a wooden spoon to make sure they don't stick to the bottom of the pot. Partially cover the pot, and cook the dumplings for about 5 minutes.

6. Remove the dumplings with a slotted spoon or skimmer onto a plate and place it in the preheated oven while you cook the second batch of dumplings. Dumplings shouldn't be kept for more than 20 minutes in the warm oven.

7. Serve 3 or 4 dumplings per serving as a side dish, or about 8 dumplings as a main dish. They are wonderful as they are, but should you have some rendered chicken or duck fat, you can sprinkle a little melted fat over them or lightly brown them in a little fat. As with the cabbage dumplings in the previous recipe, you can serve these with bits of chicken crackling sprinkled over them. It is a terrific combination.

Potato Dumplings
Erdäpfel Knödel

Potato dumplings and bread dumplings are the two most common types of dumplings in Austria and Hungary. The kind of dough used in these potato dumplings is particularly versatile. In addition to the savory dumplings made to accompany meat dishes or to be served as a meatless main dish, smaller versions of the dumplings can be served in a soup. The same dough is used in delicious dessert dumplings filled with plums, apricots, prune butter, or apricot butter (see recipe on page 130). In another dessert the dough is rolled out to make a sort of ravioli filled with prune butter. It can also be shaped into short noodles and served with ground walnuts, almonds, or poppy seeds mixed with sugar (see recipe on page 318).

If possible, don't keep this dough for more than one or two hours before cooking it, because after a few hours the potato in the dough will release moisture, making the dough sticky. At that point you have no other recourse but to add more flour, which of course would make the dumplings heavier.

YIELD: 4–6 servings (about 24 dumplings)

TOTAL TIME: about 1 hour 55 minutes (much of this is waiting time)

INGREDIENTS:
- 2 large or 3 medium russet (Idaho) potatoes (about 1¼ pounds)
- 1 large egg with 1 tablespoon of the white discarded
- 1 tablespoon canola oil, rendered poultry fat, or unsalted margarine
- ½ teaspoon kosher salt
- 1¼ cups unbleached all-purpose flour, preferably less

SPECIAL EQUIPMENT:
potato ricer
dough scraper (optional)

1. Scrub the potatoes, place them in their jackets in a medium saucepan with water to cover by about 1", bring it to a boil over medium heat, lower heat and simmer for 30–40 minutes until the potatoes are tender when tested with the tip of a paring knife or fork. Don't let the potatoes burst.

2. Drain the potatoes, let them cool a little, hold the still quite hot potatoes with a folded kitchen towel and with a paring knife pull off their skin. Place a baking sheet on your work surface. Cut the hot potatoes into 1" slices and put them through a potato ricer while holding it over the baking sheet. Spread the potatoes on the baking sheet and allow

them to cool and dry for about 1 hour. This is an important step, because the drier the potatoes are, the less flour you will need for the dough and the lighter your dumplings will be.

3. Boil 3–4 quarts of lightly salted water in a large, wide (9" or more) pot. While waiting for the water to boil, gather the potatoes into a loose heap in the middle of the baking sheet, make a well in the center, add egg, oil (or other fat), salt, and 1 scant cup flour into this well. Knead it for about 2 minutes to thoroughly blend the ingredients. If it is too sticky, add a little more flour. Don't knead it too hard or long and try to use as little flour as possible to make a workable and not sticky dough. Too much kneading or too much flour will make the dumplings heavy. Preheat oven to 175°F.

4. Lightly flour your hands and the baking sheet. Using the dough scraper or a tablespoon, cut a piece from the dough and roll it between your floured palms into an approximately 1¼" ball. Place this dumpling on the floured baking sheet until you make the other dumplings. You will end up with approximately 24 dumplings.

5. Drop about 12 dumplings into the boiling water, gently move them around a little with a wooden spoon to keep them from sticking to the bottom, lower the heat, partially cover the pot and simmer for about 5 minutes. With a skimmer or a slotted spoon, remove the dumplings to a plate and place the plate in the preheated oven until you make the second batch of dumplings. Don't keep the dumplings in the oven for more than about 15 minutes or they will become heavy.

6. Serve them immediately as a side dish with meat dishes or with a large salad as a simple main dish. If the meat dish doesn't have much sauce, you could pour a little melted chicken or duck fat, or some sautéed chopped onion over the dumplings. They are also delicious when they are browned in a little rendered poultry fat. To make this, heat about 1 tablespoon fat in a skillet and brown the dumplings in several batches for about 45 seconds on each side. The crispy browned outside of the dumpling will contrast appealingly with the soft inside.

Kohlrabi

Kohlrüben Gemüse

Kohlrabi is one of the most popular vegetables in Hungary, thus it is not surprising that this is the only vegetable included in Riza néni's collection in addition to green peas and green beans. Kohlrabi is also popular in other countries of Eastern Europe, Austria, Germany, Scandinavia, and to a slightly lesser extent in northern Italy, but it is rarely eaten in the United States and in Britain. Escoffier didn't include it among the 2,973 recipes of his *Guide Culinaire*, though it used to be common in French country cooking, too. While our *Joy of Cooking* provides only one recipe for it, most Hungarian cookbooks include recipes for it as a soup, as stuffed preparations for appetizer, as a salad, as a side dish in a few versions, and as a dish in which it is combined with chicken—a traditional and fabulous combination.

This wonderfully flavorful vegetable tastes a little like a sweeter version of turnip. Alice B. Toklas described its taste as "having the pungency of a high-born radish bred to a low-brow cucumber." Its name comes to us from German, where it means "cabbage-turnip." The first half of its German name describes it correctly as a member of the cabbage family, but it is not related to the turnip. The light green edible bulb of the kohlrabi is not a root, like the turnip is, but a swelling of the stem immediately above the ground from which the thinner stems of the leaves sprout. Its season is from spring to late summer when it is available in some of the better stores for produce, such as New York City's Fairway, though it is easier to find and much cheaper in Chinese neighborhoods. Look for small, heavy bulbs, ideally about two inches, but certainly not more than three inches in diameter. Avoid split bulbs. Try to choose kohlrabi with bright green, crisp-looking leaves. The young, tender leaves are edible and the chopped leaves can be added to the dish about five minutes before it finishes cooking. When the plant is older, it is best to discard the leaves. Sometimes late in season the greengrocers sell the bulbs with the leaves already removed.

In Hungary, the diced kohlrabi is either boiled or braised when it is prepared as a side dish. Calling it a side dish is a little misleading here because, as typical with similar vegetable dishes in Hungary, people eat a large portion of it accompanied by a small portion of meat; or sometimes they even eat it as a separate course, without any meat. Riza néni chose the braised method to prepare it, which tends to enhance its flavor, but contrary to the usual recipes for braised kohlrabi in Hungarian cookbooks, she added chopped onion and ground ginger to the dish. She also added quite a lot of sugar; in fact the original recipe called for so much sugar that I suspected it to be an error and so I cut back on it. I am not talking about the little caramelized sugar with which the kohlrabi is braised but about the sugar added later, together with the other seasonings. She clearly intended this dish to be slightly sweet, but I suggest that you start with only one teaspoon of sugar and decide whether you want to add more after tasting the dish. In Hungary people almost always add some chopped parsley and a little sour cream to this dish. I understand why Riza néni omitted sour cream from a dish made with chicken stock and rendered poultry fat: she couldn't mix dairy with meat products. But I have no idea why she left out the parsley, which I have included as an optional ingredient because its flavor goes well with kohlrabi.

YIELD: 4–6 servings

TOTAL TIME: about 1 hour

INGREDIENTS:
- 2 pounds kohlrabi
- 1 tablespoon canola oil or rendered poultry fat
- 1 medium onion, peeled and finely chopped
- 1 teaspoon sugar
- 2 tablespoons all-purpose flour
- 2 tablespoons chopped fresh flat-leaf parsley (optional)
- ¾ teaspoon kosher salt
- ½ teaspoon freshly ground black pepper
- ½ teaspoon ground dry ginger
- 1–2 teaspoons sugar
- 1 cup chicken stock or water

SPECIAL EQUIPMENT: 10" or 12" heavy-bottomed pan with a tight-fitting lid

1. Peel the kohlrabi with a paring knife. Sometimes the root end of the bulb is woody, which you can easily recognize because it is more yellowish and porous than the dense, greenish-white "good" part. Cut off and discard the woody part. Cut the peeled bulbs in half lengthwise and cut each half into ½" × ½" × ¼" pieces. Heat the oil or rendered poultry fat in a wide, heavy-bottomed braising pan or sauté pan. Add the chopped onion, stir, cover, and cook over medium heat for about 10 minutes. Check periodically; the onion should get soft and almost translucent but shouldn't brown. Push the onion to the perimeter of the pan, adjust the heat to medium-high, sprinkle 1 teaspoon sugar in the middle, and let it brown very slightly while stirring it constantly. This will take 1 or 2 minutes. Don't allow the sugar to clump into one hard piece of caramel.

2. Add the kohlrabi and 2 tablespoons water. Stir, cover, adjust heat to medium-low, and cook kohlrabi for about 25 minutes, until it is tender.

3. Sprinkle flour over the kohlrabi, stirring after each tablespoonful to make sure that the flour is evenly distributed. Cook it uncovered for 2 minutes.

4. Add the optional chopped parsley, if you wish, and a generous handful of the chopped tender leaves (stems removed prior to chopping) of the kohlrabi, if available. Also add salt, pepper, ginger, 1 teaspoon sugar, and the broth or water. Bring it to a boil, lower heat to medium-low and cook for about 5 minutes. Taste it and add more sugar, if you wish. The original dish was meant to be slightly sweet.

5. Serve it immediately to accompany roasted or braised meat, but you can also serve it by itself as light main dish.

Green Pea Purée
Erbsen Pirée

Riza néni of course made this dish with fresh peas, but the taste of frozen peas is almost as good and they are easier to find in our supermarkets. Although she didn't include it in her recipe, it is customary in Hungary to add a little sugar to green peas; it doesn't make the dish sweet but intensifies the pea flavor.

YIELD:	3 small servings
TOTAL TIME:	about 20 minutes
INGREDIENTS:	1 package frozen tiny or baby green peas (10 ounces, about 2⅓ cups)
	1 cup water
	¼ teaspoon kosher salt
	1 teaspoon sugar (optional)
	1 tablespoon canola oil or rendered poultry fat
	2 tablespoons chopped onion
	1 tablespoon all-purpose flour
	¼ cup water
	¼-½ teaspoon ground ginger
	½ medium onion, peeled and thinly sliced (about ½ cup)
	¼ cup canola oil or rendered poultry fat
SPECIAL EQUIPMENT:	hand-held blender or a food mill fitted with a fine screen

1. Place frozen peas, 1 cup water, salt, and sugar in a saucepan. Bring it to a boil, lower heat, cover, and simmer for 4 minutes.

2. While the peas are cooking, heat canola oil or rendered poultry fat in a medium saucepan, add chopped onions, sauté them over medium

heat for 3 minutes, until they turn almost translucent, sprinkle flour over the onions, stir, and cook slowly, stirring periodically, for about 2 minutes. Gradually dilute this with ¼ cup cold water, constantly stirring to avoid lumps.

3. Gradually add the peas and their cooking water, stopping a few times to stir. Add ¼ teaspoon ginger, bring the peas to a boil, lower heat, and simmer for 2 minutes, stirring periodically.

4. Tilt the pan, and purée the peas with a hand-held blender. Alternatively, you can use a food mill for the puréeing. Taste and, if necessary, adjust seasoning.

5. Separate the thinly sliced onions into threads. Heat ¼ cup canola oil or rendered poultry fat in an 8" skillet and fry the threads of onion over medium-high heat for about 3 minutes, until golden brown. It is a good idea to place a splatter guard over the skillet. Transfer the onions with a slotted spoon or skimmer onto a paper towel to drain. Alternatively, you can brown bread crumbs in a little oil or fat in a skillet until they turn golden brown, and use this instead of the fried onions for garnish.

6. Serve it hot with some fried onions or browned bread crumbs sprinkled over it.

Green Beans
Grüne Fisolen

Instead of the thin snap beans, also called string beans, most common in our supermarkets, Hungarians prefer the broad, flat-podded Italian romano beans, best known as flat beans. String beans got their name because their tough strings had to be removed, but these days this is no longer true unless the beans are really ancient. You can test them for stringiness by snapping off the top and pulling down the side to see if the string peels away. The season of green beans is from early summer through autumn; during this time I usually can find excellent flat beans in New York City's Union Square green market or Fairway supermarket. Try to buy flat green beans for this recipe, or flat wax beans, which are equally authentic, but you can also make it with the narrow kind, in which case reduce the cooking time. More than the narrow beans, flat beans retain an appealing crunch even when they are fully cooked.

The most interesting feature of Riza néni's recipe is that, while in most Hungarian recipes for this vegetable the green beans are first boiled, she cooks them practically dry, in only their natural moisture and the little water clinging to them from rinsing. I love this method of preparation, as it intensifies the flavor of the beans. Cooking green beans with vinegar is one of the traditional preparations in Austria and Hungary, but seasoning the dish with cinnamon and ginger is most unusual. It is probably another example in her recipes for an earlier style of seasoning, before paprika became the predominant seasoning in Hungarian cooking.

Riza néni must have liked overcooked green beans because according to her recipe she cooked them for the astonishing time of two-and-a-half hours. I would start testing the beans after eighteen minutes, but the actual cooking time can greatly vary depending on the age and type of green beans. I ended up cooking my flat beans for thirty minutes; string beans would take about twenty minutes. She used ground ginger, but I prefer the clean bright flavor of fresh ginger in this dish. Although her recipe didn't include parsley, I have added a little because I believe it enhances the flavor of the beans.

YIELD: 5 servings

TOTAL TIME: about 40 minutes

INGREDIENTS:
- 1¼ pounds flat green beans or snap beans
- 3 tablespoons canola oil
- 1 medium onion (about 4 ounces), peeled and finely chopped
- 2 tablespoons chopped fresh flat-leaf parsley (optional)
- 3 tablespoons all-purpose flour

¾ teaspoon kosher salt
¾ teaspoon ground cinnamon
1 teaspoon finely chopped fresh ginger (or ½ teaspoon ground ginger)
2–3 tablespoons cider vinegar
1¼ cups water
2 teaspoons sugar (optional)

SPECIAL
EQUIPMENT: none

1. Wash the green beans, cut off their ends, and cut several at once on the bias into approximately 1" pieces. You should have about 5 cups of cut green beans. Rinse them again.

2. Heat oil in a large pan or saucepan, sauté onions over medium heat for about 3 minutes, until translucent. Don't let them brown.

3. Add the optional chopped parsley and the cut green beans with the rinse water clinging to them, adjust heat to medium-low, stir, and cover. Cook for 15 minutes, stirring once or twice and checking to make sure there is still some moisture around the beans. If necessary, add 1 tablespoon water.

4. Sprinkle flour over the beans, stir to distribute, and cook uncovered for 2 minutes. Add salt, cinnamon, ginger, vinegar, and water. Bring to a boil, cover, and cook for about 3 more minutes. Check for tenderness and if necessary cook the beans a little longer. Beans should be tender but still retain some crispness to the bite. Taste them and adjust the seasoning if you think this is necessary.

5. Serve them hot. They go well with any kind of stew or braised meat; they can even be offered as a meatless main course if served together with some dumplings. In Hungary, this dish usually includes sour cream but because of Jewish dietary rules Riza néni couldn't add sour cream to a meat dish. She also left out the small amount of sugar customarily added to this dish. I, too, usually make it without sugar, but some sugar added to make it sweet and sour would be equally nice.

Fermented Dill Pickles
Wasser-Gurken

Pickles are well-known staples of traditional Jewish cuisine in the United States. Jewish immigrants from Poland, Russia, and the Ukraine, where pickles were important parts of their diet, made pickles popular here. Delicatessen stores with their barrels of pickles have long been fixtures of our Jewish neighborhoods. Even before ordering any food, bowls of pickles await us on the tables of Jewish deli restaurants. They are staples of the diet in Hungary, too, but are not associated with Jewish culture quite as closely as in the United States.

Riza néni's collection includes three recipes for pickled fruits or vegetables: pickled green walnuts, sour cherries preserved in spiced vinegar, and fermented dill cucumbers. These cucumbers are one of the most popular pickles in Hungary, but pickles made with this process, which uses no vinegar, are less widely available in the United States. Here they are called half-sour pickles or sour pickles, depending on the length of the fermentation time, and can be found in the refrigerated section of some supermarkets. Kosher dill pickles are prepared with vinegar and have a completely different taste. Riza néni's recipe is very similar to recipes in George Lang's excellent *The Cuisine of Hungary* and József Venesz's *Hungarian Cuisine*. The only difference is that they include garlic among the ingredients, while Riza néni omitted it. She must not have liked garlic, because she didn't use it in any of her recipes.

I love the interestingly complex taste and wonderful yeasty aroma of these dill pickles and their brine. In Hungary they are frequently served instead of a salad to accompany hearty meat dishes, to which they are the perfect counterfoils. They also make a terrific snack on hot summer days, eaten with some good crusty rye bread and the cold brine of the pickles as a refreshing drink on the side (as is or with a little seltzer added). This fermented pickling liquid is somewhat similar to the Russian *kvass*. The word *kvass* is related to the Slavic word that is at the root of one the Hungarian names of this pickle: *kovászos uborka* (fermented pickle).

It takes only about twenty minutes of work to make these wonderful pickles. I am sure, once you have tried them, you will be as addicted as I am.

YIELD:	16 pickles
TOTAL TIME:	about 20 minutes, plus 3–4 days fermenting time
INGREDIENTS:	16 unwaxed Kirby cucumbers, each about 4" long and 1½" thick, about 3¾ pounds in total
	2 quarts water
	2½ tablespoons kosher salt
	1 bunch of dill
	1 teaspoon all-purpose flour
	1 slice of rye bread
SPECIAL EQUIPMENT:	1 glass jar, 3 or 4 quarts capacity, or a similar capacity crock, at least 5" diameter and 11" high

1. Buy firm cucumbers of about the same size with no soft spots. Scrub them well under running water with a brush. Cut about ¼" from both ends of each cucumber. Lay them on a cutting board and with a paring knife cut through the middle of them lengthwise, stopping about ¾" short of each end. Then give them a quarter turn and make a similar cut perpendicular to the first one. Make sure you stop cutting well short of both ends of the cucumber or it will fall apart.

2. Heat 2 quarts water and dissolve the salt in it. It is better to use kosher salt that is always uniodized, as opposed to the usual iodized table salt. Let the water cool to lukewarm.

3. Wash the dill and place ½ of it on the bottom of the jar or crock. If you like garlic more than Riza néni did, you might want to add 2 peeled and slightly crushed cloves of garlic to the jar. Stand 8 cucumbers on end in the bottom of the jar. They should fit reasonably tightly in the

jar. Put another similar layer of 8 cucumbers on top of them and the remaining dill on top of the cucumbers.

4. Pour the lukewarm salted water into the jar so that it covers the cucumbers and the dill by about ½", sprinkle flour over the water, and put the slice of bread on top. Push the bread into the water.

5. Put a small plate on top of the jar and place it in a sunny place or at least in a warm place for three or four days (for example, I placed the jar on a sunny window ledge in my apartment). Don't close the jar with an airtight lid. (The plate on top merely helps to contain the smell of fermenting cucumbers.) If you have a sunny backyard put the fermenting pickles there. The water in the jar will turn cloudy, almost milky, during fermentation.

6. After three or four days transfer the cucumbers, which are similar to our half-sour pickles, to a bowl. If allowed to ferment longer they will become more sour but also softer, which I don't like. It is a good idea to test one after three days—it should be pleasingly sour and should still give a little resistance to the bite. Strain the pickling liquid and discard the dill and the bread. Put the cucumbers back into the jar or several smaller jars and pour the strained pickle juice over them to completely cover. If necessary, add a little water. Store the pickles in the refrigerator for up to three weeks—although, addicted as I am, I usually eat them all much before that.

Almond-Meringue Noodles

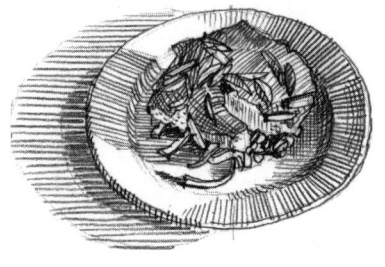

Nudel mit Souffle

There is no category in Austro-Hungarian cuisine that is as different from the cooking of other countries as the hot noodle and dumpling desserts to which this dish belongs. These desserts are almost always served hot, usually after the main course, but at times they constitute the main course of the meal. The dough or batter usually contains flour, eggs, and on occasion other ingredients, such as potatoes, cottage cheese, or farina. It can be boiled, baked, sautéed, or cooked using a combination of these methods. Outside the cooking of the former Austro-Hungarian Monarchy, Jewish cooking presents the best-known example for a similar type of dish: the *lokshen kugel* or noodle pudding, but the similarity is probably coincidental. Besides, lokshen kugel can be served either hot or cold, while most Austro-Hungarian noodle desserts are served hot. Riza néni's recipe for these almond-meringue noodles is a typical example of this category of hot desserts, but it is different from any such dish I know.

YIELD: 4–6 servings

TOTAL TIME: about 50 minutes

INGREDIENTS:
- 5 ounces dry fettuccine or tagliatelle
  Alternate: make ⅓"-wide fresh noodles from ¾ cup unbleached all-purpose flour, 1 large egg, and 2–4 teaspoons water.
- 1¼ tablespoons unsalted butter or margarine
- 1 cup blanched almonds
- ⅓ cup sugar
- ¼ cup golden raisins
- 3 large egg whites

	¼ teaspoon cream of tartar
	⅓ cup sugar
	¾ teaspoon vanilla extract
	¼ cup slivered almonds

SPECIAL EQUIPMENT: 8" × 8" × 2" gratin dish or any baking dish of about the same area
food processor

1. Preheat the oven to 325°F. Boil pasta, but it should be slightly undercooked. Dry pasta should be boiled for about 10 minutes, fresh pasta for 2–3 minutes. Toss pasta with 1 tablespoon butter or margarine.

2. Coat the baking dish with the remaining ¼ tablespoon butter or margarine.

3. Process almonds and ⅓ cup sugar in a food processor until almonds are finely ground, about 30 seconds.

4. Whip egg whites and cream of tartar to form soft peaks, add sugar and vanilla extract, then whip them a little more until they become shiny and form firm peaks.

5. Spread ½ of the noodles in the bottom of the baking dish. Sprinkle ½ of the almond-sugar mixture and ½ of the raisins over them. Then cover this with the remaining noodles and finally sprinkle the remaining almond-sugar mixture and raisins over the noodles. Spread the beaten egg whites over the noodles all the way to the sides of the dish. Strew slivered almonds on top.

6. Place the baking dish on a baking sheet and bake it in the preheated oven for about 20 minutes or until meringue is slightly brown and the slivered almonds are lightly toasted. Serve immediately. This dessert is best when fresh but you can keep leftovers for one day at room temperature or for up to one week in the refrigerator. Allow them to come to room temperature before serving.

VARIATION:

Instead of the simple meringue, make a topping similar to the famed *Salzburger Nockerl* (Salzburg soufflé): Mix 1 large egg yolk with ½ teaspoon grated lemon zest and ¾ teaspoon vanilla extract. Beat 3 large egg whites and ⅓ cup sugar to form firm peaks. Fold the egg yolk mixture into the egg white mixture and use this for the topping with the slivered almonds strewn over it.

Farina Dessert Dumplings
Grießknödel

In addition to the ubiquitous small savory dumplings made of farina and eggs, used as a soup garnish in much of Central Europe, Riza néni also made this less common dessert version.

Prune butter, or *lekvár* as such fruit butters are called in Hungary, is a very thick fruit paste. It is quite widely available in the United States either as a Hungarian import by Adro or a domestic version of it, manufactured by Simon Fischer. If you cannot find it, substitute very thick apricot jam or pitted prune plums (Italian plums).

YIELD: 4 servings (8 dumplings)

TOTAL TIME: about 45 minutes

INGREDIENTS:
- 1¼ cups water
- 1 tablespoon unsalted butter, margarine, or canola oil
- ¼ teaspoon kosher salt
- 1 tablespoon sugar
- 1¼ cups farina (I tested the recipe with the commonly available 2-minute, quick-cooking kind) or coarse semolina (see page 107 about semolina)
- 1 whole large egg

1 large egg white
¼ cup prune butter (prune lekvár)
⅓ cup walnuts
3 tablespoons sugar
½ cup sour cream (optional)

SPECIAL
EQUIPMENT: dough scraper
                food processor

1. Pour water into a medium saucepan, add butter (or margarine or oil), salt, and sugar. Bring it to a boil and slowly sprinkle the farina into the boiling water, whisking constantly to avoid lumps. It will be a very thick paste, much thicker than the usual hot farina cereal. Lower heat to medium-low and cook for 2 minutes, stirring frequently.

2. Transfer the hot farina to a large bowl, spread it on the sides of the bowl to facilitate cooling and place it in the refrigerator for 10 minutes. While the farina is cooling, boil about 4 quarts of lightly salted water in a pot about 10" wide.

3. Remove the bowl of farina from the refrigerator. Add egg and egg white; knead the mixture until it is well blended, about 5 minutes. It should be a medium-firm, slightly sticky dough. If it is very sticky or too soft, knead in a little more farina.

4. Place a small bowl of cold water on the work surface. With a tablespoon, transfer some dough to the work surface and with your slightly moistened hands form it into a 3½" square, about ⅜" thick. Place 1 teaspoon prune butter in the middle and with the help of a dough scraper fold the 4 corners of the square over the filling. Slide the dough scraper under the dough to lift it off the work surface and with your moistened hands shape the dough to completely enclose the filling. Roll the dumpling between your hands to make an approximately 2"-diameter ball. Repeat this to make 7 more dumplings from the rest of the dough and filling.

5. Gently drop the dumplings into the boiling water, carefully move them a little with a wooden spoon to make sure they don't stick to the

bottom, bring the water back to a boil, partially cover, lower heat and simmer for about 11 minutes.

6. While the dumplings are cooking, place walnuts and sugar in the bowl of the food processor and process for about 15 seconds to evenly grind the nuts. Pour the ground nuts into a soup plate.

7. With a slotted spoon or skimmer, remove the dumplings to a plate and, while they are still wet, roll them one by one in the walnut-sugar mixture. Serve them hot, 2 dumplings per person. If you serve them as part of a dairy menu or if you don't keep kosher, serve a little warmed sour cream with the dumplings.

Potato Dessert Dumplings
Erdäpfel Knödel

These dumplings have long been extremely popular in the countries of the former Austro-Hungarian Monarchy and in Germany. Riza néni's grandchildren were in seventh heaven when Paula made these dumplings for lunch in late summer or fall when the plums were ripe. Riza néni encouraged them to have dumpling-eating contests, a favorite pastime of kids in Hungary. On occasion, she served these dumplings, which are filling but not heavy if they are well prepared, as a main dish following a soup. Most often, Paula filled them with prune plums (Italian plums), less frequently with apricots. When these fruits were not in season, she used prune butter or apricot butter.

The dumplings can be either rolled in browned bread crumbs or in a mixture of ground nuts and sugar. I usually opt for the ground nuts if I am in a hurry, because they take practically no time to make in the food processor. It is customary in Hungary to serve these dumplings with some slightly warmed sour cream, but of course Riza néni couldn't use this unless the dumplings were part of a dairy menu.

YIELD:	5 servings (about 16 plum-filled dumplings or 22 prune butter–filled dumplings)
TOTAL TIME:	about 2 hours 30 minutes (of this, 1 hour is unattended)
INGREDIENTS:	1 recipe potato dumpling dough (page 113) 16 small Italian prune plums (or about ½ cup prune butter) ¼ cup sugar (omit if you use prune butter) 2 teaspoons ground cinnamon (omit if you use prune butter) 3 tablespoons canola oil, unsalted margarine or butter 1¼ cups dry bread crumbs (about 5 slices of stale white bread processed into crumbs) ½ cup sour cream, slightly warmed (optional) ½ cup confectioners' sugar
SPECIAL EQUIPMENT:	food processor

1. Prepare the dough according to the recipe for savory potato dumplings on page 113. While you prepare the dough, bring about 4 quarts water to a boil in a wide (about 10" diameter) pot.

2. Mix sugar and cinnamon in a small bowl. Wash the plums, cut them open on one side, leaving the 2 halves of the plum attached on the other side, remove the pit and fill the cavity with about ½ teaspoon of the sugar-cinnamon mixture.

3. In a heavy skillet heat oil, margarine, or butter. Add bread crumbs and brown them to even golden brown, while stirring all the time. Transfer them immediately to a soup plate to keep them from continuing to get darker in the still hot skillet. Alternatively, instead of the browned bread crumbs, use a mixture of ground nuts and sugar for coating the dumplings. To make this coating, place ½ cup walnuts and ¼ cup sugar

in the bowl of the food processor and process until finely ground, about 20 seconds. Transfer this mixture to a soup plate.

4. Divide the dough in half. Dust your work surface and rolling pin with flour, and roll out one half of the dough into a rectangle about 6" × 12" × ¼". Periodically during rolling lift up one side of the dough, throw a little flour under it, and give it a quarter turn. Cut the sheet of dough into about 3" squares. Make smaller squares, about 2½", if you decide to fill them with prune butter instead of plums.

5. Place a pitted plum (or about ¾ teaspoon prune butter) in the center of a square. With your floured fingers or with the help of the dough scraper, carefully lift up the corners of the square and fold them over the plum or prune butter. Now lift up the whole square and shape it into a ball with your lightly floured hands, completely enclosing the filling. Roll the dumpling between your floured palms to even out the dough and place it on a floured baking sheet. Repeat this with the other dough squares and with the second half of the dough. You should have about 16 plum-filled dumplings or 22 dumplings if you filled them with prune butter.

6. Drop about half of the dumplings into boiling water and move them around a little with a wooden spoon to keep them from sticking to the bottom. Lower heat to a simmer, partially cover, and cook the dumplings for about 9 minutes if they are filled with plums or 8 minutes if they are filled with prune butter.

7. Remove the dumplings from the water with a slotted spoon or skimmer and immediately roll them, while they are still wet, in either browned bread crumbs or ground walnuts. If you use a bread-crumb coating, dust the dumplings with a little powdered sugar immediately before serving them. Serve them hot. Spoon some warmed sour cream on the plate next to them, if your dietary rules allow this.

Plum-filled Bread Dumplings

Semmelknödeln mit Zwetschken gefüllt

Bread dumplings are one of the most popular savory dumplings in this part of Europe, but this dessert version is highly unusual and is another example of forgotten dishes preserved in old handwritten recipe collections, such as Riza néni's. If this book achieves nothing more than to make you take a closer look at old recipe collections handed down in your family, I will be happy, because it has served a good cause. Cooking from such old recipes might take a little more time than from modern cookbooks, but the result is definitely worth the small extra effort. It will be a tasty way to learn about your cultural heritage.

I love to read such handwritten collections even if I am not about to cook from them, because they transport me to the past and bring the person who wrote them back to life. Perhaps even better than old letters can do, certainly in a very different way, they provide a window into everyday life long ago. You can learn from them what people ate, what utensils they used in the kitchen, what ingredients they could buy in the stores, what cultural and culinary influences shaped them, and whether they were religious. Sometimes you can also learn about their social lives, because handwritten recipes frequently include the name of the person from whom the writer got the recipe. Recipes, such as *hadi Sacher* (wartime Sacher torte) in one of my family collections, tell me about shortages during war and how people tried to cope with them. I love the little quirky comments so common in such collections, such as "this recipe is not quite kosher" (which is of course like saying that somebody is a little pregnant) by a relative who started to get casual about dietary rules. I could go on citing examples, but I hope even from these few you get a sense of my passion for those old, crumbling copybooks. Such recipe collections are important parts of family traditions, but also of broader cultural traditions. They tell us the story of a vanished world and forge a link to our past and our roots.

After this long detour, let's get back to preparing the plum-filled bread dumplings. Even if the bread is not too salty, the amount of bread used in this recipe could make the dumplings taste salty, and so I suggest adding a little sugar to the dough, though this wasn't part of Riza néni's original recipe. When they are in season, use prune plums, also called Italian plums, to fill these dumplings; in off-season substitute either prune butter or apricot butter.

YIELD:	3–4 servings (9 dumplings)
TOTAL TIME:	about 1 hour
INGREDIENTS:	4 slices of white bread, cut into ½" cubes and dried for 5 minutes on a baking sheet in the 400°F oven
	2 slices of dry white bread, processed into bread crumbs (about ½ cup)
	1 tablespoon canola oil
	1 large egg
	1 tablespoon sugar (optional)
	⅓–½ cup unbleached all-purpose flour
	9 small prune plums (Italian plums) or substitute 3 tablespoons prune butter (prune lekvár)
	2 tablespoons sugar (only if you use prune plums)
	1 teaspoons ground cinnamon (only if you use prune plums)
	¼ cup walnuts
	2 tablespoons sugar
	¾ cup sour cream, slightly heated (optional)
SPECIAL EQUIPMENT:	dough scraper
	food processor

1. Place dry bread cubes in a medium bowl and soak them for about 1 minute in enough water to cover. They should be completely soft but not yet mushy. Squeeze them out well and place them in a large bowl. Add bread crumbs, oil, egg, optional sugar, and about ⅓ cup flour.

Knead the dough for about 3 minutes; if it is sticky, add a little more flour (I needed 2 tablespoons extra). Clean your hands by rubbing them together over the bowl. Gather the dough into a ball and let it rest in the bowl for at least 30 minutes.

2. Pour about 4" water into a large, about 10"-wide pot, and bring it to a boil.

3. Mix 2 tablespoons sugar and the cinnamon in a small bowl (you will not need this if you use prune butter instead of the plums). Wash and pit the plums and place about ½ teaspoon of the sugar-cinnamon mixture in the cavities. Place walnuts and 2 tablespoons sugar in the bowl of the food processor and process for about 20 seconds. Transfer the ground walnut–sugar mixture to a soup plate.

4. Using a floured rolling pin, roll out the dough on the floured work surface into a 9" square. Several times during rolling, lift it up one side of the dough, throw a little flour under it, and give it a quarter turn to keep it from sticking to the work surface. Cut it into 3" squares.

5. Place a plum (or about ¾ teaspoon prune butter) in the center of each square. If you use prune butter, make sure that it is not spread out but is in a compact little heap in the middle. Lift up a square with the dough scraper, and fold the 4 corners around the filling with your well-floured fingers. Enclose the filling, pinch to seal, and roll the dumpling between your floured palms to even it out. Place it on a floured surface. Repeat this with the remaining 8 squares.

6. Drop the dumplings into boiling water; with a wooden spoon gently nudge them a bit to keep them from sticking to the bottom; reduce heat to a simmer; partially cover, and cook for 9 minutes. With a slotted spoon or a skimmer remove the dumplings to a large plate and while they are still wet one by one roll them in the ground walnut mixture. Serve them hot, 2 or 3 dumplings per serving, with a little sour cream if your dietary rules allow this.

Napkin Dessert Dumpling with Vanilla Sauce

Servietten Knedel

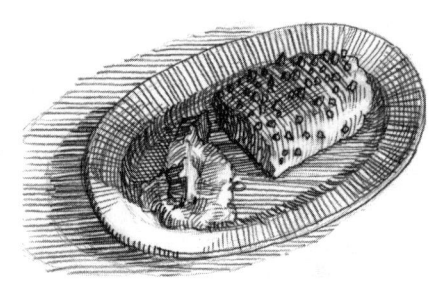

Savory dumplings boiled in a napkin are quite common in Germany and Austria, a little less so in Hungary, but I haven't come across in my research anything resembling this dessert version. This is a fabulous dessert, one of my favorites in this book. It is essentially a slightly sweet bread dumpling, which gets its wonderful airy texture from the whipped egg whites folded into the dough and from the technique of cooking the dumpling in a napkin suspended in simmering water. The crunchiness of the slivered almonds stuck into the soft dumpling provides an appealing contrast of textures. Riza néni indicated that it should be served with a dessert sauce but didn't specify the type of sauce. I love it with this vanilla sauce, but it would be equally nice with the wine sauce described in the rice and apple pudding recipe (page 145).

It is all right to use slightly salted white bread for this recipe, but try to find one that is not too salty, because the recipe contains quite a lot of bread and too much salt could upset the balance of flavors. The recipe will give you about two and a quarter cups of vanilla sauce, more than enough for the eight or nine slices of dumpling. Use the remaining sauce, which you can keep for two or three days in the refrigerator, for some other dessert or for pouring over fresh fruit.

YIELD: 8–9 slices (4 large servings or 8 modest servings)

TOTAL TIME: about 1 hour

DUMPLING INGREDIENTS:
- 1 tablespoon unsalted butter, margarine, or canola oil
- 2 large egg yolks (reserve egg whites for later use)

4 slices white bread, cut into ½" cubes, and dried on a baking sheet for 5 minutes in a 400°F oven
⅜ cup raw almonds
¼ cup sugar
½ cup dry bread crumbs, made in the food processor from stale white bread
1½ teaspoons grated lemon zest
2 teaspoons lemon juice
½ teaspoon vanilla extract
4 large egg whites (including the 2 reserved egg whites)
½ teaspoon cream of tartar
¼ cup slivered almonds

SAUCE
INGREDIENTS:
2 tablespoons all-purpose flour (1½ tablespoons if you like your sauce less thick)
2 cups milk (or water, if dietary restrictions don't allow milk)
½ vanilla bean
2 large eggs
5 tablespoons sugar

SPECIAL
EQUIPMENT:
food processor
electric mixer (optional)
smooth kitchen towel (don't use a terrycloth towel!), at least 13" × 24", preferably 14" × 30"

1. Fill a large pot, at least 10" diameter and 5" deep, with water. Cover the pot and bring the water to a boil (this will take about 20 minutes).

2. Melt butter or margarine and allow it to cool; omit this step if you decide to use oil. Place egg yolks in a large bowl and add oil, melted butter, or margarine. Whisk this mixture until frothy. Soak the dry bread cubes for 1 or 2 minutes in enough water to cover until they are completely soft but not mushy, squeeze them out, and add them to the egg mixture. Place almonds and sugar in the bowl of the food processor; process for about 30 seconds until evenly ground, and add them to

the egg mixture. Add bread crumbs, lemon zest, lemon juice, vanilla extract; mix them well with all the ingredients in the bowl.

3. Whip egg whites and cream of tartar until they form firm peaks. Stir ¼ of the whipped egg whites into the egg yolk mixture, then gently fold in the rest of the egg whites.

4. Run cold water over the kitchen towel, wring it out, and spread it on the work surface. Spoon the soft dough onto the middle of the towel, making a mound about 7" lengthwise on the towel and 4" crosswise. Fold one of the long edges of the towel over the dough, then the other long edge to overlap and enclose the dough. Tie a piece of kitchen string around the towel about 1" from one end of the filling and another piece of string about 1" from the other end. The 2 strings will be about 9" apart, enclosing the dough in the towel almost like a sausage. Lift up this "sausage" by the ends of the towel, twist one end of the towel around one handle of the pot of boiling water, then the other end of the towel around the other handle. The damp towel will not slip out of the handles. The dough sausage should be suspended between the two handles and fully submerged in the boiling water. Loosely cover the pot. Adjust the heat to medium and cook the dumpling in the simmering water for 30 minutes.

5. While the dumpling is cooking, prepare the sauce. Place the flour in a heavy, medium-sized saucepan. Add about ¼ cup of the milk or water and whisk until no lumps of flour are left in the thick liquid. Add the rest of the milk or water, whisking all the time. Slit open the vanilla bean and scrape its inside into the liquid, then add the casing of the bean, too.

6. Bring the liquid to a simmer over medium heat while constantly whisking it, immediately lower the heat, and cook the mixture for 1 minute over low heat, whisking all the time. Take it off the heat.

7. In a medium bowl, whisk together the 2 eggs and the sugar. Add a little bit of the warm liquid to this mixture and whisk to blend. Then repeat this with a little more liquid. Now, pour the mixture from the bowl back into the remaining liquid in the saucepan and whisk to blend.

8. Cook the mixture over low to medium heat, whisking all the time, for about 5 minutes until it thickens to the consistency of heavy cream. Be careful—the sauce scorches easily, especially along the perimeter of the bottom. Strain the vanilla sauce into a bowl, place a piece of plastic wrap over its surface to prevent skin from forming, and let it cool to room temperature.

9. When the dumpling is ready, remove it from the water by holding the two ends of the towel. Place it on the work surface, cut the strings, unfold the towel to expose the dumpling, and with the help of the towel flip it over so that its smoother bottom side faces up. With a large spatula, transfer it to a serving platter. Stick slivered almonds into the soft dumpling; it will look a little bit like a hedgehog. Let it cool to room temperature. When you are ready to serve, cut ¾"-thick slices from the loaf-shaped dumpling, 1 or 2 slices for each serving, and spoon some vanilla sauce around the slices.

Yeast Crêpes
Gerbenpalatschinken

No Hungarian or Austrian cookbook could be complete without a recipe for *palacsinta*, as the Hungarians call it, or *Palatschinken*, as it is called in Austria and Germany. By the way, both words derive from the Latin *placenta*, the name of a flat cake. Palatschinken are quite similar to French crêpes; the main difference is that they have fewer eggs and little or no butter in the batter. Riza néni's collection includes a recipe for the usual Palatschinken, essentially the same recipe that one can find in most Austrian and Hungarian cookbooks. Instead of repeating this, I decided to select from her collection a much less common version made with yeast. As old cookbooks and handwritten recipe collections attest, this must have been a popular recipe in nineteenth-century Austria and Hungary, but by the twentieth century it has become almost forgotten. Her yeast crêpes are a little softer and fluffier than the usual ones made without yeast, and they are appealingly laced with hundreds of pinholes. Though her original recipe didn't include it, I like to add a little sugar to the batter.

Palatschinken, just like crêpes, can be filled with a large variety of fillings. Riza néni's original recipe didn't specify the filling because she was familiar with the usual fillings of these pancakes and didn't need a recipe for them. I will suggest some traditional fillings, but you can easily invent your own.

YIELD:	4 servings (10–12 crêpes, 6" diameter each)
TOTAL TIME:	about 1 hour 45 minutes (of this 1 hour is unattended)
INGREDIENTS:	½ package active dry yeast (about 1 teaspoon)
	¼ cup barely warm (105–110°F) water
	1 teaspoon sugar
	2 tablespoons unbleached all-purpose flour
	¾ cup unbleached all-purpose flour
	¼ teaspoon kosher salt
	1 tablespoon sugar (optional)
	¾ cup barely warm water
	1 large egg
	1 teaspoon canola oil
	1 teaspoon grated lemon zest
	1 tablespoon canola oil (for brushing the skillet)
SPECIAL EQUIPMENT:	8" nonstick skillet
	pastry brush
	2-ounce ladle (preferable) or a ¼-cup measure
	narrow silicone or wood spatula

1. Sprinkle dry yeast into a bowl or cup, add ¼ cup warm water, 1 teaspoon sugar, and 2 tablespoons flour. Stir to blend and let it ferment at room temperature for 10 minutes.

2. Meanwhile, pour ¾ cup flour, salt, and the optional sugar into a medium bowl; add about half of the ¾ cup warm water and whisk for

about 1 minute to make a thick paste. Add the remaining water and whisk for another 2 to 3 minutes to eliminate all lumps of flour. Add egg, oil, and lemon zest; whisk to blend all the ingredients. Add the bubbly, fermenting yeast sponge and whisk to blend. Cover it with plastic wrap and set it aside for 15 minutes, until it becomes foamy. Uncover, whisk lightly to mix in the bubbles, cover again, and let it ferment at room temperature for 1 hour.

3. Pour 1 tablespoon oil (or melted butter if your dietary restrictions allow this) into a small bowl and place it near your cooking range. Make sure that you have a pastry brush, 2-ounce ladle (or measuring cup), spatula (a narrow silicone spatula is ideal), and a dinner plate ready near your range, because you will not have the time to search for them once you start frying the crêpes.

4. Heat the skillet over high heat for about 45 seconds, lower heat to medium high, and very lightly brush the skillet with oil. Stir the batter, fill the ladle about ¾ full, lift up the skillet with one hand and with the other hand pour the batter into the skillet near its handle. Quickly swirl the skillet in a circular motion to let the batter flow evenly around it, spreading to cover the whole skillet. Place it back over the heat and let it cook for 40–45 seconds. After about 30 seconds run your spatula under the perimeter of the crêpe to loosen it. Shake the skillet to loosen the crêpe; it usually comes loose after 35–40 seconds —a sign that it is done on that side. Even if it hasn't come loose, after 45 seconds with the help of the spatula lift up the edge of the crêpe, grab the edge, and flip it over. Look at its surface: it should be an even beige or very light golden brown color; if it is darker, cook the next one for a little less time on its first side. Cook the second side of the crêpe for about 15 seconds, then slide it from the skillet to the prepared dinner plate. Stack the finished crêpes on top of each other on the dinner plate. Don't forget to always stir the batter before dipping the ladle into it. Your goal should be to make the thinnest possible crêpes, so make sure the batter is not too thick and pour as little batter into the skillet as possible. If it fails to cover the whole skillet, you can always add a bit more. This recipe should be enough for at least 10 crêpes, but if you are skillful it will make 12 or 13.

5. Prepare one of the following fillings:

   a. The simplest filling consists of slightly thinned apricot jam (if you have some apricot schnapps or brandy, use that for thinning the jam) or red currant jam spread over the less pretty side of the crêpe, stopping about ½" short of the edges. Roll up the crêpes or fold them into quarters and dust them with confectioners' sugar.

   b. In a slightly more elaborate variation, prune butter is spread over the crêpes and this is then sprinkled with coarsely chopped (by pulsing the food processor) walnuts. Roll them up and dust them with confectioners' sugar.

   c. Place about ¾ cup walnuts and ¼ cup sugar in the bowl of the food processor, process for 20 seconds to evenly grind them. Sprinkle this mixture on the crêpes, roll them up and dust them with confectioners' sugar.

   d. Mix 2 parts cocoa with 1 part confectioners' sugar and spread this mixture on the less even-colored sides of the crêpes. Roll them up and dust them with confectioners' sugar.

   e. Cook briefly, while stirring constantly, about ¾ cup coarsely ground walnuts, ¼ cup sugar, ¼ cup water (or milk), 2 tablespoons rum, 2 tablespoons raisins, and 1 teaspoon grated lemon or orange zest. Spread this on the "private," less pretty sides of the crêpes. Roll them up and dust them with confectioners' sugar.

   f. In a medium bowl, mix ¾ cup ground poppy seeds, ½ cup sugar, and ½ teaspoon vanilla extract. Boil ½ cup water or milk. Pour some of this over the mixture in the bowl, stir well to get a thick but spreadable paste. If it is too thick, add a little more liquid, then add 2 tablespoons raisins and stir well again. Spread this mixture on the crêpes, roll them up (or fold them into quarters), dust them with confectioners' sugar.

   g. Spread applesauce on the crêpes, roll them up, dust them with confectioners' sugar.

   h. Peel, core, and thinly slice 3 Golden Delicious apples. Cook them in a mixture of ½ cup water, ½ cup white wine, 1½ tablespoons sugar, and 2 teaspoons grated lemon zest, until tender. Strain; fill crêpes with apples, leaving out the juice.

If you observe the laws of kashrut, the following fillings can only be prepared as part of a dairy menu:

i. Mix 10 ounces unsalted, not-too-dry cottage cheese with ¼ cup confectioners' sugar, 2 teaspoons grated lemon zest, ¼ cup golden raisins, and ½ teaspoon vanilla extract. Spread this mixture on the crêpes, roll them up and dust them with confectioners' sugar.

j. Put one package (7.5 ounces) unsalted farmer cheese through a potato ricer, add ¼ cup sugar, 2 tablespoons melted unsalted butter, 2 teaspoons grated lemon zest, ⅓ cup golden raisins, and 2 egg yolks. Whip 4 egg whites to form firm peaks and fold this into the cheese mixture. Spread this mixture on the crêpes, roll them up, place them in one layer in a well-buttered gratin or baking dish, top them with sour cream slightly thinned with a little milk, and bake them in a preheated 325°F oven for 20–25 minutes. Serve immediately.

k. Fill the crêpes with thick vanilla sauce (see recipe for napkin dessert dumplings on page 136).

Baked Apricot Foam
Schaumkoch

This fast, easy, and inexpensive dessert must have been popular in Moson, because in addition to Riza néni's recipe I also have a slightly different version from her older sister, the occupant of the other side of their shared house. According to Riza néni, one can use any kind of preserves for this dessert, but apricot is the best choice.

YIELD:	4 servings
TOTAL TIME:	about 20 minutes
INGREDIENTS:	1 teaspoon unsalted butter or margarine
	5 tablespoons good quality apricot preserves
	¼ cup sugar
	2 teaspoons grated lemon zest
	1 tablespoon lemon juice
	5 large egg whites
	½ teaspoon cream of tartar
	1 tablespoon sugar
	¼ cup slivered almonds
SPECIAL EQUIPMENT:	9" Pyrex or ceramic pie dish or a 14" oval stainless steel platter
	electric mixer (optional)
	16" pastry bag fitted with a ½" plain round tip (optional)

1. Preheat oven to 375°F. Coat the oval platter or pie dish with butter or margarine.

2. Place apricot preserves, sugar, lemon zest and juice in a medium-sized bowl. Stir them well until the mixture becomes pale and slightly foamy.

3. Whip egg whites and cream of tartar until they form soft peaks, add 1 tablespoon sugar and whip to form firm peaks.

4. Stir about ¼ of the egg whites into the apricot preserves mixture, then fold this into the rest of the whipped egg whites. Spoon this mixture or pipe it through a pastry bag to form 3"- to 4"-high mounds—sort of like a mountain with 3 or 4 peaks—and strew almonds over the "mountain" of whipped egg whites. Place the platter or dish on a baking sheet.

5. Bake it for 10–12 minutes, until the surface turns golden brown and the almonds are slightly toasted. Serve immediately.

VARIATION:

Lujza néni, Riza néni's sister, suggested first soaking ladyfinger biscuits (Stella D'oro is one of the domestic manufacturers; the imported Italian ones are usually called Savoiardi) in a mixture of rum and water. She then lined the bottom of an ovenproof serving dish with the soaked biscuits, spread the whipped egg white mixture over them, strewed this with slivered almonds, and baked it.

Rice and Apple Pudding with Wine Sauce
Eine kalte Schüssel von Reis

In this flavorful and refreshing dessert, rice pudding layers alternate with apple filling that has been cooked in wine. The dessert is served with a zesty wine sauce, in which I substituted a little potato starch for some of the eggs Riza néni no doubt would have used.

YIELD: 5–6 servings

TOTAL TIME: about 50 minutes

INGREDIENTS:
- 2½ cups milk
- ⅛ teaspoon almond extract
- 2 tablespoons sugar
- 1 cup Arborio-type short-grain rice
- 1 tablespoon sliced almonds
- 2 Golden Delicious apples, peeled, cored, and cut into ¼" dice

⅓ cup golden raisins
2 tablespoons sugar
½ teaspoon cinnamon
2 teaspoons grated zest of lemon
⅔ cup fruity white wine, such as Riesling
1 large egg
⅓ cup sugar
¼ teaspoon vanilla extract
1 teaspoon grated zest of lemon
1 cup fruity white wine
¼ cup water
1 teaspoon potato starch

SPECIAL
EQUIPMENT: 9" × 7" × 2" oval gratin dish or another baking dish of about the same area

1. Place milk with almond extract and 2 tablespoons sugar in a medium-sized heavy-bottomed saucepan and bring it to a simmer. Keep an eye on the saucepan because the milk boils over easily. Add rice and almonds, mix well, and bring it back to a simmer. Cover, reduce heat to very low, and simmer gently for 40 minutes or until rice is very soft. By then most of the milk should have been absorbed by the rice and the rice should be soft and creamy, not dry. Check the rice a few times during cooking to make sure there is enough moisture to keep it from burning. If necessary, add a little milk.

2. While the rice is cooking, start to prepare the filling. Put diced apples, raisins, 2 tablespoons sugar, cinnamon, zest of lemon, and ⅔ cup wine into a saucepan. Bring it to a boil, cover, reduce heat, and simmer for 8 to 10 minutes or until the apples are soft and syrup is somewhat thick.

3. Spread ⅓ of the rice about ¼" thick in the gratin or baking dish. Spread ½ of the apple filling over the rice, leaving any liquid in the saucepan. Cover the apples with another ⅓ of the rice and that with the remaining apple filling. Finally, spread the remaining rice on top. Set it aside.

4. For the sauce, beat egg with ⅓ cup sugar in a small, heavy stainless steel or enameled saucepan until it gets fluffy. Add vanilla extract, lemon zest, 1 cup wine, and potato starch dissolved in ¼ cup water. Bring the mixture to a boil while constantly stirring with a whisk. As soon as it starts to boil, reduce heat to low and simmer it for another 1 or 2 minutes, stirring constantly. The sauce should thicken as soon as it reaches the boiling point. Let the sauce cool to room temperature.

5. The rice pudding can be cut into surprisingly neat slices and transferred to a plate with a spatula. Serve it at room temperature with a little wine sauce spooned over it.

AFTERNOONS AT RIZA NÉNI'S

IN GOOD WEATHER, my mother and her sister could hardly wait to finish lunch, so they could go to swim in the Mosoni Duna, a branch of the Danube adjacent to the town. As soon as lunch was over, they grabbed their bathing suits, towels, and perhaps an apple or pear for an afternoon snack, and headed for the town beach at the Danube. In those days before air conditioning, bathing in the Danube provided an indispensable relief from the summer heat. There were usually lots of people, both grown-ups and children, on the beach; it was quite a social scene. Mother and Lili were in no great hurry to get back home; usually they spent the whole afternoon at the river and went home only around six. They had to be home before sunset, but in no case later than six-thirty.

While my mother and her sister were at the river, Riza néni took a nap, then did a little embroidery or patched some worn clothing. Just before four, she put on a good dress, because that was when neighbors dropped by for a visit. During off-season or on days when it was too cold to swim, the grandchildren were ordered to wash up and change into their best clothes for the visitors. That was bad enough, but once in a while they even had to come home early from swimming to greet these guests. They hated this.

The afternoon was the time for the more formal visits, but after dinner, if the weather was good, my great-grandparents liked to sit in front of their house, and then the neighbors might stop by again for a little informal chat. My great-grandparents were good friends with most of the middle-class merchants and professionals in town. In Moson's middle class everybody knew everybody and life was centered around tittle-tattle and gossip.

When a neighbor came visiting, Riza néni greeted her at the entrance and showed her through the entrance hall and dining room into the *szalon* (formal living room), which had a matched set of neo-Rococo–style walnut furniture. Great-grandmother offered her guest one of the upholstered small armchairs next to the round table, which she had set with her nice china. If she wanted to put on a big show, she pulled out her mother's circa 1845 elegantly simple Biedermeier-style china cups, with the wide gold band around the rim and the fancy KB initials, for Kati Baruch, on the side. Everything at my great-grandmother's: all the china, the cutlery, the tablecloths, and even the bed linens had fancy monograms on them. I don't have to take my mother's word on this, because luckily some of this china, cutlery, and linen survived and eventually found its way to me. Together with the other mementos of Riza néni's life, they have been source and inspiration in my work on this book.

The szalon was mainly for show and was used only when my great-grandparents had guests. The purpose of much of the furnishings was to serve as status symbols. This was the real function of the small, gilded and carved half-round table that stood under a large mirror between the windows facing the street and also of the collection of ornate ceramic beer mugs displayed on a small hexagonal table in the middle of the adjacent wall. All the visitors were supposed to admire those mugs and their engraved pewter lids. Just in case they were not sufficiently impressed, my great-grandparents' best china and silver in the nearby glazed display cabinet should have certainly convinced them of the elegance of the household.

Riza néni offered her visitors some cookies or small pastries from a china platter set on the table. She baked all the sweets herself. It was not only that she liked to bake, but that she didn't quite trust Paula in this respect and wanted to make sure that her recipes were accurately followed.

The grandchildren were not allowed to eat any cookies before the guests arrived, but they frequently sneaked into the szalon beforehand and stole one or two. Then they quickly rearranged the rest on the platter so that when my great-grandmother came with the visitor she wouldn't notice that cookies were missing.

After offering sweets to the visitor, Riza néni yanked the embroidered bell pull that hung next to the entrance door to signal Paula to bring the coffee. A string attached to this bell pull passed through holes in the walls from room to room to a bell in the kitchen.

As Riza néni and her friends drank their coffee, they gossiped, exchanged recipes, or played cards. In winter my great-grandparents used the adjacent dining room instead of the szalon for receiving visitors, because the szalon couldn't be heated. The dining room, on the other hand, had a nice glazed tile stove, which could be stoked from the adjacent entrance hall.

Following is a selection from the biscuits, cookies, small pastries, and cakes in Riza néni's collection. She probably served one of these or some other similar dessert for her afternoon guests.

Farmer Cheese Biscuits

Pogatscheln aus süssem Topfen für 6 Personen

There is no accurate English word for *pogácsa*, a large category of Hungarian baked products. Biscuit or scone comes close, but neither is the same as these round biscuits, which come in many sweet and savory varieties. By the way, the Italian word *focaccia* is the etymological ancestor of the Hungarian *pogácsa*, the German *Pogatsche*, and even of the Turkish *boğaça* or *poğaça*. Riza néni's ever-so-slightly-sweet biscuits are not desserts, but snacks to be eaten with coffee, tea, or wine. If you find her biscuits a bit bland, try a sweeter version or, conversely, a savory version, in which case omit the sugar, increase the salt, and possibly add some ground pepper. She specified in her German title that this recipe was for six persons. They must have been blessed with good appetites or have eaten these biscuits for days, because her original recipe produced about seventy pieces.

It is interesting to note that while there are several yeast dough recipes in Riza néni's collection, baking powder shows up as an ingredient only in some of the last recipes. She started her collection in 1869, and judging from her use of language, units of measurement, and her ingredients, it seems that at least two-thirds of it was written within the following one or two decades. But she kept adding to it, and the last recipes might have been written as late as the 1920s. Although commercial baking powder had been first introduced in the 1850s, it was hardly used in Austrian or Hungarian baking until the early twentieth century, when Dr. August Oetker started manufacturing baking powder in Austria and selling it in standardized packages. In her recipes, Riza néni usually called baking powder by its brand name, *Oetker*.

Although it contains a little yeast, the dough for these biscuits is not allowed to rise before baking, as the typical yeast dough does. Before the widespread use of baking powder, a small amount of yeast was used in this type of dough to make the biscuits lighter and flakier, but later this was usually replaced by baking powder.

YIELD: 35–40 biscuits

TOTAL TIME: about 2 hours

INGREDIENTS:
- ¼ cup barely warm (105–110°F) milk
- 1 teaspoon active dry yeast (about ½ of a standard envelope)
- 2 large egg yolks
- 2 tablespoons heavy cream
- 2 cups unbleached all-purpose flour
- 3 tablespoons sugar
- ¼ teaspoon kosher salt
- 3 tablespoons cold unsalted butter cut into ½" pieces
- 1 package (7.5 ounces) cold unsalted farmer cheese
- 1 large egg, lightly beaten (for egg glaze)

SPECIAL EQUIPMENT:
- food processor
- 1½"-round biscuit cutter (or a similar diameter brandy glass)
- 2 cookie or baking sheets (12" × 18")

1. In a cup, mix warm milk with yeast, 1 tablespoon of the flour and 1 teaspoon of the sugar. Let it proof for about 10 minutes, then add egg yolks and cream. The remaining yeast will keep for about two weeks in the resealed envelope, if kept in the refrigerator.

2. Place the rest of the flour and sugar, salt, and butter pieces in the food processor and process for about 5 seconds. Over the bowl of the food processor, break the crumbly farmer cheese into about 1" pieces and drop the pieces into the bowl. With the machine running, add the yeast-egg-cream mixture and process for about 10 seconds, until the dough comes together, forms a ball, and clears the side of the bowl. Even if it doesn't clear the bowl, stop the machine. Touch the dough,

being careful to avoid the blade. The dough should be medium-soft, but not sticky. If the dough is sticky, add 2 or 3 tablespoons more flour; if it is too dry, add a little milk by the teaspoonful and pulse a few times to incorporate the flour or the milk.

3. Transfer the dough to a floured work surface. With a floured rolling pin, roll the dough into a rectangle about 8" × 16". Fold the sheet of dough into thirds, enclose it in plastic wrap, and refrigerate it for about 20 minutes.

4. Preheat oven to 375°F. Butter the cookie sheets or line them with silicone nonstick baking mats.

5. Repeat rolling out the dough, folding it into thirds, and refrigerating it for 20 minutes. Repeat this the third time. After the dough has rested, roll it out to ¾" thickness, about 6" × 10". Cut biscuits with a 1½" diameter biscuit cutter. Cut the biscuits as close to each other as possible to minimize waste. Gather the remaining scraps of dough into a ball, roll it out, fold it into thirds, roll it to ¾" thickness, and cut it into more biscuits. Place the biscuits about 2" apart on the buttered or nonstick mat–lined cookie sheets.

6. Score the top of the biscuits about ¼" deep with a sharp knife in a lattice pattern. Brush the tops with egg.

7. Bake the biscuits in the preheated oven for 20–25 minutes, until they are light golden brown. Switch the cookie sheets halfway through baking. Transfer them to a cooling rack. Serve them lukewarm or store them, after they have completely cooled, in a cookie tin for up to one week. You can also freeze them in airtight freezer bags. However they are stored, I like to reheat them before serving.

Bread Pudding in Noodle Dough
Semmel Scheiterhaufen

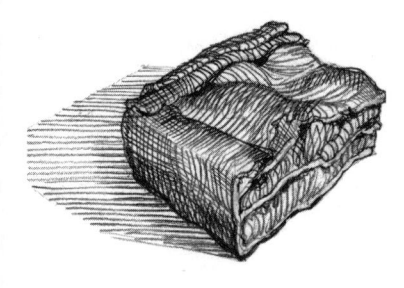

Riza néni's bread pudding, or "pyre" by its strange German and Hungarian name, is different from any Austrian or Hungarian bread pudding recipe I know. I haven't seen another version that calls for layering the bread pudding between sheets of noodle dough and for soaking the stale slices of bread in wine before dipping them into a mixture of eggs and sugar. The noodle dough casing helps keep it moist and makes for tidier-looking slices than the usual bread pudding, and the wine gives it an interesting sweet-and-sour taste.

Though boiled noodle dough is frequently used in Austro-Hungarian hot noodle desserts, such as Riza néni's almond-meringue noodles (see recipe on page 126), her use of baked noodle dough in layered desserts, such as this bread pudding, is unusual. Equally unusual is her use of baked noodle dough to encase her apple kugel (see recipe on page 251) or to wrap the filling in such desserts as her apple-filled noodle dough "wheels" (see recipe on page 163). Typically, one would use pastry dough or yeast dough for such desserts in Austria and Hungary. Some traditional Jewish desserts are made with boiled noodles or noodle dough, for example the *lokshen kugel* (though it is questionable whether one can consider it a dessert) or the *kreplach* and *varenikes*, Ashkenazi Jewish filled dumplings that exist in both sweet and savory versions. But it is difficult to find comparable examples of baked noodle dough, unless one considers an early form of Jewish *fladen*, layered pastry squares, which as some sources suggest was made with it. Perhaps the simple reason for her idiosyncratic use of noodle dough in some of her desserts might be that it was easier and less expensive to make than other types of dough.

She suggests poppy seeds or almonds as alternates to the walnut filling; you might want to try this, too. She also suggests that it can be served with a sauce, though she doesn't specify the kind of dessert sauce. In my opinion, this moist bread pudding is terrific by itself, but if you wish to serve it with a sauce, a vanilla sauce (see recipe for napkin dumpling with vanilla sauce on page 136) would go nicely with it. In adapting Riza néni's recipe for the modern kitchen, I decided to cut back on the number of eggs into which the bread slices are dipped.

Bread pudding came about to make use of leftover stale bread. Riza néni, like most women of her time, was thrifty and always tried to find ways to recycle leftovers in another dish. Of the hundred and thirty recipes in her collection, twelve call for stale bread soaked in some liquid, and many more recipes call for bread crumbs. According to Riza néni, the biggest crime her grandchildren could commit was to leave food on their plates.

The best bread for this recipe is the ubiquitous and inexpensive long Italian loaf without seeds, or a not-too-thick-crusted baguette. Don't use any bread with a thick crust. The usual packaged and sliced white bread is not good for this recipe, because it will turn into mush when soaked. Should you have leftover stale challah, this would be your best option, even better than Italian bread.

YIELD: 6 servings

TOTAL TIME: about 1 hour 15 minutes

DOUGH INGREDIENTS:
1½ cups unbleached all-purpose flour
⅛ teaspoon kosher salt
1 teaspoon sugar
1 large egg
1½ tablespoons canola oil or rendered poultry fat
¼–⅓ cup water or white wine

OTHER INGREDIENTS:
1½ cups fruity white wine
3 large eggs
¼ cup milk or water
2 tablespoons sugar
½ teaspoon vanilla extract
¼ cup sugar
½ teaspoon ground cinnamon
½ cup golden raisins
¼ cup ground walnuts

¼ cup chopped walnuts
¼ cup apricot jam
½ tablespoon white wine or water
2 tablespoons melted unsalted butter or rendered poultry fat
1 teaspoon unsalted butter or rendered poultry fat (to grease the baking dish)
20 slices of stale bread, cut from a long Italian loaf or a baguette, each slice about 2" x 4" x ⅜" thick

SPECIAL EQUIPMENT:
food processor
8" x 8" x 2" baking pan, Pyrex baking dish, or a gratin dish of about the same area

1. To make the dough, place flour, salt, sugar, egg, oil or poultry fat, and ¼ cup water or wine in the bowl of a food processor. Process for 1 minute. The dough should form a ball on top of the blade. If it doesn't form a ball, add a little more water or wine by the ½ tablespoonful and briefly process to mix it into the dough. Transfer the dough to a lightly floured work surface and knead it for about 5 minutes by hand, until it is very smooth and elastic. If it is sticky, knead in a little more flour. The dough should be a touch softer than the usual firm noodle dough. Wrap it tightly in plastic and let it rest for about 15 minutes. You can save time and effort if you have a pasta machine by using it for kneading and rolling the dough. Many pasta machines, however, can only produce a maximum 5½" wide sheet of pasta, so you would have to join your pasta sheet from 2 pieces to be able to cover the 8" x 8" baking dish, as described in step 5.

2. While the dough is resting, pour 1½ cups wine into a medium-sized bowl. Beat 3 eggs in another medium-sized bowl, add the milk or water, 2 tablespoons sugar, and vanilla extract, and mix them well. In another small bowl or a cup, mix ¼ cup sugar with cinnamon. Put the raisins and walnuts into separate bowls or cups. I used my nut grinder for half of the walnuts and chopped the other half with a knife, but you could also put all the walnuts into the food processor and pulse a few times to get the desired mixture of finely and coarsely chopped nuts. Be careful not to over-process, or the nuts will turn into

oily paste. Dilute the apricot jam with a little wine or water in a cup or small bowl. In yet another bowl or cup, melt 2 tablespoons butter or poultry fat, which you will use for brushing the dough. Line up these 6 bowls or cups neatly near your work surface; this will make assembling the bread pudding faster.

3. Grease an 8" × 8" × 2" baking pan or Pyrex baking dish. Preheat the oven to 375°F.

4. Divide the dough into halves. On a floured work surface, roll out one half of the dough with a floured rolling pin into a very thin (similar to thin pasta) sheet of about 9" × 17". Repeat the same with the other half of the dough. Cut each sheet to 8" × 16", or twice the size of your baking dish. Cut an 8" × 12" piece from one of the sheets and lay it in the bottom of the baking dish so that it also covers two sides of the dish. From the remaining 4" × 8" piece of dough cut 2 strips to cover the other two sides of the dish. Brush the dough with some of the melted butter or poultry fat.

5. Soak a few slices of stale bread for about 1 minute in wine then dip them into the egg mixture. Place them tightly next to each other in the bottom of the baking dish. There should be as little space between the slices and around the perimeter as possible. Sprinkle ½ the sugar-cinnamon mixture, ½ the walnuts, and ½ the raisins evenly over the bread slices and dot it with about ½ the jam. Spoon a little more egg mixture over the slices but leave about ½ of the original amount for the next layer.

6. Cut the second 8" × 16" sheet of dough into half crosswise and lay one 8" × 8" piece over the slices in the dish. Brush it with melted butter or poultry fat. Make another layer of bread slices soaked in wine and dipped into eggs, sprinkle it with the remaining sugar, walnuts, raisins, dot it with the remaining jam and pour the remaining egg mixture over it. Cover it with the remaining 8" × 8" piece of dough and brush it with the remaining melted butter or poultry fat.

7. Place the baking dish on a baking sheet and bake it in the preheated oven for 35 minutes. Allow the pudding to cool in the baking dish set

on a cooling rack, cut it into 6 equal parts in the dish and serve it lukewarm or at room temperature. It will keep for about two days at room temperature. If you must refrigerate it, allow it to return to room temperature before serving.

Jam or Almond Turnovers

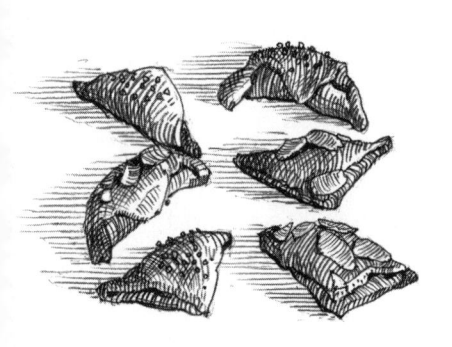

Gleichgewicht und Schnellgebäck

This is a terrific and most versatile dough. You can use it for jam- or almond-filled turnovers or fabulous jam-filled crescents. Though the baked dough doesn't form distinct leaves and rise quite to the degree of puff pastry, it does puff up a bit and has a similar airy, flaky texture. It is also much easier to make. You can use it for savory pastries, too, if you leave out the sugar from the dough. The German name of this dough is "equal weight" because the original recipe uses equal weights of flour, butter, and cheese. In adapting the recipe, I slightly increased the amount of flour because our farmer cheese tends to be a little more moist than European pot cheese (the German *Topfen*). But even this can only be a general guideline. As is true with all types of dough, you might have to adjust the actual amount of flour to accommodate variables, such as the moisture content of the cheese and the flour. If you are in a hurry, you can omit step 2 (twice rolling, folding, and chilling the dough) and, after step 1, proceed with step 3. The baked dough will be still wonderful, but perhaps not quite as puffed up and airy.

Riza néni offered the alternative of filling these turnovers with either apricot jam or almonds. The recipe for almond filling is included, following the basic recipe.

YIELD:	about 36 turnovers
TOTAL TIME:	about 2 hours 30 minutes (much of this is waiting time)
INGREDIENTS:	1¾ cups unbleached all-purpose flour
	7.5 ounces (1 stick and 7 tablespoons) unsalted butter, cold, cut into ½" pieces
	1 package (7.5 ounces) unsalted farmer cheese, drained
	¼ teaspoon kosher salt
	1½ tablespoons sugar
	½ cup very thick apricot jam or, even better, apricot *lekvár*
	1 large egg
	¼ cup sliced almonds
	2 tablespoons turbinado or other coarse sugar (choose either the sliced almond or the coarse sugar topping)
SPECIAL EQUIPMENT:	food processor
	marble pastry board (not essential but handy to keep the dough cool)
	2 baking sheets (12" × 18")
	pastry brush

1. Place flour and cold butter pieces in the bowl of the food processor and process for 6 seconds. Holding it over the bowl of the processor, break or cut the farmer cheese into small pieces and let them fall into a bowl. Add salt and sugar; process for about 10 seconds, until the dough forms a ball on top of the blades. Transfer the dough to the work surface. The dough will be quite soft, but it shouldn't stick to the work surface or your hands. If it is sticky, knead in a little more flour. Work quickly and handle the dough as little as possible. Transfer it to a piece of plastic wrap about 15" long; shape it with the help of the plastic into a rectangle about 5" × 8" and wrap it tightly. Place it in the refrigerator for at least 1 hour.

2. Unwrap the dough; reserve the plastic. Lightly flour your work surface and your rolling pin; roll the dough into a rectangle about 10" × 16". Work quickly to keep the dough cool. Fold both 10" ends of the rectangle toward the center of the rectangle so they meet in the middle, making 2 layers over the whole surface. Now fold the dough again on this center seam, creating a rectangle about 10" × 4" that has 4 layers. Wrap this in the plastic and refrigerate it for 30 minutes or place it in the freezer for 10 minutes. Repeat rolling out, folding, and chilling the dough.

3. Adjust the oven racks to divide the oven into thirds; preheat the oven to 350°F. Break the egg into a small bowl or cup, add 1 tablespoon water and beat it lightly with a fork. Cut about ⅓ off the dough, rewrap the remaining part and return it into the refrigerator. Sprinkle your work surface and rolling pin with flour and roll out the dough into a 9" × 12" rectangle. Cut this with a dough scraper into 3" squares; you should have 12 squares. Place about ½ teaspoon jam or lekvár in the center of each square and fold each of them diagonally to enclose the jam. Transfer the turnovers with the help of the dough scraper to a baking sheet, keeping them about 1" apart. Keep the turnovers refrigerated until you prepare the next batch. Make the next batch using the second third of the dough, then the last batch using the remaining dough. Continue on the second baking sheet after the first one has filled up. Press the seams of the turnovers on the baking sheets to make sure that jam will not ooze out during baking (a problem you will not have if you use lekvár). Brush the turnovers with egg, sprinkle them with coarse sugar or paste sliced almonds on them—the almonds will adhere to the egg glaze. Riza néni recommended using both sugar and almonds, but two kinds of topping on the small turnovers seemed to me too much.

4. Bake the turnovers for 17–20 minutes, until light golden brown. Remove them with a metal spatula to a cooling rack. Serve them slightly warm or at room temperature. Store them at room temperature in a cookie tin. They can be reheated, if you wish.

VARIATIONS:

1. Use the following almond filling in place of apricot jam:

YIELD: ½ cup

INGREDIENTS: ½ cup blanched almonds, toasted
¼ cup confectioners' sugar
1 tablespoon unsalted butter, at room temperature
¼ teaspoon almond extract
1 tablespoon egg white

Place almonds and sugar in the bowl of the food processor; process until almonds are finely ground. Add butter, almond extract, and 1 tablespoon egg white; briefly process to mix. The filling keeps in the refrigerator in an airtight container for up to one week. Use ½–¾ teaspoon filling in each turnover.

2. Make small apricot jam- or almond-filled crescents. With a floured rolling pin and on a lightly floured work surface, roll out ⅓ of the dough to about a 14" × 11" rectangle. Work quickly to keep the dough cool. If it starts to get sticky, transfer it to a cookie sheet and place it for a short while in the freezer. Cut the dough rectangle into about 3½" squares; you should have 12 squares. Place ½"–¾" teaspoon apricot jam or almond cream filling near one corner of each square and, starting from that corner, roll them diagonally into cigar shapes. Pinch the ends closed and bend them into crescent shapes. Place the crescents on a baking sheet and refrigerate them until you prepare the next batch. When you have used up all the dough, brush the top of the crescents with egg glaze and sprinkle them with coarse sugar or decorate them with sliced almonds. Bake them in the preheated 350°F oven for about 17–20 minutes, until light golden brown. If you are in a hurry, you can omit the coarse sugar or almond decoration and dust the crescents with confectioners' sugar shortly before serving them.

Apple-filled Noodle Dough "Wheels"

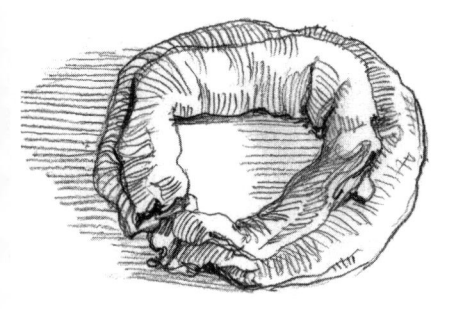

Apfelräder

These apple "wheels" are another example of Riza néni's unusual habit of using noodle dough in the type of desserts in which most people in Austria and Hungary would use pastry or yeast dough. In my research of Austrian and Hungarian cookbooks, including several books exclusively devoted to desserts, I couldn't find any recipe resembling this one. These five- or six-inch diameter "wheels," filled with a mixture of chopped apples and ground almonds, are quite filling, and one piece is sufficient for a satisfying dessert portion. The faint taste of wine in the noodle dough casing is terrific with the apple filling. Though the original recipe didn't call for golden raisins, I decided to add some, because I felt they would enhance this dessert and had been used by Riza néni in similar apple fillings. The original recipe used rendered goose fat instead of butter and oil. Though Riza néni was certainly no pioneer of low saturated fat and cholesterol diet, this dessert is appropriate even for the diet-conscious, because one huge portion of it contains only a sixth of an egg and a quarter tablespoon butter.

YIELD: 6 large servings

TOTAL TIME: about 1 hour 10 minutes

INGREDIENTS:
2½ cups unbleached all-purpose flour
1 tablespoon sugar
¼ teaspoon kosher salt
1 teaspoon grated lemon zest
½ teaspoon vanilla extract
1 large egg
1 tablespoon canola oil

½–¾ cup fruity white wine
1 teaspoon unsalted butter or margarine (for greasing the baking sheets)
1½ tablespoons unsalted butter or margarine, melted
2 tablespoons canola oil
½ cup blanched almonds
¼ cup sugar
2 large or 3 small Golden Delicious apples, peeled, cored, and cut into ¼" dice (about 3 cups)
1 teaspoon ground cinnamon
2 tablespoons sugar
3 teaspoons grated lemon zest
⅓ cup golden raisins (optional)

SPECIAL
EQUIPMENT: food processor
2 baking or cookie sheets (12" × 18")

1. Place flour, sugar, salt, and 1 teaspoon lemon zest in the bowl of the food processor and pulse to blend. Add vanilla, egg, 1 tablespoon oil, and ½ cup of the wine and process for 1 minute. The dough should gather on top of the blade. If it doesn't come together, add a little more wine by the tablespoonful and briefly process to mix it into the dough. In low humidity, I needed 3 more tablespoons of wine. Transfer the dough to a lightly floured work surface and knead it for about 5 minutes, until it becomes very smooth and elastic. If it is sticky, knead in a little more flour. The dough should be a little softer than the usual firm noodle dough. Wrap the kneaded dough tightly in plastic and let it rest at room temperature for about 15 minutes while you prepare the filling. If you have a pasta machine, you can use it for kneading and rolling out the dough. Although I have such a machine, I opted to knead the dough by hand and roll it out with a rolling pin, because I felt that by the time I took out and set up the machine I could just as easily do the whole thing manually.

2. Adjust oven racks to divide the oven into thirds; preheat the oven to 375°F. Grease the baking or cookie sheets or line them with parchment paper.

3. Wipe clean the bowl and the blade of the food processor but it is not necessary to wash them. Place almonds and ¼ cup sugar in the bowl and process for about 10 seconds. The almonds should be coarsely ground with some ⅛" pieces remaining among them.

4. In a small bowl, mix melted butter or margarine with oil. In another small bowl, mix cinnamon with 2 tablespoons sugar. Place lemon zest and raisins in separate small bowls. Line up these 4 bowls near your work surface.

5. Cut the dough into 6 equal parts. Lightly flour your work surface and rolling pin and roll 1 portion of the dough into a rectangle about 6" × 12". Periodically lift up the dough rectangle and throw a little flour under it so the dough doesn't stick to the work surface. Lightly brush the top of the dough with the butter-oil mixture. Centered lengthwise on the rectangle of dough, pile about ⅙ of the diced apple to make a 1½" × 11" mound, leaving about ½" clear at both ends of the rectangle. Sprinkle the apple with ⅙ of the almond-sugar mixture, cinnamon-sugar mixture, lemon zest, and the optional raisins. Lift the dough on one of the long sides of the rectangle and bring it to cover the filling; repeat from the other side. The dough should enclose the filling and overlap about ½" on top of it. Fold back the open ends of this "sausage" by about ¼" and press these hems to seal them. Place one of the buttered baking sheets nearby, and holding the "sausage" by its ends, gently lift it up and transfer it to the baking sheet so that the seam faces up. Bend it on the baking sheet into an about 5" circle with the ends slightly overlapping. Make sure there is space left on the baking sheet for two more such "wheels."

6. Repeat the same procedure of rolling out, filling, transferring, and bending into a circle with the other 5 portions of the dough. When the first baking sheet has filled up, continue on the second sheet. Generously brush the "wheels" with the butter-oil mixture. Bake them in the preheated oven for 30–35 minutes, until they turn rich yellow and the edges become light golden brown. Reverse the two baking sheets halfway through the baking. Transfer the pastries onto a cooling rack.

7. Serve them lukewarm or at room temperature. Dust them with a little vanilla sugar or confectioners' sugar, if you wish. Ideally, they should be served not long after they have been baked, but they will keep for one or two days at room temperature if tightly wrapped in plastic. After that, the wonderfully delicate dough, which contains very little fat, will dry out.

Fruit Cake
Catalaner Brot

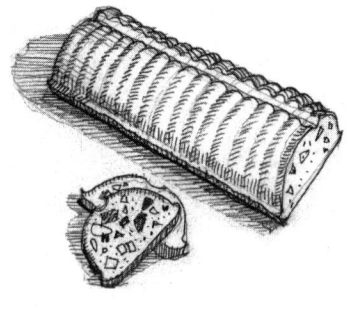

This cake must have been one of Riza néni's favorites, because I have no fewer than five versions of it from her. In addition to the three versions in her copybook, there are two more, marked as coming from Riza néni, in her daughter's recipe collection. This is a fascinating opportunity to follow the development of a recipe from the first version, which was probably dictated by Riza néni's mother in 1869, to the last one, which in turn was dictated by Riza néni to her daughter sometime in the early twentieth century.

This cake is known in today's Austria and Hungary as "bishop's bread," but only her last version refers to it as that. "Catalonian bread," the title of her earlier versions, made more sense because some of the candied fruit in it came from Catalonia, a region of northeast Spain. It is harder to figure out why it became known as bishop's bread, and different books come up with different explanations. Some claim that it has been a favorite of clergymen, others give the slightly more convincing explanation that it has been a popular dessert in homes and coffeehouses on Sundays, after returning from church. As the cake stays fresh for a long time, it could be prepared the day before.

It is equally elusive to describe this cake, because I don't know another Austro-Hungarian cake that has so many radically different versions. I could say that it is a type of sponge cake, but there are versions containing butter, and there is even a version in which baking powder substitutes for eggs. Some versions, such as Riza's first two recipes, don't separate the eggs, others, like her three later versions, start with the yolks and add the whipped egg whites at the end. The best definition I could think of is that it is long, narrow cake, served in thin slices, and made with candied fruit and almonds, less frequently with nuts. This almost works, but there is the improbably named "Gypsy bishop's bread," which contains no candied or dried fruit, but only sugar, eggs, flour, nuts, and cocoa. I can't resist giving here a few additional examples for the many Austro-Hungarian pastries containing chocolate or cocoa and named after dark-skinned people: for Gypsies there is this cake and the famed *Rigó Jancsi*, for African people, *Mohr im Hemd*, for Hindus, *Indianerkrapfen*.

Riza néni's earlier recipes add extra yolks to the whole eggs, emphasizing richness over lightness. After years of experimenting, she must have realized that her *Catalaner Brot* would be lighter if she left out the extra yolks, separated the remaining eggs, and added the whipped egg whites at the end. In my updated recipe, I combined what I felt were the best features of her five versions.

Traditionally, this cake is baked in a so-called saddle of venison form: a long, narrow, half-cylinder–shaped form, which is made to resemble a saddle of venison by its cross ribs and a lengthwise depression where the "backbone" should be. My thirteen-inch-long form with its five-cup capacity could accommodate the amount of dough from this recipe, but a fourteen-inch form would have been even better. If you don't have such a "saddle of venison" form, a five- or six-cup ring mold or loaf pan will do just as well.

YIELD: 32 slices

TOTAL TIME: about 1 hour 10 minutes

INGREDIENTS:
- 1 teaspoon unsalted butter or margarine (to grease the baking form)
- 2 tablespoons unbleached all-purpose flour (to flour the baking form)
- 6 large egg yolks
- 1 tablespoon water

⅓ cup sugar
3 ounces (3 squares) bittersweet chocolate, cut into about ¼" pieces
¾ cup blanched whole almonds
1 teaspoon grated lemon zest
2 tablespoons lemon juice
¼ cup golden raisins
¼ cup candied lemon or citron peel, diced
¼ cup candied orange peel (optional)
¼ cup pitted dates, chopped (or substitute some other dried or candied fruit)
¼ cup pitted prunes or dried apricots, chopped
1 tablespoon unbleached all-purpose flour (to sprinkle over the candied or dried fruit)
1 cup unbleached all-purpose flour
6 large egg whites
½ teaspoon cream of tartar
⅓ cup sugar

SPECIAL
EQUIPMENT: "saddle of venison" form (5- or 6-cup capacity) or a similar-capacity ring form or loaf pan
electric mixer (optional)

1. Center a rack in the oven and preheat the oven to 350°F. Grease and flour the baking form. Beat egg yolks, water, and ⅓ cup sugar for about 5 minutes by machine or 10 minutes by hand until the yolks turn very pale and fluffy. Mix in the chopped chocolate, almonds, and lemon zest and juice.

2. Place all the dried and candied fruit in a bowl and sprinkle them with 1 tablespoon flour. Separate the pieces that stuck together and toss them to coat each piece with flour. Stir them into the egg yolk mixture. Add 1 cup flour in 2 batches and stir to mix evenly.

3. Whip egg whites and cream of tartar to form soft peaks, add ⅓ cup sugar, and continue whipping until the egg whites become shiny and form firm peaks. Stir about ⅓ of the whipped egg whites into the very

thick egg yolk mixture to lighten it, then gently fold in the rest of the whites.

4. Pour this dough into the greased and floured form, place the form on a baking sheet, and transfer it into the preheated oven. Prop the oven door slightly open with a wedged-in knife and bake the cake this way for 10 minutes in order to allow moisture to escape. Then close the oven door tightly and bake the cake for another 35–40 minutes. After about 35 minutes test the cake by gently poking the top of it with your finger. When the cake springs back, it is done. If your finger leaves an indentation in the surface, bake the cake for another 5 minutes.

5. Cool the cake for about 30 minutes in the form set on a cooling rack, then turn it out and continue cooling it for another hour or so. When it is completely cool, wrap it in wax paper and keep it for one full day at room temperature before cutting it.

6. Shortly before serving, slice it with a serrated knife into ¼"–⅜" thick slices and serve it sprinkled with confectioners' sugar. Don't cut more slices than you wish to serve at the same time. Store the remainder of the cake for up to four days at room temperature, wrapped in wax paper or plastic.

Sour Cherry Cake

Weichselkuchen

In his *The Cuisine of Hungary*, George Lang published a recipe he called "My mother's cherry cake." For many years this has been one of my favorite desserts; I have made it so many times that the book opens by itself at this recipe. When I started to recreate my great-grandmother's recipes, I was delighted to discover that generations earlier she had loved this cake, too. Hers is not exactly the same as Lang's cake, because it is made with sour cherries and it includes lemon zest and juice in the dough, but they are close relatives.

The Turks introduced cherry and sour cherry to Hungary in the sixteenth and seventeenth centuries, when they occupied much of the country. One can find excellent cherries in the United States, but it is impossible to find the kind of large, juicy, intensely flavored, dark-burgundy sour cherry that is grown in Hungary. According to George Lang, "Perhaps it is worth considering a Turkish Occupation of the United States to change the lamentable quality of this fruit that one buys in the supermarket here." Short of that, we have to make do with the paler variety that is grown here, though its flavor is quite different from Hungarian sour cherry. To add insult to injury, even this pale version of the real stuff is hard to find in our stores. In the absence of good fresh sour cherries, I suggest using canned morello cherries, imported from Hungary and quite easily found in better delicatessen stores, even in some supermarkets, at least in New York City. They are sold in jars, 25 ounces net weight, and the lightly sweetened deep-red liquid in which they are preserved makes for the most wonderful, intensely fruit-flavored drink. True, these canned sour cherries are softer than the fresh ones, but this is a small compromise considering their wonderful flavor. If you cannot find canned Hungarian sour cherries, use pitted Bing cherries or use cranberries. Of course, cranberries have nothing to do with sour cherries, but at least they are tart, red, and easily available.

The only change I made in adapting Riza néni's recipe was to separate the eggs and fold in the whipped egg whites at the end, a method she had used in several other recipes.

YIELD: 16–18 servings

TOTAL TIME: about 40 minutes

INGREDIENTS:
- 1 teaspoon unsalted butter (to grease the baking pan)
- ¼ cup bread crumbs, made in the food processor from stale white bread (to coat the baking pan)
- 1 stick (4 ounces) unsalted butter, softened
- ½ cup sugar

AFTERNOONS AT RIZA NÉNI'S

    3 large egg yolks
    1 pinch of kosher salt
    1 teaspoon grated lemon zest
    1½ tablespoons lemon juice
    1¼ cups unbleached all-purpose flour
    4 large egg whites
    ½ teaspoon cream of tartar
    ¼ cup sugar
    15 ounces pitted sour cherries, preferably canned Hungarian sour cherries drained from the canning liquid (use a little more than half the cherries from a 25 ounce jar and don't forget to reserve the liquid)

SPECIAL EQUIPMENT: 6½" x 11½" x 1¾" or 8" x 8" x 2" baking pan
food processor (for making bread crumbs)
electric mixer (optional)

1. Grease the baking pan, pour bread crumbs into it, and tilt it in all directions until the whole inside is evenly coated. Pour out the excess crumbs. Center a rack in the oven and preheat the oven to 375°F.

2. With an electric mixer or by hand with a wooden spoon, beat butter until it is fluffy, add ½ cup sugar and continue beating until the mixture becomes almost foamy. Add egg yolks, salt, zest and juice of lemon, and mix well. Add half the flour, mix to incorporate it, then repeat this with the second half.

3. Whip egg whites and cream of tartar to form soft peaks, add ¼ cup sugar, and continue whipping until egg whites become shiny and form firm peaks. Stir about ½ of the egg whites into the egg yolk mixture to lighten it, then with a rubber spatula carefully fold in the remaining whites.

4. Using the spatula, transfer the dough into the baking pan and gently tap the pan to level the dough in it. Evenly distribute the sour cherries on top of the dough, place the baking pan on a baking sheet and that in the preheated oven. Bake it for 30 minutes.

5. Allow it to cool in the baking pan set on a cooling rack. Cut it in the pan into approximately 2" × 2" squares or turn it out onto a cutting board, flip it over so that its top faces up again, and cut it into squares. It is best eaten on the day you bake it, but it will keep at room temperature in an airtight box for two or three days. Shortly before serving, dust the squares with confectioners' sugar.

Poppy Seed Squares
Mohnbitter

Lots of people in our country, England, or France only know poppy seed as sprinkles on bread or rolls. Though hardly known in European countries west of Austria and Germany, desserts made with poppy seeds are very popular in Austria, Hungary, Germany, and the Slavic countries. Ashkenazi Jewish baking adopted many of these desserts and came up with some typically Jewish ones, such as *kindli*, *flódni*, and *hamantaschen*.

Riza néni's strange German name for these pastries has nothing to do with bitter, but is a distortion of *pite*, the Hungarian word for filled pastry squares. In these pastries the filling—fruit, cottage cheese, nuts, or poppy seeds—is spread over a layer of dough and is either covered with another layer of dough or with a latticework made of dough, but there are *pite*s in which the top layer is missing altogether. The word *pite* is of Turkish origin, where it is called *pide*; it came to the Hungarian language during the Turkish occupation of Hungary in the sixteenth and seventeenth centuries, and is ultimately related to the Greek pita.

In adapting Riza néni's recipe, I substituted two egg yolks for her one whole egg because this makes for more tender dough. The yeast alone provided sufficient leavening for the dough and made baking powder, which was also included in the original recipe, superfluous. She recommended rolling the dough to the thickness of one's pinkie, but I prefer it slightly thinner.

You can buy poppy seeds by the pound in ethnic groceries selling German, Hungarian, Polish, Russian, or Jewish specialties. Try to find a store that is equipped to grind the seeds; they have a smoother texture and stronger taste when ground, more accurately crushed, in a special grinder between two metal discs. Store poppy seeds, especially the ground ones, in airtight plastic bags for up to four months in the refrigerator or indefinitely in the freezer, because they quite easily go rancid unless refrigerated. Ground poppy seeds can also be ordered from some mail-order spice dealers such as The Spice House (tel.: 847-328-3711).

YIELD: 20 pastry squares

TOTAL TIME: about 2 hours 15 minutes (1 hour more if you allow the dough to rest for 2 hours)

INGREDIENTS:
- 1¼ teaspoons active dry yeast (about ½ of a standard envelope)
- ¼ cup barely warm (105–110°F) water
- 1 teaspoon sugar
- 1 tablespoon unbleached all-purpose flour
- 2¼ cups unbleached all-purpose flour
- 7 tablespoons unsalted butter or margarine, cut into ¼" slices
- 3 tablespoons sugar
- 2 large egg yolks
- ¼ teaspoon kosher salt
- ¼ teaspoon ground cloves
- ¾ pound ground poppy seeds (about 4 cups)
- 1 cup water
- ½–⅔ cup sugar
- 3 tablespoons unsalted butter or margarine
- 1 Golden Delicious apple, peeled, cored, and coarsely grated
- ½ teaspoon ground cloves

½ cup dark or golden raisins
3 teaspoons grated lemon zest
1 tablespoon apricot jam
1 teaspoon water
1 large egg, lightly beaten

SPECIAL
EQUIPMENT: food processor
baking pan, 12" × 8" × 1½" or a different pan
   of about the same area and depth
baking sheet
pastry brush

1. In a bowl or measuring cup, dissolve yeast in ¼ cup warm water, stir in 1 teaspoon sugar and 1 tablespoon flour. Allow this mixture to ferment at room temperature for about 15 minutes. (Reseal the envelope of dry yeast; the remaining yeast will keep in it for about two weeks, if refrigerated.) Grease the sides, but not the bottom, of your baking pan with a little butter or margarine.

2. Place 2¼ cups flour and the butter or margarine pieces in the bowl of a food processor; process for 8 seconds, until the mixture resembles coarse cornmeal. Add 3 tablespoons sugar, egg yolks, salt, cloves, and the fermented yeast mixture, and process for about 15 seconds. If the dough doesn't form a ball on the blades, add water by the tablespoonful and process for a few seconds to see if the dough comes together. I had to add 2 tablespoons of water, but this can vary depending on the moisture in the air. The dough should be a little softer than noodle dough and shouldn't be sticky. Transfer the dough to the lightly floured work surface and knead it for 5–8 minutes, until it becomes smooth and elastic. Alternatively, you can knead it in a stand mixer with the dough hook attachment. Place the dough in a large bowl, cover the bowl with plastic wrap, and let the dough rest at room temperature for at least 1, but preferably 2 hours.

3. In the meantime, prepare the filling. Place poppy seeds in a large bowl. Place 1 cup water, sugar, and butter or margarine in a small saucepan; bring it to a boil and stir to mix. Pour the hot liquid over the

poppy seeds, and stir to evenly moisten the seeds. I made my filling with only ½ cup sugar because I like the slightly bitter flavor of poppy seed. Taste the filling; if it is not sweet enough for you, add a little more sugar. Add grated apple, cloves, raisins, and lemon zest; stir to mix thoroughly. If the mixture doesn't stick together like wet sand, add 1 tablespoon water. Place apricot jam in a small bowl and dilute it with 1 teaspoon water.

4. Center a rack in the oven and preheat the oven to 375°F. Divide the dough into halves; place one half on the lightly floured work surface, and with a floured rolling pin roll it out into a rectangle, about ½" larger in both directions than your baking pan. Loosely roll the dough rectangle on your rolling pin and unroll it over the baking pan. Gently tuck the dough into the pan and trim it to fit the bottom. The elastic dough can be carefully stretched a little if the fit is not perfect. Brush it with the diluted apricot jam.

5. Using a rubber spatula, evenly spread the filling over the dough in the pan. Roll out the other half of the dough and cover the filling with this. Brush the top with beaten egg; let it dry slightly for 1–2 minutes; then lightly scratch a diagonal grid pattern into the egg glaze with the tines of a fork; use the fork to prick the top layer of dough at approximately 2" intervals. Place the pan on a baking sheet and bake it in the preheated oven for about 30 minutes, until golden brown.

6. Allow it to cool for 15 minutes in the baking pan set on a cooling rack. Run a knife along the edges to release the pastry, then place a cutting board on top of the pan. Holding the pan and the board together, invert the pastry onto the board. Now place the cooling rack upside-down on the pastry and holding the pastry between the cutting board and the rack, invert it again so that it faces up on the rack. When it is completely cool, transfer it to the cutting board, and cut it with a long serrated knife into 4 strips in width and 5 strips in length to make 20 squares. Serve them at room temperature. Store them for up to 3 days at room temperature in a cookie tin in layers separated by wax paper.

Walnut Squares

Diós lepény

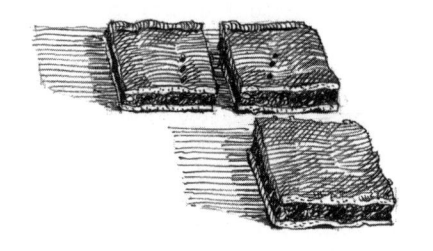

This is one of the last recipes in Riza néni's collection and one of the few that she wrote in Hungarian. She long resisted the trend among the German-speaking Hungarian Jews to switch to Hungarian, the language of the government, newspapers, literature, and the Gentile majority. But by the 1910s, when she must have received this recipe from a Hungarian-speaking friend, she occasionally used Hungarian. Her final switch to this language happened when as an old women she moved to live with her daughter in Budapest, and her son-in-law, although he knew German, insisted on speaking Hungarian at home. Like most Jews in Hungary, he was very patriotic, and as an assimilated Jew he wished to use at home the official language of the country. All her life Riza néni thought that important as traditions were, family came first, and now she felt that avoiding tensions was more important than using the language she was used to.

The almost soufflé-like filling of these walnut squares is quite unusual; this is another wonderful recipe that would have been forgotten had it not been preserved in handwritten collections like hers. The whipped egg whites in the filling will puff up during baking and lift the top layer of dough. Although it subsides during cooling, the filling never looses its light, airy texture. Riza néni didn't include any sugar in the dough, almost as if it were a pie dough, but sugar is customarily added to this type of dough, and I decided to add a little as an optional ingredient.

YIELD: 20 pastry squares

TOTAL TIME: about 1 hour 30 minutes

INGREDIENTS: 2 cups unbleached all-purpose flour

1½ sticks (6 ounces) cold unsalted butter or margarine, cut into ½" cubes (Riza néni probably used goose fat)
2 large egg yolks
2 tablespoons cold milk or water
¼ teaspoon kosher salt
2 tablespoons sugar (optional)
1½ cups walnuts
½ cup sugar
5 large egg yolks
3 tablespoons sugar
1 tablespoon dark rum (optional)
5 large egg whites
½ teaspoon cream of tartar
1 tablespoon sugar
2 tablespoons confectioners' sugar

SPECIAL EQUIPMENT:
food processor
electric mixer (optional)
12" × 8" × 1½" baking pan or a different pan of about the same area and depth
parchment paper
baking sheet
small strainer

1. Place flour and cold butter or margarine pieces in the bowl of the food processor; process for 6–8 seconds. Add 2 egg yolks, salt, optional sugar, and cold milk or water. Process for 8–10 seconds, until the dough clumps together. If the dough doesn't stick together, add 1 more tablespoon liquid, pulse about three times, and see if that does it. The goal is for the mixture to form lumps, not a smooth ball. In fairly humid weather, I didn't need any additional liquid for the dough but probably I would need a little more when the air is dry. Transfer the dough to a piece of plastic wrap about 12" long and use the wrap to shape it into a slab, about 4" × 6" × 1". There should be small specks of white butter visible in the beige dough. Enclose it in plastic and refrigerate for at least 45 minutes.

2. Center a rack in the oven and preheat the oven to 375°F. After the dough has rested, start to prepare the filling. Place walnuts and ½ cup sugar in the food processor and process for about 20 seconds to finely and evenly grind the nuts. Beat egg yolks and 3 tablespoons sugar with an electric mixer or by hand until the mixture becomes foamy and turns pale. Add ground nuts and optional rum; mix them well.

3. Grease the sides of your baking pan. Divide the chilled dough into halves, rewrap one half and put it back into the refrigerator. Cut a piece of parchment paper about 18" long, lay it on the work surface and place the unwrapped half of the dough on it. Cut a piece of plastic wrap about 18" long, cover the dough with it, stretch the plastic smooth and align it with the parchment paper in the bottom. Roll out the dough between the sheets into a rectangle about ½" larger in both directions than your baking pan. Flip the dough over, peel off the parchment paper and with the help of the sheet of plastic invert the dough over the baking pan and lower it to cover the bottom of the pan. Use the plastic to gently tuck the dough into the corners of the pan. Peel off the plastic, cut and remove any excess dough along the sides of the pan. The dough should completely cover the bottom of the pan. Refrigerate the baking pan.

4. Take the remaining chilled half of the dough and repeat the procedure of rolling it out between sheets of parchment paper and plastic wrap. Place it on a baking sheet with the plastic wrap in the bottom, peel off the parchment paper and place the baking sheet in the freezer.

5. Finish preparing the filling. Whip egg whites and cream of tartar to soft peaks, add 1 tablespoon sugar, and continue whipping until the whites form firm peaks. Stir about ⅓ of the whipped egg whites into the walnut mixture, then gently fold in the rest. Remove the baking pan from the refrigerator, pour the filling in the middle of the pan, and with a rubber spatula spread it evenly over the dough. Remove the baking sheet with the sheet of dough on it from the freezer and use a dough scraper to trim the dough to the exact size of your baking pan without cutting the plastic. With the help of the plastic, invert the cold and stiff dough over the pan and carefully lower it to completely cover the filling. Use the plastic to tuck the edges of the dough into the pan

without crushing the soft filling. Peel off the plastic, and with a fork, prick the top layer of dough at about 2" intervals.

6. Place the baking pan on a baking sheet and bake it in the preheated oven for about 25 minutes, until light golden brown. The filling will puff up—especially in the center of the pan—during baking and will lift the top layer of dough by as much as 1". Cool the baked pastry for about 20 minutes in the pan set on a cooling rack. Run a knife along the sides of the pan to release the pastry. If your baking pan is 1½" deep or slightly less, place a cutting board over the top of the baking pan and invert the pastry to the cutting board. If your baking pan is more than 1½" deep, cut a piece of cardboard to the size of your pan, lay it on top of the pastry, and holding it between the pan and the cardboard invert it to the cardboard. In either case, place another cutting board on the inverted pastry and, holding it sandwiched between this cutting board and the cardboard or the other cutting board, re-invert it so that the top side faces up again. Cut it lengthwise into 4 strips, then each strip into 5 pieces, making 20 squares. Transfer the squares to the cooling rack to finish cooling. Dust the squares, when serving, with confectioners' sugar tapped through a small strainer. Store leftover squares, without the sugar dusting, at room temperature in a cake tin between layers of wax paper.

Almond Macaroons
Weisse Mageron

The idea and the name of macaroons come from sixteenth-century Italy, though they have been known in France for almost as long. The original macaroons were made with ground almonds, sugar, and egg whites, but in some later versions other nuts substituted for almonds. Both the Ashkenazim and the Sephardim adopted this dessert centuries ago because it could easily accommodate Jewish dietary restrictions. As these cookies don't contain any fat, they can be served with either meat or dairy dishes, and as they don't contain flour, they can be eaten during Passover, too. As a result, macaroons have long been traditional Jewish desserts for Passover and Purim, and to a slightly lesser degree at other time of the year as well.

Riza néni's collection well documents the popularity of these cookies among Jews, because it includes eleven recipes for various versions of macaroons, a large share of the eighty-five dessert recipes in the collection. The slightly soft and chewy Viennese-style macaroons of this recipe are quite different from the better-known French version because they include a little flour and lemon juice among the ingredients. The lemon juice, combined with the more customary grated zest of lemon, lends complexity to the flavor. But the most distinctive feature of these macaroons is their interesting texture, the result of using a mixture of ground and slivered almonds. For Passover, Riza néni made different kinds of macaroons without flour.

Riza néni suggested decorating the macaroons with sour cherries. Unfortunately, fresh sour cherries can rarely be found in our stores and even if they are available they pale (literally, because they are a different, paler variety, and figuratively, because their flavor is not as intense) next to the kind available in Hungary. Instead of fresh sour cherries you could use Hungarian or Bulgarian canned sour cherries, which are available in jars in many delicatessen stores, or could substitute pitted fresh Bing cherries. You could even use cranberries to decorate the cookies.

YIELD: about 30 pieces

TOTAL TIME: about 35 minutes

INGREDIENTS:
- 1 cup blanched almonds
- ⅓ cup granulated sugar
- 2 tablespoons all-purpose flour
- 1½ teaspoons grated zest of lemon
- 1 cup slivered almonds
- 2 large egg whites
- ¼ teaspoon cream of tartar

½ cup confectioners' sugar
1 tablespoon lemon juice
½ teaspoon vanilla extract
30 sour cherries (fresh or canned), Bing cherries, or cranberries

SPECIAL
EQUIPMENT: food processor
2 nonstick baking mats or parchment paper
2 baking sheets (12" × 18")

1. Line two baking sheets with nonstick baking mats or parchment paper. Adjust oven racks to divide the oven into thirds and preheat the oven to 300°F.

2. Place almonds, sugar, flour, and lemon zest in the food processor. Process for about 20 seconds, until the almonds are finely ground. Transfer the mixture into a large bowl; add slivered almonds and mix to distribute them.

3. Whip the egg whites and cream of tartar until they almost form firm peaks. Sprinkle the confectioners' sugar onto the whites and continue whipping for a few seconds until the whites become shiny and form firm peaks. Stir in the lemon juice and vanilla. Stir ½ of the whipped egg whites into the dry ingredients in the bowl then fold in the remaining whites. It will be a thick, sticky mixture.

4. Place heaping teaspoonfuls of the mixture at least 1½" apart on one of the baking sheets and with the help of another teaspoon shape them into high, compact heaps, each about 1"–1¼" diameter. You will have 3 rows of 5 cookies on each sheet. With your fingertip, push back any slivered almond that sticks out of the round heaps. Place a sour cherry, Bing cherry, or cranberry on top of each heap.

5. Bake the macaroons in the preheated oven for 15 minutes, switching each baking sheet to the other rack about halfway through this time. Raise the heat to 450°F and bake them for another 5 minutes, until the edges are the lightest golden but the centers still pale. Check 2 minutes before the end of baking time to see if they are done.

6. Slide the baking mats or sheets of parchment with the macaroons on them from the baking sheet to a cooling rack. After 5 minutes, use a spatula to remove the cookies from the mat or paper and place them directly on the cooling rack to finish cooling.

Sponge Dough Discs

Pletzel

Sponge dough, used in these cookies and also in sponge cakes, consists mainly of eggs, sugar, and flour. Typically, it contains no shortening and gets its light, airy texture solely from the leavening power of eggs. Unlike the way these cookies are prepared, the eggs are usually separated and the whipped egg whites are added at the end to the mixture of egg yolks, sugar, and flour. Though some versions of sponge dough are enriched with a little butter, those are exceptions, because most versions include no fat. As a result, Jewish people can serve them with both meat and dairy dishes, which may be the reason for their popularity among Jews. Among the eighty-five desserts in Riza néni's collection, twelve recipes use different versions of this dough, and this doesn't even include her flourless tortes, which are really variations of the idea.

I cannot think of any cookies that are easier and faster to make than these sponge dough discs. In about twenty minutes from starting to make the batter, you can serve these elegant pale-yellow cookies, appealingly light brown around the edges, decorated with a dainty strip of lemon zest in the middle. The only change I had to make in adapting Riza néni's recipe for these *Pletzel*, or *Plätzchen* as they are called in today's Austria, was to add a little water to the batter in order to make it more workable.

YIELD: 24 cookies

TOTAL TIME: about 20 minutes

INGREDIENTS:	1 teaspoon unsalted butter or margarine
	2 tablespoons unbleached all-purpose flour
	8 strips of lemon zest, each about 2" × ¼"
	2 large eggs
	½ cup sugar
	1 teaspoon grated lemon zest
	1 teaspoon vanilla extract
	1 tablespoon water
	¾ cup unbleached all-purpose flour
SPECIAL EQUIPMENT:	2 cookie sheets or baking sheets (12" × 18")

1. Adjust oven racks to divide the oven into thirds and preheat the oven to 375°F. Grease the cookie or baking sheets with butter or margarine and dust them with flour. Alternatively, line the sheets with parchment paper. With a vegetable peeler, cut eight 2" × ¼" strips of zest from a lemon. Cut each strip into 3 parts to make 24 pieces of zest, each about ⅝" × ¼".

2. Break the eggs into a bowl; add sugar, grated lemon zest, vanilla, and water. Beat them well with an electric mixer or by hand until the mixture turns pale and becomes foamy. Gently fold in the flour. Make sure that there are no lumps of flour left in the batter, which should be a little thicker than pancake batter.

3. Make little heaps of 1 full teaspoon batter, which will immediately spread into 2"–2½" discs. Keep about 2" of space between them. There should be 12 discs (3 rows of 4) on each cookie sheet. Divide any remaining batter among the discs and place a piece of lemon zest in the middle of each.

4. Bake them in the preheated oven for about 10 minutes. Start checking the cookies after 7 minutes and don't leave the kitchen while they are in the oven. The cookies are ready when the edges are slightly brown but the center is still pale yellow. With a spatula, transfer the discs, while they are still warm and soft, from the cookie sheet to a cooling rack for about 10 minutes. The cookies are best when they are fresh, but can be kept for up to 3 days in an airtight box.

VARIATIONS:

1. Proceed as described above, but with the back of a teaspoon spread the batter into 3" discs. Bake them for only 5–8 minutes. While the thin cookies are still hot and pliable, you can form them into cones, which you can later, shortly before serving them, fill with fresh raspberries or whipped cream. If you decide to leave them flat, these thinner cookies will be a little crisper than the slightly thicker ones.

2. Omit the lemon zest from the cookies and make sandwich cookies by pressing 2 pieces of about the same diameter together with a thin layer of apricot jam or chocolate cream between them.

Evening Flowers
Pletzl

The batter for these cookies, one of my all-time favorites, is made the same way as the previous recipe, but they are so different from the sponge dough discs that I follow Riza néni's example of including them as different cookies, not just a variation. To make them, the discs of unbaked batter are allowed to dry on the baking sheet overnight, or for at least 3 or 4 hours. They get their name from this method of preparation: because they are usually prepared at night and baked the following morning, they are called *estike* (evening flower). I like to decorate them with a small pinch of anise seeds instead of the strips of lemon zest. Bake them in a preheated 275°F oven for about 14–18 minutes or until the edges of the cookies start to turn golden. The cookies will have an appealingly brittle, almost meringue-like consistency, quite different from the cookies that are not left to dry and baked at a higher temperature. They even look different because of their speckled, slightly shiny surface.

YIELD:	24 cookies
TOTAL TIME:	about 25 minutes, plus overnight drying
SPECIAL EQUIPMENT:	2 cookie or baking sheets (12" × 18")

Hazelnut Slices
Haselnuss Schnitt

Although I couldn't find the actual source of this recipe in my research of late-nineteenth- and early-twentieth-century Hungarian cookbooks, I found several related recipes, indicating that similar cookies must have been popular at that time and place. In these cookies a coating of meringue covers the dough, which is a mixture of finely ground hazelnuts, sugar, and egg whites. I love the intense hazelnut flavor of these easy-to-make cookies; their aroma is so intense that just opening the cookie tin and catching a whiff of these cookies is enough to make me feel in heaven. When I tested the recipe I substituted toasted and blanched hazelnuts for the raw hazelnuts of the original recipe, because that was the kind I happened to have at home. Use the kind of hazelnuts you have at home or available in your neighborhood; the cookies will be terrific with either.

YIELD:	36 cookies
TOTAL TIME:	about 1 hour 10 minutes
INGREDIENTS:	1 heaped cup of raw or toasted and blanched hazelnuts
	⅓ cup sugar

1½ teaspoons grated lemon zest
2 large egg whites
¼ cup sugar (preferably superfine sugar)

SPECIAL
EQUIPMENT: food processor
parchment paper
baking or cookie sheet (12" × 18")

1. Center a rack in the oven and preheat the oven to 200°F. Line a baking or cookie sheet with parchment paper. Alternatively, butter and flour a baking or cookie sheet. Place hazelnuts and ⅓ cup sugar in the bowl of a food processor. Process until the hazelnuts are finely and uniformly ground. Add lemon zest and pulse to mix it in. Place egg whites in the bowl that you will use for whipping them.

2. Transfer the ground hazelnuts into a bowl, add 2 tablespoons of the egg whites, stir to evenly distribute them and knead the mixture for a short time until it sticks together. The dough should be neither too crumbly nor too soft. If necessary, add ½ tablespoon more egg white.

3. With an electric mixer or by hand, which I prefer for such small quantities of egg whites, whip the remaining egg whites until they form almost firm peaks, add sugar, fold it in and whip for a few seconds until the whites become shiny and form stiff peaks.

4. With a lightly floured rolling pin, roll out the dough into a 9" square, about ⅛" thick. The rolled-out dough can be easily patched to make a neater square.

5. With a spatula or a long, straight knife, evenly spread the whipped egg whites on top of the dough. Using a dough scraper or a long, straight knife, cut off a 1"-wide strip from the dough and divide the strip crosswise into 4 equal pieces, each about 1" × 2¼". One by one, transfer the pieces to the prepared cookie sheet by sliding the dough scraper or spatula under the soft cookie and using a knife to push it onto the cookie sheet. Leave about 1" space between the cookies. Now cut another 1" × 9" strip from the dough, divide it into 4 equal parts, and repeat the whole process. You will end up with 36 cookies.

6. Bake the cookies in the preheated oven for about 50 minutes. The meringue topping will absorb some of the color from the hazelnuts and turn light brown. Transfer the cookies to a cooling rack. If you wish to keep them for more than a day, store them at room temperature in an airtight box.

Meringue-coated Almond Sandwich Cookies
Tortlette

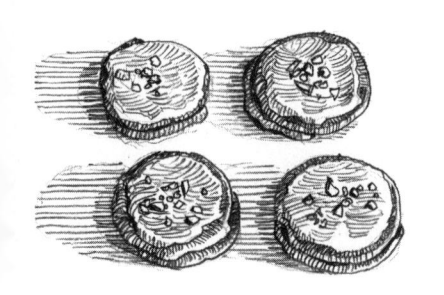

Similar to some other recipes in her collection, this one allows us to follow how a recipe developed before achieving its more or less codified form. Riza néni's recipe for these delicious cookies preserves an earlier version of the *non plus ultra* (Latin for "none better than this") cookies, one of the most elegant cookies invented in the former Austro-Hungarian Monarchy. The only differences are that her dough includes some ground almonds and the meringue coating of her cookies isn't flavored with lemon juice but sprinkled with coarse sugar and chopped almonds. I make these cookies a little thinner than she recommended, because I believe they are daintier and prettier this way.

Riza néni would have been amazed seeing our modern kitchen equipment. She would have admired the food processor, which can grind the almonds and mix the dough for this recipe in a fraction of the time this took for her. Not having a refrigerator or freezer, not even an icebox, she could have no idea of icebox cookies, a technique that makes it faster and a lot easier to prepare these little round cookies. Seeing this, she would have remembered how much skill it took for her to quickly roll out the dough and cut discs from it before the dough would warm up and become unmanageably sticky.

One doesn't have to think of history to enjoy these divine cookies, in which the airy brittleness of the meringue contrasts unforgettably with the softness of the cookie dough. No wonder that the children stole from the tray of cookies their grandmother set out for her guests. I would have done the same.

YIELD:	about 22 sandwich cookies
TOTAL TIME:	about 2 hours 10 minutes, but this includes 1 hour of waiting for the dough to chill
INGREDIENTS:	¼ cup blanched almonds
	1 cup unbleached all-purpose flour
	2 tablespoons sugar
	¼ teaspoon kosher salt
	1 stick (4 ounces) unsalted butter, softened and cut into ½" pieces
	1 large egg yolk
	3 tablespoons slivered almonds
	2 tablespoons turbinado sugar (or other coarse sugar)
	1 large egg white
	1 small pinch of cream of tartar
	¼ cup superfine sugar (available in the baking section of supermarkets but you can also make your own finer-grained sugar by placing regular granulated sugar in a food processor and processing it for about 1 minute)
	3 tablespoons thick but not chunky apricot jam
SPECIAL EQUIPMENT:	food processor
	2 cookie sheets (14" × 18")
	¾"-wide offset spatula (optional)

1. Place almonds, flour, 2 tablespoons sugar, and salt in the bowl of the food processor. Process for about 30 seconds, until the almonds are finely and evenly ground. With the machine running, add pieces of butter and egg yolk; process for about 15 seconds, until the mixture starts to form a ball on top of the blade. (When the air is very dry, you

might have to add 1 or 2 teaspoons more water for the dough to come together.)

2. Transfer the dough onto an 18" piece of plastic wrap and use the plastic to shape it into a 9" by 1½" round sausage. Wrap it in the plastic and shape it so that the ends are flat and perpendicular to the sides. Carefully, without distorting its round shape, transfer to a cookie sheet, and place in the freezer for 1 hour.

3. Position oven racks to divide the oven into thirds and preheat the oven to 350°F. Place 3 tablespoons of slivered almonds in the food processor and pulse a few times to chop them into pieces about ⅛". Transfer the pieces to a small bowl and place the coarse sugar in another small bowl.

4. Unwrap the hard dough sausage and lightly score it to divide it into 9 equal parts. Slice it with a sharp, narrow knife into thin slices, about 5 slices for each of the 9 marked sections, making a total of about 45 slices. Rotate the sausage a few times during cutting to prevent it from getting flattened. Try to work quickly and make neat slices of uniform thickness. If the dough sausage starts to get soft, put it back into the freezer for a short time. Place about 22 slices on each cookie sheet, keeping the slices about 1" apart.

5. Bake the cookies for 13–14 minutes, until their edges are the lightest golden brown but their middles are still pale. About halfway through the baking, rotate the sheets top-to-bottom and left-to-right to ensure even baking.

6. While the cookies are baking, prepare the meringue. Place egg white and cream of tartar in a bowl; whip it until it almost forms firm peaks. Add sugar in 2 batches, stir and whip briefly until the meringue is stiff and shiny. It is easier and gives better results to whip such small quantities of egg whites by hand than by machine.

7. Remove the sheets from the oven and adjust oven temperature to 175°F. Leave the cookies on the cookie sheets and allow them to cool slightly for a few minutes.

8. Use an offset spatula or a knife to evenly spread the meringue about ⅛" thick over the entire surface of the cookies on the sheets. Sprinkle a pinch of chopped almonds in the middle of 22 meringue-coated cookies and a pinch of coarse sugar on the remaining cookies. Riza néni sprinkled both almonds and coarse sugar on each cookie but I believe it looks more elegant if almonds and sugar are not mixed and if they are sprinkled only in the middle, leaving much of the white meringue untouched. Place the sheets in the oven for about 30 minutes to dry the meringue, which should remain white.

9. Allow the cookies to cool a few minutes on the sheets, then transfer them with a metal spatula to a cooling rack. When the cookies are cool, spread a little apricot jam on the uncoated bottom side and gently press another cookie against it to make a sandwich. The meringue will be visible on both sides of the sandwich cookie. Fill only as many cookies as you are planning to serve, and store the remaining unfilled cookies at room temperature in a cookie tin for up to four days. I am sure they will be consumed well before that.

Rainy Afternoons at Riza Néni's

In bad weather, my mother and her sister spent the afternoon at home, where Riza néni kept them busy with projects. She taught them to sew, make dolls, handbags, or pillows. She also taught them to play the piano. Once my mother knew how to play, Riza néni selected some easy four-hand music from the chest of sheet music that was behind the big standing mirror in the corner of the formal dining room, where the piano stood, and my mother had to play four hands with her.

Another project she invented for them was to put on a play in one of the granaries, which was empty at the time. The audience, which consisted of my great-grandparents' neighbors, had to pay admission, and the money from the tickets went to benefit victims of a flood. The children made the curtain out of blankets. My mother played a male role and wore trousers borrowed from Imre Herz, a boy who was courting her at the time. He didn't act in the play, only his trousers made their appearance on stage!

Touring theater groups rarely came to Moson, because Győr and Vienna were so close that people could easily go there for theater. A few times a year there was a ball in the ballroom of the Weisses Rössl (White Horse) Inn, and once in a rare while a concert. The only other cultural events were the concerts of the local fire brigade's band and the lectures and charity events organized by the Hebrew Ladies' Society of Moson. Lujza néni was the president of this society and she was insufferably stuck-up with her "important position."

Carl Flesch, whose first violin teacher was the violinist-conductor of the Moson fire brigade's band, tells an anecdote about the Moson cultural life, which he heard from his older friend, the conductor Arthur Nikisch (1855–1922). Nikisch, one of the greatest conductors of his generation, was born in a village only about fifteen miles from Moson. According to Flesch his friend never tired of repeating this anecdote every time they met: "You are from Wieselburg" (the German name of Moson), Nikisch began in his broad Swabian-Magyar dialect, "that reminds me a of a funny story. When I was a young man I often played piano trios with the violinist 'Pepi' Hellmesberger and the cellist Karl Lasner, I at the piano. We also held a number of provincial engagements. Now, in Wieselburg there was a lawyer named Bókay, who once engaged us for a trio recital in the Rössl inn. Well, we drove out in the afternoon; there were still two hours to the concert, and so we sat down in the parlor and had something to eat. Suddenly, we heard a tremendous row going on in the main street. Pepi ran to the window and shouted: 'Come and look boys, here comes our audience!' Lasner and I ran to the window and saw about a hundred cattle coming along the street and making a frightful noise. Well, you can guess how we laughed." This anecdote also makes it clear that in the 1870s when Riza néni moved to Moson and this concert took place, Fő utca (Main Street), part of the Budapest–Vienna highway, wasn't exactly the busy highway we envision today.

One of the children's favorite pastimes on cold or rainy afternoons was to go up to my great-grandparents' part of the attic. Each family had a closed area in the attic, in addition to the large common area. So many exciting things were stored up there! In a corner stood a mannequin made of cane that looked like an ugly birdcage. A large stuffed parrot perched nearby. The trunk containing the Passover dishes stood there too, as well as the crates in which walnuts were drying. The children loved to eat the walnuts, a special thin-shelled variety, called *papír dió* (paper walnuts).

Next to the crates in a cabinet the children found old books and dresses. In a drawer of that cabinet they discovered bundles of old letters and postcards with gorgeous old stamps on them. The oddly formal greetings on the cards were written in old-fashioned, spiky Gothic German script: "To the most esteemed Miss Therese Baruch." First the children read the funny old texts aloud and then they soaked off the nice stamps for their stamp collections. In another drawer they found fancy *cotillions*, little souvenirs made of paper, which my great-grandmother got at balls when she was young. Once, when the children were already slightly older, they found there in the attic a corsage made of silk flowers. They took it down to show to Riza néni, who told them that she used to wear it stitched to the train of her long ball dress. And so many hats in a chest! There were lots of ostrich feathers, loose and on hats. The children laughed their heads off trying on those silly old hats.

One day they found a hairpiece in one of the drawers. They all tried it on before asking Riza néni what it was. "This was great-grandmother's *sheitel*," she answered. "But what is a sheitel?" the children asked. Then Riza néni showed them how her mother put it in her hair to partially cover her head instead of a full wig, and she told the children that she used to wear a similar hairpiece when she was a young wife, but later gave it up. An oil portrait made in 1840 of Riza néni's grandmother shows her wearing what looks like a black cap under her traditional silk flower–decorated tulle headdress. Married Jewish women used to cut off their hair and wear a wig to cover their heads, because they were not allowed to expose their hair to anyone but their husband. From Riza néni's description we can follow how increasing assimilation has gradually eroded this old custom: her grandmother had cut her hair off, her mother kept her hair but wore a hairpiece in it, and Riza néni—at least in later life—ignored the custom altogether.

DINNERS AT RIZA NÉNI'S

THE SHADOW of the horse-chestnut tree in the courtyard was getting longer; people and animals were feeling tired and looking forward to dinner. Bizsu (bijou), my great-grandparents' fat dog, who looked like a cross between a dachshund and a cow, was in a mellow mood. During the day he chased the family's cat up the tree, but now as he lay on the floor of the entrance hall, he allowed the cat to nap on top of him.

The children, who had spent the afternoon at the Danube and who had to be home by 6:30, felt pleasantly tired as they walked home after all the swimming and running; the evening breeze felt great on their sun-parched skin. They were hungry and could hardly wait to get home and see what was cooking for dinner. Of course, their first trip was to the kitchen, where Riza néni, after allowing them a quick peep into the pots on the stove, ushered them to the washstand. While they washed their hands, she asked them about their adventures at the Danube and whom they had seen at the beach. Perhaps it was due to self-consciousness about her weight, but she, herself, never went to the beach. But she didn't want to miss out on any of the gossip the children could report from this center of social life in Moson. They kept chattering as they helped Riza néni and Paula to set the table in the informal living room, the room next to the kitchen.

In the meantime, my great-grandfather came in from the porch, then Frigyes bácsi arrived; they also washed their hands, and everyone sat down at the table. Dinner, which in Hungary is a lighter meal than lunch, was always at seven o'clock sharp. After Paula brought the steaming bowl of cabbage noodles to the table, Riza néni ladled it onto the plates, my great-grandfather mumbled a blessing over the bread, and they all began to eat.

Usually, there was warm food for dinner and it was always something different from what they had had for lunch. For a meat dinner they might eat a stew, goose cracklings with mashed potatoes, or scrambled eggs with little bits of smoked beef in them. For a dairy dinner they might get cauliflower topped with bread crumbs and sour cream, rice cooked in milk and sprinkled with cocoa, or noodles with farmer cheese. Other times they had pickled herring or anchovy eggs (see recipes on pages 200 and 204).

Once in a while, they had cold dinners and ate homemade sausage, chopped calves' liver (see the following recipe and the recipe on page 198), or *inarsz*, a kind of goose "bacon" made of fat cut from the neck or breast of the goose. This lump of hard fat was removed from under the skin, rubbed well with garlic, and rolled in paprika. It looked exactly like "paprika bacon," and was similarly sliced thin and eaten with bread. Unlike paprika bacon, however, the inarsz wasn't cooked but only very well chilled.

This goose "bacon" is an interesting example of an attempt to make an acceptable Jewish equivalent of an inherently non-kosher dish. Paprika bacon—a cooked, garlic-flavored bacon made from white pork fat that has no meat streaks in it and is coated with paprika—has long been one of the most popular types of bacon in Hungary. This bacon is never used in cooking but eaten in thin slices, like a cold cut, on bread.

Diced Pickle and Carrot Sausage
Fleischwurst zu Assiet

In Hungary life is not worth living without bacon, sausages, or salami. Jewish people were unwilling to be deprived of this pleasure. After overcoming the difficult challenge of making "kosher" paprika bacon, devising this recipe for sausage was, dare I say it, a piece of cake.

Riza néni suggested slicing the sausage like salami, but this strikes me as overly optimistic, unless she liked her salami ½" thick. Though she recommended eating it cold, I like it equally as much warm, if it is served with a warm salad or her cabbage dumplings (see recipe on page 108). I borrowed this technique of sausage-making from one of Jacques Pépin's cookbooks.

YIELD:	5 or 6 servings
TOTAL TIME:	about 50 minutes, plus 2–3 days curing
INGREDIENTS:	½ pound beef stew meat
	½ pound veal stew meat
	3 tablespoons crushed ice
	1 tablespoon rendered or finely chopped raw chicken fat
	1 medium carrot, peeled and cut into ⅛" dice (about ⅓ cup)
	2 slices stale white bread, crust removed, cut into ½" cubes
	1 cup white wine or water or a mixture of the two
	2 whole kosher dill pickles cut into ⅛" dice (about ¾ cup)
	2 tablespoons lemon juice
	2 teaspoons grated lemon zest
	½ teaspoon freshly ground black pepper
	1½ teaspoons kosher salt
SPECIAL EQUIPMENT:	food processor
	10" to 12" diameter pan with a lid

1. Cut about ⅓ of both beef and veal into 1" pieces, place them in the bowl of the food processor and add the crushed ice. Process for about 30 seconds to emulsify the mixture. Cut the rest of the meat into ¼" cubes; place them in a large bowl; add chicken fat and the meat purée from the processor.

2. Parboil diced carrots for 2 minutes in boiling water, drain them and add them to the bowl. In a medium bowl, soak dry bread cubes for 1 or 2 minutes in wine or water and squeeze them out. Add them and all the other ingredients to the meat in the bowl and mix them well.

3. Select a large pan with a lid or a roasting pan at least 3½" deep with a cover. From the size of your pan decide how long the sausage can be. Spread a 15"-long piece of plastic wrap on your work surface, spoon

the sausage mixture onto it, and use the plastic to shape it into a sausage that is about 9½" long and 2"–2½" thick. If your pan is smaller then 10", make 2 shorter sausages on separate pieces of plastic wrap. Enclose the sausage tightly in the plastic wrap, allowing no air bubbles or voids and twist the ends to close. Roll this package into a piece of aluminum foil about 15" long and seal it as tightly as possible. Place it in the refrigerator for 2 or 3 days to cure before cooking. The salt and lemon juice will keep the meat from spoiling.

4. Place the foil-wrapped sausage in the selected pan or roasting pan with enough cold water to cover it. Place an inverted plate over the sausage to keep it submerged. Bring the water to a boil, cover, lower heat, and simmer very gently, for 10 minutes. Remove the pan from the heat and let the sausage sit in the hot water for at least 15 minutes, but you can leave it there for up to 1 hour. Remove the sausage from the water, but be careful not to bend it while lifting it. Unwrap it and serve it warm in ½" or ¾" slices, or let it cool, as Riza néni recommended, before slicing it with a serrated knife. It is easier to cut it into neat slices when it is chilled. Serve it with a vinaigrette-type potato salad, potato-watercress salad, lentil salad, or green salad.

Chopped Calves' Liver
Leberpastete

While chopped liver is one of the best known Jewish foods in the United States, it occupies a less central role in Hungary. Jewish jokes, one of our best sources for the study of Jewish culture, reflect this difference. I am not aware of Hungarian equivalents to the many American jokes about chopped liver or turns of phrases such as our "he is not chopped liver" (he is not inferior) or "What am I, chopped liver?" (when somebody feels left out). The best modern book about Hungarian Jewish cooking, *Old Jewish Dishes* by Zorica Herbst-Krausz, doesn't include chopped liver and doesn't mention it as typical food for the Sabbath or any other holiday. Nevertheless, it was a popular dish and is included in Riza néni's collection.

These days chopped liver usually means chopped chicken liver, but this wasn't always so. Riza néni raised her own chickens and there was no practical way for her to gather enough chicken liver for chopped liver. Even at the kosher butcher she couldn't have bought it. The liver from their geese was baked, sliced, and eaten with bread, but never made into chopped liver. For her, chopped liver meant chopped calves' or beef liver.

Although it is more expensive, I prefer calves' to beef liver. The superior tenderness of calves' liver is of less importance here, but I prefer its milder flavor and believe it is healthier. Because of its role in the body, liver tends to absorb and store undesirable medicines, hormones, and chemicals from the animal's diet. It seems logical that the older the animal is, the greater the accumulation of such substances is in the liver. If possible, try to find liver from calves raised without hormones.

YIELD:	about 1½ cup
TOTAL TIME:	about 1 hour
INGREDIENTS:	3 tablespoons canola oil or rendered poultry fat
	1 large onion (8 to 10 ounces), peeled and finely chopped
	½ pound calves' liver cut into slices about ½" thick
	¼ teaspoon kosher salt
	2 large eggs
	¼ teaspoon kosher salt
	⅛ teaspoon freshly ground black pepper
	1–2 teaspoons Dijon mustard
SPECIAL EQUIPMENT:	food processor

1. Heat oil or fat in a large skillet and sauté chopped onions over low heat for about 45 minutes until they become light brown and almost translucent.

2. While the onions are cooking, remove the broiler pan and preheat the broiler. Cut out all veins, skin, and connective tissue from the liver and lightly salt both sides of the slices. Place a large piece of aluminum foil

on the broiler pan or a baking sheet and turn up the edges of the foil. Place the liver on the aluminum foil and place it about 4" from the heating element of the broiler. Broil the liver for 2 to 3 minutes on each side or until it changes color and no trace of pink is left. Pat it dry with a paper towel. Cut it into chunks about ½".

3. Boil about 1 quart water in a medium saucepan. Prick the wide ends of the eggs with a pin. Gently lower them into the boiling water, adjust heat to medium-low and simmer for 10 minutes. Pour out the hot water, shake the pan to crack the eggshells, add a few ice cubes, fill the pot with cold water, let eggs cool completely, then shell them. Cut them into halves, remove the yolks and cut the whites into ⅛" dice.

4. Place the chunks of liver, sautéed onion (including the oil from the skillet), salt, pepper, and mustard in the bowl of the food processor. (You might also add the hard-cooked egg yolks, but I left them out.) Pulse about 10 times, checking frequently to make sure you don't process the liver into mush. It should be finely chopped but not turned into paste. Remove the blade and with a rubber spatula mix in all but 1 tablespoon of the diced egg whites. Taste and adjust seasoning, if necessary. Transfer it to a small serving bowl, smooth the top surface with a knife and decorate it by placing the reserved egg whites in the center. Serve it at room temperature (not cold out of the refrigerator) on crackers, small thin slices of dark bread, or cocktail rye.

Pickled Herring
Angemachte Häringe

Since the Middle Ages, herring has been one of the staples of the diet in much of Northern Europe. In those times, before refrigerated trucks and airplanes, smoked or salted herring and dried cod were the most common saltwater fish eaten, because fresh fish was available only in fishing ports. The dominance of herring in the fish trade is shown by the fact that in twelfth-century France dealers of all saltwater fish were called *harengères*, herring sellers, even if they were also selling other types of saltwater fish. It is hard to believe today, when it is sold in fancy delicatessen stores, but herring used to be the cheapest fish and as a result became the food of the poor.

In the nineteenth century, salt herring preserved in brine was transported in barrels by rail from Holland, Scandinavia, and, surprisingly, even from as far away as Scotland to the remote inland areas of Central and Eastern Europe. Jews were prominent in this herring trade. According to the Jewish dietary laws, fish may, with some restrictions, be eaten in either *fleischig* (meat) or *milchig* (dairy) menus. Salt herring keeps well, and after the salt is soaked out, the herring can be pickled for a cold snack or prepared for a hot meal. This flexibility, combined with its cheapness, made herring one of the most important foods in the diet of the Jews. There are numerous accounts of Jews in some areas eating herring in some shape or form several times a week. Perhaps I can be forgiven for repeating a rather well-known Jewish joke, but it illustrates better than anything does the reputation of herring as Jewish food:

A man asks the owner of a delicatessen, "What makes you Jews so clever?" "Because we eat pickled herring every day." The man comes back every day to buy pickled herring. After doing this for three months, he storms in angrily one day and shouts, "I just found out I can buy herring for half price in another store nearby!" "You see," says the owner, "it is working already!"

Herring is part of a large family of saltwater fish, which includes, among others, sardines, anchovies, and the largest member of the Clupeidae family, the American shad. The common herring is rarely more than twelve inches long and can be found in the cold waters of the Atlantic and the North Sea. It is an oily fish; fats account for at least 6 percent of its weight. All herring usable for pickling at home is cured in brine and sold from barrels; though these days the barrels are made of plastic instead of wood. Some of the varieties of cured herring are: schmaltz herring, an especially fat kind of herring; matjes herring, a reddish-colored young, tender herring that is almost always sold skinned and filleted; and salt herring, which in my opinion makes the best pickled herring because of its firm texture. In the United States salt herring is usually imported from Canada, Iceland, or Norway. The biggest obstacle to making pickled herring at home is finding a store that sells salt herring. There are lots of delicatessens selling pickled herring, and a few of them even prepare their own from salt herring, which they buy wholesale—but they don't sell salt herring retail. In New York City, as far as I know, one can buy salt herring only in some of the Polish, Russian, or Jewish neighborhoods of Brooklyn. Getting to know these fascinating neighborhoods better was a nice added benefit to my herring-hunting expeditions. In spite of the obstacles, finding a source for salt herring is worth the effort, because homemade pickled herring is easy and inexpensive to make. In addition, it is not only superior in quality to the commercially available, but many traditional varieties, such as this recipe made with the fish milt stirred into the pickling liquid, are not available in the stores. The pre-spawning herring, especially one that is carrying milt (*miltz* in Yiddish), the sperm and seminal fluid of the male fish, is the most desirable for pickling. Jewish recipes frequently refer to such herring as milch herring. Try to buy plump herring with big milt sacs and firm flesh. Test the firmness by squeezing the fish.

YIELD: about 24 pieces

TOTAL TIME: about 30 minutes, plus 3 days soaking and 2 days pickling

INGREDIENTS:
- 6 salt herring, whole and unopened (at least 4 of them with milt)
- 2 cups distilled white vinegar, plus 1 tablespoon vinegar to mix with milt
- 2 tablespoons sugar
- 1 cup water
- 2 teaspoons drained small capers
- ½ teaspoon dried thyme
- ½ teaspoon whole black peppercorns
- 4 bay leaves
- 3 cloves
- 3 medium onions, peeled and thinly sliced
- 1 lemon, thinly sliced
- 1 tablespoon canola oil

SPECIAL EQUIPMENT: 1 glass jar, 3 quarts capacity, or a similar capacity crock with a lid. *Note*: Any porous material, rubber, or plastic will permanently absorb herring odors. If you are using a patent jar, remove the rubber gasket from the lid.

1. About 5 days before you wish to serve the fish, place salt herring in a large stainless steel stock pot or deep glass bowl, fill with cold water, cover and let the fish soak in the refrigerator for at least 3 days, changing the water twice a day.

2. When you are ready for pickling, place in a stainless steel saucepan 2 cups vinegar, 1 tablespoon of the sugar, and all the water, capers, thyme, peppercorns, bay leaves, and cloves. Bring it to a boil, reduce heat, and simmer for 5 minutes. Add sliced onion and lemon to the hot liquid and set it aside to cool.

3. Cover your kitchen counter with a disposable plastic sheet or several layers of brown wrapping paper. Remove the herring from the water and, using scissors, trim off all fins. With a sharp, narrow, pointed knife cut open its belly and carefully remove the insides. Set aside the 4"- to 5"-long pinkish beige sacs of milt and discard the rest of the insides. On a large ceramic or glass plate, cut off the head and tail of the fish and discard them. I don't like using my plastic cutting board for herring because it tends to absorb the odor. Some people like to fillet the fish and remove its skin. I definitely prefer to leave the skin on, because I think the texture of the pickled fish is much better that way. I have less strong feelings about leaving in the bones, although I usually leave them in. If you wish to fillet the fish, pry one end of the backbone loose with your fingers and lift it out. Most of the small bones will come out with it. Rinse the fish under cold running water and slice it crosswise into about 1½" sections, cutting through the backbone if you haven't removed it.

4. Place the milt glands on another large ceramic or glass plate, and with the tines of a fork press out their thick, creamy content. Discard the empty outside membranes of the sacs. If you have trouble fishing out all bits of the membrane, press the contents through a strainer. Transfer the creamy substance of the milt to a glass bowl and stir in the remaining sugar, 1 tablespoon vinegar, and the oil.

5. With a slotted spoon or a skimmer, transfer the onion and lemon slices from the pickling liquid to a bowl or a plate. Mix the puréed milt into the cooled liquid.

6. Put the herring in alternate layers with the onion and lemon slices into a large glass jar. Pour the pickling liquid over it. Cover the jar and place it in the refrigerator to pickle for at least 2 days, preferably 3 or 4 days.

7. Serve it at room temperature with good crusty rye bread or small boiled potatoes. Pickled herring was frequently served at dairy meals in a sauce of sour cream mixed with pickling liquid. If you wish to serve it this way, a few hours before serving mix about 1 cup sour cream with 2 tablespoons of the pickling liquid in a bowl and place some of the herring and onion in this. Cover it and let the herring marinate in the refrigerator. Remove it from the refrigerator about 15 minutes before serving.

Anchovy Eggs

Sardellen Eier

This tasty and easy-to-prepare appetizer must have been popular in Riza néni's family, because I found an almost identical version of it in the recipe collection of her niece. I also found a similar recipe in a collection that used to belong to Katharina Schratt, Emperor Franz Joseph's lady friend. According to that recipe, she decorated each anchovy egg with a teaspoon of caviar. Well, this was one of the many differences between the Emperor and Riza néni, his subject.

It takes only about twenty minutes to prepare this appetizer, which can be served in either fleischig or milchig menus. The salt-preserved anchovies Riza néni bought by the piece at the grocer were larger than the small, oil-packed, flat fillets commonly available today in cans. Therefore, I substituted one and a half small fillets or the equivalent amount of anchovy paste for her larger anchovy.

YIELD:	3 first course servings
TOTAL TIME:	about 20 minutes
INGREDIENTS:	3 large eggs
	1½ tablespoons grated or very finely chopped onion
	¾ teaspoon anchovy paste or 1½ olive oil–packed flat anchovy fillets
	1–1½ teaspoons distilled white vinegar
	2–3 teaspoons canola oil
	½ teaspoon sugar
	⅛ teaspoon freshly ground black pepper
	3 leaves of Boston lettuce (each leaf about 4")
	2 teaspoons chopped chives
	6 blades of chive
SPECIAL EQUIPMENT:	none

1. Bring about 3 cups of water to a boil in a medium saucepan. While the water is heating, puncture the wide ends of the eggs with a pin. Gently lower the eggs with a spoon into the boiling water. As soon as the water returns to a boil, reduce heat and very gently simmer the eggs for 10 minutes. Drain the water from the pan and shake the pan to crack the eggshells. Fill the pan with ice cubes and cold water; allow the eggs to cool completely. Shell the eggs under running water. Carefully cut them in half lengthwise. Remove the egg yolks without breaking the egg white halves.

2. With a spoon, press the egg yolks through a coarse strainer into a medium bowl. Place the chopped onion in a small strainer and briefly run cold water over it. Drain the onion, dry it in a paper towel, and add it to the egg yolks in the bowl. Add ½ teaspoon vinegar, 1 teaspoon oil, anchovy paste, sugar, and ground pepper. I prefer to use anchovy paste

for the small amount of anchovies in this recipe because it requires no puréeing. But if you don't mind opening a can of anchovies, purée 1½ fillets and use them instead of the anchovy paste. Leftover anchovies can be kept in the refrigerator in a small covered jar of olive oil.

3. Thoroughly mix the ingredients in the bowl. Taste the mixture and, if you prefer stronger anchovy taste, blend in another ¼ teaspoon anchovy paste or ½ of a fillet, puréed. With a teaspoon or your fingers, fill the egg whites with the egg yolk mixture, reserving about 2 teaspoons of stuffing in the bowl.

4. Place the eggs filled side down on a dinner plate or a cutting board. Dilute the remaining stuffing in the bowl with ½ teaspoon vinegar and 1 teaspoon oil to create a sauce of about the consistency of pancake batter. If the sauce is too thick, add a little more vinegar and oil. Using the back of a teaspoon, coat the egg whites with this sauce.

5. Place a lettuce leaf on each serving plate and, with the help of a knife or a spatula, transfer 2 eggs with their filled side down onto each. Sprinkle chopped chives over the eggs and lay 2 blades of chive across each plate for decoration. Serve them at room temperature. You can prepare the stuffed eggs and the sauce ahead of time, but don't coat the eggs with the sauce until they are ready to be served.

Evenings at Riza Néni's

Dinner was over by about eight. After Paula cleared away the dishes and turned down the beds, she and Frigyes bácsi carried the bench, which stood in the vaulted front entrance during the day, to the sidewalk in front of the house. My great-grandparents and their siblings, Lujza néni and Sándor bácsi, sat on this bench on one side of the arched gate. On the other side of the gate sat the two servants, Paula and Ilka. During the day they had frequently quarreled, almost as if they had tried to imitate the behavior of their mistresses, but by now this was all forgotten and harmony ruled. Bizsu, my great-grandparents' dog, also came out and lay down in front of their bench.

Masters and servants chatted there for a while, gossiped, and discussed the way of the world. Frequently a neighbor stopped by and joined in the conversation. Then another friend came and joined in; Mrs. Stadler joined in; Frida Sommer joined in; soon they had to bring out additional chairs to accommodate everybody. In the easy-going, jovial atmosphere of Moson, time seemed to move slower than in the cities and people always had time for amusing anecdotes about the past and present inhabitants of this small town. My mother recalled hearing from Riza néni stories about the night watchman, an institution I usually associate with the sixteenth-century

On the other side of the gate sat the two servants.

Nuremberg of Wagner's *Die Meistersinger von Nürnberg* but which still had been a fixture of Moson in the 1880s. During the day he served as the gravedigger and guard of the Catholic cemetery; at night his duty was to announce each hour between nine and three in winter, ten and two in summer. For example, at ten he stopped at eight places along Fő utca to sing:

> Alle meine Herr'n, ich muss Euch sag'n,
> Der Hammer hat zehne g'schlag'n.
> So loben wir Gott und unsere liebe Frau.

(To all gentlemen I must announce
that the hammer has struck ten.
So, we should praise God and the Holy Mother)

She went to spend time with the neighborhood boys on the korzó.

At the end of the night he announced in a slightly different song that "all gentlemen be jolly and awake because the day is driving away the dear night."

When my mother was a teenager, after dinner she would go with Lili, her older sister, to spend time with the neighborhood boys on the *korzó*. This was what they called a stretch of a few blocks along Fő utca (Main Street) where young people walked up and down in the evenings. There, Lili would stroll with her suitor and my mother with hers. They didn't go to the coffeehouse, because my great-grandparents didn't allow this, but it wouldn't have occurred to them to go there in any case, because they preferred to be outside.

In the evening, Frigyes bácsi usually visited his lady friend, Ilka néni, or went to the "Mocca" coffeehouse on Fő utca. As usual in coffeehouses, newspapers attached to the traditional cane holders were hanging between the mirrors that lined the walls of one room in the café; a billiard table stood in the middle of the other room. The clientele was mainly but not exclusively Jewish. The owner, Pál Koppi, a district judge, was a Gentile. In the "Mocca," Frigyes bácsi usually played billiards and chatted with Holdi, his best friend, whose real name was Reinhold Teutsch, the son of the Catholic, "Swabian" owner of the town pharmacy.

My mother and her sister had to be back from the korzó by no later than ten o'clock, because this was their bedtime. By that time, Frigyes bácsi was usually back also. But even if he wasn't back yet, the other grownups went to sleep around ten, my great-grandfather sometimes even a little earlier. They would carry the bench back to the entrance passage before they got ready to go to bed.

The Holidays at Riza Néni's

SABBATH AT RIZA NÉNI'S

PREPARATIONS for the Sabbath started on Thursday, when Riza néni bought the fish and Paula prepared the dough for the challah, allowing it to rise overnight. Occasionally, a fishmonger brought the fish to my great-grandmother's house, but usually she bought it at the Thursday market on Main Street.

Friday morning Paula and Riza néni were up earlier than usual, because much work was to be done to get everything ready by the evening for all the meals of the Sabbath. Paula set fire in the stove and braided four loaves of challah from the risen dough. Riza néni tore off a small piece from the dough, threw it into the fire, and mumbled a prayer over it. Unlike the bread, which they took to the baker for baking, they always baked the challah at home.

Now, Paula killed the fish, which had been swimming in the bathtub since the day before, and made poached carp, which she served in a vinegary broth with horseradish (see recipe on page 220) or some other similar fish dish for the traditional first course of the Friday evening meal. Gefilte fish is considered one of the quintessential Jewish dishes in the United States, but my mother couldn't recall ever eating it at Riza néni's, not even on Sabbath. The idea of chopping fish, making a kind of fish forcemeat from it, and baking or cooking this mixture stuffed into fish skin, had originally come from medieval Germany, but Riza néni was unaware of this ancient history. While her avoidance of gefilte fish could have been merely a whim of personal taste, I suspect she associated gefilte fish with the Jews of Poland, Russia, and the Ukraine, where this dish had become most popular, and she was more interested in assimilated "western"—mainly Austrian—customs. A look at old Hungarian Jewish cookbooks confirmed my suspicion that gefilte fish was less common among Jews in nineteenth-century Hungary, certainly in western Hungary, than in some other countries. These cookbooks never called stuffed fish by its Yiddish name, gefilte fish, and similar to local Gentile cookbooks, stuffed fish was awarded no special place in them, but was merely one of thirty or fifty fish recipes. As a matter of fact, some of them copied the recipe from Gentile cookbooks.

Thursday or Friday morning, Paula tied up the goose or chicken intended for the holiday menu and gave it to my mother to take it to the *shochet*. After my mother returned with the killed bird, Paula koshered it, and on Friday she roasted it. She also prepared the soup, cholent, kugel, and whatever else was on the menu for the Sabbath meals. While Paula was busy cooking, Riza néni baked cakes, usually a strudel or a torte from her recipe collection.

Friday lunch was a lighter, simpler meal, typically consisting of dairy dishes. The reason for this was that they didn't want to stuff themselves before the big dinner and also because Riza néni and Paula were too busy preparing everything for the Sabbath meals to be able to cook another elaborate meal. Such dairy lunches could start with sweet milk soup with noodles, fruit soup, potato soup, or green bean soup made with butter and sour cream. After the soup, they could have, for example, noodles with farmer cheese or, in warm weather, cold sweet-and-sour squash with sour cream mixed into the dill sauce. Frequently, there was also dessert, such as warm noodles topped with meringue or rice and apple pudding served with wine sauce (see recipes on pages 126 and 145).

In the early afternoon, Paula polished the silverplated candlesticks and the silver cup for the wine. Riza néni changed into a holiday dress and took out the embroidered Sabbath tablecloth and challah cover from the wardrobe. Paula, who after spending decades in Riza néni's household was an expert in Sabbath customs, set the table in the informal living room with the holiday china and silver. She stuck new candles into the candlesticks, placed them at the head of the table, put two loaves of challah next to them, and laid the pretty challah cover over the loaves. Riza néni embroidered this cloth in the 1870s when she was a young wife, decorating it with a naïve depiction of the challah surrounded by the words that her husband always recited on Friday evenings: "A woman of worth is hard to find, for she is more precious than rubies" (Proverbs 31:10–31).

In the afternoon my great-grandfather hurriedly smoked his last cigar

She moved her hands around the flickering flame of the candles.

before the holiday, then took his *bájtli* (from the German *Beutel*, bag), a velvet bag containing his tallith, and set out for the synagogue. Frigyes bácsi, who was much less religious, frequently stayed home or went only later to join his father on the way home. When it was time for the Sabbath ceremony, my great-grandmother covered her hair with a lace scarf. The children and Frigyes bácsi, if he was not in the temple, gathered at the head of the table around Riza néni and watched as she lit the candles. With a smile of satisfaction on her face, she moved her hands around the flickering flames of the candles as if she wished to embrace all the brightness of the holiday, then covered her eyes and said a benediction to greet the Sabbath.

As my great-grandfather entered, he sang in his raspy voice the traditional song greeting the angels, who, according to the legend, accompanied him on his way home from the synagogue. Standing at the table, he placed his hands first on Frigyes bácsi's then the grandchildren's bowed heads to bless them, then said a kiddush, a blessing, over the wine in the fancily engraved ceremonial beaker. Now, everybody went to the washbasin and poured water over their hands from a two-handled cup that was traditional for this ritual. After they returned to the table, he cut a piece from the end of the challah, broke it into smaller pieces, dipped each into salt, gave one to each member of the family and blessed the challah pieces, too, by saying: "*hamotzi lechem min haretz*" (who brings forth the bread from the earth).

Listening to my secular mother's description of how she stood in front of the ample body of her grandmother during the candle-lighting ceremony and her account of the other details of the holiday, I could sense how much the memory of Sabbath in her grandmother's house meant to her even if she could only recall this fragment of the blessing over the challah.

As they all sat down to eat, Riza néni finally relaxed after all the bustle of the day and enjoyed the conversation and good food. The meal usually started with fish, after which Paula removed all the plates and the cutlery used for it, as they couldn't be used for the rest of the meal. Occasionally, usually in winter, they would have chicken or beef soup (see recipe on page 88) instead of the fish. Roast goose or chicken, which they sometimes stuffed (see recipe on page 229), followed the first course, and potatoes or dumplings went along with them. For dessert they had strudel, cake, or stewed fruit.

Butter Challah

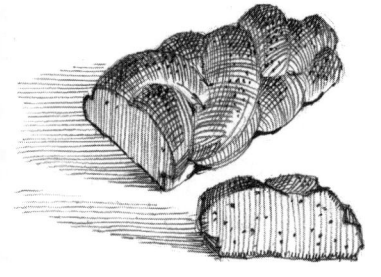

Barches

Challah (Hebrew for "dough"), the holiday bread, plays a most important role in the observance of the Sabbath ritual. It is perhaps the best example of special foods becoming integral parts of Jewish religious festivals. Bread has great symbolic significance in other religions, but Judaism is perhaps unique in its tendency to create symbols out of almost any ordinary act. As Rabbi Harold Kushner puts this: Judaism "is the science of making the mundane holy."

To understand the significance of the Sabbath challah we have to go back about two thousand years to the period prior to the destruction of the Second Temple in Jerusalem. Jews were required to give a portion of their bread dough, a "challah," to the *kohanim* (priests) every Sabbath. In addition, every week twelve loaves of bread, symbolizing the twelve tribes of Israel, were placed in the Temple. These small round and flat loaves were made of unleavened dough, similar to a small pita. After the destruction of the Temple, the home table replaced the altar (in fact, the home is called *mikdash me'at*, a small temple, in Hebrew), and the two loaves of Sabbath bread replaced the twelve loaves required in the Temple. The two loaves are usually thought to represent the double portion of manna gathered for the Sabbath. Manna is the wonderful "bread from heaven" sent by God to feed the Israelites during the years of Exodus, the wandering in the desert. The portion of the bread that used to be given to the kohanim is now burned to avoid the appearance of personally benefiting from it.

The custom of our familiar oval braided challah started when German Jews adopted this popular type of Sunday loaf from local Gentiles as their Sabbath bread. The German Jews called it *berches* or *barches*, which might be a corruption of *broches*, "blessings" in Yiddish. John Cooper cites another explanation in his *Eat and Be Satisfied*: that the name was derived from the first word of a Hebrew phrase frequently engraved on the knives used to cut the Sabbath bread: "The blessings of the Lord, it maketh rich"

(Proverbs 10:22). Hungarian Jews also adopted the name barches, and later it came to mean any similar braided loaf in Hungary, Jewish or not. According to John Cooper, "one of the earliest references to the word berches was contained in the writings of Rabbi Kirchan, who lived at the end of the seventeenth century." In Poland, Russia, Lithuania, and many other areas challah continued to be the name of the Sabbath bread. While the oval-shaped, braided challah became common among Ashkenazi Jews, round Sabbath loaves continued to be baked by the Sephardim. With increasingly affordable sugar in the nineteenth century, sweeter versions of challah became popular, especially in southwestern Poland. On the other hand, most German, Austrian, and Galician (southeastern Poland) Jews continued to prefer a leaner and much less sweet version.

Hungarians and Austrians tend to be very demanding when it comes to the quality of their bread and yeast cake. So it is not surprising that Charles Fleischmann, a young Hungarian Jewish immigrant experienced in brewing and distilling, upon arrival to the United States in 1865 was displeased with the quality of American bread made with unreliable home-brewed starters and leaveners. Bakers in Europe by that time were using a superior type of yeast produced by what was then called the Hungarian method. He formed a partnership with his brother and a local yeast maker to produce yeast. This company was the first to produce compressed baker's yeast, active dry yeast, and quick-acting yeast. Fleischmann's Yeast became a household name and made most American breads and yeast cakes distant cousins to the ones in Hungary.

The following recipe comes from Julia Pollák, Riza néni's best friend in the 1870s and the recipient of some of her letters quoted in the first part of this book. It is about as lean as any challah I have seen, because its dough contains relatively little fat and no eggs. Butter challahs, such as this, were prepared for Saturday breakfasts, for dairy meals at any time during the year, or for the customary dairy meals during Shavuot, a religious festival. For a fleischig version, substitute water for milk and about seven teaspoons peanut oil for three tablespoons butter.

Don't let the lengthy description of how to braid the challah scare you away. Doing it is easier than describing it. Nevertheless, I would suggest practicing it beforehand with pieces of thick string. Try to do this a few hours or a day before attempting your first challah. This is a lot better than doing it when the dough is ready for braiding and the guests are about to arrive expecting the home-made challah you promised them.

YIELD:	1 approximately 13" loaf (1½ pounds) or 2 smaller loaves
TOTAL TIME:	about 4 hours 15 minutes
INGREDIENTS:	1 cup and 1 tablespoon milk
	1 envelope active dry yeast
	1 teaspoon sugar
	3 tablespoons unsalted butter, cut into ½" pieces
	2 teaspoons sugar
	1 teaspoon kosher salt
	3¼ cups unbleached all-purpose flour
	½ teaspoon canola oil
	1 large egg yolk
	1 tablespoon cold water
	1 teaspoon poppy seeds
SPECIAL EQUIPMENT:	food processor, at least 7-cup capacity
	parchment paper or silicone nonstick baking mat
	baking sheet (12" × 18")

1. Warm milk in a small saucepan to barely warm (105–110°F). Make sure the milk isn't warmer than that, because hot liquid kills the yeast culture. Pour ⅓ cup of it into the bowl of the food processor, add yeast and 1 teaspoon sugar; pulse to mix and allow the mixture to ferment for 10 minutes, until small bubbles appear on the surface.

2. To the remaining (about ¾ cup) milk in the saucepan, add butter pieces, 2 teaspoons sugar, and salt. Heat them gently for a few minutes, then remove the saucepan from the heat and wait until the butter dissolves and the liquid cools to barely warm.

3. Add flour to the fermented yeast in the processor. With the machine running, pour in the cooled liquid from the saucepan. Process for 20 seconds, wait 3 minutes, then process for about 10 more seconds until the dough sticks together, cleans the inside of the bowl, and forms a ball.

4. Turn the dough out onto the lightly floured work surface and knead it for about 5 minutes, adding more flour as needed for a smooth and elastic dough that springs back when you make an indentation with your finger. In low humidity, I had to add about 1 tablespoon more flour. Knead by pressing down into the dough with your hands, pushing forward, folding the dough back on itself, giving it a quarter turn, then repeating this sequence.

5. Take a bowl that is deep enough to allow room for the dough to rise. Coat the inside of the bowl with ½ teaspoon canola oil. Shape the dough into a ball, place it in the bowl and roll it around to lightly coat it with the oil. Cover the bowl with plastic wrap or a lid and let the dough rise at room temperature until it doubles in bulk, 1 to 1½ hours.

6. Deflate the risen dough by bringing its outer edges to its center with your hand and pushing down on the dough. Cover the bowl again and allow the dough to rise a second time until it doubles in bulk again, 45 minutes to 1 hour.

7. Deflate the dough again the same way, transfer it to the lightly floured work surface and knead it briefly. Divide it into 4 equal pieces and form each piece into a ball. Cover them with the inverted bowl or with plastic wrap and let them rest for 10 minutes to relax the gluten and make it easier to shape the dough. Shape the balls into ropes about 12" long by rolling them back and forth between your palms and letting the dough hang down. Extend the ropes by rolling not by stretching. Once you have short ropes, finish rolling them on the work surface to about 16" in length and lightly dust them with flour.

8. Lay the 4 ropes perpendicular to the edge of the work surface and about ½" apart; pinch the ropes together at the end furthest away from you. Now start braiding. Take the rope on the far right and pass it over the 2 ropes on its left, then back under the one now on its immediate right. Now do the mirror image of this on the other side: take the rope on the far left and pass it over the 2 ropes on its right, then back under the one now on its immediate left. Continue doing this on alternating sides, always working with the outside ropes. Braiding should be neither too loose nor too tight. Be careful not to stretch the dough.

When you have finished braiding, pinch the ends together and gently tuck both ends of the loaf under so you cannot see the pinched ends. Gently push the loaf with your hands from both ends to slightly compact it and make it higher in the center.

9. Line a baking sheet with parchment paper or nonstick mat, transfer the braided loaf to it, cover it with a flour-dusted kitchen towel, place it in a warm, draft-free place, and let it rise for 1 hour. Center a rack in the oven and preheat the oven to 375°F. In a cup or small bowl, mix egg yolk with water and brush the loaf with this mixture. Sprinkle it lightly with poppy seeds. Reserve the remaining egg-water mixture.

10. Bake it for 20 minutes. Take the baking sheet out, but don't turn off the oven. Some of the inner dough will be exposed, because the loaf has expanded in the oven. Brush these newly exposed parts with the remaining egg wash and put the challah back into the oven to bake for 15 to 20 minutes longer, until it is golden brown and sounds hollow when you tap it on the bottom. Transfer it to a rack to cool for about 1 hour before slicing it. Reduce baking time if you decide to make 2 small loaves instead of 1 large one.

11. Once cut, it should be kept in a plastic bag, where it will keep for 2 days. You can also freeze it. The tightly wrapped loaf in a sealed plastic bag will keep in the freezer for several months. Thaw it in the bag at room temperature. Stale challah makes excellent French toast or bread pudding.

Poached Carp in Vinegary Broth with Horseradish

Heiszgesottener Karpfen

For practical and symbolic reasons fish dishes have always played a prominent role in Jewish cooking. Eating shellfish or fish that doesn't have scales and fins is forbidden, but otherwise Jewish dietary laws make fewer restrictions on cooking or eating fish than for meat and dairy products. Fish doesn't have to be ritually slaughtered and salted like meat. In addition, it can be eaten at the same meal with either meat or dairy dishes, although it must precede the meat dish and cannot be put on the same plate with meat. Several of the traditional fish preparations are eaten cold, which makes it easier to serve them during Sabbath when one cannot light a fire. But there are also symbolic reasons for the ancient custom of serving fish, usually as the first course, on Friday night at the first Sabbath meal. Close to two thousand years ago, during the Talmudic age, a fish course was one of the highlights of the Friday evening meal. Both the Mishnah and the Talmud refer to the close connection between Sabbath and eating fish. According to tradition, Sabbath gives us a foretaste of the Messianic age when the tranquillity of Sabbath will be universal. If all the Jews could keep the Sabbath completely, the Messiah would come. When that happens the righteous will join the Messiah in a new world order and feast on the flesh of the giant fish, the leviathan. Fish is also prominent at other holiday meals, especially on Yom Kippur, Purim, and Shavuot.

The Jewish tradition of eating freshwater fish came from Eastern European Jews who lived in landlocked areas. In those areas, one could only get locally caught fresh fish, of which carp and pike became the most common in Jewish cooking. It was usually kept for Sabbath and other holidays, while pickled or cooked cured herring, which in many places was cheaper than fresh fish, was eaten on weekdays as well.

Riza néni probably bought fish for the Sabbath at the town market. One of her former neighbors told me that in the 1930s Árpád Gróf, a Jewish fishmonger, sold fish every Thursday from a bag at the market. Jewish fishmongers used to be quite common in Hungary and also in Poland and

Russia. In many regions Jews were involved in fish farming. As Claudia Roden wrote in *The Book of Jewish Food*, "Carp was associated with Jews because Jewish traders on the silk route were involved in introducing carp from China to Central and Eastern Europe in the seventeenth century, and it was Jews who first farmed carp in Poland. They managed fishponds and also bred fish from the Black, Azov, and Caspian seas and from the river Don. It was carp, which traveled easily live in tanks, that they adopted as their fish."

Carp was usually sold live from tanks, crates, or even bags, where it can survive for a few hours. People took the live carp home in a bag and kept it for a day or so in clean water in their bathtub. Carp lives in ponds or slow-moving rivers and occasionally acquires a slightly musty taste from muddy water, which one can get rid of in the clear water at home. Keeping a live carp in the bathtub is not so common these days; but even in the 1950s, much after Riza néni's time, I recall sharing our bathroom in Budapest with a carp for a day. I loved the strange but jolly sight of the carp swimming happily in our bathtub.

These days, the carp one can buy is almost always farmed fish in the five- to eight-pound range, available at a reasonable price as a whole fish or steaks. Only in a few fish stores or in Chinatown can one buy it live. The firm-textured flesh of this meaty fish has excellent delicate flavor, especially between November and April, when the water is cold. Carp has many small bones and, contrary to the recommendation of several Hungarian cookbooks, I wouldn't suggest filleting it. The bones give flavor and it is almost impossible to extricate all of them. If you can find live carp, buy it, but I have had such good luck with killed fish that I don't take the time to go to Chinatown for live carp. I recommend buying a whole fish, which is much cheaper per pound than steaks. Choose a plump fish with a thick body, which is the most likely to have roe or milt. Even if you can find fish weighing less than five pounds, don't buy it, because the larger fish is easier to eat, as it has less closely spaced bones. Like all fish, it shouldn't be kept long, but if you must, you can keep it in the refrigerator for a day or two in a plastic bag set in a large bowl filled with ice cubes. Freeze the head and the tail, which are not used in this recipe, for later use in fish stock or jellied fish, such as pike in sour aspic (see recipe on page 225).

I am very fond of Riza néni's poached carp recipe. From her options of either poaching the fish in one piece or cut into pieces, I chose the latter method. I happen to have a fish poacher, but unless it is for some festive party where the impressive looks of the whole fish matter, I find it much more convenient to poach the carp in slices. This way I can fit the pieces snugly into a large sauté pan or other large-diameter pan and poach them in the least amount of liquid, which gives the best-flavored sauce. I suspect she made her own vinegar, but regardless of whether she did so or bought it in the store, it was milder than the kind available today. Unfortunately, I can only guess how much milder and had to use my judgment to adjust the water to vinegar ratio. She used the unaltered cooking liquid as the sauce, but I decided to add a little butter to it. If you don't want to use butter, you can use the broth straight, just as she used to do, or add a little oil. Alternatively, you can thicken the sauce by stirring in half a teaspoon of potato starch or cornstarch, dissolved in one tablespoon of cold water, and turning off the heat as soon as the sauce comes back to a boil and thickens. I don't know whether this dish was served hot or cold on Friday night, but, as it was the first course, it shouldn't have been difficult to keep it warm until mealtime. I prefer to eat it warm, but like most poached fish it is also good cold. If you serve it cold, omit the potatoes and spoon some gelled broth around the fish. Eat it with good crusty bread.

YIELD: 4 or 5 servings

TOTAL TIME: about 1 hour 15 minutes

INGREDIENTS:
- 4 carp steaks, each about 1½" thick, about 2 pounds total weight. After cleaning it and cutting off its head and tail, the 5-pound carp I used gave me 5 such steaks weighing 2¾ pounds total. I decided to use all 5 steaks in this dish, but you might decide to freeze the extra steak for later use.
- 1 teaspoon kosher salt (to salt the fish)
- 6 cups water (or enough to cover the fish)
- ½ cup distilled white or white wine vinegar
- 1 medium onion (4 to 5 ounces), peeled and thinly sliced
- 8 strips of lemon peel, removed with a vegetable peeler and cut into narrow julienne strips
- 2 cloves

¾ teaspoon black peppercorns, coarsely crushed with
  the bottom of a heavy skillet
½ teaspoon whole allspice berries, coarsely crushed
½ teaspoon dried thyme
½ teaspoon kosher salt
2 bay leaves
1 celery stalk cut into 3" to 4" pieces
3 parsley sprigs, tied in a bundle with the celery
  stalks and the bay leaves
3 large or 4 medium Yukon Gold potatoes, about
  1½ pounds
1 tablespoon unsalted butter
1 piece of horseradish, about 3" long, cut into very
  thin long slices with a vegetable peeler
2 tablespoons chopped chives
7 chive blades, cut into halves (to about 4")
8 thin slices of lemon

SPECIAL
EQUIPMENT: 10" or 12" sauté pan or similar wide pan

1. Sprinkle the fish slices with salt, place them on a plate, cover with plastic, and refrigerate for 30 minutes to 2 hours.

2. Select a wide pan to accommodate all the slices in 1 layer, with little room to spare; a large sauté pan is ideal. Place the slices in and add enough water to cover by about ¼". Transfer the slices back to the plate, but leave the water in the pan. To the water, add vinegar, onion, lemon peel, cloves, crushed peppercorns and allspice berries, thyme, salt, and the bundle of celery, parsley, and bay leaves. Bring it to a boil, reduce heat, and simmer for about 20 minutes.

3. Rinse the potatoes, place them in a saucepan, add water to cover by about 1", and bring it to a boil. Reduce heat to medium, and gently simmer uncovered for 25 to 30 minutes, or until the potatoes are tender. Pour off the water, cover the saucepan, and set it aside to cool. When the potatoes are cool enough to handle, pull off their skins and cut them into ⅜" slices. Place them on a plate and keep them warm in the 180°F oven. Place 4 dinner plates in the oven.

4. Pour the broth and everything that cooked with it into a bowl. Discard the bundle of parsley, celery, and bay leaves. Place the fish slices in 1 layer in the pan and return the hot broth, onion, and so forth to cover the fish. Add a little water, if necessary. Bring the broth to a boil, then reduce the heat so that the liquid barely simmers. Make sure the fish slices stay completely submerged. After 15 minutes of simmering, gently lift them out with a slotted wide spatula or lifter and transfer them to a large plate or platter. You have to lift the fish slices carefully, because they are very fragile. Put the plate with the slices into the oven to keep warm until serving time.

5. Ladle enough fish broth from the pan into a bowl to leave about 2 cups of liquid and all the onion in the pan. Let the bowl of broth cool, cover and refrigerate it for later use. Boil the remaining liquid in the pan rapidly over high heat until it is reduced to about 1 cup. Taste it and, if necessary, adjust the seasoning by adding a little salt or, if you find it too sour, a little sugar. Mix in the butter and let it melt.

6. At serving time, place about 5 slices of potato in 1 layer in the middle of a prewarmed dinner plate to create a platform. Ladle a little sauce on top and lay 4 strips of horseradish over the potatoes. Place a fish steak on top of the horseradish slices and ladle more sauce over the fish. Sprinkle the fish with chopped chives and lean a few stalks of chive against it. Garnish it with slices of lemon and serve immediately.

7. If you have to reheat leftovers, first bring the reserved 3 or 4 cups of broth to a boil, then put the fish slices and potatoes into it briefly to reheat. Store and reheat the sauce separately in a small saucepan.

Pike in Sour Aspic
Gesulzte Fische

Cold poached fish, usually made from carp or pike and served in its own aspic, was another traditional dish frequently prepared for the Sabbath. Its aspic in Poland was usually sweetened with sugar and could include almonds and raisins, while an elegant Russian version was made with white wine. But in its most common form the aspic was flavored with herbs, root vegetables, and perhaps a little vinegar in addition to the obligatory onions and fish bones, which were necessary for the gelling of the aspic.

Riza néni's recipe is quite unusual, because even if I consider that she used milder vinegar than is customary today, her aspic is more sour than any version I have seen. Some Austrian versions and the "Scharfe Fish" in Mimi Sheraton's *From My Mother's Kitchen* are somewhat similar, but none are as tart as Riza néni's. I like it a lot; it would be a great first course at any time of the year, and its refreshing tartness makes it most appropriate for a cold lunch in summer.

Pike is a freshwater predator fish. It is easily recognizable by its slim body, long pointed head, large mouth, and lots of ferocious-looking teeth. For centuries its lean, firm, and low-fat white flesh has been popular in most European countries. According to the *Larousse Gastronomique*, it used to be raised in the Louvre fish ponds for the French royal table. In Jewish cooking, too, it has been one of the most popular fish. Gefilte fish is frequently made of pike, and pike in walnut sauce (see recipe on page 315) has been a traditional dish in both Jewish and Gentile cooking in Hungary. There are several varieties of fish in the pike family. The most common kinds available in the United States are the northern pike, weighing usually three to five pounds, and the slightly smaller walleyed pike, also called yellow pike or pike perch. To be absolutely correct, the walleyed pike is a pike only in name as it belongs to the perch family. Pike is occasionally available in some of the better fish stores, such as New York City's Citarella, but at most places it is only available before Rosh Hashanah and some of the other Jewish holidays. At other times your safest bet is to look in Jewish neighborhoods, such as the Russian Jewish neighborhood of Brighton Beach in New York City. When buying pike, look for one with bright silvery rather than brownish scales and for a fairly large fish, because its bones will be less closely spaced.

In adapting Riza néni's recipe I decided to simplify her technique of preparation, which I thought was unnecessarily complicated. As Chef Louis Szathmáry wrote in one of his cookbooks, "Never forget that people don't eat methods; they enjoy results." After cooking the vegetables and the fish, my great-grandmother removed the fish, puréed the sauce, and then clarified it with egg whites. Considering that the pulp in the liquid will be eliminated when it is clarified, I see no advantage to puréeing the sauce as opposed to simply straining it. The vegetables and the fish have already transmitted much of their flavor and natural gelatin to the stock during cooking; puréeing cannot appreciably intensify the flavor or make the stock gel better. Her suggestion of clarifying the stock is more logical, because it produces a prettier aspic, but if you have a fine strainer and find that the speed of preparation is more important than the clarity of the aspic, you may decide to skip this step, too.

I used some leftover carp pieces from my freezer in addition to the head and backbone of the pike to prepare the aspic and even with no gelatin added it gelled beautifully, as it should have. Nevertheless, if you want to be absolutely sure that the aspic gels properly, I suggest adding a small amount of gelatin to the stock. This dish can also be prepared with carp or whitefish.

YIELD: 6 to 8 servings

TOTAL TIME: about 2 hours, plus at least 12 hours refrigeration

INGREDIENTS:
- 1 pike weighing about 4 pounds; ask the fishmonger to clean it and to remove the head, tail, and backbone, provided that you don't want to do this yourself. Save the removed parts.
- 2 teaspoons kosher salt
- 6 large onions (about 2 pounds), sliced
- 15 black peppercorns, coarsely crushed with the bottom of a heavy skillet
- 3 bay leaves
- 1 lemon, the zest removed in strips with a vegetable peeler

2½ quarts water
1 cup apple cider vinegar (the original recipe used even more)
2 large carrots, cleaned and sliced
2 envelopes (½ ounce) unflavored gelatin (optional; see page 261 for information about pareve kosher gelatin)
2 large egg whites
1 small, narrow green pepper (optional), seeds and veins removed through the stem end, and sliced crosswise into very thin (⅛") unbroken rings (for decoration)

SPECIAL
EQUIPMENT: 9½" × 14" × 2" Pyrex glass dish or a porcelain or pottery baking dish of about the same area

1. Although Riza néni left the backbone in, I suggest removing it, if you can do this neatly before slicing the fish; but don't bother removing the small bones: it would make a mess of the flesh. Use a sharp, narrow knife and scissors to remove the backbone. I prefer to do this myself, but if it seems to be too much of a task for you, ask the fishmonger to do it or leave the backbone in the fish. If the backbone is removed, keep it for the stock. Cut the fish into 1" slices, salt the slices, put them on a plate, cover with plastic wrap, and refrigerate for 30 minutes to 2 hours. Place the empty baking dish in the refrigerator.

2. Place onions, peppercorns, bay leaves, strips of lemon zest, together with the head, tail, and backbone of the fish in a large stainless steel pot. Add water and vinegar, bring it to a boil, lower heat, and simmer for ½ hour. Strain it through a fine-mesh strainer into a bowl, press the solids with a large wooden spoon to extract as much liquid as possible, and discard the solids. Pour the strained stock back into the pot.

3. Add carrots to the stock, bring it back to a boil, lower heat, and simmer for 5 minutes. Add the fish slices, return it to a boil, then reduce heat to low and gently simmer for 10 more minutes. Transfer the fish to a plate, strain the stock into a large bowl, and place the carrots on another plate. Place the plates with the fish and carrots in the refriger-

ator until they are thoroughly chilled. Taste the stock and adjust the seasoning. Riza néni used even more vinegar in her recipe; you can also add more but for me this seemed about right. Conversely, her recipe also suggests adding a little sugar if one feels the stock is too sour.

4. Place the optional gelatin and the egg whites in a large saucepan. Add about ¼ cup cold water and mix them well. Then add the stock, mix well, and bring it to a boil while mixing frequently to keep the ingredients in suspension. As soon as the mixture comes to a strong boil, stop stirring, reduce heat to low, and gently simmer for 10 minutes, making sure that you don't shake or disturb the pot.

5. Remove the pot from the heat and let it stand undisturbed for 15 minutes. Line a large strainer or colander with paper towels and carefully strain the stock into a stainless steel bowl. Place it in the refrigerator to chill until it gets syrupy, but don't allow it to gel. Or chill it by placing the bowl of stock into a larger bowl filled with ice cubes and slowly stirring the stock until it becomes syrupy.

6. Remove the well-chilled baking dish, carrots, fish, and stock from the refrigerator. Ladle a little stock into the dish and allow it to gel in a thin layer on the bottom. If the stock doesn't want to gel, place the dish back in the refrigerator for a short while. Distribute the fish slices over the layer of gelled stock in the dish, place carrot slices around them and rings of green pepper on top of them. Ladle enough chilled stock into the dish to cover the fish.

7. Refrigerate it for at least 12 hours. Serve the fish on chilled plates surrounded by its own aspic and some of the sliced carrots. Eat it with good crusty bread.

Chicken or Squab Stuffed under the Skin
Gefüllte Hühner und Tauben

This tasty stuffed chicken, in which the stuffing under the skin subtly flavors the meat and helps to keep the breast meat moist, might well have been one of the dishes Riza néni served for the first Sabbath meal on Friday evening. Though, as usual, she didn't specify quantities for some of the ingredients, this is one of the more detailed recipes in her collection, and I adapted it virtually unchanged for the modern kitchen. The only change I made was, that instead of cutting the skin on the breast and sewing it closed after stuffing the chicken, as she suggested, I spoon the stuffing under the skin, which has been loosened but not cut. This way it is not necessary to sew the skin closed.

YIELD: 4 servings

TOTAL TIME: about 1 hour 40 minutes

INGREDIENTS:
- 1 chicken, about 3½ pounds
- 1 tablespoon canola oil (or rendered chicken fat)
- ½ cup chopped onion
- ⅔ cup bread crumbs (made in the food processor from 2–3 slices of stale white bread)
- 4 tablespoons fresh parsley, coarsely chopped
- 1½ teaspoons finely chopped fresh ginger (or ¾ teaspoon ground ginger)
- 1 pinch kosher salt
- ¼ teaspoon freshly ground black pepper
- ½ teaspoon sweet paprika, preferably Hungarian
- ½ large egg
- ¼ teaspoon kosher salt (for sprinkling on the chicken)

SPECIAL
EQUIPMENT: "Regency" professional reusable parchment or regular parchment paper
heavy roasting pan or 12" skillet
baking sheet

1. Cut the wings at the "elbow" joint leaving only the first meaty section. Place the chicken on its back and lift up the skin at the neck. Slide a sharp paring knife along each side and the top of the V-shaped wishbone and pry it out by hooking your fingers behind it near the top.

2. Remove the lumps of fat from inside the cavity and some of the loose skin around the cavity openings. Cut this into small pieces. Heat 1 tablespoon oil or previously rendered chicken fat in a saucepan, put the removed lumps of chicken fat and skin in the saucepan, and sauté them over medium heat, stirring occasionally, for about 10 minutes until the fat is rendered and the skin is golden brown. Strain the fat into a bowl and reserve the cracklings for another use, such as sprinkling them over a salad or eating them with bread as a snack. If you are in a hurry, omit this step and use oil or margarine instead of rendered fat in the filling and for brushing on the chicken.

3. Spoon 3 tablespoons of rendered chicken fat back into the saucepan (or place oil or margarine in a skillet) and heat it until the fat is hot but not smoking. Add chopped onion and sauté it over medium heat for 4 minutes. Add bread crumbs and cook, stirring occasionally, for another 4 minutes, until bread crumbs are light-medium brown. Add chopped parsley, ginger, and seasonings; cook them for 1 more minute. Set the mixture aside to cool slightly.

4. Place the chicken on its back and insert your finger between the skin and the flesh at the neck opening. Gently push in your hand to loosen the skin around the breast and on the sides of the chicken, being careful not to puncture the skin. Continue pushing your fingers into the thighs, too. Do not loosen the skin on the back.

5. Adjust a rack to the lower third of the oven and preheat the oven to 425°F. Thoroughly mix egg into the cooled stuffing. Stand the

chicken with the neck opening up in a large (1 quart) measuring cup or bowl, and stuff it by spooning the bread crumb mixture between the skin and the flesh. Use your hand to distribute the stuffing evenly around the breast and the sides. Lay the chicken on its back and finish distributing the stuffing, pushing some into the thighs, too.

6. Use a 30" piece of cotton kitchen twine to truss the chicken. Place the chicken on its back. Slide the twine under the tail end of the chicken and bring the ends of the twine up next to the tips of the drumsticks. Then cross the twine above the chicken and slide both ends of the twine under the tips of the drumsticks to create a figure X. Pull the ends of the twine to pull the legs together. Make sure that the legs are pulled snugly against the chicken in order to push the breast up.

7. Bring each end of the twine around the sides of the chicken, over the wings, and over the neck end. The twine should go over the neck bone to prevent it from slipping off the chicken. Tuck the hanging skin of the neck under the twine. Turn the chicken on its side, tighten the twine, and tie a knot on one side of the chicken to secure the trussing.

8. Brush the skin of the chicken with some of the remaining rendered fat (or oil or margarine) and sprinkle it with ¼ teaspoon salt. I like to place an 8" square piece of "Regency" professional reusable parchment (not paper but a thin fabric with a nonstick coating, it comes in a 13" × 17" sheet from which one can cut any size piece) in the pan under the chicken. It is great because it never sticks to the skin. But you can also use an approximately 8"-square piece of regular parchment paper, which you generously coat with chicken fat. In either case, place the parchment in a heavy-bottomed aluminum roasting pan or large skillet, placed on a baking sheet to catch some of the inevitable splattering. Place the chicken on its side on the parchment.

9. Roast the chicken for 25 minutes lying on one side, then with the help of an oven mitt turn it to its other side. (I don't like to use kitchen tongs to turn the chicken because they tend to tear the skin.) Roast it on the second side for an additional 25 minutes. Finally, turn it on its back, baste it, and allow it to cook for another 10 minutes. By now, the chicken has cooked for a total of 1 hour. Lift up the chicken and pour

the juice from the cavity into a cup or small bowl. The chicken is done when the juice is clear without any trace of pink.

10. Remove the chicken from the oven, turn the oven thermostat down to 150°F, and leave the oven door open for a few minutes. Transfer the chicken, breast side down, to a platter and place it uncovered to rest in the oven for 15 minutes.

11. Scrape off the solidified juices from the parchment and save the reusable parchment, if that is what you used. Tip the roasting pan or skillet, pour off as much fat from the top of the juices as possible, add a little white wine, vermouth, chicken stock, or water, and bring to a boil. Scrape up all the solidified juices from the bottom and pour the juices and drippings into a cup.

12. Remove the trussing twine and carve the chicken, giving each person a piece of thigh or drumstick and a piece of the breast. Spoon some of the juices over the meat. Riza néni recommends serving it with fresh peas, green beans, or new potatoes, but I think it would also be terrific with a green salad, perhaps Boston lettuce or watercress, using some of the remaining chicken fat in the dressing and sprinkling chicken cracklings on top.

Chestnut Torte
Kastanien Torte

I am glad that Riza néni's collection includes a chestnut torte, because even such a personal compilation of recipes with no claim to comprehensiveness couldn't give a fair idea of Austro-Hungarian baking without at least one dessert made with chestnuts. In the United States, imported chestnuts are widely available for quite reasonable prices during fall and winter. We typically eat them roasted, or cooked with vegetables such as Brussels sprouts, or use them in turkey or game dishes, perhaps in savory soups, but rarely in desserts. I don't know the reason for this neglect, because this naturally sweet, starchy nut lends itself so well to desserts. Chestnut desserts can be found in France and Italy, but certainly not the seemingly endless variety invented by Hungarian and Austrian pastry chefs. There, in any self-respecting pastry shop, one finds chestnut balls, sausages, loafs, pyramids, all made of chestnut purée, sponge cake rolls or pastry crescents with chestnut filling, and cups filled with layers of riced chestnut purée and whipped cream. But the most inventive use of chestnut is in the flourless, or nearly flourless, tortes, such as this recipe. These tortes, in which chestnut replaces flour, benefit from both its wonderful flavor and starchy quality.

When buying chestnuts, select large, relatively heavy pieces; avoid any with a small hole, the telltale sign of a worm. The main obstacle to using chestnuts in cooking or baking is not availability, nor price, but the task of cleaning them, a nuisance job, if there ever was one. Different cookbooks tout different methods, each claiming its own method to be fast and easy. I tried most of them, and I am afraid the only easy way is to open a can of puréed chestnuts. But while chestnuts are not expensive, canned purée is pricey, and the quality is rarely as good as the homemade one. Using the following method, somewhat less frustrating than most others, I can clean a pound of chestnuts in about twenty minutes, not counting the time required for roasting the nuts. The surest way to keep up your spirits while cleaning the nuts is to think of the wonderful flavor of chestnut purée. I usually clean about one-and-a-half or two pounds of chestnuts at a time, because it takes almost the same amount of time to clean and purée this larger amount than to do only one pound. The leftover purée can be used for some other dessert or savory dish. You can cook and purée the chestnuts a few days before making the torte, because tightly wrapped puréed chestnut will keep for about a week in the refrigerator. Store leftover purée in the freezer for up to two months.

Though Riza néni's original recipe used chestnuts in place of most of the flour in the dough, it also included a small amount of flour. I decided to replace the flour with ground almonds, because this made her almost flourless torte a real member of this fabulous group of Austrian desserts. The small quantity of ground almonds will not change the flavor of her torte, which will be still dominated by the chestnuts. The only other change was that I substituted whipped cream for the whipped egg whites she had used for the filling. She probably used whipped egg whites in order to avoid using cream in a torte served as part of a fleischig meal. I prefer the taste and mouth-feel of whipped cream and wished to avoid the risk, however small, of eating uncooked egg whites.

YIELD: 12 servings

TOTAL TIME: about 3 hours 35 minutes, plus up to a day drying time before slicing the torte into layers

INGREDIENTS:
- 1 pound fresh chestnuts (about 30 large, plump pieces)
- 5 large egg yolks
- ⅓ cup sugar
- 1½ teaspoons vanilla extract
- 1 tablespoon dark rum (optional; it wasn't in the original)
- 1 teaspoon grated lemon zest
- ½ cup whole blanched almonds
- 2 tablespoons sugar
- 6 large egg whites
- ½ teaspoon cream of tartar
- 1 tablespoon sugar
- ½ pint (1 small carton) heavy cream, preferably not ultra-pasteurized (you can usually find it in health food stores)
- 1 package "Whip it," manufactured by Oetker (optional)
- 2 tablespoons sugar, preferably confectioners' sugar
- ¼ cup sugar (for the chestnut in the filling)
- ½ teaspoon vanilla extract (for the chestnut in the filling)
- 1 tablespoon dark rum (for the chestnut in the filling)

SPECIAL EQUIPMENT: baking sheet

food mill
9" spring form
food processor
electric mixer (optional)

1. It is best to bake this torte the day before, but to put off filling it until shortly before serving. Preheat oven to 400°F. Holding a sharp paring knife by its blade, so that only about 1" of the blade sticks out, cut with the point of the knife an "X" into the flat side of each chestnut. The blade should penetrate the chestnut only about ¼" to cut through the shell and inner skin. Place the chestnuts on a baking sheet and bake them in the preheated oven for 30 minutes. Remove them but don't turn off the oven.

2. Hold a hot chestnut by a kitchen towel and with your other hand split off its outer shell and inner skin. The chestnuts must be still quite hot, otherwise it will be much harder to clean them. If they get too cool and you have trouble pealing off their inner skin, put them back into the oven for a short time. On most pieces this inner skin will come off easily, but there are always a few recalcitrant ones. Sometimes the inner skin penetrates between the lobes of the chestnut. Try to poke it out, but if you cannot remove every last bit, don't worry, most of them will float to the surface of the cooking water and the food mill will keep any remaining piece out of the purée. Cut off any moldy, blackened or otherwise damaged parts of the chestnuts. Turn off the oven.

3. Place all the cleaned chestnuts in a medium saucepan and add enough water to barely cover them. Bring to a boil, lower heat, skim off the few bits of inner skin that float to the surface, and simmer for about 1¼ hours. The chestnuts will absorb some water, so you must add a little water a few times while cooking them. The object is to cook them in the least amount of water possible, without burning them.

4. Drain the chestnuts. I like to drink the little remaining cooking water, which has a nice chestnut flavor. This is the cook's bonus. Press the still hot and moist chestnuts through the fine screen of a food mill into a large bowl. It is easier and faster to do this in small batches. You will end up with about 4 cups (1 pound) of riced chestnuts. The absorbed

water makes the cooked chestnuts weigh about the same as the unshelled ones.

5. Center a rack in the oven and preheat the oven to 350°F. Butter and flour the spring form.

6. With an electric mixer or by hand beat egg yolks with ⅓ cup sugar until the mixture turns very pale and becomes fluffy. Mix in vanilla, rum, lemon zest, and 2½ cups of riced chestnuts. Process the almonds and 2 tablespoons of sugar in the food processor until the almonds are finely ground. Stir this into the egg yolk mixture.

7. Whip egg whites and cream of tartar to form soft peaks, add 1 tablespoon sugar and continue whipping until they form firm peaks. Stir about ⅓ of the whipped egg whites into the egg yolk mixture to lighten it, then with a rubber spatula gently fold in the rest.

8. Pour the dough into the buttered and floured spring form, even out the top surface with the rubber spatula, and bake it in the preheated oven for 50 to 60 minutes. During the first 10 minutes of baking, prop the oven door slightly open by wedging a knife or spoon behind it. The torte will be ready when its edges start to pull away from the side of the form and the top of the cake springs back when poked with a finger. Don't overbake.

9. Run a paring knife between the cake and the side of the spring form, then remove the side ring of the form and allow the torte to cool on a cooling rack. When the torte has cooled, run a long narrow knife or spatula under the torte to separate it from the metal base of the form, and slide the cake onto a 9"-round cardboard or a large flat serving plate. If, as usual, the bottom side of the torte is more even than the top, turn it upside down. Cover it with a kitchen towel and keep it at room temperature until cutting it into layers and filling it.

10. If possible, wait a day to cut the cake into 2 layers. Insert a 10" or 12" serrated knife horizontally into the cake, hold the knife stationary and level, and place your other hand on the cake to rotate it. Don't remove the blade until the cutting is complete.

11. Shortly before you intend to serve the cake, pour the very cold heavy cream and the optional "Whip it" into a well-chilled bowl and whip them to soft peaks, add the confectioners' sugar, and continue whipping to get firm peaks. Don't over-whip or the cream will turn into butter. ("Whip it," manufactured in Canada by Oetker and available in some delicatessen stores in the United States, helps whipped cream keep its shape longer.) In a little bowl, mix the remaining (about 1½ cups) riced chestnut with ¼ cup sugar, ½ teaspoon vanilla, and 1 tablespoon rum. Spread about ⅓ of the whipped cream on the bottom layer of the cake and evenly strew it with about ⅓ of the chestnut mix. Cover it with the top layer and spread the remaining whipped cream over the sides and the top of the torte. Make 12 little balls, each about ¾" diameter, from the remaining chestnut mix and distribute them evenly along the perimeter of the torte. You probably will have a little chestnut purée and whipped cream left; put them in a cup as a bonus dessert for the cook. Preferably, serve the torte soon after filling it, but leftovers will keep for another day in the refrigerator. After that, the whipped cream will not keep its form, especially if you didn't add "Whip it" to the cream. I used "Whip it" and the leftover slices of my torte were still presentable the day after, although the whipped cream seemed to get a little denser and drier.

VARIATION:

If you wish to prepare the cake with an icing that retains its looks longer than whipped cream or want to avoid using dairy products in the torte, fill it with apricot jam and cover it with a shiny chocolate glaze. Decorate it with little balls of chestnut purée or purée shaped to look like unshelled chestnuts and dipped into melted chocolate to complete the illusion.

Saturday Mornings and Lunches

On Saturday morning, Paula lit the stove to warm both the milk for breakfast and the food for lunch. Sabbath breakfast was similar to what my great-grandmother's family ate weekdays, only they had butter challah (see recipe on page 215) instead of bread with their coffee. Riza néni then accompanied her husband to the synagogue and once in a while my mother went along, too, to play with the other children in the synagogue courtyard. My great-grandmother, who was religious but not quite as strict in such matters as my great-grandfather, would occasionally skip Saturday services after her husband's death. But even when she went with him to the temple, she would return before the end of the long Saturday morning service for house cleaning.

Riza néni didn't sew or allow the children to climb the tree in the garden on Saturdays, but strangely she didn't mind that the big weekly house cleaning in her house was done on that day. Paula did most of it, but Riza néni helped, too. Somehow she didn't consider this to be work or thought that it was permissible as long as they carried the furniture only to the porch, which was still part of her house. She probably also thought this was a practical day for the house cleaning, because on Saturday they had more time, as they couldn't shop or cook. However she rationalized it, it is a fact that all the chairs were carried out from the formal living and dining rooms to the arcade facing the courtyard. They cleaned these rarely used rooms only once a week, though they cleaned the other rooms every day.

The main dish for Saturday lunches in my great-grandparents' house was usually *cholent* (see the following recipe), cooked in the oven of their wood-burning stove on Friday and heated up on Saturday. My mother especially loved the *halsli* (see recipe on page 244), the stuffed goose neck, which was frequently cooked in the same pot as the cholent. Sometimes it was filled with meat, but my mother liked it most when it was filled with a mixture of semolina, flour, onions, paprika, and lots of goose fat. Occasionally, whole eggs and onions were cooked in the cholent, which colored them brown. Frequently, they also had *kugel*—a savory or slightly sweet one to go along with the cholent or served as a separate course. Made in a traditional kugel form, which looked a bit like a wide but not too deep flowerpot. Of the kugels, my mother's favorites were Riza néni's slightly sweet bread kugel with apples and raisins in it and the sweeter apple kugel. Usually there was cake, too. Great-grandmother baked wonderful cakes. Her apple torte, meringue torte, lemon-almond torte, and potato torte were all terrific. (See pages 255–267 for the kugel and torte recipes.)

Cholent
Bohnen Scholet

Cholent, an ancient Jewish dish, was created to satisfy two seemingly conflicting requirements: though the Bible mandates that "You shall kindle no fire throughout your habitations upon the Sabbath day," it is at the same time a *mitzvah*, a religious obligation, to eat a hot meal on Saturday. A hint at the solution to this dilemma was given by the Mishnah, the third-century codification of the oral law. It suggests, according to a phrase that was incorporated into the Friday evening service, that hot foods should be covered before the arrival of the Sabbath to retain their heat. The Hebrew phrase for this was *tomnin et ha'hamin* and throughout the Diaspora most of the names for the Sabbath stew are translations of the words "hot" or "covered" from this. The Sephardim call it *hamin*, from the Hebrew word for hot, or *dafina*, which comes from the Arabic word for covered. In Morocco it is called *skhena*, which also means hot. The Ashkenazim call it cholent or *shalet*, probably both from *chauld*, the Old French word for hot. To make it, the food is at least partially cooked in a tightly sealed pot on Friday before the onset of the Sabbath and it usually finishes cooking overnight in very low heat that is not adjusted after the arrival of the Sabbath. The cooking process is the essential feature of this dish, not the specific ingredients, though at least the main ingredient is common to most versions: fresh or dried legumes. Cholent was usually made with chickpeas and meat in the Sephardi world and with dried beans and meat among the Ashkenazim, to which grains, potatoes, and whole hard-cooked eggs could be added.

According to John Cooper, "Among the Ashkenazim the first reference to the Sabbath stew, cholent, was by Rabbi Isaac of Vienna (1180–1250) . . . who reported what he had witnessed in his teacher's home at the end of the twelfth century in France." By the fifteenth century the cholent tradition was already quite similar to that in the nineteenth and early twentieth century. To quote again John Cooper, "The disciples of Rabbi Israel Isserlein (1390–1460) described how Jews in fifteenth-century Austria brought cholent to the bakery on a Friday afternoon, where it was slowly cooked in an oven until collected by an aide or a child for the midday meal on the Sabbath."

Jewish literature reflects the significance of cholent in the Sabbath tradition. For writers, like for all Jewish people, waking up to the fabulous aroma of cholent baking in the oven signified the traditional Jewish home, and the mere thought of it could instantly recall the festive atmosphere of Sabbath. Heinrich Heine (1797–1856), the great German Jewish poet, wrote: "Börne [German Jewish writer, 1786–1837] assures me that, no sooner will the renegades who go over to the new faith get a whiff of schalet than they'll begin to feel homesick again for the synagogue." This didn't keep Heine, a complicated man full of ambiguities, from becoming a Protestant. Even wittier is his parody of Schiller's "Ode to Joy" (An die Freude) included in the poem "Princess Sabbath" (Prinzessin Sabbat), an affectionate and at the same time ironic retelling of the Sabbath:

> Schalet, schöner Götterfunken,
> Tochter aus Elysium!
> Also klänge Schillers Hochlied,
> Hätt er Schalet je gekostet.
> Schalet ist die Himmelspeise
> Die der liebe Herrgott selber
> Einst den Moses kochen lehrte
> Auf dem Berge Sinai...
> Schalet ist des wahren Gottes
> Koscheres Ambrosia...

(Cholent, beautiful divine spark, maiden from Elysium! That is how Schiller's ode would sound had he ever tasted cholent. Cholent is the heavenly food that the Lord God himself once taught Moses to cook on Mount Sinai... Cholent is the true God's kosher ambrosia...) I have to be careful not to think of this when I listen to Beethoven's Symphony no. 9, the last movement of which is a setting of Schiller's poem, and giggle because I imagine hearing "Schalet, schöner Götterfunken" instead of "Freude, schöner Götterfunken."

Cholent is a wonderfully satisfying dish in which the aromas of meat, seasonings, and beans are blended and heightened by the long cooking process, but diet food it is not. George Lang tells the following story in *The Cuisine of Hungary*: "The Jewish rabbi and the Catholic priest were very friendly in a village in Hungary. The priest complained to the rabbi that he was unable to sleep and the latter suggested the cholent recipe as a cure for insomnia. A few days later they met again, and to the eager question of the rabbi came the rueful answer from the priest: 'I understand how you fall asleep after you eat this dish, but what puzzles me is: how do you get up?'" No wonder it was traditional following Saturday lunch to either take a nap or take a walk, which was called *Sabbatspaziergang*. They needed one or the other after eating cholent.

Even within Hungary there were many versions of cholent. Bean cholent was by far the most common, but I have also found recipes for rice, pea, or crushed barley cholents in old Hungarian cookbooks. If the cholent included pearl barley in addition to beans, it was usually called *ricset*. It could be made with beef or goose, either of which could be fresh or smoked. Some people used small white beans to make the cholent, others, like my great-grandmother, the large spotted-red kind. According to an old Yiddish saying: "One shouldn't look too closely into the cholent or a marriage."

Riza néni's cholent is an almost classically pared-down version, both in cooking technique and ingredients. Contrary to some fancier recipes, it doesn't call for initial sautéing of the onion or browning of the meat. I tried the recipe both with and without browning the meat and, defying my expectation, it was just as good when prepared the simpler way. According to George Lang, the closer one got to Vienna, the more barley one found in the cholent. But even this couldn't have been an absolute rule, because Riza néni's recipe doesn't include any barley in spite of the fact that in Hungary it was hard to get much closer to Vienna than Moson, where she lived. Even more idiosyncratically, she doesn't use garlic, though in Hungary it is always a part of cholent. I like garlic a lot more than she seemed to, but I must say I don't miss it in this strongly flavored stew. I included it, however, among the optional ingredients. You could serve fermented dill pickles (see recipe on page 123) with the cholent and the halsli; it is a terrific combination. Heine was right: cholent is kosher ambrosia.

YIELD: 4 servings

TOTAL TIME: about 4 hours 40 minutes

INGREDIENTS:
- 1¼ cups dried beans (red-spotted large Roman beans, small white navy beans, or a mixture of the two)
- 1 large onion, chopped
- 1 teaspoon paprika
- ¼ teaspoon ground ginger
- ¼ teaspoon freshly ground black pepper
- 1 teaspoon kosher salt
- 1½ tablespoons all-purpose flour
- 1 pound beef short rib or flanken, cut into 4 pieces
- 3 cups water (approximate)

OPTIONAL:	½ pound smoked goose or turkey, breast or drumstick
	1 clove garlic, chopped
	1 small onion, ends cut off, peeled, and left whole
	2 large eggs in unbroken shells, washed
SPECIAL EQUIPMENT:	5- or 6-quart capacity heavy pot with a tight-fitting lid

1. Boil the beans in about 2 quarts of water for 2 minutes, then turn off the heat and let them soak in the hot water for 1 hour. Drain them in a colander and rinse them under running water.

2. Select an enameled cast iron casserole or some other heavy pot with a tight-fitting lid. Put the beans, chopped onion, the optional chopped garlic, and the seasonings in the pot. Sprinkle flour over the ingredients in the pot and mix to distribute evenly. Push the ingredients to the side and place the pieces of beef with the rib down on the bottom of the pot. If you decide to use the optional smoked meat and whole onion, bury them also in the bean mixture.

3. Add water; it should barely cover the ingredients. Bring it to a boil, adjust heat to very low, cover, and cook, barely simmering, for 1 hour.

4. Bury the optional eggs, carefully so they don't break, in the hot liquid among the beans. Place the optional halsli and/or ganef (see the next recipe) on top of the ingredients in the pot. Cover, making sure that everything fits comfortably under the lid.

5. Bake it in a 225°F oven overnight or in a 325°F oven for 2½ hours. Check the cholent during baking and add a little water if it looks dry. By the time the dish is ready, the beans should have absorbed most of the liquid, but the cholent should still be moist, not dry. Shell the optional eggs and cut them into halves. Cut the optional whole onion into quarters.

6. Serve the cholent with a piece of the meat placed on top of the beans and the optional egg, onion, halsli or ganef arranged around the beans.

7. Should you wish to make this dish ahead for later serving or wish to warm up leftovers, be very careful because the cholent, like all bean stews, tends to thicken with time. You might have to thin it with a few tablespoons of water. Don't leave the cholent unattended during reheating, because it burns easily. (Perhaps you can guess how I found this out.)

Stuffed Goose Neck and Cholent Dumpling
Halsli and Ganef

Remembering a simple dish from our childhood often can, better than anything else, evoke memories of long-gone people and the whole environment where we first tasted the dish. It is a strange thing with such early taste memories: they seem deeply imprinted on our unconscious and carry great emotional significance. Both my mother and aunt were enthusiastic about the stuffed goose neck their grandmother had prepared for the Sabbath. But as I couldn't eat it at Riza néni's table, it cannot mean as much for me, although I enjoy it as a most pleasant side dish, especially when it is permeated by the wonderful flavor of the cholent. I also like to eat room-temperature leftover halsli with bread, pickles, or salad.

The word *halsli*, or *helzel* as it is more commonly called in Ashkenazi cooking, comes from Yiddish, but originally from *Hals*, the German word for neck. It thriftily makes use of the skin of the neck, an item that otherwise might go to waste. It is one of several possible delicacies cooked and served with the cholent; others are: stuffed *kishke* or *derma* (stuffed beef casing, the small intestine of a cow), *cholent knaydl*, also known as *cholent kugel*, and *ganef*; all of them are really dumplings. There are many kinds of traditional stuffing for goose neck: most of them include flour, onion, and some poultry fat in addition to other ingredients. A fancy version printed in George Lang's *The Cuisine of Hungary* doesn't include flour, but this is more than compensated for by the inclusion of goose meat and goose liver.

Riza néni's version is a lot simpler, but it is also quite unusual. Contrary to the dozen or so versions I have seen in various cookbooks, its main ingredient is semolina. The coarse semolina expands when it absorbs moisture and the large kernels make this filling less dense than the mainly flour-based varieties. Farina is a poor substitute to semolina here because its texture is much less interesting. The biggest obstacle to recreating this dish is finding a goose neck, because no supermarket sells separate goose or turkey necks. Goose is expensive in the United States and it is not practical to buy a whole bird, not even the more affordable turkey, for the neck. Besides, birds in supermarkets rarely have necks. One would imagine that these are special breeds without necks, heads, or feet. Chicken necks, when they are available with the skin on, are too small for stuffing. The most practical solution I can think of is to use the skin of the commonly available and quite inexpensive fresh turkey drumstick. To make the deal still better: one can make a nice turkey soup out of the drumstick after its skin has been removed.

Another, even simpler, solution is to forget about the skin and make a ganef, a dumpling without casing, from the same stuffing used in the halsli. As one of the traditional accompaniments to cholent it is almost as authentic as halsli, though my mother didn't specifically mention eating it at her grandmother's. There is no difference in taste, because the thin skin casing of the halsli, while it looks pretty, has no perceivable flavor. In addition to its simpler preparation, ganef has the added appeal of an endearingly odd name: it means "thief" in Yiddish, because as it cooks on top of the cholent it steals its flavor.

YIELD: 4 to 6 servings

TOTAL TIME: about 2 hours if baked separately, 3 hours if baked with the cholent

INGREDIENTS:
- 1 large or 2 medium-size turkey drumsticks (they should be completely covered by intact skin) or, as a less convenient alternative, 2 large chicken legs with intact skin
- 3 tablespoons canola oil
- 1 medium onion, finely chopped or grated
- ½ cup coarse semolina (see page 107 about semolina) or farina
- ⅓ cup boiling water

2 tablespoons finely chopped raw chicken fat (my preference), rendered poultry fat, or canola oil
¾ teaspoon paprika
½ teaspoon ground ginger
½ teaspoon kosher salt
¼ teaspoon freshly ground black pepper
2 tablespoons all-purpose flour

OPTIONAL: 1 tablespoon chopped fresh flat-leaf parsley

SPECIAL EQUIPMENT: sewing needle and white thread

1. With your fingers reach under the skin at the upper end of the turkey drumstick and roll it down, like rolling down a stocking. You might have to use a paring knife to cut away the membrane that is under the skin and sometimes is attached to it at a few places, but be very careful not to puncture the skin. Sew the opening at the narrower end of the removed skin closed with a fairly large sewing needle and thread. (You can substitute the skin of 2 chicken legs for that of the turkey drumstick, but this is less practical because, not only will you have to remove and sew closed 2 skins instead of 1, you will also have to sew up the long slits where the thighs used to be.)

2. Heat oil in a skillet and sauté the chopped onion for 5 minutes over medium heat, until it becomes soft. Don't allow it to brown.

3. Spread semolina or farina in a skillet, add boiling water, mix it, cover, and set it aside for 5 minutes to absorb the moisture. Transfer the semolina or farina to a medium-size bowl; add the sautéed onion and all the remaining ingredients; mix them well.

4. Loosely stuff the filling into the skin and sew it closed. It is important not to stuff it too tightly, because the filling will expand during cooking. If you decided to make a ganef instead of the stuffed skin, shape the stuffing into a sausage about 2" in diameter. Should you have stuffing left after filling the skin, make a small ganef of it.

5. Simmer the halsli for 10 minutes in water to cover. Then transfer it and/or the ganef to the top of the ingredients in the cholent pot, and

make sure they fit under the lid. Bake them with the cholent and serve them in approximately ½" slices.

6. You can also make halsli without making cholent and serve it warm with meat dishes or cold with salad or pickles. In this case, after the halsli has simmered in water, coat a baking dish with 1 tablespoon canola oil, then peel and slice a medium onion and spread it in the dish. Place the halsli on the onions, cover with aluminum foil, and bake it for about 1½ hours in a 350°F oven. Remove the foil during the last 10 minutes of baking to allow the halsli to brown.

Bread Kugel with Raisins and Diced Apples
Semmelkugel

In much of the Ashkenazi world, including Hungary and Austria, the traditional Sabbath pudding is called a *kugel*, the Yiddish and German word for a sphere or ball. In its original form, it indeed was a large ball-shaped dumpling, which was baked in the same pot with the cholent, sort of like the ganef (see previous recipe) is done today. By the nineteenth century, however, most people baked it in a round clay form that they sometimes placed in the cholent pot, but they more typically baked it separately. It might not be quite as ancient a dish as cholent, which can be traced back to the thirteenth century, but its roots also reach back centuries, and together with cholent it has long been part of the second Sabbath meal. The name kugel is an abbreviation of *Schalet Kugel*, the way it used to be called in Germany centuries ago. This earlier name also attests to its close relationship with cholent. Even today, apple or bread kugels are frequently called shalet, obviously a variation of the word cholent.

Among the many different kinds of kugel, bread kugel is one of the oldest. In the sixteenth century a German rabbi mentioned *Weck Schalent* (bread kugel) together with *Vermicelles Schalent* (noodle kugel) and *Matzo Schalent*. These days potato or *lokshen* (noodle) *kugel* is more common than bread kugel. But potato kugel is a relatively recent, nineteenth-century, innovation, and, as we have just seen, bread kugel is at least as old as lokshen kugel. I agree with John Cooper, the author of *Eat and Be Satisfied*, that it seems probable that the custom of making bread kugel and apple kugel spread from Germany to Poland and Lithuania with eastward migrating German Jews. When it came to the idea of combining these two kinds of kugels into one, as it is done in this recipe, the influence moved in the opposite direction: it spread from Poland and Lithuania to Western Europe.

Jewish authors have commented on the importance of kugel in traditional Jewish life. Heinrich Heine wrote in 1825 with his typical combination of irony and seriousness to the editor of a new Jewish magazine: "Kugel, this holy national dish, has done more for the preservation of Judaism than all three issues of your magazine." Geographically closer to Riza néni, the Hungarian-born Austrian humorist Moritz G. Saphir (1795–1858) commented ironically on kugel and the Jews' supposed lack of physical courage: "More than once the fighting courage of the seed of Jacob has been impugned by slanderers who say: 'They are afraid of the kugel, the cannonball.' For that reason many Jews go through battle practice every Sabbath by advancing in the face of the kugel with serenity and bravery."

Making a dairy version of her recipe, I substituted butter for her combination of finely chopped beef fat and hard goose fat, which I thought would be unappealing and impractical for the modern cook. Use margarine for a version to go with meat dishes. The only other change was that, as she had done in several analogous recipes, I decided to separate the eggs and add the whipped egg whites at the end, because this made for a lighter kugel. Riza néni had baked her kugel in a special kugel form, but as I don't have such a form I substituted a soufflé dish.

At my great-grandmother's, this slightly sweet dish was served at the second Sabbath meal either with the cholent or as a separate course after it. Eating the savory Sabbath stew of cholent with a sweet side dish sounds quite strange today, but centuries ago this pairing of savory and sweet used to be very popular. Jewish cooking in its adherence to tradition merely preserved an idea here that has mostly fallen out of favor elsewhere. Tradition, history, and all the other good things notwithstanding, I prefer to eat it as a dessert, whether for Sabbath or for any other meal.

YIELD:	8 generous servings
TOTAL TIME:	about 1 hour 30 minutes, plus cooling time
INGREDIENTS:	6 slices of white bread, cut into ½" dice
	4 tablespoons unsalted butter, margarine, or rendered poultry fat, softened
	3 tablespoons sugar
	4 large egg yolks
	¾ teaspoon ground cinnamon
	¼ teaspoon kosher salt
	2 teaspoons lemon zest, grated or very finely chopped (optional)
	⅓ cup golden raisins
	2 Golden Delicious apples, peeled, cored, and cut into ⅜" dice
	½ cup fruity white wine, such as Riesling
	½ cup water
	1 cup dry bread crumbs, made in the food processor from about 4 slices of stale white bread
	⅓ cup coarse semolina (see page 107 about semolina) or farina
	1 teaspoon unsalted butter or canola oil (to grease the soufflé dish)
	4 large egg whites
	½ teaspoon cream of tartar
	1 tablespoon sugar
SPECIAL EQUIPMENT:	baking sheet
	food processor
	electric mixer (optional)
	7" soufflé dish, charlotte mold, or a similar-diameter pot about 3½" deep
	parchment paper

1. Center a rack in the oven and preheat the oven to 350°F. Place bread cubes on a baking sheet and dry them without allowing them to brown, about 7 minutes. Don't turn off the oven.

2. In a fairly large bowl, beat butter, margarine, or rendered poultry fat by hand or with the help of an electric mixer until it gets foamy. Add sugar and egg yolks, then continue beating until the mixture becomes fluffy and very pale. Mix in cinnamon, salt, and optional lemon zest, then fold in raisins and diced apples.

3. In another bowl, soak bread cubes for about 2 minutes in a mixture of wine and water, squeeze them out and discard the remaining liquid. Add the moistened bread to the first bowl and mix well.

4. Gently fold bread crumbs and semolina or farina into the bread and apple mixture and let it rest for about 10 minutes for the semolina or farina to absorb some of the moisture. Meanwhile, generously grease the soufflé dish, line its bottom with parchment paper, then flip the paper over so that its top surface is greased, too.

5. Whip egg whites and cream of tartar to soft peak, add sugar and continue whipping until they form firm peaks. Stir about ½ of the whipped egg whites into the thick and chunky bread mixture to lighten it, then gently fold the remaining egg whites into the mixture.

6. With a rubber spatula, transfer the mixture into the soufflé dish, making sure that there are no voids, and use the spatula to smooth the top surface. Cut a round piece of parchment paper to fit inside your soufflé dish and lay it on the mixture in the dish. Place the dish on a baking sheet.

7. Bake it in the preheated oven for 25 minutes; remove parchment paper from the top and continue baking for an additional 25 minutes. Let it cool for 10 minutes in the dish set on a cooling rack; run a knife along the side of the dish to release the kugel, and invert the kugel onto a large plate. Peel off the parchment from its bottom and allow it to cool for another 15 minutes. Place an inverted serving plate over it,

and with the help of the plates carefully flip it over to transfer it onto the serving plate, so that its top side faces up.

8. Serve it lukewarm or at room temperature. It is terrific by itself, but you could also serve it with a little raspberry syrup, which would go well with the slightly sweet kugel and provide visual contrast to it.

Apple Kugel
Apfelkugel

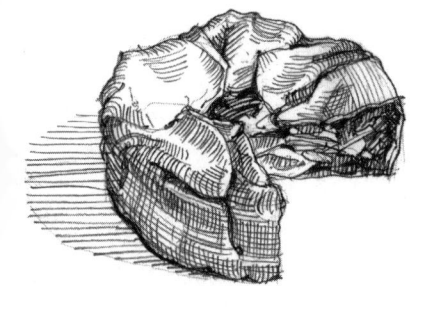

While the previous bread kugel was usually eaten with cholent, the sweeter apple kugel was one of the traditional desserts at the Sabbath meal. Like all other kugels, this Sabbath pudding also used to be called *schalet* and this is what it is called even in some contemporary cookbooks, such as Claudia Roden's *The Book of Jewish Food*. Gentiles must have liked it, too, because it was primarily for them that Auguste Escoffier included it under the name *"schâleth à la juive"* in his *Guide Culinaire*, his classic work on French cooking, first published in 1903.

Like bread kugel, it was first made in Germany, probably in southern Germany. John Cooper describes in his *Eat and Be Satisfied* a schalet or *Apfelbuwele* (little apple boy), a southern German Sabbath dessert. Though that was different from Riza néni's version, like *Apfelkuchen*, another German dessert, it had the same basic idea: apple filling encased by dough.

While most recipes in Riza néni's collection needed little interpretation, this was hardly more than a description of an idea: "roll strudel dough to be thicker than what you would use for a strudel; fill it with apple strudel filling; bake it in a well-greased and paper-lined kugel form." But my reconstruction isn't arbitrary, because it is based on the traditional apple strudel recipe and on similar fillings from other recipes in her collection. Instead of rolling the filling into the dough and then bending this to fit the round kugel form, I decided to line the form with the dough and encase the filling with it, because this is a little easier to make and can be cut into more uniform slices. I used Golden Delicious apples for the filling, but you could make it with Granny Smith apples, which would emphasize the appealing contrast between the sweet and sour flavors. This is one of my favorite desserts in this book, and it is one that contains little saturated fat or cholesterol. With even more justification than her bread kugel, which originally was not intended to be a dessert, it can be served with a fruit sauce.

YIELD: 8 generous servings

TOTAL TIME: about 2 hours, plus cooling time

INGREDIENTS:
- 4 Golden Delicious apples, peeled, cored, and cut into ¼" slices
- ⅓ cup sugar
- 2 tablespoons lemon juice
- 1⅓ cups unbleached all-purpose flour
- 1 teaspoon sugar
- ¼ teaspoon kosher salt
- 1 large egg
- 2 tablespoons canola oil
- 1 tablespoon white wine or 1 teaspoon distilled white vinegar
- 1–3 tablespoons water
- 1 teaspoon unsalted butter or margarine (to grease the dish)
- ½ cup walnuts
- 2 tablespoons sugar
- ½ tablespoon unsalted butter or margarine
- ½ cup bread crumbs, made in the food processor from stale white bread
- ½ cup golden raisins
- 2 teaspoons grated lemon zest
- 1 teaspoon ground cinnamon

2 tablespoons unsalted butter or margarine, melted
1 teaspoon unsalted butter or margarine (to dot the top of the kugel)

SPECIAL
EQUIPMENT: food processor
7" soufflé dish, charlotte mold, or a similar-diameter pot about 3½" deep
parchment paper
baking sheet

1. Place sliced apples, sugar, and lemon juice in a large bowl; mix them well; let them rest for at least ½ hour, but preferably 1 or 2 hours. The apples will release liquid.

2. Place flour, sugar, and salt in the bowl of a food processor and pulse to blend. Add egg, canola oil, wine or vinegar, and 1 tablespoon water. Process it for about 30 seconds; if the dough doesn't form a ball on top of the blade add more water by the ½ tablespoonful and process it very briefly to incorporate the water. It should be slightly softer than pasta dough. As soon as the dough forms a ball, transfer it to the lightly floured work surface and knead it for 3 to 5 minutes until it is satiny smooth and elastic. If it is sticky, knead in a little flour. Flatten the dough into a 1"-thick disc, wrap it in plastic wrap, and let it rest for at least ½ hour.

3. Center a rack in the oven and preheat the oven to 350°F. Grease the soufflé dish and line it with parchment paper.

4. Wipe out the bowl of the food processor—but this should hardly be necessary, because if the dough was the right consistency it should have left the bowl practically clean. Place ¼ cup of the walnuts and 2 tablespoons sugar in the bowl of the machine and process until the nuts are finely ground. Add the remaining ¼ cup nuts and pulse briefly a few times to coarsely chop them. Heat ½ tablespoon butter or margarine in a heavy skillet, add bread crumbs and lightly brown them while continuously stirring. Pour the approximately ¼ cup liquid produced by the apples into a small saucepan and boil it down to a thick syrup. Pour it back into the bowl of apples; add walnuts, toasted

bread crumbs, raisins, zest of lemon, cinnamon, melted butter; mix them together.

5. Unwrap the dough and place it on a lightly floured work surface. With a floured rolling pin, roll it out into an about 17" diameter circle. Periodically during rolling, lift up one side of the dough, throw a little flour under it, and give the dough a quarter turn to make sure it doesn't stick.

6. Loosely roll up the dough circle around the rolling pin and unfurl it centered on the soufflé dish. Lift up the edges of the dough to gently lower the middle part into the dish so that it completely covers the bottom. Let the edges of the dough hang over the side of the dish. Fill the dough with the apple filling, leaving any liquid in the bowl, and tap the filling down. Fold the overhanging part of the dough to almost enclose the kugel, leaving a small vent hole in the center. If the dough flap is slightly short on one side, you can gently stretch this wonderfully elastic dough a little to cover most of the filling. Dot it with ¼ tablespoon butter or margarine cut into small pieces. Cover it with parchment paper cut to size.

7. Place the dish on a baking sheet and bake it in the preheated oven for 25 minutes. Remove the parchment paper cover and bake the kugel for another 20 to 25 minutes or until the top is slightly browned at places but still quite light overall. Set the dish on a rack and allow it to cool for 15 minutes. Unmold it onto a large plate and put an inverted serving plate on top. Holding the kugel between the 2 plates flip it over so the serving plate is on the bottom. Let it cool to lukewarm before slicing. Serve it lukewarm, which is my preference, or at room temperature.

Apple Torte

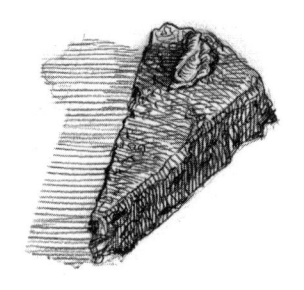

Apfeltorte

This intensely apple-flavored and wonderfully moist torte is quite unusual. Although there are many flourless cakes in Austro-Hungarian cuisine, I haven't found a similar recipe in my research of Austrian and Hungarian cookbooks. Like most flourless tortes, this one could easily be adapted for Pesach if matzo meal was substituted for bread crumbs.

Riza néni suggested slicing the torte into two layers, filling it with apricot jam, and coating it with rum icing. Cutting the approximately one-inch-high soft torte into layers would be difficult and in my opinion unnecessary because it is tasty and moist enough to require no filling. Instead of filling and icing it, I recommend brushing the top of the torte with apricot jam, sprinkling ground walnuts over this, and decorating each slice with a piece of walnut—a treatment borrowed from one of Riza néni's other tortes.

YIELD: 12 servings

TOTAL TIME: about 1 hour 30 minutes

INGREDIENTS:
- 3 large Granny Smith apples, peeled, cored, and grated with the coarsest side of a box grater
- 1 tablespoon lemon juice
- 3 tablespoons sugar
- 1 teaspoon unsalted butter or margarine (to grease the form)
- ¼ cup dry bread crumbs, made in the food processor from stale white bread (to coat the form)
- 1 cup walnuts
- ¼ cup sugar
- 3 large egg yolks

1 tablespoon sugar
½ cup dry bread crumbs, made in the food processor from stale white bread
 2 tablespoons dark rum
 4 large egg whites
½ teaspoon cream of tartar
 1 tablespoon sugar
 2 tablespoons strained apricot jam (optional)
 1 teaspoon dark rum (optional)
¼ cup walnuts (optional)
 1 tablespoon sugar (optional)
 6 walnut halves, split lengthwise (optional)

SPECIAL
EQUIPMENT: baking sheet
food processor
9" spring form

1. Peel and core the apples and grate them on the coarsest side of a box grater into a bowl. Stir in lemon juice and ¼ cup sugar. Gather the apples in the center of the bowl, place a small plate weighed down by a heavy can on top of them and let them rest for at least 20 minutes to release some of their juices.

2. Center a rack in the oven and preheat the oven to 350°F. Grease the spring form and coat it with bread crumbs.

3. Process walnuts and ¼ cup sugar in the food processor until finely ground, about 25 seconds. In a large bowl, beat egg yolks and 1 tablespoon sugar with an electric mixer or by hand until they turn pale and fluffy. Stir in the ground walnuts.

4. Strain the grated apples in small batches over the sink and use the back of a spoon to press out as much juice from them as you can. Add the grated apples, ½ cup bread crumbs, and rum to the egg-walnut mixture and mix them well.

5. Whip egg whites and cream of tartar to form soft peaks, add 1 tablespoon sugar and continue whipping until firm peaks form. Stir about

⅓ of the whipped egg whites into the apple mixture, then fold in the rest of the egg whites.

6. Pour the batter into the spring form and smooth the top with a rubber spatula. Place the form on a baking sheet. Bake it for 15 minutes in the preheated oven with the oven door kept slightly ajar by a wedged-in knife, then for another 40 minutes with the door completely closed.

7. Let the torte cool for 10 minutes in the form set on a rack. Run a paring knife along the inside of the form to release the sides, remove the side ring and let the torte cool for another 20 minutes on the rack. Run a long narrow knife or spatula under the torte to release it from the metal base of the form. Place a large plate over the torte and invert it so the plate is on the bottom. Let the bottom of the torte dry for at least 1 hour. Place an inverted serving plate on top of the torte and, holding the 2 plates, flip it over so that its top faces up.

8. In a small bowl, dilute strained apricot jam with rum and brush the top of the torte with this. Grind walnuts and sugar in the food processor and evenly sprinkle this over the top of the torte. Cut it into 12 slices and decorate each slice with a split walnut.

Meringue Torte with Almond Cookie Dough Base

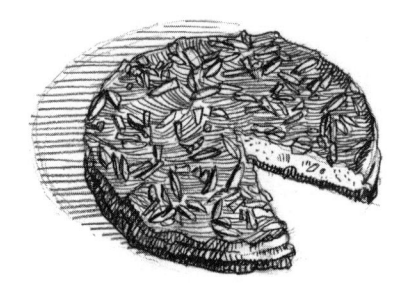

Eistorte

Tortes were Riza néni's pride and joy. It was not enough for her to have an amazing variety of macaroons and meringues in her repertory, she wanted to be able to make a macaroon and a meringue torte as well. This meringue torte is another dessert whose idea seemed so obvious to me that I was sure I would find several versions of it in my cookbooks. But no, I found only one similar recipe, in a Hungarian book collecting more than eight hundred (!) desserts of "our grandmothers," and it was for a torte in which whipped and sweetened egg whites were merely spread on the pastry base, not baked as they are in Riza néni's recipe. This is an impressive and tasty torte that one can eat without feeling too guilty about high cholesterol, because a slice of it contains only a twelfth of an egg yolk and a third of an ounce of butter.

The only changes I made in adapting the original recipe were substituting butter or margarine for "fat" (probably goose fat) and cutting back slightly on the amount of sugar in the pastry base. I used a cake ring to make the torte, but this is not absolutely necessary. Although it will not be so perfectly shaped, you could make this torte on a cookie sheet without using such a ring. Just roll the dough into a circle, transfer it to the cookie sheet, form a raised edge around the disc of dough, and proceed as described in the recipe. In this case, pipe the meringue with a pastry bag that has no metal tip in which the almonds could get stuck. It is a little more cumbersome, but you could also make this torte in a nine-inch spring form. Should you use a spring form, make sure the bottom disc of the form doesn't have a raised edge, which would make removal of the torte difficult.

YIELD: 12 slices

TOTAL TIME: about 55 minutes, plus cooling time

INGREDIENTS:
- ½ cup blanched almonds
- ¾ cup unbleached all-purpose flour
- 3 tablespoons confectioners' sugar
- ⅛ teaspoon kosher salt
- 1 stick (4 ounces) unsalted butter or margarine, softened and cut into ½" pieces
- 1 large egg yolk (reserve the egg white for the meringue topping)
- 1–2 teaspoons water, depending on the moisture in the flour

¼ cup (or less) of seedless raspberry or red currant preserves
5 large egg whites (including the reserved egg white)
½ teaspoon cream of tartar
½ cup sugar
1 teaspoon vanilla extract
1 teaspoon zest of lemon, grated or very finely chopped
1 cup slivered almonds

SPECIAL EQUIPMENT:
food processor
cookie sheet
reusable silicone nonstick baking mat or parchment paper
9" or 9½" diameter × 1½" deep cake ring (optional)

1. Center a rack in the oven and preheat the oven to 375°F. Line your cookie sheet with baking mat or parchment paper.

2. Place almonds and ¼ cup flour in the processor bowl and process until the almonds are finely ground, about 25 seconds. Add the remaining ½ cup flour, 3 tablespoons sugar, and salt; pulse to mix. Add butter and process for 10 seconds. Add egg yolk and 1 teaspoon water. Process for 5–10 seconds, until the dough starts to come together on top of the blade. If the dough doesn't come together, add another teaspoon water and briefly process.

3. Place an 18"-long sheet of plastic wrap on your work surface. Transfer the soft and sticky dough to the plastic and with the help of the plastic shape it into a disc about 6" in diameter. Stretch another 18"-long sheet of plastic wrap on top of it and align it with the bottom sheet. With a rolling pin, roll the dough between the sheets of plastic into a 10½" circle, approximately ⅛" thick. Peel off the top layer and with the help of the bottom layer invert the dough onto the baking mat or parchment paper. Peel off the remaining sheet of plastic.

4. Place the cake ring in the middle of the dough circle and very lightly press to score the dough. Remove the ring and fold the approximately half-inch of dough outside the score mark back on top of the dough within the score mark. Place the cake ring to surround the dough circle and with your fingers shape the folded back dough into about a half-inch high and wide raised border against the cake ring. The border should be triangle-shaped, wide at the base and narrow at the top. With a fork, prick the circle of dough at 1" or 2" intervals.

5. Bake it in the preheated oven for 23–25 minutes, until light golden brown. While the dough is baking, whip egg whites with cream of tartar to soft peaks. Add vanilla and gradually add sugar while whipping until the whites form firm peaks. Using a rubber spatula, gently fold in ⅔ of the slivered almonds, as well as the optional lemon zest, should you decide to include it.

6. Don't turn off the oven when you remove the cookie sheet with the pastry base on it. Lift off the cake ring and coat its inside with butter or margarine. While the pastry base is still hot, spread a thin glaze of preserves over it. Put the ring back around it and evenly spread the whipped egg whites over the warm dough inside the ring, making especially sure that there are no air bubbles along the perimeter. Strew the remaining slivered almonds over the top of the egg whites.

7. Return the cookie sheet to the oven and bake the torte for 15 minutes, until much of the meringue becomes light brown and the slivered almonds on the top are lightly toasted.

8. Set the cookie sheet and the torte on a rack in a draft-free place to cool. Most of the meringue has probably pulled away from the ring, but to make sure, run a paring knife along the inside and remove the ring. If you didn't use a baking mat you will have to run a long spatula or slicing knife under the bottom of the torte to loosen it. Carefully, so that you don't break its cookie dough base, slide the torte onto a serving plate. The very crisp base of the torte can easily break when it is sliced. Cutting the cake with a long, serrated knife minimizes this risk. The torte is best served on the day of baking, because later the soft meringue will "weep" at the bottom, eventually making

the dough soggy. For a more stable meringue you could use an Italian meringue, in which cooked sugar syrup is beaten into the whipped egg whites.

Lemon-Almond Torte
Citrom torta

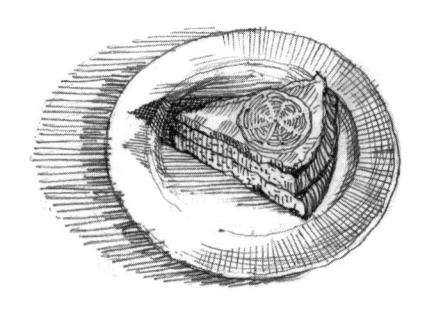

This is a very flavorful variation of the classic Austro-Hungarian sponge torte. Most Austrian and Hungarian cookbooks include one or more versions of this torte. Riza néni's collection also includes the basic version under the name *Piskoten Torte*, but her interesting lemon-almond torte is quite unusual. Like all flourless cakes, it can be made for Pesach, but as this torte includes no fat, it has the added advantage of going equally well with fleischig (meat) or milchig (dairy) menus.

Though some sponge tortes are enriched with a little butter, most are made from a dough containing no fat, but only eggs, sugar, and flour, which in this recipe is replaced by ground almonds. This type of dough is only leavened by the tiny air bubbles in the whipped eggs that expand in the oven, making the dough rise to become light and fluffy. The problem is that when the torte cools it tends to partially deflate, especially in the center, producing an uneven sunken surface. This can be minimized if you follow the instructions, a version of a traditional Austro-Hungarian technique for slowly driving the moisture out of the dough and allowing the torte to firm up.

The recipe is long but making the dough is really very simple. If you are in a hurry, omit the clear gelatin topping from the torte. It will not look quite as spectacular, but the taste will be almost the same. Omit the gelatin topping, too, if you keep a kosher kitchen, or make it with kosher gelatin. For pareve (usable with either meat or dairy) kosher gelatin, it is best to stick with a product made from a non-animal source, such as the Kojel brand of vegetarian kosher gelatin.

YIELD: 12 slices

TOTAL TIME: about 1 hour 40 minutes, plus time to dry and cool the torte

INGREDIENTS:
- 1 teaspoon unsalted butter or margarine (to grease the spring form)
- 2 tablespoons all-purpose flour (to coat the spring form)
- 1 cup blanched almonds
- ¼ cup sugar
- 5 large egg yolks
- ⅓ cup sugar
- 3 teaspoons grated lemon zest
- 3 tablespoons lemon juice
- 6 large egg whites
- ½ teaspoon cream of tartar
- 1 tablespoon sugar
- ¼ cup lemon marmalade
- 1 lemon

OPTIONAL:
- ¾ cup water
- 3 tablespoons sugar
- 3 tablespoons lemon juice
- 1 tablespoon water
- 1 envelope unflavored gelatin

SPECIAL EQUIPMENT:
9" spring form
food processor
electric mixer (optional)
baking sheet

1. Center a rack in the oven and preheat the oven to 350°F. Grease the spring form and coat it with flour.

2. Place almonds and ¼ cup sugar in the food processor; process for about 20 seconds, until finely and evenly ground. Carefully reach into the bowl, avoiding the sharp blades, to make sure there are no bigger pieces of almond left.

3. Beat egg yolks and sugar at fairly high speed for about 5 minutes with the mixer or 10 minutes by hand until the yolks become fluffy and turn very pale. Fold in the ground almonds, lemon zest, and lemon juice.

4. Whip egg whites with cream of tartar to soft peak. Add 1 tablespoon sugar and continue whipping until egg whites become shiny and form firm peaks. Stir about ¼ of the whipped egg whites into the egg yolk mixture to lighten it, then gently fold in the rest of the whites.

5. Pour this batter into the spring form. Tap the form to even out the batter in it and place it on a baking sheet.

6. Bake it in the preheated oven. For the first 10 minutes, prop the oven door slightly ajar with a knife wedged in to allow moisture to escape. Remove the knife, close the door completely, and bake the torte for another 20 to 25 minutes. Check after 20 minutes by pressing the top surface with your finger. If the top springs back and is light golden brown, and its edge starts to pull away from the form—the torte is done.

7. Use a small fine strainer or a duster cup to dust the top of the hot torte in the form with a little flour. Place a large, flat, pre-warmed plate upside-down on the form and while holding them together invert the form onto the plate. Allow the torte to cool slowly under the form for about 30 minutes.

8. Chances are that the cake dropped from the form onto the plate, but if it is still stuck in the form, remove the sides of the form, and with a long straight spatula or knife remove the bottom disc of the form. In either case, the cake should rest upside down on the plate. Cover it loosely with a kitchen towel and let it continue firming up at room temperature for a few hours, preferably overnight.

9. Slide a long, wide spatula under the cake to separate it from the plate and turn it over. Part of the thin brown "skin" probably stuck to the plate. Carefully peel off the remaining brown "skin" from the top surface of the torte; it should come off easily and evenly. You should end up with an even, not sunken, and uniformly yellow top surface. Place the torte on a serving platter or a 9" cardboard round.

10. Cut the cake into 2 layers with a long serrated knife the following way: insert the knife horizontally into the cake, and while holding the knife stationary use your other hand to rotate the cake until you have cut all the way through it. Don't remove the knife until you have finished cutting. Spread the lemon marmalade on the bottom layer and replace the top layer to its original position. Cut 10 very thin (1/16") slices of approximately the same diameter from the center of a lemon and remove the seeds from them. Use a mandolin or a very sharp knife to cut the slices. Decorate the torte with the slices of lemon; I managed to fit 8 slices along the perimeter and 1 more in the center.

11. Optional: Boil ¾ cup water with 3 tablespoons sugar in a small saucepan. Pour 3 tablespoons lemon juice and 1 tablespoon cold water into a bowl, sprinkle gelatin over the cold liquid and let it stand for 1 minute. Add hot liquid and stir until gelatin is completely dissolved. Place the bowl in the freezer for 15 to 20 minutes, checking periodically to see if it has become syrupy, but don't allow it to gel. Quickly spread the syrupy glaze in an even layer about ⅛" thick on top of the torte so that it covers the lemon slices, too. Try to make the top of the glaze perfectly level and smooth. You must work fast while the glaze is neither too runny nor too firmly gelled. Discard the remaining gelatin glaze or save it for your next torte. Refrigerate the torte for at least 2 hours. Slice it with a long thin knife.

Potato Torte

Erdäpfel Torte

Cooked and grated potato is what makes this flourless torte so moist, in spite of the fact that it is made with no butter and only three egg yolks. Austro-Hungarian cooking has invented seemingly endless varieties of tortes made without flour. People in that part of the world could have eaten a different kind of flourless torte every week of a year and still have a few other varieties left for the next year. Potato torte is one of the more unusual members in this family of tortes, although I wouldn't say it is the oddest. That prize belongs to the dry bean torte. Your guests probably will not be able to guess your "secret ingredient" and will be interested hearing about it. For Pesach substitute matzo meal for the bread crumbs. As the torte contains no fat or dairy products, it can be part of either meat or dairy menus. In this last combination consider serving it with a little sour cream, crème fraîche, or lightly sweetened whipped cream.

YIELD:	12 servings
TOTAL TIME:	about 2 hours 25 minutes, plus several hours drying time
INGREDIENTS:	1 very large or 2 medium Idaho potatoes, about 12 ounces total
	1 teaspoon unsalted pareve margarine (to grease the form)
	½ cup bread crumbs (about 2 slices of stale white bread processed into fine crumbs)
	½ cup shelled walnuts
	¼ cup sugar

3 large egg yolks
⅓ cup sugar
¼ teaspoon kosher salt
2 teaspoons grated lemon zest
1½ tablespoons lemon juice
4 large egg whites
½ teaspoon cream of tartar
1 tablespoon sugar
⅓ cup seedless raspberry jam or red currant jelly
2 tablespoons of dark rum or water
6 walnut halves, split lengthwise (for decoration)
¾ cup sour cream, crème fraîche, or lightly sweetened whipped cream (optional)

SPECIAL EQUIPMENT:
9" spring form
food processor
electric mixer (optional)
baking sheet

1. At least 1 hour before you wish to bake the torte, rinse the potatoes and cook them in their jackets for about 25 minutes. The potatoes should be slightly undercooked. Drain the potatoes and when they are cool enough to handle peel them. Let them get completely cold or chill them in the refrigerator, then coarsely grate them. It is important that the potatoes are completely cold or they will fall apart when you grate them. You should have about 2 loosely packed cups of grated potatoes.

2. Center a rack in the oven and preheat the oven to 350°F. Grease the spring form and coat it with bread crumbs. Reserve the remaining (about ⅓ cup) bread crumbs for the batter of the torte.

3. Place walnuts and ¼ cup sugar in the food processor. Process for about 30 seconds until they are finely and evenly ground.

4. Beat egg yolks and ⅓ cup sugar with an electric mixer or by hand until the yolks turn very pale and fluffy. Add about ⅔ of the ground walnuts

(reserve the rest for coating the baked torte), the remaining bread crumbs, the potatoes, salt, lemon zest and juice, and mix them well.

5. Add cream of tartar to egg whites and whip them to form soft peaks. Add 1 tablespoon sugar, and continue whipping until egg whites become shiny and form firm peaks. Stir about ⅓ of the whipped egg whites into the egg yolk mixture to lighten it, then gently fold in the rest.

6. Pour this batter into the spring form and tap the form to level the batter. Place it on a baking sheet and bake it in the preheated oven. Prop the oven door slightly ajar with a wedged-in knife and bake the torte this way for 10 minutes to allow moisture to escape. Remove the knife and close the door completely. Bake the torte for another 50 minutes or until it starts to pull away from the form and the top surface springs back when pressed with your finger.

7. Cool the torte in the form set on a cooling rack. After about ½ hour, run a paring knife along the inside and remove the side ring. Leave the torte on the metal base of the form, cover it with a kitchen towel, and let it firm up for a few hours or overnight.

8. Place jam or jelly in a small bowl and dilute it with 2 tablespoons of dark rum or a similar amount of hot water. Brush the top and the side of the torte with the diluted jam or jelly and coat it evenly with the remaining ground nuts. Run a long straight knife or spatula under the approximately 1"-high torte to release it from the bottom of the form, and with the help of a large, broad spatula transfer the torte onto a large serving plate. Decorate the torte with a 12 pieces of split walnut distributed evenly along the perimeter. Serve it at room temperature by itself or with a dollop of sour cream, crème fraîche, or lightly sweetened whipped cream next to it.

Saturday Afternoons and Evenings

On Saturday afternoons, the children played games while the grownups took a nap and then waited for visitors to arrive. While Frigyes bácsi, ignoring the Sabbath restrictions, played billiards in the Mocca coffeehouse, my great-grandfather went to the synagogue for the afternoon service, where he had his third Sabbath meal together with the other men. The *shammas*, the synagogue beadle, served this light snack, usually con-

Riza néni gave my mother a candle.

He stared at his fingernails in the candlelight.

sisting of cooked egg, challah, and fruit. While the men were in the temple, Riza néni and the grandchildren at home also had their meal, which was lighter and simpler than the one at noon. They usually ate cold food, such as diced pickle and carrot sausage, pickled herring, pike in sour aspic (see recipes on pages 196, 200, and 225). Most of the time there was also leftover dessert from lunch.

At the end of the Sabbath, when she could see three stars in the sky, Riza néni said a prayer, lit the candles again, and exclaimed "A good week, a full week, a fortunate week . . ." to welcome in the new week. Great-grandfather arrived home saying the same greeting: "A good week . . ." Everybody gathered around the table again for the *havdalah* (Hebrew for "separation"), the ceremony that separates the Sabbath from the weekdays. Riza néni gave my mother a candle made of braided strands of thin candles, lit it, and told her to hold it as high as she could "to get a tall bridegroom." Some of the thin strands of candles in the braid were white, others red, which made the pattern of the braid even prettier. Great-grandfather poured wine into the silver beaker. "A full week," he said while allowing the wine to overflow onto a plate. He said a benediction over the wine and the beautiful silver container that stood on the table and was filled with cloves, cinnamon, and other spices. It had a nice smell and the children were told to sniff from it. Then my great-grandfather cupped his hands and stared at his fingernails in the candlelight while saying another blessing, this time over the light of the candles. As he explained to my mother, he was trying to see from the white spots of the fingernails if the coming week would be lucky. He extinguished the candles in the spilled wine on the plate, then dipped his finger in the wine and brushed this on his eyelids and forehead, to gain knowledge and foresight. He also stuck the same finger into his pocket, in the hope that this would bring lots of money. Finally, everybody sang a song for the departure of the Sabbath.

Now they got something to eat again, at times even warm food, but nothing heavy. After all the eating during the Sabbath, nobody was very hungry. Sometimes at this meal or at the afternoon meal before it, they had a kind of spice cake or spice strudel (see the following two recipes). Afterward, if the weather was good, everyone sat for a while on the bench in front of the house to talk with each other and watch the passersby.

Spice Cake or Torte
Gewürzkuchen oder Torte

Spice cakes were usually eaten on Saturday evenings, at the end of the Sabbath. During the *havdalah* service, which signifies the end of Sabbath, all participants smell a mixture of pleasant spices, called *besamim*. The spices, some of which are also used in the spice cakes, represent the wonderful "fragrance" of Sabbath and they are meant to revive the body after the departure of the special Sabbath soul. Supposedly, during Sabbath the special Sabbath soul moves into people and increases their appetites. Now they have to eat for two: for themselves and the Sabbath soul. Therefore, on Sabbath it is considered a mitzvah, a religious obligation, to eat three main meals, not including breakfast. I love this justification for making our noble duty to eat three good meals in succession!

Adapting the original recipe was a fairly straightforward job, though in an effort to come up with the best version I made some minor adjustments, such as exchanging one egg yolk for an egg white to lighten the torte, and adding a little applesauce to make it more moist. As in several other recipes, I had to guess how much citron and chocolate Riza néni could buy for ten kreuzer. From Riza néni's alternatives of baking this cake in either a square or a round form, I chose the round form, which I think is prettier. She didn't specify the glaze or icing for coating the torte, but I think a chocolate glaze would be most appropriate. The wonderfully compatible combination of flavors of ground almonds, spices, chocolate, and citron peel make this dessert an unforgettable taste experience. It can sure revive the body—not only after the departure of the Sabbath soul but on any other occasion.

YIELD:	12 servings
TOTAL TIME:	about 1 hour 30 minutes, plus time to dry the torte
INGREDIENTS:	1 teaspoon unsalted butter or margarine (to grease the form)
	1¼ cups raw almonds
	⅓ cup sugar
	3 ounces bittersweet chocolate
	5 large egg yolks (reserve egg whites)
	¼ cup sugar
	½ teaspoon vanilla extract
	1¼ teaspoons ground cinnamon
	½ teaspoon ground cloves

2 tablespoons lemon juice

2 teaspoons lemon zest, grated or very finely chopped

⅔ cup dry bread crumbs (about 2 slices of stale white bread processed into crumbs)

⅓ cup applesauce (optional)

½ cup candied and diced citron (or substitute candied, diced lemon or orange peel)

7 large egg whites (including the 5 reserved egg whites)

¾ teaspoon cream of tartar

1 tablespoon sugar

¼ cup seedless raspberry or currant jam

6 ounces bittersweet chocolate (for the optional glaze)

½ cup heavy cream (for the optional glaze)

SPECIAL EQUIPMENT:
9" spring form
electric mixer (optional)
baking sheet

1. Center a rack in the oven and preheat the oven to 350°F. Grease the spring form.

2. Place almonds and ⅓ cup sugar in the bowl of the food processor and process until finely and uniformly ground, about 40 seconds. Transfer the almond mixture into a small bowl. Cut chocolate into chunks about ¾", place them in the food processor and process them into ⅛" granules, about 30 seconds.

3. Beat egg yolks and ¼ cup sugar in a large bowl with an electric mixer or by hand until the mixture becomes fluffy and very pale. Stir in vanilla, cinnamon, cloves, lemon juice and zest, ground almonds, dry bread crumbs, applesauce, candied citron, and chopped chocolate.

4. Add cream of tartar to egg whites and whip them to form soft peaks, add 1 tablespoon sugar and continue whipping until they form firm peaks. Stir about ½ of the whipped egg whites into the thick mixture

to lighten it, then gently fold in the remaining whites in 3 batches. Don't over-mix, a few streaks of egg whites are OK. Pour the mixture into the greased form, tap the form to even out the batter in it, place it on a baking sheet, and transfer it into the preheated oven.

5. Prop the oven door slightly ajar with a knife wedged in and bake the torte this way for 10 minutes to allow moisture to escape. Remove the knife, close the door completely, and bake the torte for another 30–35 minutes, until the top springs back when you press it with your finger and the torte pulls away from the form.

6. Cool the torte for 10 minutes in the form set on a rack. Run a paring knife around the torte and remove the side ring. Let the torte continue cooling on the base of the form for another 20 minutes. Run a long knife under the torte to release it from the metal base and with the help of a large spatula transfer it to a large flat plate. Cover it with a kitchen towel and let it continue firming up for several hours or overnight.

7. Turn the torte upside down because the bottom surface tends to be smoother than the top. Cut the torte into 2 layers and fill it with seedless raspberry or currant jam. Dust the top with confectioners' sugar or vanilla sugar. If you are more adventurous, coat the torte with a beautiful, shiny chocolate glaze.

8. In preparation for it, place the cake on a flat plate or cardboard disc slightly smaller than the cake, and push another plate under it to elevate it about ¾" above the work surface. Dilute seedless raspberry jam slightly with water and brush the torte with it. Cut the chocolate into ¾" pieces and process them for about 30 seconds in the food processor into very small pieces. Transfer the chocolate into a medium bowl. Bring heavy cream to a boil in a small heavy-bottomed saucepan and pour it over the chocolate, then cover the bowl and wait for about 3 minutes until the chocolate melts. Stir the mixture with a small whisk until it becomes perfectly smooth, but be careful not to whip air into the mixture. Wait until the mixture has slightly thickened but is still quite liquid. Pour most of it over the center of the torte and smooth it with the back and forth motion of a long metal spatula while

the glaze is still liquid. Move the spatula across the whole top; don't try to "touch up" parts of the glaze. Take a small spatula and quickly spread glaze over the still bare parts of the side, but don't touch the top again. Let it set for about 2 hours. After the glaze has hardened, cut the torte into 12 equal parts.

Spice Strudel
Gewürtz Strudel

Luckily, Riza néni's small collection of recipes includes examples for almost all major types of Austro-Hungarian desserts. It is especially lucky that the one strudel recipe in the collection happens to be unusual. I have not found a similar recipe in my research of cookbooks. The Turks introduced the paper-thin strudel dough, which they used in baklava and other similar desserts, to Hungary when they occupied much of the country for a hundred and fifty years in the sixteenth and seventeenth century. The German word *strudel* means whirlpool, which the cut side of the dessert vaguely resembles. It can be made with other types of thin dough, so don't be surprised to read about yeast-dough or pastry-dough strudels.

Of course, Riza néni, like all Hungarian housewives before World War II, used homemade strudel dough. Making it required great skill, as this dough had to be stretched by hand until it was so thin that one could almost see through it. In addition to the skill required, making the dough needed a large kitchen or someone who didn't mind flour all over the floor around her dining table, because the dough had to be stretched on a free-standing table. Today, most people in Hungary, as in our country, use store-bought dough for strudel. In the United States, factory-made phyllo, filo, or strudel (the names are used interchangeably) is available in the frozen food section of many supermarkets. One package usually contains about twenty sheets, the size of which can vary slightly from brand to brand, but it will not be much different from the size used in the recipe. It is easy to compensate for the small difference in size by varying the overlap of the layers of leaves; it is a much harder problem to deal with the variance in the quality of the product. Some brands are better than others, but how the packages have been handled by the store can make an even bigger difference. My best advice is to buy from a store that sells a great many, because then there is less chance that the sheets have stuck together as a result of improper storage. Occasional small tears don't matter—the layering of the dough will take care of that—but if you see that the sheets stick together, are brittle or full of tears, don't waste your time finishing the strudel but exchange the package or buy another one in a different store.

The original recipe didn't specify the kind of fat used for brushing the dough. I substituted a mixture of butter and oil for the rendered goose fat that I am sure Riza néni used.

YIELD: 8 servings

TOTAL TIME: about 1 hour, plus 10 minutes cooling time

INGREDIENTS:
⅔ cup raw almonds
2 tablespoons sugar
4 large egg yolks
3 tablespoons sugar
⅔ cup golden raisins, coarsely chopped
⅔ cup dark raisins, coarsely chopped
1 tablespoon lemon juice
2 teaspoons grated lemon zest
1 teaspoon ground cinnamon
½ teaspoon ground cloves
2 large egg whites
¼ teaspoon cream of tartar
1 tablespoon sugar
5 tablespoons unsalted butter or margarine
2 tablespoons canola oil

7–10 strudel (filo or phyllo) leaves, each 13½" × 17", taken from a thawed package of phyllo leaves (phyllo must always be thawed in the refrigerator because the leaves tend to stick together when they are thawed at room temperature)

SPECIAL
EQUIPMENT: cookie sheet (14" × 18")
food processor
electric mixer (optional)
smooth-weave kitchen towel, 18" × 25" or larger

1. Center a rack in the oven and preheat the oven to 350°F. Place almonds and 2 tablespoons sugar in the food processor and process for 50 seconds, until finely and evenly ground.

2. Beat egg yolks and 3 tablespoons sugar with an electric mixer for about 3 minutes or by hand for about 5 minutes. Add ground almonds, chopped golden and dark raisins, lemon juice and zest, cinnamon and cloves, and mix it all together.

3. Add cream of tartar to egg whites and whip them at medium speed to form soft peaks, add 1 tablespoon sugar and continue whipping at high speed until the whites become shiny and form firm peaks. Stir about ⅓ of the whipped egg whites into the egg yolk mixture to lighten it, then gently fold in the rest of the whites.

4. Place butter and oil in a small saucepan or heat-resistant bowl, and heat it until the butter melts. Place it and a large pastry brush near your work surface. Brush the cookie sheet with fat. Spread the kitchen towel sideways on your kitchen counter. Open the package of thawed phyllo leaves and place 7 to 10 leaves on top of each other on the dry and clean work surface or on a tray near the kitchen towel. Immediately cover the removed sheets completely with plastic wrap to keep them from drying out and becoming brittle. Reseal the phyllo package.

5. Place 1 sheet of the 17" wide phyllo so that it covers one end of the 18" wide kitchen towel. Keep the remaining sheets covered with the plas-

tic wrap. Brush well an approximately 2"-wide strip along the 4 edges of the phyllo on the kitchen towel with fat, then brush the inside of the sheet much more lightly. Place another sheet on top of the first sheet and repeat the step of brushing it with fat. Now place a third sheet so that it covers the other end of the kitchen towel and overlaps the first 2 sheets of phyllo by about 3". Brush this sheet also, especially the edges. Don't use too much fat on the inside of the sheet or the strudel will be greasy. Now, put a second layer of phyllo on top of this sheet and brush it lightly. Finally, place a sheet on top of the first 2 sheets, and brush this, too. You now have half of the 18" × 25" kitchen towel covered with 3 layers, the other half with 2 layers of phyllo. If the sheets had lots of tears in them, add 1 more layer to both halves.

6. Spoon the fairly soft filling over the 3-layered area, but be careful to leave a 3"-wide bare strip on 3 sides around the filling. Don't spread any filling over the 2-layered half of the phyllo rectangle. With the help of the cloth, fold the 17"-long bare strip over the filling, being careful not to crush it, and brush this hem with fat. Now, with the help of the cloth, fold the 2 longer sides of the phyllo rectangle and brush these hems, too. Again, be careful not to crush the filling. You should be left with a sheet of dough about 12" × 22", half of it covered with filling and 3 of its edges folded to form hems.

7. Holding the cloth at the narrower side, start rolling the strudel from the end where the filling is but roll it very loosely, allowing about ½" of slack at each turn (this is very important) to give room for the filling to expand. As you roll the strudel, stop at each turn to brush it with fat, so that the whole surface gets coated. Don't worry if the strudel looks flat; it will rise during baking when the eggs swell in the filling, so it will be nicely shaped when it is finished. On the other hand, if you roll it too tightly, you run the risk that the strudel might burst. When you finished rolling the strudel, brush the top with fat, lift it up by cradling it in the kitchen towel and gently roll it onto the greased baking sheet so that the seam of the strudel is on the bottom.

8. Bake it in the preheated oven for about 35–40 minutes, until golden brown. Transfer the cookie sheet with the strudel on it to a cooling rack and allow it to cool until warm. Carefully slide the strudel from

the cookie sheet onto a cutting board and slice it 1½" thick on the bias with a long, serrated knife. Dust the slices with confectioners' sugar and serve them warm. Store leftovers at room temperature and reheat them before serving.

ROSH HASHANAH AND YOM KIPPUR AT RIZA NÉNI'S

ON THE HIGH HOLY DAYS, when my mother and her siblings got ten days off from school in Budapest, they always went by train to visit their grandparents in Moson. They arrived for Rosh Hashanah, the Jewish New Year, and returned to Budapest after Yom Kippur, the Day of Atonement. Frigyes bácsi, their favorite uncle, picked them up at the train station and took them home in one of the fiákers, elegant, Viennese-style horse-drawn carriages, that waited for hire in front of the train station for arriving passengers. In Judaism Rosh Hashanah and the following days are the time when God examines the deeds of each person and decides their fate for the coming year. For the past several days in preparation for these holidays, my great-grandparents had been going to the synagogue every morning for prayers of forgiveness. They were just ending their morning fast when the children arrived in the early afternoon.

The next day, while Riza néni and her husband were in the synagogue,

Paula finished preparing the festive midday meal. She baked sweet challah loaves with raisins in them. Contrary to the elongated, braided Sabbath challah, these were round, perhaps to represent a well-rounded year to come and the continuity of life. To make the year sweet, Riza néni served lots of sweet things for Rosh Hashanah lunch. The meal started with chicken, goose, or beef soup, followed by a main course with something sweet to go with it, such as soup meat served with raisin sauce, roast poultry or meat with fruit, or goose fricassee with chestnut sauce. Riza néni had told Paula to include the head of the poultry, which she served to my great-grandfather to express his place as the head of the family and the hope that in the coming year he would be a leader among men. Conversely, she had told Paula to throw away the poultry's giblets and feet, which had been valued parts of the soup at other times; but my mother couldn't explain the reason for this custom. There was always at least one dish made with carrots on the table, because, in addition to being sweet, carrots were associated with gold and this would bring prosperity in the new year. Carrots were also omens of fertility and increasing valor, as *mehren*, the Yiddish word for carrots is similar to the one for "multiply." Mother was not very fond of carrots, but according to Riza néni merely looking at them was already beneficial. They never had anything with tomatoes for their holiday dinner because the tomatoes would have soured the new year. For dessert there was apple strudel, apple compote, or apple-filled pastry squares. The squares didn't include the customary walnuts because Riza néni followed the local custom in forgoing walnuts between New Year and the last day of Sukkot, three weeks later. Probably she was unaware of it, but the reason for this custom was the almost identical numerical value of the Hebrew words for walnuts and sin.

In the afternoon, as the whole family walked the short distance on Duna utca (Danube Street) from Main Street to the nearby branch of the Danube, they met many of their Jewish neighbors all heading the same way. When they got to the river they could see about thirty or forty people already standing along the bank, praying and throwing bread crumbs into the water as symbols for casting their sins into the depths of the sea. Some even turned their pockets out to make sure that no crumb was lurking there from the previous year. They wished to start the year with a clean slate, or at the very least with clean pockets. Of course, my mother and her sister thought that this scene at the river was great fun: all the grownups were feeding the fish.

For the children, one of the highlights of the holiday season was watching their grandparents perform a ceremony in the courtyard of their house on the morning before Yom Kippur. First, Paula tied the legs of a white hen and rooster, which of course were protesting at the tops of their voices. She then gave the hen to Riza néni and the rooster to my great-grandfather, who swung them a few times around their heads to transfer their sins to the unfortunate birds. The children laughed their heads off when the rooster managed to get away and began to hop around furiously flapping his wings. Immediately after the ceremony, the shochet, whom

Riza néni had asked to come to their house, killed the fowl. These were then donated to charity, with the paradoxical result that the poor ate the poultry carrying the sins of the well-to-do.

Traditionally, lunch that day was beef soup with *kreplach*, meat-filled noodle dough pockets, in addition to dishes like those served for Rosh Hashanah. Dinner, the last meal before the fast, was a lighter meal, usually chicken soup followed by stuffed chicken, which Paula prepared with less salt than usual to minimize thirst during the fast. After dinner Riza néni lit two candles, one for the dead and another for the living, and blessed each. She looked sadly at the candle, thinking of her three children who had died young. This day and Rosh Hashanah were the only times of the year when she wore a white dress instead of her usual long black dresses, while her husband put a white robe over his suit because white was traditionally worn in the temple on these holidays. In addition, they wore slippers instead of leather shoes during the fast. Even Frigyes bácsi, who otherwise paid little attention to religious tradition, fasted and went to the temple with his parents. The children stayed home in the evening with Paula, watching the candles and playing. The next day on their way to visit Riza néni in the synagogue they walked through the gate of the tree-shaded yard of the synagogue complex, entered the temple through the women's entrance, and climbed the curving stair to bring

flowers to their grandmother. More than seventy years later, my mother was still perplexed over how her religious grandmother could allow them to carry flowers on Yom Kippur, when—similar to the Sabbath restrictions—labors are prohibited.

When my mother and her sister were a little older, they were allowed to sit with the women on the balcony, which was separated from the rest of the temple by a rather widely spaced screen. "It was quite a scene there on the balcony!" my mother recalled, "Next to the less well-to-do, elegant ladies sat there and showed off their jewelry. I've never heard so much gossiping in all my life. Downstairs, grandfather was beating his chest to purge his sins. When I was a teenager, Fenákel, the cantor, courted me. I tried to find a seat near the end of one of the side wings of the balcony, because this was the closest to where he stood downstairs, and exchanged glances with him during the service. He looked up, I looked down: it was great fun. I will never forget how gorgeously he sung the Kol Nidre. I lost track of him in later years, but I believe he was deported and killed during World War II.

"You can imagine how little patience we had for sitting in the temple all day." she continued, "So, we went out to the courtyard of the synagogue to chat and fool around. Then my grandfather would come out from the service to tell us 'Go home and check if there is any mail. If there is something that looks important, ask Paula to open it and tell you what it is.' We always laughed at grandfather, who couldn't wait until the end of the holiday to find out what was in the letters."

As the stars began to appear in the sky, after saying the concluding prayers of Yom Kippur and the blessing for the appearance of the New Moon, Riza néni and her family returned home. Riza néni had always baked a gugelhupf (see recipes on pages 288–295) the day before, to be cut up and eaten when the fast was over. First they sipped a little schnapps, then ate the cake with coffee. They had gugelhupf at other times, too, but it was a must at the end of the long fast.

Honey Cookies

Honigpusserl

Honey is frequently mentioned in the Bible, though instead of bees' honey, in most cases this was probably syrup extracted from dates or figs. Before the widespread use of cane sugar, honey was the most common and sometimes the only sweetener. As a result, baked goods made with honey are some of our oldest kinds of desserts.

For centuries they have been popular among Ashkenazi Jews, too, as is attested by the "Machzor Vitry," a compilation of prayers and other religious texts prepared in eleventh-century France, which describes how Jewish people gave honey cakes to their children on the first day of religious school. The "Machzor Vitry" then goes on to tell the next step in this pedagogical use of honey: "after reading him [the child] the letters, they covered the blackboard with honey and told him to lick it off." They probably intended this to be an incentive to learn, but it sure wouldn't make me love school.

Honey cakes and cookies have become associated in Ashkenazi Jewish life with life-cycle events, such as engagement, wedding, or circumcision, and with festivals, such as Shavuot, Purim, or Chanukah. Honey's association with Rosh Hashanah, however, is closer than with any other festival. Already during kiddush—the prayer that starts the holiday—there is a bowl of honey on the table to represent the desire to have a sweet New Year, and following the kiddush the family dips bread and apple slices into this. Throughout the holiday, cakes and cookies made with honey are traditionally served with the meals.

All the dozen or so versions of these cookies I have seen in my research of Austrian and Hungarian cookbooks add ground cinnamon to the dough and many of those versions, especially the older ones, use a mixture of rye and wheat flours to make the dough. Although Riza néni left both cinnamon and rye flour out of her recipe, I decided to include them as optional ingredients because their flavors go wonderfully well with honey. I also offer the option to either decorate these tasty cookies with sprinkles of coarse sugar, as Riza néni recommended, or with split almonds.

YIELD:	about 60 cookies
TOTAL TIME:	about 1 hour (half of this is unattended)
INGREDIENTS:	1⅓ cups all-purpose unbleached flour, or ⅓ cup rye and 1 cup all-purpose unbleached flour (you can usually buy rye flour in health food stores)
	¾ teaspoon baking soda
	1 teaspoon ground cinnamon (optional)
	4 tablespoons (¼ cup) honey
	⅓ cup superfine sugar
	1 large egg
	1 large egg white
	2 tablespoons coarse white or multicolored cake-decorating sugar
	¼ cup blanched almonds, split lengthwise with a knife (optional, instead of the coarse sugar)
SPECIAL EQUIPMENT:	food processor
	dough scraper (optional)
	cookie sheet (14" × 18")
	parchment paper or nonstick silicone baking mat
	1¼"-diameter round cutter (or use a similar-diameter small brandy glass to cut the cookies)

1. Place flour, baking soda, and cinnamon in the bowl of the food processor and pulse once to mix them. Place honey and sugar in a small saucepan and stir them over medium heat for about 2 minutes, until they turn into a homogeneous syrup. Add this syrup to the flour mixture in the processor, making sure that you don't pour it over the center shaft. Process for about 20 seconds until the dry ingredients have completely absorbed the syrup, no lumps are left, and the mixture resembles slightly damp sand. Wait about 2 minutes for the mixture to cool a bit. Add the whole egg and process for about 20 seconds until the dough starts to gather on top of the blades and clear the bowl. The

dough should be medium-soft and slightly sticky. Place an 18"-long piece of plastic wrap on the work surface, transfer the dough onto it, and use the plastic to shape the dough into a slab about 4" × 5" × 1". Wrap it in plastic and let it rest at room temperature for at least 30 minutes.

2. Adjust a rack to the middle of the oven and preheat the oven to 300°F. Line a cookie sheet with parchment paper or baking mat.

3. Roll out the dough with a floured rolling pin on the floured work surface into a ¼"-thick sheet, about 10" × 7". Periodically during rolling lift up one and then the other side of the sheet of dough with a dough scraper and throw a little flour under the dough to keep it from sticking. Use the dough scraper to press the edges of the dough into neat lines. Cut little discs from the dough and place them about 1" apart on the cookie sheet. Gather the scraps of dough into a ball, roll it out again, cut discs from it, and continue this way until you have used up all the dough. I had 8 rows of cookies on my cookie sheet, 63 cookies in total.

4. Brush the cookies with lightly beaten egg white and sprinkle them with a small pinch of coarse sugar (Riza néni's recommendation) or press a split blanched almond in the middle of each.

5. Bake the cookies in the preheated oven for 15 minutes. Slide the parchment paper or baking mat with the cookies on it onto a cooling rack to cool for about 5 minutes. Remove the cookies from the paper or mat and place them on the rack to finish cooling, about another 5 minutes. Store the pleasantly chewy and very tasty—especially so if you made them with rye flour—cookies in an airtight tin or jar, where they will keep for at least a week. In fact, I like them best when they are three or four days old.

Rich Gugelhupf
Englisher Kugelhopf

Jewish people long ago adopted *gugelhupf*, the archetypal cake served during the Viennese *Jause*, the afternoon tea. This coffeecake stays fresh for a long time; in fact it is best a day or two after baking it, which makes it ideal for the Sabbath and for breaking the fast of Yom Kippur. *Kugel*, the German word for "ball," is at the root of gugelhupf, the untranslatable name of this cake that is baked in a special form. The gugelhupf (or kugelhupf as it is sometimes called) form is a deep tube form with a fluted pattern on its sides that vaguely recalls the swirling folds of a Turkish turban. Viennese bakers supposedly created this form in 1683 to celebrate the defeat of the Turkish army at the gates of Vienna. Most gugelhupfs are made with yeast dough, frequently with chocolate, raisins, candied fruit, or slivered almonds mixed into it, but there are also sponge dough gugelhupfs and even some that are made with baking powder. The traditional dusting of confectioners' sugar beautifully accentuates its distinctive shape as it settles on it as light snow settles on the ornaments of a classical building.

I don't know why Riza néni called this recipe "English gugelhupf." The only gugelhupf recipe I recall seeing with this name in one of my cookbooks is a completely different version made without yeast. While most gugelhupfs contain three to six eggs, her original recipe called for twelve eggs, which I decided to cut back to a "mere" nine: three whole eggs and six yolks. I thought that the cake would still be sufficiently rich this way, especially because in addition to the eggs it also includes heavy cream and more than the usual amount of butter. I use mostly yolks because this makes the cake even more moist. Riza néni left out the usual raisins from the dough, but I prefer to include them.

A slice of this cake might look plain, but one bite is enough to convince anybody that it is in fact the ultimate of luxury. Its fine moist texture, wonderfully rich mouth-feel, and seductive flavor are all unforgettable.

I can't think of a better way to celebrate the pleasures of eating after the long fast.

YIELD:	16 servings
TOTAL TIME:	about 2 hours 20 minutes (of this 1 hour is unattended)
INGREDIENTS:	½ cup milk
	1½ envelopes (1 envelope plus 1 teaspoon) active dry yeast
	1 tablespoon sugar
	1 cup unbleached all-purpose flour
	½ tablespoon unsalted butter, softened (to grease the form)
	⅓ cup fine bread crumbs, made in the food processor from stale white bread (to coat the form)
	16 blanched almonds (to decorate the form)
	½ cup heavy cream
	3 large eggs
	6 large egg yolks
	1½ teaspoons vanilla extract
	½ cup sugar
	½ teaspoon kosher salt
	2 tablespoons grated lemon zest
	2 sticks (8 ounces) unsalted room-temperature butter, cut into ½" pieces
	⅓ cup plump, soft golden raisins (optional)
	¼ cup plump, soft dark raisins (optional)
	2½ cups unbleached all-purpose flour
	1 envelope (5/16 ounce) vanilla sugar (by Oetker) or your own vanilla bean–infused confectioners' sugar (see step 7 for how to make it)
SPECIAL EQUIPMENT:	gugelhupf form (9" diameter × 4" deep, 12-cup capacity) or 12-cup capacity Bundt pan or other tube pan
	food processor, at least 7-cup capacity
	baking sheet

1. Heat milk to barely warm (105–110°F) and transfer it to a medium-size bowl. Stir in yeast, 1 tablespoon sugar, and 1 cup flour. Cover it with plastic wrap and let it ferment for 20 minutes at room temperature.

2. Generously butter a gugelhupf form or Bundt pan (use a piece of wax paper to spread the room-temperature butter), and lightly coat it with bread crumbs by pouring them into the form, turning it to coat the entire inside, and shaking out the excess crumbs. Sprinkle crumbs over the center tube. Lay a blanched almond in the bottom of each fluted section of the gugelhupf form.

3. Use a metal blade in the processor. Place heavy cream, eggs, yolks, vanilla, ½ cup sugar, salt, lemon zest, and pieces of butter in the bowl of the machine. Pulse about 10 times, until the butter is incorporated, then process for 30 seconds.

4. With a rubber spatula, scrape the risen yeast sponge into the processor bowl and add 2½ cups flour. Pulse 5 times by letting the machine run for about 2 seconds, then waiting about 2 seconds, and repeating. Scrape down the accumulated flour from the perimeter, then pulse another 5 times or until all the flour is incorporated. Process for 10 seconds. Strew the raisins over the dough and pulse a few times to distribute them. The soft and sticky dough will not clear the side of the bowl.

5. With a rubber spatula, transfer the dough into the form, making sure you don't dislodge the almonds in the bottom of the form. The dough will fill about ⅔ of the form. Even out the top of the dough with the spatula. Tightly cover the form with plastic wrap and let the dough rise in a comfortably warm place until it is close to the rim or slightly above, about 1 hour. Remove the plastic wrap when the dough starts to get close to the rim. About 15 minutes before the end of rising time, set the oven rack to the lowest position, remove the other racks, and preheat the oven to 400°F.

6. Place the form on a baking sheet and bake the cake for 10 minutes. Don't open the oven door during this time. Reduce the temperature to

350°F and continue baking for 20 minutes. Loosely cover the top of the cake, which has risen well above the top of the form, with a piece of aluminum foil, and continue baking for an additional 20 minutes. By now, you have baked it for a total of 50 minutes. Test it with a cake-testing pin; the cake is done when the pin comes out clean.

7. Cool the gugelhupf in the form set on a cooling rack for 5 minutes. Turn it out onto the cooling rack to finish cooling, about 2 hours. Shortly before serving, dust it with vanilla confectioners' sugar by rubbing the sugar through a small fine strainer. You can make vanilla confectioners' sugar by burying a vanilla bean in a jar of confectioners' sugar for a few weeks, or use a mixture of vanilla sugar (manufactured by Oetker and sold in small envelopes) and regular confectioners' sugar. Slice the cake so that each slice has an almond in it and cut only as many slices as you wish to serve. Store it for up to three or four days at room temperature in the covered gugelhupf form or in a plastic bag.

Chocolate Gugelhupf
Chokolade Kugelhopf

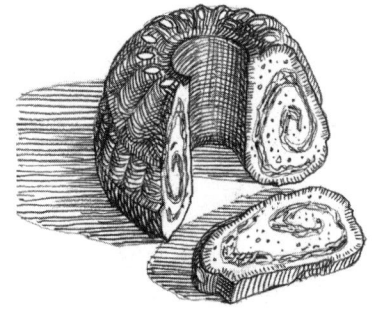

This recipe is not the usual marbled gugelhupf, but a yeast-dough strudel baked in a gugelhupf form. The filling of this strudel is the same dough as the casing, only it has been mixed with chocolate. The unbaked strudel is placed into the gugelhupf form and as it rises it fills the form resulting in elegantly alternating stripes of light and dark dough swirling in each slice of this cake. After admiring its spectacular looks, one can enjoy its wonderfully light texture and a taste that combines chocolate with the flavor of buttery yeast dough.

I have seen poppy seed or nut-filled versions of this recipe, though even they are quite rare, but I have never encountered a similar gugelhupf of alternating ribbons of light and dark dough. Like so many other recipes in this book, this points up the importance of old handwritten recipe collections: they preserve a tradition of cooking and baking that otherwise would have been forgotten. Aside from having to guess how much chocolate she could buy in the 1870s for fifteen kreuzer (coins of low value), the only hurdle in updating this recipe, one of the more detailed in the collection, was to adapt it to the food processor.

YIELD: 16 servings

TOTAL TIME: about 4 hours

INGREDIENTS:
- ⅔ cup milk
- 2 envelopes active dry yeast
- 1 teaspoon sugar
- 1 cup unbleached all-purpose flour
- ½ tablespoon unsalted butter, softened (to grease the form)
- ⅓ cup fine, dry bread crumbs, made in the food processor from stale white bread (to coat the form)
- 16 blanched almonds (to decorate the form)
- 2 large eggs
- 2 large egg yolks
- 1½ teaspoons vanilla extract
- ⅔ cup sugar
- ½ teaspoon kosher salt
- 2 teaspoons grated lemon zest
- 1 stick plus 2 tablespoons (5 ounces total) unsalted, room-temperature butter, cut into ½" slices
- 2¾ cups unbleached all-purpose flour, plus 1–4 tablespoons more flour to knead and roll the dough
- 4 ounces (4 squares) bittersweet chocolate, coarsely chopped into about ½" pieces

1 envelope (⁵⁄₁₆ ounce) vanilla sugar (by Oetker) or your own vanilla bean–infused confectioners' sugar (see step 7 of the previous recipe)

SPECIAL
EQUIPMENT: gugelhupf form (9" diameter × 4" deep, 12-cup capacity) or a 12-cup-capacity Bundt pan or tube pan
food processor, at least 7-cup capacity
baking sheet

1. Heat milk to barely warm (105–110°F) and pour it into a medium-size bowl. Stir in yeast, 1 teaspoon sugar, and 1 cup flour. Cover with plastic wrap and let the mixture ferment at room temperature for 20 minutes.

2. Generously butter the gugelhupf form or Bundt pan. Use a piece of wax paper to spread the butter in the form. Lightly coat it with bread crumbs by pouring them into the form, turning it to coat the entire inside, and shaking out the excess crumbs. Sprinkle crumbs over the center tube. Lay a blanched almond in the bottom of each fluted section of the gugelhupf form.

3. Use the metal blade in the processor. Place eggs, yolks, vanilla, ⅔ cup sugar, salt, lemon zest, and the butter pieces in the processor bowl. Pulse about 10 times to form a paste, which will look curdled. Process for 30 seconds to make the paste smoother.

4. Lift out the metal blade and replace it with a plastic one if you have a 7-cup machine; leave the metal blade in place if you have a larger processor. To minimize leakage, place the plastic blade where the metal blade left a void in the paste. With a rubber spatula scrape the risen yeast sponge into the processor bowl and add 2½ cups flour. Pulse until a soft and sticky dough has formed, then process for 15 seconds. Add ¼ cup more flour and process for another 10 seconds. The dough will not clear the side of the bowl.

5. Use a rubber spatula to transfer the soft and sticky dough to your well-floured work surface. Gather the dough, sprinkle a little flour over it,

and start kneading. The soft, butter-rich dough should be slightly sticky, but not so sticky as to stick to your hands or the work surface. If the dough is too sticky, gradually add a little flour. (In low humidity I didn't have to add any, but this can vary depending on the weather.) Knead it for about 2 minutes by pressing down into the dough with your hand, pushing forward, folding the dough back on itself, giving it a quarter turn, and repeating this sequence. The kneaded dough should be silky smooth, elastic, and it should slowly spring back when pressed with your finger. Very lightly butter the inside of a large bowl. Shape the dough into a ball, place it in the bowl, cover with plastic wrap, and let the dough rise at room temperature until it swells to about 1½ times its volume, about 45 minutes.

6. Wipe out the bowl of the food processor—it is not necessary to wash it. If you used the plastic blade for the dough, switch to the metal one. Place coarsely chopped chocolate in the machine and process for about 20 seconds, until finely ground. Transfer the risen dough to the lightly floured work surface; divide it with a dough scraper or knife into 2 parts, one slightly smaller than the other. Add the smaller part to the chocolate in the processor. Pulse 5 times, then process for about 10 seconds, until the dough has absorbed the chocolate and but still has some blond streaks. Turn it out to the lightly floured work surface and knead it very briefly to finish distributing the chocolate.

7. With a floured rolling pin on the floured work surface, roll out the blond dough into an 8" x 16" rectangle. Repeat the same with the dark dough. Rolling the rectangles next to each other with their long sides perpendicular to the edge of the work surface makes it easy to roll them to the same size without much measuring. Place the dark rectangle on top of the blond one, and roll them up into a 16" long and about 3"-diameter roll. If the dough has contracted, gently roll the dough-sausage under your hands on the work surface to make it 16" long. Carefully pick it up so that the seam is on the top and, starting at the middle of the sausage, lay it in the bottom of the form so that it reaches all the way around the center tube of the form and the ends ever so slightly overlap. Be careful not to dislodge the almonds in the bottom of the form. Even out the top surface of the dough, because if the dough is higher on one side of the form the finished cake will be also

lopsided. The dough will fill a little less than half the depth of the form. Tightly cover the form with plastic wrap and set it to a comfortably warm place to rise until it has risen to the top of the form or close to it, about 2 hours. The degree of rising is what matters, not the time it takes. About 15 minutes before the end of rising set a rack to the lowest position in the oven, remove the other racks, and preheat the oven to 400°F.

8. Place the form on a baking sheet and bake the cake in the preheated oven for an initial 10 minutes. Don't open the oven door during this time. Reduce the temperature to 350°F and continue baking for 20 minutes. Loosely cover the top of the cake, which has continued to rise in the oven, with a piece of aluminum foil and continue baking for an additional 20 minutes.

9. Cool the cake for 5 minutes in the form. Turn out the cake to the cooling rack to finish cooling, about 2 hours. The cake is the prettiest if before slicing you present it whole, lightly dusted with vanilla confectioners' sugar. Sprinkle the sugar over the cake by rubbing the sugar through a small fine strainer. Don't try to cover the entire surface evenly, but let the sugar fall over the cake like light snow. Store the cake for up to 3 or 4 days at room temperature in the covered gugelhupf form or in a plastic bag.

SUKKOT AT RIZA NÉNI'S

BY THE TIME my mother lived with them, my elderly great-grandparents no longer erected a sukkah. This is the name of the makeshift hut, or booth as it is frequently translated, where religious Jews eat and the most pious also sleep during the holiday of Sukkot to remind them of the way their ancestors dwelt while wandering in the desert during their exile in Egypt. Instead, my great-grandparents used the *szaletli*, a gazebo in their garden. One couldn't see the stars through the roof of the gazebo, as one can see through the loosely laid branches or reed in a real sukkah that conforms to religious requirements, but Riza néni felt this was close enough to the ideal and a lot simpler than constructing a sukkah.

She helped my mother decorate the szaletli prettily for the occasion with fruits and tree branches hanging from its sides and roof and taught her to make garlands from colored paper, which they hung from branches in the roof. She also taught my mother to puncture small holes in eggs, blow out their insides, and glue paper heads and feathers on the empty eggshells to make birds from them. Riza néni's family ate their meals in the szaletli, which was only a few steps from their kitchen, but never slept there.

She asked my mother to make a sign and write on it "Liebe Ahnen, sei willkommen in unserer Hütte" (Dear ancestors, be welcome in our hut). They hung this sign at the entrance of the gazebo so that Abraham, Isaac, Jacob, Joseph, Moses, Aaron, and David could find their way to visit them, though the biblical visitors would have been surprised to find a German sign instead of the Aramaic *ushpizin* (invitation; literally: "guests") prescribed by religious tradition. While my mother was making the sign, her grandmother entertained her with stories about Riza néni's grandfather Abraham and his brother Jacob, namesakes of the patriarchs, whom she as a young girl had visited in Körmend, a small town near the Austrian border. As I listened to my mother telling me about the Sukkot of her childhood, it struck me how such stories provide a personal connection to the distant past: after all, I was listening to stories about my ancestors who were born in 1767 and 1771.

Lujza néni's family, who didn't have direct access to the garden from their apartment, erected a sukkah on their side of the courtyard between the two walnut trees, with the side of it against the porch to be near their kitchen. Riza néni and her husband visited their siblings to admire their sukkah and sit in it for a while, but as usual, the two families ate separately, each in their own part of the house.

The last day of Sukkot was Simchat Torah, "rejoicing of the Torah," the joyful day associated with the conclusion of the annual reading of the Torah. At this time all the Torah scrolls were taken out of the ark and paraded around the synagogue by the dancing and singing male congregants. They even took the scrolls up to the women's balcony. Mother fondly remembered this festival when girls and young women were also allowed to enter the main part of the synagogue to participate in the joyous procession. She and the other kids carried flags mounted on sticks on the top of which were hollowed out large apples with candles burning inside.

The congregation selected two *hatanim*, Hebrew for bridegrooms, of the Torah: one to read the last words of the Torah, the other one to read the first words of Genesis, the first of the five books of Moses that comprise the Torah, thus initiating a new cycle in the annual reading. While the two "bridegrooms" hosted a Simchat Torah party for the whole congregation, the children gathered in the courtyard of the synagogue and waited excitedly for what was for them the culmination of this holiday. They cheered when at long last one of the balcony windows of the temple opened and the shammas (synagogue beadle) leaned out. He showered them with walnuts from two baskets, then smiled broadly at the sight of the kids scampering to grab as many nuts as possible. The children were unaware of the origin of this unusual custom, which, in tune with the wedding symbolism that permeated so much of the Simchat Torah festivities, borrowed a feature from a Hungarian Jewish wedding tradition, in which the bridegroom was showered with walnuts, a symbol of fertility.

Wine Cake
Weinkuchen

Sukkot, also known as the Festival of Tabernacles, which is celebrated in late September or early October, is among others a joyous thanksgiving festival, the celebration of the bounty of the harvest. In keeping with harvest time, during this holiday it is traditional to serve stuffed grape leaves or stuffed cabbage, a modern version of the dish. Other stuffed preparations also became associated with Sukkot, for example kreplach, stuffed noodle dough dumplings served in chicken soup. Desserts, such as compotes, strudels, or pies make use of the fruit available in autumn; dishes and desserts made with wine are further reminders of harvest time. Braised veal tongue (see recipe on page 104) is a good example of such dishes, as is this wine cake of the desserts prepared for this holiday.

Riza néni's wine cake is a kind of sponge cake, a name doubly appropriate in this case, because it not only describes the type of dough, but it is also true in the most literal sense: a sponge to soak up the mulled wine poured over it. It is a wonderfully tasty cake, which, as Riza néni was careful to point out in her recipe, will keep moist for several days. Desserts made with wine or other alcoholic drinks are nothing unusual: wine soufflés or puddings are fairly common in Austria and Hungary, and rum-soaked yeast cakes, such as rum babas or savarins, are traditional in France. But no matter how I searched in cookbooks, I couldn't find any cake similar to Riza néni's wine-soaked sponge cake, another great cake that has somehow become forgotten in the intervening one hundred and thirty years.

YIELD: 12 servings

TOTAL TIME: about 1 hour 15 minutes

INGREDIENTS:
- 1⅓ cups fine bread crumbs (made in the food processor from about 5 slices of stale white bread)
- 1 teaspoon unsalted butter or margarine (to grease the cake pan)
- ¼ cup raw almonds
- 2 tablespoons sugar
- 5 large egg yolks
- ½ cup sugar
- 1 teaspoon ground cinnamon
- ½ teaspoon ground cloves
- 3 teaspoons grated lemon zest
- 7 large egg whites
- ¾ teaspoon cream of tartar
- 1 tablespoon sugar
- 1⅓ cups fruity white wine, such as Riesling
- 2 teaspoons ground cinnamon
- 2½ tablespoons sugar

SPECIAL EQUIPMENT:
food processor
9" × 9" × 1½" or 2" cake pan
electric mixer (optional)
baking sheet

1. Center a rack in the oven and preheat the oven to 350°F. Place bread crumbs in a bowl. Grease the inside of the cake pan, pour ¼ cup of the bread crumbs into it, tilt the form in all directions to lightly coat the entire inside with crumbs and shake the excess crumbs back into the bowl.

2. Place almonds and 2 tablespoons sugar in the food processor and process them for about 40 seconds, until finely and evenly ground. In a large bowl, beat egg yolks and ½ cup sugar for about 5 minutes with an electric mixer or 10 minutes by hand, until they become very pale and fluffy. Mix in the bread crumbs, ground almonds, cinnamon, clove, and lemon zest. It will be a very stiff, thick mixture.

3. Place egg whites in a large bowl, add cream of tartar, and whip whites to form soft peaks. Add 1 tablespoon sugar and continue whipping until they form firm peaks. Stir about ½ of the whipped egg whites into the egg yolk mixture to lighten it, then gently fold in the rest. Pour the soft batter into the cake form; use a rubber spatula and tap the form to even out the batter in it.

4. Place the cake form on a baking sheet and transfer it into the preheated oven. Prop the oven door slightly ajar with a wedged-in knife and bake this way for 10 minutes to allow moisture to escape. Remove the knife, close the oven door completely and continue baking the cake for another 18–20 minutes, until its top surface springs back when lightly pressed with your finger and its edges pull away from the form.

5. Place a cooling rack upside-down on the cake form and while holding them together carefully invert the form and let the cake drop onto the cooling rack. Allow the cake to cool this way, upside down, for about 30 minutes.

6. While the cake is cooling, pour wine into a small saucepan, add 2 teaspoons cinnamon and 2½ tablespoons sugar, and heat them until the sugar dissolves. It is not necessary to bring it to a boil.

7. When the cake is cool, put it back into the form, and pour about ⅓ of the hot liquid evenly over its top surface. Wait until the cake has

soaked up most of the liquid; repeat this with the second third of the liquid; and after further waiting for the liquid to be absorbed, pour the remainder of the hot liquid over the cake. After it has absorbed all the wine mixture, transfer it to a platter or a cutting board and cut it into 12 slices. Keep leftover slices in the refrigerator in the cake form tightly covered with plastic wrap.

CHANUKAH AT RIZA NÉNI'S

IN RIZA NÉNI'S HOUSE Christmas was not considered a holiday, but when her daughter, my grandmother, moved to Budapest, she decided to follow the example of virtually all assimilated Jews there and celebrate Christmas as a secular holiday. On Christmas Eve, while her children were told to wait in their room behind closed

She lit a candle on the tree stump in the window.

doors, she set up and decorated a tree in the living room and placed presents under it. She then rang the doorbell, let the children into the living room, and told them that they had just missed the angel who had rung the bell and brought the tree and the presents. The children knew who the resident angel was, but played along and pretended to believe the story. My grandmother and her family skipped church, of course, but otherwise they celebrated Christmas the same way as Gentiles.

But Chanukah was very much a holiday at Riza néni's. She set the beautiful brass menorah in the window of the formal dining room facing the street, while on the courtyard side of the house she set a simple tree stump on the window ledge of the informal living room. Because the walls of their old house were so thick, the window ledge was close to two feet deep and could comfortably accommodate the stump. The candles stuck on it were Riza néni's personal take on the Chanukah tradition. She certainly could have afforded a second menorah, but must have felt that in the window facing her unpaved courtyard the rustic stump was more appropriate.

On the first night of Chanukah the whole family gathered at the menorah in the formal dining room, where following a blessing by my great-grandfather Riza néni helped my mother to light the first candle. Then they sang a beautiful old hymn about the holiday, and my mother was told to light the candle on the tree stump in the other room, too. She melted the bottom of a little colored candle and stuck it on the stump. A separate candle was the *shammash*, the "servant" light, because it was used to light the others. After dinner Riza néni and Frigyes bácsi played dreidl with my mother. Each of them put a nut into the "pot," then they took turns spinning the dreidl, a four-sided top made of cast lead and decorated with the Hebrew letters *nun*, *gimel*, *heh*, and *shin* on its sides. These letters stood in the old German version of this toy for *nichts* (nothing), *ganz* (all), *halb* (half), and *stell ein* (put in). Of course, the conversation was in German, and when Riza néni disappointedly said "stell ein" upon seeing that the dreidl had landed on the letter *shin*, she probably had no idea that she was recalling the German origins of this Chanukah tradition. Every night during the eight days of Chanukah my mother lit one more candle, until at the end, all eight candles were burning festively in both windows to commemorate the victory of the Jews and the rededication (the meaning of the Hebrew word *chanukah*) of the Temple.

Pastry Fritters

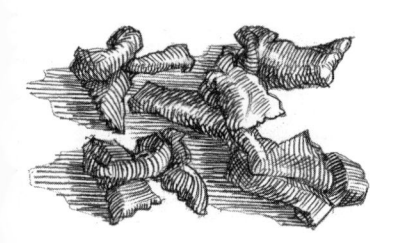

Fritteln

Fried chicken, potato latkes, doughnuts, fritters, and other deep-fried food have long been eaten during Chanukah as reminders of the "miracle of the oil."

While the story of the miracle is apocryphal, it relates to a historical event, the return of Judah Maccabeus and his army to Jerusalem following their victorious uprising against the Greek oppressors of Jews. In 165 B.C.E., the Jews returned to Jerusalem to find the Temple and all its oil vessels desecrated, except for one small vessel, which still contained consecrated olive oil, but only enough to burn for one day in the candelabrum. They poured it into the candelabrum, lit it, and miraculously it lasted eight days, enough for the priests to cleanse the Temple and get a new supply of holy oil. Riza néni's pastry fritters and the following recipe for candied apple fritters are typical examples of deep-fried desserts prepared for this holiday.

Such desserts are most typical of Chanukah, but they are prepared for other holidays, too. The so-called Haman's ears, one of the traditional Purim desserts, are really very similar to these pastry fritters. They are made of the same dough, cut into similar strips; the only difference is that in Haman's ears the dough strips are pinched together in the middle instead of slit like the pastry fritters. Not a difference worth getting excited about.

Deep frying needs quite a lot of oil: even in a relatively small, eight-inch-diameter pot, such as the one I used here, I needed about three cups of it. Luckily, canola oil is relatively inexpensive and you can reuse it after straining it through a paper towel–lined strainer. The used oil will keep for a week or two in a jar, though it is best to discard it after the second use.

YIELD: about 24 fritters

TOTAL TIME: about 45 minutes

INGREDIENTS:
- 1 cup unbleached all-purpose flour
- 1½ teaspoons sugar
- ¼ teaspoon kosher salt
- 1½ tablespoons unsalted butter or margarine, cut into ¼" pieces
- 1½ teaspoons grated lemon zest
- ½ teaspoon vanilla extract
- 2 large egg yolks
- 2–4 tablespoons white wine
- ¼ cup confectioners' sugar
- 2 teaspoons ground cinnamon

3 cups canola oil
⅓ cup apricot jam
1 tablespoon rum, orange juice, or water

SPECIAL
EQUIPMENT:
food processor
fluted pastry cutting wheel (optional)
deep fryer or an about 8"-diameter and 3" to 4" deep pot
deep-frying thermometer (unless your fryer has a thermostat)
cooling rack (optional)

1. Place flour, sugar, and salt in the bowl of the food processor. Pulse once to mix them. Add butter or margarine pieces and process for 10 seconds. Add lemon zest, vanilla, egg yolks, and 2 tablespoons of wine. Process for about 20 seconds. The dough should form a ball on top of the blades of the machine; if it doesn't, add more wine by the tablespoonful and process briefly until the dough comes together. The dough should be fairly soft but not sticky. As soon as it has formed a ball, remove the dough from the processor, wrap it in plastic, and let it rest for at least 15 minutes.

2. Divide the dough into halves. Place one half on the lightly floured work surface, and with a floured rolling pin roll it out into a rectangle about 6" × 12". Lift up the dough a few times during rolling and sprinkle a little flour under it so it doesn't stick. With the fluted pastry wheel, or with a knife or dough scraper, cut the sheet of dough into 6" × 1" strips. Cut a 2½"–3" slit in the middle of each strip. Thread one end of a strip through the slit in the middle, then thread the other end through the same slit, but this time from the opposite side of the strip. It will vaguely resemble a bow tie. Repeat this with all the strips, then roll out the second half of the dough, and repeat the whole procedure. You will have about 24 pieces. Keep them on a lightly floured surface.

3. Lay a large piece of paper towel near your range and place a cooling rack over it. If you don't have a cooling rack, the paper towel alone will do. Mix confectioners' sugar with cinnamon and spread this mixture

on a plate. In a small bowl, dilute apricot jam with a little rum, juice, or water and set it aside.

4. Of course, deep frying is easiest in a thermostatically controlled deep fryer. If you are among those—as I am—who don't have such a deep fryer, pour about 1" oil into an 8" diameter and 3"–4"-deep pot or sauté pan and clip a candy/deep-fry thermometer—a fairly inexpensive gadget—to the side of the pot. Make sure the end of the thermometer is completely immersed and the tip doesn't touch the bottom. Heat the oil over medium heat to 375°F. It is important that the oil be the right temperature because if it isn't hot enough, the fritters will be greasy, and if it is too hot, it will start to decompose while the fritters will be too dark and have an unpleasant burned taste. As soon as the oil has reached the temperature of 370°F, adjust the heat to medium-low, because the pot's residual heat will keep raising the temperature of the oil for a few seconds. If you don't have a thermometer, drop a ½" cube of white bread into the hot oil; if it browns to a uniform golden color in 40 seconds, the oil is about 375°F. When the oil is the right temperature, drop as many dough strips, one by one, into the hot oil as the pot can accommodate without crowding, about 6 pieces. After about 45 seconds, when their first side has turned golden brown, flip the fritters over with tongs to allow their second side to brown, which should take less time than the first side. Watch them carefully that they don't get too dark. As soon as a piece is ready, remove it from the oil and transfer it to drain on the cooling rack or paper towel. When you have finished frying the first batch, wait to bring the oil back to 375°F, test the temperature and fry the second batch of fritters, and so on until all are done.

5. Roll the fritters in the sugar-cinnamon mixture and serve them by themselves or with a small bowl of diluted apricot jam for dipping. The fritters are best when freshly made, but they will stay crisp in an airtight box for about two days.

Candied Apple Fritters
Kandierte Äpfel

Strangely, while I couldn't find any similar recipe in my Hungarian and Austrian cookbooks, I found a related recipe in Maida Heatter's *New Book of Great Desserts*, one of her excellent dessert books. It is slightly different from Riza néni's version because it uses whole slices instead of little discs of apples for the fritters and uses baking powder in the batter instead of yeast, but the overall idea is the same. The use of baking powder also shows that hers is a twentieth-century descendant of Riza néni's version. Commercial baking powder had been around since the 1850s, but at least in Austria and Hungary it had rarely been used before the beginning of the twentieth century, when it began to be sold in standardized packages. In the nineteenth century, people used a small amount of yeast in the kind of batter or dough that today would be prepared with baking powder. According to Maida Heatter, her recipe comes from her mother, Saidie Heatter. The recipe detective in me would love to know where Saidie Heatter got her recipe and whether it can be traced back to some Austro-Hungarian source.

These apple fritters are best when they are fresh, but only the frying and broiling needs to be done shortly before serving; preparing the batter and coating the apple pieces can be done up to an hour earlier.

YIELD: 5 servings

TOTAL TIME: about 55 minutes

INGREDIENTS:
- 3 tablespoons unsalted butter, melted
- ⅓ cup half-and-half
- 1 teaspoon active dry yeast (about ½ of a standard envelope)
- ½ tablespoon sugar
- ¼ cup unbleached all-purpose flour

3 Granny Smith apples, peeled, cored, and cut crosswise into ¼" slices
¾ cup unbleached all-purpose flour
2 tablespoons sugar
1 large egg yolk
3 cups canola oil
1 teaspoon unsalted butter (to coat the aluminum foil)
3 tablespoons sugar

SPECIAL
EQUIPMENT: 1"- or 1¼"-diameter cutter, or a similar-diameter brandy glass
deep fryer or pot about 8" diameter and 3" to 4" deep
deep-frying thermometer (unless your fryer has a thermostat)
baking sheet
cooling rack (optional)

1. Melt the butter in a small bowl or cup and set it aside to cool to lukewarm. Heat half-and-half to barely warm (105–110°F), pour it into a 2-cup bowl, sprinkle yeast over it and mix it with ½ tablespoon sugar and ¼ cup flour. Set it aside for 10 minutes to ferment at room temperature.

2. With a cutter or brandy glass, cut discs from the apple slices, keeping the smallest slices for snack, as they will be too small for cutting 1" discs from them. You should have about 70 little discs.

3. In a large bowl, mix ¾ cup flour, 2 tablespoons sugar, egg yolk, lukewarm melted butter, and fermented yeast mixture; whisk them until the batter becomes smooth. It should have the consistency of thick pancake batter.

4. Cover a large cutting board or the counter top next to your range with wax paper. One by one, dip the little apple discs into the batter to coat them on all sides, place them about 1" apart on the wax paper, and let them rest for about 15 minutes. The batter should be enough for 60 to 70 fritters.

5. Postion an oven rack about 6" under the heating element of the broiler and preheat the broiler. Spread a large piece of paper towel on the kitchen counter near your range and place a cooling rack over it. If you don't have a cooling rack, the paper towel alone will do. Line a baking sheet with aluminum foil, coat it with butter, and place it next to the cooling rack or paper towel.

6. Pour about 1" oil into a pot or sauté pan 8" in diameter and 3"–4" deep. Heat the oil over medium heat to 375°F. See the description in step 4 of the previous recipe about the use of a thermometer or a more approximate alternate procedure for judging the temperature of the oil. As soon as the temperature of the oil has reached 375°F, with a spatula slide as many coated apple pieces, one piece at a time, into the hot oil as the pot can accommodate without crowding, about 10 pieces. After the first side of the fritters has turned golden brown, about 45 seconds, flip them over with tongs (avoid piercing the fritters) or a wire skimmer to brown the other side, which should take less time. Watch them carefully so that they don't get too dark. As soon as a piece is ready, remove it from the oil and transfer it to drain on the cooling rack or paper towel. When all the pieces from the first batch are done, wait to bring the oil back to 375°F, test the temperature, and fry the second batch of fritters. Repeat this until all the coated apple pieces are done.

7. Place the fried fritters tightly against each other on the buttered foil. Generously sprinkle them with granulated sugar and place them under the preheated broiler. Keep the oven door open and watch when the sugar on the fritters starts to bubble and melt, because within seconds it can turn into a dark burned mess. As soon as the sugar melts, remove the baking sheet from the oven. Serve immediately, while the fritters are still hot.

PURIM AT RIZA NÉNI'S

MOTHER LOVED to accompany her grandparents to the synagogue during Purim. She and the other children brought rattles, toy trumpets, and other noisemakers to the temple to make noise whenever the name Haman was mentioned during the reading of the scroll of Esther—thereby making his hated name inaudible. According to the legend, Haman, a minister to the Persian king, had sought to exterminate all the Jews of the Persian Empire, who had been saved by Esther, the Jewish-born queen.

On Purim morning, Riza néni helped her select a costume from the old hats and other clothing kept in the attic. She also helped my mother make a paper mask and sent her together with her sister or another little girl to carry trays of pastries as gifts to their Jewish neighbors and to perform improvised Purim skits. One year they pretended to be gypsy fortunetellers, another year beggars or visitors from a faraway land. Mother usually took her violin to provide musical accompaniment. Sometimes they ended the performance with a little verse, actually a German version of a traditional Yiddish jingle:

> Heute ist Purim,
> Morgen wird's aus.
> Gib mir ein paar Kreuzer,
> Und wirf mich heraus!

(Today is Purim, tomorrow it will be over. Give me a few pennies and throw me out!) The children put the pennies, fruit, and cookies received from the neighbors for their performance into the basket they carried.

Though my mother had been too young to attend balls when she lived in Moson, she told me that Frigyes bácsi had always gone to dance with Ilka néni, a Catholic widow, at the Purim ball. The Hebrew Ladies' Society organized this ball and used the income from it to support the poor. It was a high point of the social season for the status-conscious Lujza néni, who was the president of the Society and could feel "important" directing the preparations during the weeks leading up to this event. The place of the ball varied: in some years it was in the second floor ballroom of the Weisses Rössl (White Horse) Inn, in other years in Mr. Tóth's restaurant, opposite my great-grandparents' house. The Catholic Tóth family was on friendly terms with my great-grandparents and all their other Jewish neighbors and found it perfectly natural to host the Purim ball. In addition to the grownups, lots of teenagers, dressed in the colorful Purim costumes, attended the ball, which started around eight in the evening. They waltzed merrily until the wee hours of the morning to the music of Pista Farkas' gypsy band while the mothers who accompanied the teenage girls sat along the walls of the room and gossiped.

Sending gifts to friends and relatives, giving to charity, and participat-

Frigyes bácsi went to dance at the Purim ball.

ing in the festive Purim meal are some of the mitzvot (commandments) associated with Purim. Like all Jewish families in Moson, Riza néni baked lots of cakes for Purim, both for her family and to give as gifts. She made *kindli* (see recipe on page 320) and pinched the top of the dough to give it the traditional ribbed shape. She also baked *fládni* (see recipe on page 325) and the same spice torte (see recipe on page 270) that she sometimes made for the end of Sabbath. For dinner, which had to begin while there was still daylight, she usually prepared fish with a sauce of puréed vegetables and chopped walnuts (see the following recipe) and soup with kreplach (noodle turnovers filled with ground meat). After my mother had started school in Budapest, she rarely went to Moson for Purim because she had only one day off from school for this holiday, but Riza néni always sent the family in Budapest a big package of kindlis for Purim.

Fish with Walnut-Vegetable Sauce
Diós hal

This fish dish and the following two desserts, *kindli* and *fládni*, come from a collection of Passover and Purim recipes written by Riza néni's niece. According to my mother, Riza néni frequently prepared this fish dish for Purim and for the first Sabbath meal. Even within Ashkenazi Jewish culture, a dish that is most typical in one country can be quite peripheral in another. While chopped liver occupies a less central role in Hungarian Jewish cuisine than in the United States, the situation is reversed in the case of fish in walnut sauce, which is one of the best-known Jewish dishes in Hungary but is hardly known in our country. This dish might be a rare example of Sephardi influence in Hungarian Jewish cooking, because the few similar recipes I found in American Jewish cookbooks listed them as typical Sephardi dishes, mainly from Georgia, Turkey, or Iran. If it indeed shows Sephardi influence, this would be quite unusual in the predominantly Ahkenazi Jewish culture of Hungary. But regardless of its origin, it has certainly been popular among Hungarian Jews: the book *Old Jewish Dishes* by Zorica Herbst-Krausz, the best modern book about the history of Hungarian Jewish cooking, includes three versions of it, and there is another version in George Lang's *The Cuisine of Hungary*. Although most popular among Jews, fish with walnut-vegetable sauce hasn't been an exclusively Jewish dish in Hungary.

In all versions of this dish, carp or pike is first poached in a court bouillon made with root vegetables, then the bouillon is thickened with a little flour, and sometimes with egg yolks, too, and finally chopped or ground walnuts or almonds and a little sugar are added to the sauce. There are differences: some versions include garlic, others don't; some purée the vegetables, others leave them in slices; some add sour cream to the sauce (of course, only if it is not eaten as part of a fleischig meal), but the basic idea is the same in all the different variations. I love the complementary flavors and contrasting textures of the puréed root vegetables and the coarsely chopped walnuts in the sauce; it is a great combination, both rustic and sophisticated at the same time.

The only change I made in adapting the original recipe was to cut the fish into thick slices instead of poaching it whole. This eliminated the need for a fish poacher and produced a more flavorful sauce because the slices could be poached in less liquid than a whole fish. Although a four- to five-pound fish makes for five servings instead of the customary four, I suggest you don't buy a smaller fish, because the more closely spaced bones of a small fish make eating difficult. In addition, it is more economical to buy a whole fish than separate slices, and you have the bonus of the head, which you can freeze for later use in fish stock or jellied fish. The original recipe offered the option of using either carp or pike for the dish; I like equally the more assertive flavor of carp or the delicate flavor of pike.

YIELD:	5 servings
TOTAL TIME:	about 1 hour 10 minutes
INGREDIENTS:	1 whole pike or carp, 4 to 5 pounds, scaled and gutted
	1½ teaspoons kosher salt
	1 medium onion, peeled and thinly sliced
	1 large carrot, cleaned and sliced
	1 small parsnip, cleaned and sliced
	1 bay leaf
	¾ teaspoon black peppercorns, coarsely crushed with the bottom of a heavy skillet
	½ teaspoon kosher salt
	1½ quarts water
	2 large egg yolks
	1½ tablespoons all-purpose flour
	1 cup walnuts
	2–4 teaspoons sugar
	3 tablespoons chopped fresh flat-leaf parsley

SPECIAL
EQUIPMENT: sauté or other pan approximately 10" in diameter
                    with a tight-fitting lid
                wire whisk
                hand-held blender (optional)
                food processor

1. Cut off the head and tail of the fish and freeze them for later use. Cut the fish into 5 or 6 slices, each about 1½" thick. Rinse the fish slices, pat them dry with a paper towel, and sprinkle them with 1½ teaspoons salt. Place them on a platter, cover with plastic wrap, and refrigerate for 30 minutes to 2 hours.

2. Meanwhile, clean and slice the vegetables and put them into a 10" sauté pan. Add bay leaf, crushed peppercorns, ½ teaspoon salt, and 1½ quarts water. Bring it to a boil, lower heat, and simmer for 25 minutes. Preheat oven to 180°F.

3. Add the fish to the court bouillon in the pan and carefully place the slices on their cut sides so that they can be submerged in the least amount of liquid. If necessary, add a little more water to barely cover the fish slices. Bring the liquid back to a boil, lower heat, cover, and gently simmer for 12 minutes. With a spatula, carefully lift the slices out of the liquid, transfer them onto a large platter, loosely cover them with aluminum foil and place them in the preheated oven to keep warm.

4. Place 2 egg yolks in a medium bowl, whisk them, add flour, and whisk well to make a smooth paste. With a ladle, little by little add about 2 cups court bouillon, allowing each time for the hot liquid to cool in the ladle and always stopping to whisk the egg mixture to make sure that there are no lumps of flour in it.

5. Bring the remaining court bouillon to a strong boil and boil to reduce it by about half. To accurately measure how much you have to boil away, stick the handle of a wooden spoon into the liquid and mark its depth before starting to boil it. Remove and discard the bay leaf. Purée vegetables in the pan with a hand-held blender, tilting the pan to make

sure that the head of the blender stays completely submerged in the liquid. If you don't have a hand-held blender, you can purée the vegetables in a regular blender, a food processor, or with a food mill.

6. Very slowly add the diluted egg mixture to the puréed vegetables and stir to distribute. Slowly warm the sauce in the pan over low heat, constantly stirring it. Don't bring it to a boil or the eggs will curdle. Stop as soon as the sauce has thickened enough to coat the back of a spoon.

7. Place walnuts in the bowl of the food processor and pulse a few times to chop them into ⅛" pieces. Add the coarsely chopped walnuts to the sauce. Stir 2 teaspoons sugar into the sauce, taste it and decide whether to add more. The sauce should be slightly sweet, but not cloyingly so. Adjust the rest of the seasoning, if you feel this is necessary.

8. Serve it with small boiled potatoes or boiled egg noodles. Place a fish slice on each preheated serving plate, ladle a little sauce over it, sprinkle it with a little chopped parsley, enjoy the wonderful earthy fragrance of the sauce, and wait for the compliments of your guests.

Potato Noodles with Poppy Seed

Sweets made with poppy seed have long been part of the Purim tradition. This is usually explained by the similar-sounding names of the German *Mohntaschen* (poppy seed pockets) and *Hamantaschen*, a Purim pastry, which is frequently—but not always—filled with poppy seed and is named after Haman, the villain in the Purim story. However, the association of poppy seed with Purim seems to predate the custom of making hamantaschen, because already in the twelfth century Abraham Ibn Ezra recorded in a religious poem the eating of poppy seeds and honey as a Purim sweetmeat.

The poppy seed noodles of this recipe are frequently served during Purim, but they are popular among both Gentiles and Jews in Hungary at other times, too. If possible, don't keep the dough for more than one or two hours before cooking it—the less, the better—because the dough tends to get sticky if it is allowed to sit too long. Instead of poppy seeds, the same noodles can be served sprinkled with a mixture of ground walnuts and sugar. In Hungary, these noodles, similar to other hot noodle desserts, are frequently served as the main course of a light lunch, preceded by soup and accompanied by salad.

YIELD:	4 dessert or 3 main course servings
TOTAL TIME:	about 2 hours, but much of this is waiting time
INGREDIENTS:	1 recipe potato dumpling dough (see page 113)
	⅔ cup ground poppy seeds (see page 173 for buying and storing ground poppy seeds)
	⅓ cup sugar
	1–2 teaspoons unsalted butter or margarine
SPECIAL EQUIPMENT:	potato ricer
	baking sheet
	dough scraper (optional)

1. Prepare the dough according to the recipe for potato dumplings (see page 113). While you are preparing the dough, boil about 4 quarts water in a wide pot, about 10" in diameter. In a medium bowl, mix ground poppy seeds and sugar. Preheat oven to 175°F.

2. Divide the dough into halves. Lightly dust your work surface and rolling pin with flour and roll out half of the dough to an 8" x 9" rectangle, about ¼" thick. Periodically lift up one side of the dough, throw a little flour under it and give it a quarter turn to keep it from sticking to the work surface. With a dough scraper or knife, cut a strip about ⅜" wide from the rolled-out dough, and then cut this strip into 1" pieces. Lightly roll each piece between your floured palms to shape

them into cigar-shaped noodles about 1" by ⅜". Place them in 1 layer on a flour-dusted large chopping board. Repeat until you have made noodles from the entire sheet of dough. Now roll out the other half of the dough and make noodles from this, too.

3. Drop about half of the noodles into the boiling water and move them around a little with a wooden spoon to keep them from sticking to the bottom or to each other. Bring it back to a boil, partially cover, lower heat to a simmer, and cook the noodles for 4 to 5 minutes.

4. Remove the noodles from the water with a slotted spoon or skimmer and very briefly rinse them in a colander under running water. Transfer the cooked noodles into a heat-resistant bowl, add butter or margarine, gently toss the noodles to coat them with the fat, and place the bowl in the preheated oven until you cook the second batch. You can keep the noodles in the preheated oven for up to 30 minutes, though the less time they sit there, the better they are.

5. Pour off any liquid that may have collected at the bottom of the bowl, sprinkle noodles with poppy-sugar mixture, and carefully turn the noodles with a serving spoon to evenly coat them with the mixture. Serve immediately.

Kindli

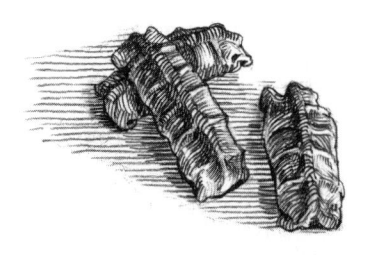

Kindli, which together with *fládni* (see recipe on page 325) are the most common pastries made for Purim in Hungary, is a local specialty, a fact rarely noted even in Hungarian Jewish cookbooks. The shape and traditional pattern of the pastry supposedly represents a baby, the meaning of the German-Yiddish *kindli*, wrapped in swaddling clothes.

Unfortunately, some books about the history of Jewish cooking substitute unfounded theories and guessing for factual research. True, it is usually difficult to prove conclusively when a certain recipe appeared in a country, and where it came from. But few writers on the topic tried to mine old cookbooks for such information. Whether a recipe does or doesn't show up in one old Jewish cookbook cannot prove much. But if it does not appear in three or four such books of the same country and the same period, a period when far fewer cookbooks were published than today, this makes it highly unlikely that it could have been a popular recipe at that place and time.

I used this method to check two statements that frequently crop up in the literature about the history of kindli. One statement claims that this pastry has been popular in Hungary for a very long time. The local Jewish cookbooks tell a different story. It cannot be found in three late-nineteenth-century cookbooks, which probably represent all or most of the Jewish cookbooks published in Hungary in that period. On the other hand, it appears in virtually every such book published there in the first half of the twentieth century. Therefore, it is likely that it became popular in Hungary in the last years of the nineteenth or the first years of the twentieth century.

According to another commonly repeated claim, it came to Hungary from Germany and Austria. I checked in three large Jewish cookbooks published in Germany between 1875 and 1888, as well as in a similarly comprehensive German-language cookbook published in 1898 in Prague, but couldn't find any trace of kindli in them, not even a crumb of it. I would love to check whether I could find kindli in Yiddish cookbooks of the period, perhaps from the area of Mukachevo (Munkács), formerly part of the Monarchy, now in the Ukraine, but unfortunately I haven't yet been able to locate such a book.

It is possible that the original idea of this pastry is of Polish origin. John Cooper in his *Eat and Be Satisfied* tells about Rabbi Joel Serkes (1561–1640), who described that for Purim "people kneaded the kreplekh [a sheet of dough wrapped around some filling] with goose fat and filled them with raisins and nuts." This pastry wasn't called kindli and didn't have its traditional shape, but the basic idea was quite similar.

Another unsolved puzzle is what the child or baby, that lent this pastry its name and inspired its shape, has to do with Purim. Two of the best and most famous Hungarian Jewish folklorists offer equally unconvincing explanations. One of them claims that it refers to Haman's sons. But according to the Scroll of Esther, Haman's ten sons were adults, not babies in swaddling clothes when they were hanged. The other explanation states, without the slightest shred of proof, that the kindli was borrowed from a pastry made by German Gentiles for the ancient German New Year, which was in March.

Kindli is filled with either nuts or poppy seeds, which are usually wrapped in the type of dough used in *beigli* or *pozsonyi kifli*, two versions of a popular Hungarian pastry. This type of dough includes a little yeast, in addition to flour, eggs, and butter or lard. Less common is the type of dough used by Riza néni, made without yeast. Her dough, which is rolled to be almost paper-thin, is wonderfully tender and delicate. It is made with wine, consistent with the importance of wine during Purim, the one day during the Jewish year when the people are encouraged to drink—and a lot of it. According to one talmudic scholar, a person is supposed to drink during this holiday until he cannot distinguish between the phrases "cursed be Haman" and "blessed be Mordecai," the villain and the hero of the Purim story.

YIELD: 14 pastries

TOTAL TIME: about 1 hour 30 minutes

DOUGH INGREDIENTS:
- 2½ cups unbleached all-purpose flour
- 1 pinch of kosher salt
- 2 teaspoons sugar
- 5 tablespoons unsalted butter or margarine, softened
- 3 large egg yolks
- 7 tablespoons white wine (or a mixture of wine and water)

FILLING INGREDIENTS:
- 1¾ cups walnuts
- ¼ cup sugar
- 2 teaspoons grated lemon zest
- 1½ teaspoons lemon juice
- ½ teaspoon vanilla extract
- ¼ cup finely chopped golden raisins
- 2–3 tablespoons water

	2 tablespoons sugar
	1 tablespoon unsalted butter, margarine, or canola oil
FOR BRUSHING:	1 tablespoon honey
	3 tablespoons unsalted butter, canola oil, or a mixture of the two
SPECIAL EQUIPMENT:	food processor
	pastry brush
	2 baking sheets (12" × 18")

1. Place flour, salt, and sugar in the bowl of a food processor and pulse once to mix. Add butter or margarine cut into ½" pieces and process for about 15 seconds, until they are fully incorporated. Add egg yolks and wine; process for about 20 seconds. Transfer the contents, which will be still granular, to a large sheet of plastic wrap and use the plastic wrap to press them into a ball. Knead the dough by hand on the work surface for about 5 minutes, until it becomes satiny-smooth and elastic. The dough should be slightly softer than noodle dough. Wrap it in plastic and let it rest for about 30 minutes.

2. While the dough is resting, prepare the filling. Place walnuts and ¼ cup sugar in the bowl of the food processor and process for about 15 seconds until the nuts are finely and evenly ground. Transfer them into a bowl; add grated lemon zest, lemon juice, vanilla, and chopped raisins; stir to blend. Place 2 tablespoons water, 2 tablespoons sugar, and 1 tablespoon butter, margarine or oil in a small saucepan and heat until the sugar and fat dissolve. Add this to the walnut mixture and stir. The filling should stick together and be slightly soft. If necessary, add a little more water by the teaspoonful.

3. In a small heat-resistant bowl, heat honey and butter or oil. Adjust racks to divide the oven into thirds and preheat the oven to 350°F.

4. Divide the dough into halves, roll each half into a sausage about 9" long, cut each sausage into 7 approximately equal parts, and shape

each part into a ball. You should have 14 little balls of dough. Using a rolling pin, roll one ball into a very thin circle, 6"–6½" in diameter. If the dough is the right consistency, it will not stick or tear and you will not have to flour the rolling pin or your work surface. Lightly brush a 3"-diameter area in the center of the dough circle with the honey mixture. Place about 2 teaspoons filling in the middle to form a mound that is about 2½" long and 1" wide. Lift up the dough on 1 side of the filling and loosely fold it over the filling, tucking it in on the other side. Roll this package to loosely wrap the dough around the filling and continue rolling until the seam faces down. Fold under about ½" of the dough at one open end of the package to create a hem and press to seal it, then repeat this at the other end. The filling inside the package should be about 1" from each end, allowing plenty of room for expansion during baking. Pinch the dough on the top of the package simultaneously from both sides between the index finger and thumb of one hand and the index finger and thumb of the other hand to create a ridge about ½" high running lengthwise and shorter ribs crosswise. Then move your hands to repeat this until you created one continuous long ridge running the full length of the pastry and five or six crosswise ribs on both sides of this ridge, as shown in the drawing. The ridge and the cross ribs should sharply protrude above the top of the pastry and there should be no filling in the folds of dough. You will have to pinch the dough pretty hard to make the dough on the sides of the folds adhere to each other. If you don't press hard enough, the pattern on the top of the pastries will tend to smooth out during baking.

5. Using a dough scraper or spatula, transfer the dough package to the baking sheet and repeat the procedure with the remaining balls of dough. Leave about 1½" between the pastries. If you run out of space on the first baking sheet, use another sheet for the remaining pastries. Lightly brush the top of the pastries with the honey mixture. Bake them in the preheated oven for 20 minutes, then brush them again with the honey mixture and put them back into the oven to bake for another 10–15 minutes, until they are light golden brown. Don't overbake or the thin dough will dry out. Transfer them to a cooling rack and store them at room temperature in an airtight container for up to 3–4 days.

Fládni

The name *fládni* (the title of the original recipe) or *flódni* (the more common variant of the name in Hungary) comes from the German *Fladen* and originally from the medieval Latin *flado*, a flat cake. Jewish cuisine long ago adopted from Gentile cooking the idea of making a pastry in which some filling is sandwiched between layers of dough. A cheese-filled version seems to be the earliest in Jewish cooking; it is mentioned in a tenth-century source about a discussion between two rabbis. Judging from its frequent mention in early documents, it must have been one of the most popular pastries among French, German, and Austrian Jews in the Middle Ages. Later, fladen became less common, which is documented by the fact that it doesn't appear in nineteenth-century German Jewish or Hungarian Jewish cookbooks, at least in the four German and three Hungarian books I had access to.

But it never disappeared completely, and Riza néni's collection recorded a nineteenth-century version, which she called *Fledel-Fächer* (it is almost untranslatable, but "layered flat pastry" is close). This recipe, which she probably wrote around 1870, is a precursor both to *flódni*, a multilayer version that is a popular Purim dessert in Hungary, and to an Austrian torte, called *Fächer Torte*. Instead of her somewhat confusingly written recipe, which has two layers of filling, I decided to update a version preserved in the recipe collection of her niece, who used the same kind of dough but added layers of poppy seed and jam to Riza néni's walnut and apple filling. My great-grandmother's dough doesn't include yeast, as the dough used for 'flódni' in Hungary usually does, and it is not the kind of short dough (*Mürbteig* in German) that is used in some other versions of flódni and in the Viennese Fächer Torte. Her wonderfully elastic dough is rolled very thin to make the most delicate flódni and kindli, the previous recipe for which she used the same kind of dough. I changed the red currant jam of the original recipe to prune butter, because I think its flavor goes even better with poppy seed, which is the layer underneath it, and it has less tendency to run during baking.

In Hungary, flódni is one of the most traditional desserts made for Purim, less frequently for Sukkot, and it is included in virtually all twentieth-century Hungarian Jewish cookbooks. The flódni in those books shares only its name and the basic idea of a filled flat pastry with the *floden* recorded in medieval documents, and it is filled with layers of walnut, apple, poppy seed, and sometimes jam. How it has become so closely associated with Purim is not clear; perhaps it has something do with the tradition of making kindli for this holiday. They seem to have appeared at about the same time in Hungarian Jewish cooking, they are usually made of the same kind of dough, and they share the walnut or poppy seed filling. Perhaps these pastries came to Hungary from the same area, but I was unable to prove or disprove this hypothesis. Flódni's close association with Purim is probably unique to Hungary. None of the older sources I have seen from other countries mention it as a Purim dessert, with the sole exception of a book of Jewish holiday recipes published around 1910 in Neu-Isenburg, Germany. This, however, could have been a Hungarian influence as it was published after flódni had become popular in Hungary.

YIELD: 18 slices

TOTAL TIME: about 2 hours, plus 2½ hours cooling time

DOUGH INGREDIENTS:
2½ cups unbleached all-purpose flour
1 pinch of kosher salt
2 teaspoons sugar
5 tablespoons unsalted, room-temperature butter or margarine
3 large egg yolks
7 tablespoons white wine (or a mixture of wine and water)

APPLE FILLING:
1½ pounds Golden Delicious apples (3 large or 4 medium apples)
1 tablespoon lemon juice
2 tablespoons sugar
¼ teaspoon ground cinnamon

WALNUT FILLING:	1¾ cups walnuts
	¼ cup sugar
	2 teaspoons grated lemon zest
	1 teaspoon lemon juice
	½ teaspoon vanilla extract
	¼ cup raisins, chopped
	2–3 tablespoons water
	½ tablespoon unsalted butter or margarine
POPPY SEED FILLING:	1½ cups ground poppy seeds (see page 173 about buying and storing poppy seeds)
	3 tablespoons sugar
	2 teaspoons grated lemon zest
	¼ teaspoon ground cinnamon
	½ Golden Delicious apple, peeled, cored, and coarsely grated
	¼ cup raisins, chopped
	2 tablespoons water
	½ tablespoon unsalted butter or margarine
PRUNE BUTTER FILLING:	½ cup prune butter (prune lekvár)
FOR BRUSHING:	1 tablespoon unsalted butter or margarine
	1 tablespoon canola oil
EGG GLAZE:	1 large egg, lightly beaten
	1 tablespoon water
SPECIAL EQUIPMENT:	food processor
	pastry brush
	8" x 8" x 2" baking pan with vertical (not sloping) sides and sharp corners. If you have such a baking pan with removable bottom, it is even better.
	dough scraper
	baking sheet

1. Prepare the dough the same way as for kindli, the previous recipe. Wrap the dough in plastic and allow it to rest for at least 30 minutes. Meanwhile, prepare the fillings.

2. Peel, core, and halve the apples; slice them crosswise into ⅛" slices. Stack 5 or 6 slices at a time and cut them into slivers about ¼" wide. Place the cut-up apples in a medium saucepan, add sugar, lemon juice, and cinnamon. Stir to mix; cover and cook over medium heat for 10 minutes. Transfer about half the apples into a strainer and press them with the back of a wooden spoon to extract as much juice as possible. Place them in a medium bowl and repeat with the remaining apples. Set the bowl aside until you prepare the other fillings.

3. Place walnuts and sugar in the bowl of the food processor and process for about 15 seconds, until the nuts are finely and evenly ground. Transfer them to a bowl; add grated lemon zest, lemon juice, vanilla, and chopped raisins. Mix well. Place 2 tablespoons water and ½ tablespoon butter or margarine in a small saucepan and heat until the fat melts. Add this to the walnut mixture in the bowl and mix to get a filling that sticks together and is slightly soft. If necessary, add a little more water by the teaspoonful.

4. In another bowl, mix ground poppy seeds, sugar, grated lemon zest, cinnamon, grated apple, and chopped raisins. In the previously used small saucepan heat 2 tablespoons water and ½ tablespoon butter or margarine until the fat melts. Pour this over the poppy seed mixture and mix well until the filling sticks together and is slightly soft. If necessary, add a little more water by the teaspoonful.

5. In a small heat-resistant bowl, heat butter and oil. Center a rack in the oven and preheat the oven to 350°F.

6. Divide the dough into 5 approximately equal parts. Roll out 1 part into a square about 9". Place the baking pan over this square and trim the dough to extend about ¼" beyond the pan on all sides. Use the dough scraper to carefully loosen the dough square, pick it up and transfer it to line the bottom of the baking pan. Adjust it to lie flat and

cover the whole surface. Lightly brush it with the butter-oil mixture and using a rubber spatula spread the walnut filling in an even layer approximately ¼" thick over the dough.

7. Roll out another part of the dough into a similar 9" square, trim it and carefully transfer it to cover the walnut filling. Brush it with the butter-oil mixture and spread the apple filling with the rubber spatula in an even layer over it. Lightly pat the apples with the spatula to compact them a little.

8. Prepare another 9"-square sheet of dough, trim it, and lay it to cover the apples in the baking pan. Brush it with the butter-oil mixture and with the rubber spatula spread the poppy seed filling in an even layer over it.

9. Prepare another 9"-square piece of dough, trim it, and lay it to cover the poppy seed filling. Brush it with the butter-oil mixture and spread the prune butter in a much thinner, approximately ⅛", even layer over the dough. Prepare the final 9"-square piece of dough, trim it, and cover the prune butter filling with it.

10. In a small bowl or cup, lightly beat the egg and dilute it with 1 tablespoon water. Brush the top of the fládni with it and allow it to dry slightly for about 5 minutes. Use the tines of a fork to scratch a diagonal grid (about 1") pattern into the egg glaze. Prick the top layer of the dough with the fork in the middle of each square in the grid. Place the baking pan on a baking sheet and bake it in the preheated oven for at least 1 hour, until the egg glaze turns light golden brown.

11. Cool it in the baking pan set on a cooling rack for 1 hour. Run a narrow knife around the perimeter of the cake to loosen it from the sides of the pan. Place a cutting board over the pan, and holding the board to the pan, carefully invert the cake onto the board. Re-invert the cake, carefully so it doesn't crack or break, to the cooling rack and allow it to cool completely, which will take another 1½ hours or so. Using a long serrated knife, trim about ¼" from the cake on all sides to make the edges tidier and to remove the bits of dried

filling. First cut the cake into 3 strips, careful not to crush it, then cut each strip, one strip at a time, into 6 slices. You can dust the top with powdered sugar, though I prefer to omit this as it covers the pretty pattern of the egg glaze. Serve immediately or store it at room temperature in an airtight box for up to three days.

Cookies as in Brno
Brünner Küchel

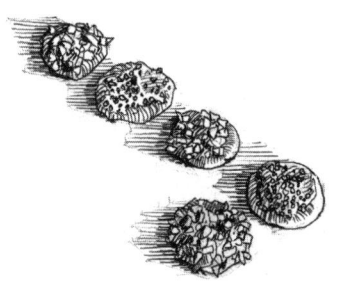

I wish I could ask Riza néni what these cookies have to do with Brno, a city in the Moravian region of the Czech Republic. While we are at it, I would also ask her about the shape of the cookies. *Küchel* is one of several possible names for cookies in old German cookbooks, but it is a general term, not of a specific shape. In her recipe, Riza néni called for making little dough balls, coating them with whipped egg whites, and baking them so that the coating stayed white. The problem is that by the time the dough is baked all the way through, the coating is no longer white. One solution would be to apply the coating after the balls have almost finished baking, but that was not what she described. Alternately, one could assume that she forgot to write that the balls of dough should be flattened; obviously, the thinner the dough is, the faster it will bake. This seems all the more probable because one of the decorating options she offered was to place a sour cherry in the middle of the cookies. She didn't write the recipes for others but as memory aids to herself, and so she occasionally skipped such steps that seemed obvious to her.

But even if their shape is only my best guess, these cookies are terrific. They are so tender as to almost melt in your mouth and their pretty decoration—especially the one with the colorful sugar sprinkles—look appropriate for the joyous holiday of Purim. I substituted butter or margarine for the "fat" (probably goose fat) of the original recipe.

YIELD:	32 cookies
TOTAL TIME:	about 50 minutes
INGREDIENTS:	1¼ scant cups unbleached all-purpose flour
	¼ cup sugar
	1 pinch kosher salt
	2 teaspoons grated lemon zest
	6 tablespoons unsalted butter or margarine, softened and cut into ½" pieces
	1 large egg yolk
	1 tablespoon milk or water
	1 teaspoon vanilla extract
	⅓ cup slivered almonds
	3 tablespoons cake-decorating coarse sugar in assorted colors ("confetti" sugar)
	2 large egg whites
	1 tablespoon sugar
SPECIAL EQUIPMENT:	food processor
	2 baking sheets (12" × 18")
	parchment paper or 2 nonstick baking mats
	dough scraper

1. Place flour, sugar, salt, and lemon zest in the bowl of a food processor. Pulse to mix. Add butter or margarine, egg yolk, milk or water, and vanilla. Process for about 10 seconds, stopping a few times for a split second, until the dough starts to come together into small lumps. Spread a large piece of plastic wrap on the work surface and pour the bits of dough in the middle. Use the plastic to press the dough into a slab about 6" × 3" × 1", wrap it in plastic, and refrigerate for at least 15 minutes.

2. Line 2 baking sheets with parchment paper or silicone nonstick baking mats. Adjust oven racks to divide the oven into thirds and preheat the oven to 325°F.

3. Chop the slivered almonds into pieces about ⅛", and place them in a small bowl. Place cake-decorating sugar in another small bowl. Whip

egg whites until they form soft peaks, sprinkle 1 tablespoon sugar over them and continue whipping until egg whites become shiny and form firm peaks.

4. Cut off ¼ of the dough, rewrap the remaining part and put it back into the refrigerator. Divide the cut-off portion into halves, then each half into 4 approximately equal pieces, 8 pieces in total. Make a little ball, about ¾" diameter, from 1 of the pieces and flatten this ball into a 1¾"- or 2"-diameter disc on the work surface. Lift it up with the dough scraper, spread about an ⅛"-thick coat of egg whites over it, hold it over the bowl of colored sugar and sprinkle sugar over the coating. Place it on the parchment-lined baking sheet. Repeat this with the remaining 7 pieces of dough, alternating almond and sugar sprinkles for decoration. Space the cookies about 1" apart.

5. Now, cut off the second quarter of the dough, return the rest to the refrigerator and make another 8 cookies as described above. Repeat this until you have used up all the dough and made a total of 32 cookies, 16 of them decorated with colored sugar, the rest with chopped almonds.

6. Bake the cookies in the preheated oven for 15–17 minutes, switching the baking sheets halfway through to make sure that the cookies bake evenly. The coating on the cookies should stay mostly white, with only a few places starting to get a little color. Use a spatula to transfer the cookies to a cooling rack and allow them to cool completely before serving. Store them in a cookie tin with parchment or wax paper between the layers.

Nut Hoop

Nussenbeigel

If this flat cake resembles a round tray or board, this is no coincidence: it serves as an edible tray for cookies and pastries. During Purim one must send at least two "portions" of delicacies to friends; this is the *mishlo'ah manot*, Hebrew for "sending of portions." According to religious law, one cannot hand over these gifts personally but must send them by a messenger. On Purim morning, Riza néni piled an assortment of her Purim cookies on such nut hoops and told my mother to take them to the Stadlers and other good friends, who ate the presents, tray, and all.

YIELD: 1 large or 2 smaller cakes

TOTAL TIME: about 25 minutes, plus cooling time

INGREDIENTS:
1½ cups walnut halves
1⅓ cups unbleached all-purpose flour
½ cup sugar
¾ teaspoon ground cinnamon
½ teaspoon ground cloves
1 tablespoon lemon juice
2 large egg yolks
3 large eggs
2 large egg whites
¼ teaspoon cream of tartar
1 tablespoon sugar
1 tablespoon coarse multicolored cake-decorating sugar

SPECIAL EQUIPMENT: food processor

cookie sheet (14" × 18")
parchment paper or nonstick baking mat
16" pastry bag with about ⅝" plain tip (optional)

1. Line a baking sheet with parchment paper or nonstick mat. Center a rack in the oven and preheat the oven to 350°F.

2. Place walnuts, flour, sugar, cinnamon, and cloves in the bowl of the food processor. Process for 10 to 15 seconds, until the walnuts are finely ground. Add lemon juice, egg yolks, and whole eggs. Process for about 10 seconds, until the dough comes together; it will not clear the bowl. Use a rubber spatula to transfer the sticky dough into a large bowl.

3. Whip egg whites and cream of tartar until they form soft peaks, add 1 tablespoon sugar and continue whipping until the whites become shiny and form firm peaks. Using a rubber spatula, stir ⅓ of the egg whites into the dough, then gently fold in the rest.

4. Fold down the top of the pastry bag to form a deep cuff, tuck the bottom of the bag into the tip to keep the soft dough from coming out while you fill the bag. Stand the bag in a tall jar and use a rubber spatula to fill it. Pipe the dough in a spiral onto the parchment- or baking mat–lined cookie sheet to form a 9" circle with a 1½" hole in the middle, which will get a little smaller when the soft dough spreads. Sprinkle the top with coarse sugar. Alternately, make 2 approximately 7"-diameter circles with a 1½" hole in each. If you don't have a pastry bag, you can shape the dough with a spoon or rubber spatula but it will not be possible to do it as neatly as with a bag.

5. Bake it in the preheated oven for about 15 minutes, until the top of the cake springs back when gently pressed with your finger. Slide the parchment or the baking mat to a cooling rack and allow the cake, still on the paper or mat, to cool and firm up for 15 minutes. Remove it from the mat or, if you used parchment, carefully place the cake upside down on the work surface and peel off the paper. Place the cake on the cooling rack to finish cooling, about 20 more minutes.

✂ PESACH AT RIZA NÉNI'S ✂

UNLIKE PURIM, when the short vacation in school usually forced them to stay in Budapest, my mother and her siblings always spent the week of Pesach, or Passover by its English name, in Moson. The house was full of people, because in addition to the children their parents and governess also came to join my great-grandparents and Frigyes bácsi in celebrating this holiday. Sometimes Dezső bácsi, the second of Riza néni's surviving three sons, who lived in Budapest, and his wife came, too.

A day or two before Pesach, Paula and my great-grandmother removed everything from the cupboards in the kitchen and scrubbed the empty shelves. They carried all the regular food supplies, like flour and sugar, from the pantry out to one of the granaries. They emptied and scrubbed the *Handspeiz*, the pantry-closet in the hallway next to the kitchen door. Special Pesach dishes were brought down from a big trunk in the attic along with the special pots, pans, china, and cutlery. On the night before Pesach eve, my great-grandfather took an old wooden spoon in one hand and a goose feather in the other and went to look through all nooks and crannies of the house for leaven, anything that might ferment. Riza néni, who held a candle, accompanied him on the search, and my mother tagged along enjoying this strange scene. Of course, my great-grandfather was merely going through the motions, because he knew that the house had been scrubbed clean of all offending material except for the few crumbs of bread Riza néni had previously placed on pieces of paper in conspicuous places for her husband to find. He used the feather to brush the crumbs onto the wooden spoon, which Riza néni then stuck into a paper bag, ready to be burned on the following morning in the traditional burning of the leaven.

They bought special potato flour and staples like sugar or salt, which had been packaged and certified to be free of any impurity that could ferment, because even one bread crumb or one particle of flour accidentally dropped into them would render them unacceptable. They ordered the Passover wine and the boxes of matzo. Mr. Miksa Löwin, who lived a few houses from my great-grandparents on Fő utca, made matzo for the whole Moson Jewish community with the help of two or three women.

He started baking the matzos in his brick oven already five or six weeks before the holiday. Mr. Löwin gave tense, short commands to his helpers as they all hurried to get the matzo into the oven, because, according to rabbinical rules, a batch of matzos had to be baked within eighteen minutes from the time they started mixing the dough. In addition, they had to be constantly on the watch to make sure that nothing contaminated the dough or the matzo and had to frequently wash their hands and the pots used in the work. Contrary to the machine-made square matzo common today, Mr. Löwin's matzo was round, about seven inches in diameter. My great-grandparents ate only matzo during Pesach, but they ordered bread for their children and grandchildren, who liked matzo but wanted to eat bread, too. Riza néni made sure that on the table in the first granary there should be bread, even pork sausage, though the children were not allowed to bring these into the apartment.

In the afternoon of the first day of Pesach, while my great-grandfather and his sons were at the temple, my great-grandmother and Paula prepared the formal dining room for the Seder, Hebrew for "order": the order of the ceremonial meal. They rarely ate in this room; only the Seder and birthday dinners were held here. Occasionally, Riza néni played the piano, which stood between the two windows, and once in a rare while a guest slept on the bed. But most of the time the oil portraits of ancestors on the wall could only look at each other, not a live person using the room.

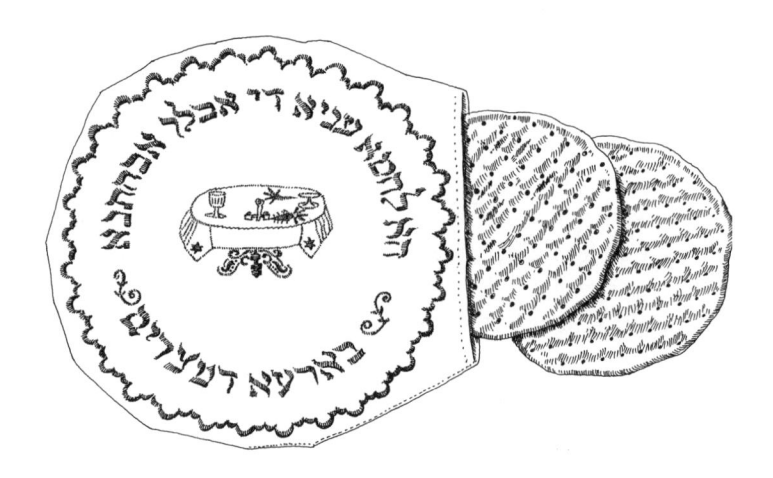

Riza néni and Paula covered the large oval table with the embroidered Seder tablecloth and placed the two-tiered, silver-plated, round Seder plate in the center. The Seder plate had a handle above its top tray and three short legs under its bottom tray. Riza néni stuck three sheets of matzo into a round bag, its shape designed to fit the round matzo, and put it behind the curtain that surrounded the bottom tray. I was happy to hear from my aunt that this matzo bag still exists; it is in the collection of The Jewish Museum in New York, to which she had given it some decades ago. In the museum, a curator pulled it out from storage for me and I could admire the charmingly naïve picture of the Seder table and the Aramaic text "This is the bread of affliction," which my great-grandmother had embroidered on it in the 1870s.

Five arms projected from the upper part of the Seder plate, and each one held a little plate of its own for the symbolic foods that are part of the holiday tradition. Riza néni's grandson, who inherited her Seder plate, was not religious and for a while stored it in his cellar. Around 1960 he threw it out because he couldn't sell it—there were few practicing Jews in those years in Hungary—and neither he nor anybody else in the family wanted to keep the bulky plate.

The Seder table was set with a wineglass for everybody and an extra glass for Elijah the Prophet, who might drop by to announce the arrival of the Messianic age. There were three haggadah books on the table for the ceremony. Great-grandfather and Frigyes bácsi arrived from the synagogue and were eager to eat. Great-grandfather Bernhard, who wore a white robe over his suit, said a blessing over the wine. After the ritual of pouring water over their hands, they ate slices of celeriac and parsley leaves, which they dipped in a dish of salt water that stood next to the Seder plate. The children were most interested in the haroset, one of the symbolic foods made of grated apples, chopped walnuts, sweet spices, honey, and wine, which was their favorite and from which they already noshed before the Seder. Great-grandfather removed the middle matzo from the bag in the Seder plate, broke it into two pieces, wrapped one of them in a napkin, and "hid" it behind his chair. Later, when he went to wash his hands again before the actual meal, Riza néni whispered to my mother that she should "steal" the wrapped matzo and hide it, which my great-grandfather pretended not to notice. Toward the end of the meal, my mother returned the stolen matzo and got a present in exchange.

Now my mother had to ask, "How is this night different from all others?" This was the *"mah nishtanah,"* but she could rarely say it all by heart and had to look it up in the book. Great-grandfather answered her question by reading the Passover story from the haggadah, a book whose

Hebrew name means "narration," as it tells the story of the liberation of the Jews from slavery in Egypt. He read the story in a strange singsong Hebrew while leaning on his left elbow, which amused my mother, because Riza néni always scolded the children if they leaned on their elbows during a meal.

Mother struggled to explain to me, "It is the story of marching out or marching in, but I would be lying if I told you that I know exactly what it is. But it is interesting and it would be good to know it, because it is, after all, history." She continued in the same vein: "We children followed the text from a book that had one side printed in Hebrew and the other in German. Although we knew a few words of Hebrew, you bet we read the German instead of the Hebrew. When we saw somebody turn the page, we turned ours too. Later in high school we learned some Hebrew, but by then we outgrew our interest in religion." My secular mother recalled the

Seder in her grandparents' home with great affection and even remembered short fragments of Hebrew text from the haggadah, but she obviously had only the vaguest of notions about the religious and historical significance of the Passover story.

When my great-grandfather got to the story of the ten plagues, the retribution inflicted by God upon the Egyptians for the sufferings of the Israelites, he showed the children the woodcuts in the haggadah depicting those horrors. Then he spilled some wine from the cup—one drop for each plague—to remind them that sadness should be felt for any human suffering, even for that of the oppressors.

I love to look at Riza néni's old haggadah and admire its crimson leather binding on which gold-embossed letters proclaim "T. [Therese] Berger" as the owner. Like many old books, the object has a story independent of the one printed between its covers. The haggadah was published in 1878 in Vienna, and Riza néni must have bought it not much later. Inside the book, I was surprised to find what looked like the draft of a contract. It read: "Contract zum Verkaufe des Chamez" (Contract to sell the chametz). I am embarrassed to confess my ignorance, but as I am not a practicing Jew, I didn't know that Chamez, or "chametz" as it is spelled in the United States, refers to bread, leaven, and the utensils touched by them. But after rereading the text more carefully I understood why this document had been included in the haggadah: it is the draft of a contract to symbolically sell everything that is not allowed in the house during Pesach to a non-Jew who will later, after the holiday, return it to the original Jewish owner.

I was also surprised by the incongruously old-fashioned woodcut illustrations, which looked like crude copies of Renaissance or Baroque originals. This intrigued me enough to look up other old editions of the Passover haggadah. It soon became obvious that illustrations in many of those editions had simply been copied from edition to edition for almost three hundred years, from the early seventeenth until the end of the nineteenth century. Similar precursors to the pictures of Riza néni's 1878 Vienna edition could be found in a 1711 German, a 1695 Italian, and a 1695 Dutch haggadah. An even earlier edition, a 1609 Venetian one, contained the prototypes of the woodcuts depicting the ten plagues.

I cannot think of a similar example in the history of printed books. What could be the reason for this? Perhaps it has something to do with the fact that old Jewish books rarely had illustrations because Jews tradition-

The crossing of the Red Sea
from a 1695 Dutch haggadah.

The same scene in
Riza néni's 1878 Viennese haggadah.

ally associated pictures with idolatry. Although haggadoth were exceptions to this, because they weren't taken to the synagogue, nevertheless, both the publishers and the users were more comfortable with the tried and true old images. The authority of traditions has always been very strong in Judaism and people must have felt that the layout of early printed editions of the haggadah and their illustrations were almost as much part of the Passover tradition as the printed text or the "order" of the home service

Two of the plagues in a
1609 Venetian haggadah.

The same two plagues in
Riza néni's 1878 Viennese haggadah.

and meal. This doesn't explain, however, why this custom died out at the end of the nineteenth century.

I smiled when I got to the "This is the bread of affliction" and the four questions that follow it. What I saw in my great-grandmother's haggadah confirmed my mother's account of trying to follow the Hebrew text during Seder, despite not being able to understand it. Somebody had drawn some vertical lines in ink in the German text and at corresponding places in the Hebrew text on the facing page to make it easier to follow the readings.

"Arthur Berger, second year student, Mosony (the old-fashioned spelling of Moson)," read the childish script on the first page of the haggadah. I got rather emotional when I noticed this, because I remembered my mother telling me that Arthur, Riza néni's second son, had died in April 1887, when he had been only seven years old. He must have written this in the haggadah only a few days before his death. As the family's youngest child, he must have used the book to ask the four questions at what was to be his last Seder.

At the beginning of the long evening my great-grandfather followed all the rules of the traditional ceremony. But as the hours went by, the children became ever more unruly, rattling their spoons and making a racket because they were bored with the long readings. They also started to feel some of the hunger experienced by their ancestors while wandering in the desert. Finally, after the lengthy story they were told to wash their hands again, which the children knew meant that at long last, mealtime was near. Great-grandfather said yet another blessing, and everybody ate first from the matzo, then from the grated horseradish on the Seder plate to remind them of the bitter times of slavery.

When my great-grandmother saw that the first part of the Seder was nearing its end, she yelled towards the kitchen: "Paula, man kann die Knedel einkochen!" (Paula, you can start cooking the matzo balls!). That was what the children had been waiting for. Generally, Paula had the matzo balls in the pot even before my great-grandmother said a thing, because she knew the whole script of the Seder as if she had been raised a Jew herself. Dinner started with roasted eggs, another one of the symbolic foods on the Seder plate, followed by chicken or meat soup with Paula's famous matzo balls (see recipe on page 344) in it. Then came a roast goose or a fricassee of goose with horseradish sauce or applesauce. The side dish was one of Riza néni's slightly sweet matzo kugels (see recipes on page 347 and 350) or mashed potatoes and some vegetable, such as puréed carrots.

"Paula, you can start cooking the matzo balls!"

Everybody was supposed to drink four glasses of special Pesach wine during the Seder ceremony, but except for Frigyes bácsi, they didn't really drink the wine but only stuck one finger in the glass and licked it off. For dessert they had potato flour torte, macaroon torte (see recipes on pages 360 and 362), chocolate-matzo torte, or layered matzo made with wine, eggs, ground nuts and sugar.

After dinner they should have sat down to read some more from the haggadah. If my great-grandfather did this at all, he excerpted what was already a sped-up version and the whole thing was over in ten minutes. He could see that the children were impatient and the grownups were eager for them to go to bed. Frigyes bácsi and Dezső bácsi could also hardly wait for the ceremony to be over and had been teasing my great-grandfather all through the reading: "You are wrong, this is not where we stopped. We were already two pages farther along."

Towards the end of the Seder, after the recovery of the *afikoman*, the "stolen" matzo, they sipped a little more wine, poured wine into the cup set out for Elijah, and opened the door to the hallway. They were expecting Elijah, the forerunner of the Messiah, who supposedly visits every Jewish home during Seder and offers his protection to the household. While the children looked toward the door, Riza néni spilled a little wine from the Prophet's cup trying to convince the kids that he had indeed sneaked in unnoticed and drunk from his cup. But instead of the Prophet entering, the children could only see Paula coming to clean off the table. After this, they sang some hymns, and then the children went to bed, but the grownups lingered at the table for a while to chat.

Next morning, they had coffee with matzo in it, their usual breakfast fare during Passover. They broke the matzo into pieces, put them in a mug, poured hot milk and coffee over them, and finally placed an extra piece of matzo on the thick skin of the milk. Of course, the matzo immediately gets soft in the coffee. It was wonderfully filling and all the grandchildren loved it.

Mother kept referring to Passover as Easter and this was no mere slip of tongue, because Riza néni and the rest of her family had frequently done the same—a practice quite common in Hungary, Austria, and Germany. Even such local Jewish cookbooks that take the rules of kashrut seriously use the word *Oster* or *húsvét*, German and Hungarian for Easter, instead of the Hebrew Pesach. The literal translation of the original German names of Riza néni's following two recipes is Easter dumpling and Easter kugel. One could say that this was only a question of word usage, because neither Riza néni nor the rest of our family kept Easter as a religious holiday. But I see in this casual interchangeability of the names of Christian and Jewish holidays the beginning of a process in which her descendants gradually stopped observing Pesach, and a few of them actually adopted some nonreligious Hungarian Easter customs.

On Easter Sunday for example, when I was a child, I followed the example of the other kids in my neighborhood and went from door to door sprinkling perfumed water on women and receiving little presents for it. Naturally, this is not a Christian custom but the vestige of an old fertility rite. Although it is not a religious ritual, in Hungary it had become part of the Easter tradition and I was eager to join my Gentile friends in this.

Matzo Balls
Osterknedel

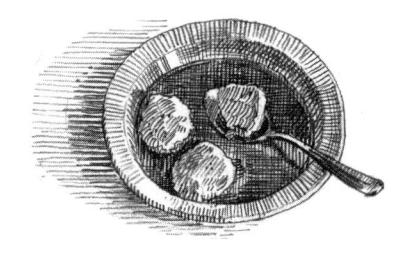

Matzo balls—originally created as a Passover specialty—are one of the great success stories of Jewish cuisine. They have become so popular among Jews that they make them throughout the year. Gentiles couldn't resist their lure either, and they became fairly standard fare in both the United States and Hungary, where one can find matzo ball soup on the menu of many nonethnic restaurants.

Riza néni's matzo balls will be a revelation to anybody who only knows the pleasant but fairly bland white soup dumplings made from matzo meal. Her dumplings can compete in lightness with any matzo ball but they are slightly darker than the usual kind because they are mainly made of broken pieces of matzo and contain very little matzo meal. This also makes their texture more interesting than the uniform fluffiness of the more common version.

In addition to Riza néni's recipe, I have another version from her older sister, Lujza néni. They could have organized a contest between them for the best matzo balls. In my updated recipe, I decided to include ground pepper and chopped parsley from Lujza néni's version. I also took from her the idea of allowing the dumplings to rest before cooking them, which is in addition to the usual resting of the dough before shaping the dumplings. I believe this produces unusually moist and tender dumplings without running the risk of their falling apart in the boiling water. They had cooked their matzo balls in chicken soup, but I prefer adding them to the soup after they have been cooked in water because the dumplings tend to absorb a great deal of cooking liquid and one would need a lot of extra soup to compensate for this. I use unsalted matzo to make these dumplings for the same reason that I prefer to use unsalted butter in savory dishes: I can control the saltiness better by adding the salt separately.

YIELD:	about 14 dumplings
TOTAL TIME:	about 1 hour 40 minutes
INGREDIENTS:	3 sheets (7" × 6½") or 4 sheets (6" × 6") of unsalted matzo
	1 cup low-salt or unsalted chicken broth or water
	2 large egg yolks
	2 tablespoons rendered chicken fat or canola oil
	3 tablespoons chicken broth or seltzer
	¾ teaspoon kosher salt
	¾ teaspoon ground ginger (or 1½ teaspoons finely chopped fresh ginger)
	¼ cup unsalted matzo meal
	2 tablespoons finely chopped fresh parsley (optional)
	¼ teaspoon freshly ground black pepper (optional)
	2 large egg whites, whipped
	¼ teaspoon cream of tartar
	1 tablespoon kosher salt (to salt the cooking water)
SPECIAL EQUIPMENT:	food processor

1. Break half of the matzo into about 1" pieces, place them in a medium bowl, add 1 cup chicken broth or water, soak them for about 8 minutes, squeeze them out well, and strain the broth for reuse or discard the water. Break the other half of the matzo into about 2" pieces, place them in the bowl of the food processor, and process them into approximately ¼" pieces, about 10 seconds.

2. While the matzo is soaking, whisk egg yolks, chicken fat or oil, and broth or seltzer in a large bowl until they are slightly foamy. Add salt, ginger, soaked matzo, coarsely ground matzo, matzo meal, and the optional parsley and ground pepper. Mix them into a medium-soft dough.

3. Whip egg whites with cream of tartar until they form firm peaks. Thoroughly stir half of the whipped egg whites into the dough, then fold in the remaining egg whites. The dough should be soft, almost runny. Let it rest for ½ hour; the dough will get firmer as it rests.

4. Check the consistency of the dough; it should be medium-soft, barely firm enough to shape it into dumplings. If it is too dry, mix in a little broth or water. Place a bowl of cold water near your work surface, dip your hands into it, then take about 1 heaped tablespoon of the dough and form it between your damp palms into a ball about 1½" in diameter. Place it on a cutting board and proceed to make the remaining dumplings until you have used up all the dough. Periodically moisten your hands to keep the dough from sticking. You should have about 14 dumplings. Let them rest on the cutting board for another ½ hour. Boil about 3" of salted water in an at least 10"-diameter pot.

5. Use a spoon to gently lower the dumplings into the boiling water, reduce heat, cover, and cook them in simmering water for 23–25 minutes if you plan to serve them immediately, about 2 minutes less if you plan to reheat them. Carefully stir them halfway through the cooking. The dumplings will expand to almost 2" in diameter during cooking. Remove them from the water with a slotted spoon and serve them immediately in hot chicken soup or keep them on a plate and reheat them for 2 minutes in simmering soup.

Apple-Matzo Kugel
Osterkugel

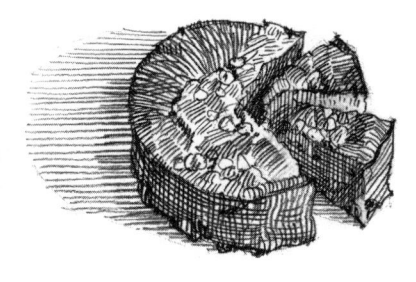

Many old documents used the same name for *kugels* and cholent: they uniformly called them *cholent, schalet,* or *schalent,* because kugel, the Sabbath pudding, was inseparable from cholent at Saturday lunch. Only the adjective before the noun *cholent* indicated that these were really kugels: bread cholent, apple cholent, rice cholent, noodle cholent, and so on. Later, they came to be called *Schalet-Kugel* and according to John Cooper, "at some point the shortened Yiddish term *kugel* was substituted in Poland for the German name Schalet-Kugel."

Matzo kugels are one of the oldest types of kugel, as is attested by the fact that—quoting again John Cooper—"a matzah cholent was reported from Austria in the fifteenth century." People made them for Sabbath during the week of Passover. Matzo kugels must have been popular in the shared Moson house of Riza and Lujza néni because I have four different recipes—some of them in several versions—from the two sisters for such kugels. Both matzo kugel recipes selected for this book had originally been intended to be side dishes, not desserts. In this apple-matzo kugel, apple is the dominant ingredient; in the following recipe, matzos and sliced potatoes are more important than the small quantity of apple.

I substituted chopped chicken fat for the chopped beef fat of the original recipe, because I thought this would be more practical and appealing for the modern cook. Using raw animal fat in baking is unusual today, but there is no reason to be squeamish about it because the heat will cook and melt the finely chopped raw fat, which will be completely absorbed by the dough. But if it bothers you, omit it, and increase the amount of rendered chicken fat in the dish by three tablespoons or use margarine instead. When I make a chicken dish, I always save the chicken skin and fat that I trimmed from the meat and freeze it, so I can later use it for making rendered fat and cracklings, or for dishes such as this kugel. Before chopping the raw fat, cut off the skin and save it for making cracklings.

Riza néni baked her kugels in a round clay dish with slightly tapering sides, sort of like a shallow flowerpot with a cover. I used a soufflé dish for baking my kugel and covered it with a piece of parchment paper cut to the size of the dish and laid directly on the dough. If you don't have such a dish, use a similar-size charlotte mold or pot.

I love how the crunchy bits of almond provide appealing contrast to the airy, moist texture of this kugel and how the flavors of apple, wine, matzo, and a touch of cinnamon blend in a most harmonious way in it. Probably at Riza néni's it was a side dish to savory meat dishes on the Sabbath table, but I like to serve this slightly sweet pudding as a dessert by itself or in a pool of raspberry or plum sauce. Fruit compote would be also terrific with it.

YIELD: 8 servings

TOTAL TIME: about 1 hour 35 minutes, plus cooling time

INGREDIENTS:
- 3 small or 2 large Golden Delicious apples, peeled, cored, and cut into ¼" dice (about 3 cups)
- 1 tablespoon lemon juice
- ¼ cup sugar
- 2½ sheets (7" × 6½") or 3 sheets (6" × 6") unsalted matzo
- 1 cup water
- 1 cup white wine
- 1 teaspoon rendered chicken fat, margarine, or canola oil
- ⅔ cup raw almonds
- ⅓ cup unsalted matzo meal
- 5 large egg yolks
- 2 tablespoons rendered chicken fat
- ¼ cup sugar
- ¼ teaspoon kosher salt
- ½ teaspoon ground cinnamon
- 3 tablespoons very finely chopped raw chicken fat
- 2 tablespoons unsalted matzo meal
- 2 teaspoons grated lemon zest (optional)

| | 6 large egg whites |
| | ½ teaspoon cream of tartar |

SPECIAL
EQUIPMENT: 7" or 8" soufflé dish or a charlotte mold or pot of similar size
food processor
electric mixer (optional)
parchment paper
baking sheet

1. Place diced apple, lemon juice, and sugar in a medium bowl; mix them well and let them rest for at least ½ hour. Drain them in a strainer, use the back of a wooden spoon to press the liquid out of them, and set them aside. Break matzos into 2" pieces, place them in a medium bowl and soak them in a mixture of water and wine for about 8 minutes. Squeeze them out and set them aside.

2. Grease the soufflé dish with a little rendered fat, margarine, or oil, and line its bottom with parchment paper. Center a rack in the oven and preheat the oven to 350°F.

3. Place almonds and ⅓ cup matzo meal in the food processor and process for 10 to 15 seconds until coarsely ground. Place egg yolks, rendered chicken fat and ¼ cup sugar in a large bowl; beat them for a few minutes until the mixture gets foamy. Stir in the almond mixture, the diced apples, the soaked pieces of matzo, salt, cinnamon, chopped chicken fat, 2 tablespoons matzo meal, and optional lemon zest.

4. Whip egg whites and cream of tartar with a balloon whisk by hand or with an electric mixer until the egg whites form firm peaks. Stir about ½ of the egg whites into the apple-matzo mixture then fold in the rest of the egg whites.

5. Transfer the batter into the soufflé dish and lay a piece of parchment paper cut to fit the dish over the batter. Place the dish on a baking sheet and bake it in the preheated oven for 50 minutes. Peel off the paper from the top and continue baking it for another 15 to 20 minutes,

65 to 70 minutes in total, until the top of the kugel springs back when gently pressed in the center with your finger.

6. Let it cool for about 20 minutes in the baking dish set on a cooling rack. Run a knife around the kugel in the baking dish, place a large dinner plate upside down on the dish, hold them together, invert them and let the kugel drop onto the plate. Remove the baking dish, peel off the paper from the bottom, place a large flat serving plate over the upside-down kugel, and while holding the kugel sandwiched between the plates, invert it to the serving plate. Serve it lukewarm—as Riza néni probably did—or let it finish cooling on the serving plate.

Matzo Kugel

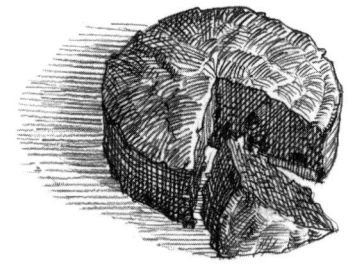

Laska kugli

Though all the kugels in Riza néni's repertoire included sugar, she served most of them as accompaniments to savory dishes. On occasion some could take the place of desserts on her Sabbath table, but I doubt that she would have ever offered this kugel as a dessert—it is most emphatically a side dish. The idea of serving such a slightly sweet pudding with savory dishes sounds odd today, but it used to be quite common in Ashkenazi Jewish cuisine. Much as I love culinary history, when I spend hours preparing a dish only to find it unappealing, it gives me little consolation to read that centuries ago people used to love it. But as the saying goes, the proof is in the pudding. And, well, in my opinion, this pudding would go very nicely—just to pick an example—with roast or stuffed chicken (see recipe on page 229) and a salad. It would also be great as a meatless main course if served with Riza néni's mildly sour, ginger- and cinnamon-flavored green beans.

This is again a recipe of which I have slightly different versions from

Riza néni, her older sister, and her niece. Riza néni lined the bottom of her kugel form with fatty chicken skin over which she placed a layer of sliced potatoes, but I preferred to follow her sister's suggestion of using only potatoes without the chicken skin as the base. I also took from her sister's recipe the idea of adding a small amount of grated apple to the dough, because I thought this made the kugel moister and less dense. Instead of the chopped hard beef fat in the original recipe, I used chopped raw chicken fat. Though it gets cooked and completely absorbed during baking, should you have qualms about adding raw fat to the dish, you can substitute rendered chicken fat.

YIELD: about 8 servings

TOTAL TIME: about 2 hours, plus cooling time

INGREDIENTS:
- 2½ sheets (7" × 6½") or 3 sheets (6" × 6") unsalted matzo, broken into about 1" pieces
- 1 cup fruity white wine
- ½ cup water
- ¾ cup walnut halves
- ⅓ cup sugar
- 1 teaspoon rendered chicken fat or canola oil
- 1 large Yukon Gold potato (about 5 ounces) cut crosswise into ⅛"–¼" thick slices (about 10 slices)
- ¼ cup rendered chicken fat, softened
- 5 large egg yolks
- 1½ teaspoons grated lemon zest
- 1½ tablespoons lemon juice
- 2 tablespoons white wine
- ⅓ cup sugar
- 1 pinch kosher salt
- ½ teaspoon ground cinnamon
- ¼ cup very finely chopped raw chicken fat
- ¼ cup golden raisins
- ½ Golden Delicious apple, peeled, cored, and coarsely grated
- 1 cup unsalted matzo meal

	1–2 tablespoons white wine
	6 large egg whites
	½ teaspoon cream of tartar
SPECIAL EQUIPMENT:	food processor
	7"- or 8"-diameter soufflé dish (about 3½" deep) or a similar-sized round pot
	electric mixer (optional)
	parchment paper
	baking sheet

1. In a medium bowl, soak the matzo pieces in a mixture of wine and water for about 8 minutes then squeeze them out and set them aside. Discard the soaking liquid. Place walnuts and ⅓ cup sugar in the bowl of a food processor and process for about 10 seconds, until finely ground.

2. Grease the soufflé dish with rendered fat or oil. Place slices of potato in 1 layer tightly against each other to cover most of the bottom of the dish. Center a rack in the oven and preheat the oven to 350°F.

3. Place softened rendered fat, egg yolks, lemon zest and juice, 2 tablespoons wine, ⅓ cup sugar, salt, and cinnamon in a large bowl. Whisk to blend and continue whisking for a few minutes until the mixture gets slightly foamy. Add soaked matzo, ground walnuts, chopped chicken fat, raisins, grated apple, and matzo meal, then stir to blend. Let it rest for about 20 minutes for the matzo meal to absorb some of the moisture. The mixture should be slightly soft, not dry. If necessary, stir in a little more wine by the tablespoonful to get the right consistency.

4. Whip egg whites and cream of tartar until they form firm peaks. Stir half of the egg whites into the matzo mixture, then carefully fold in the remaining whites. It should be a very soft batter. Pour the batter into the soufflé dish, even out the top by gently tapping the dish, cut a piece of parchment paper to fit inside the dish and lay it over the batter, place the dish on a baking sheet and bake it in the preheated oven for 1 hour. Remove the parchment cover and continue baking the kugel for additional 15 to 20 minutes.

5. Place the dish, with the kugel still in it, on a cooling rack for about 20 minutes. Run a knife around the kugel to release it, place a large inverted dinner plate on top of the dish, hold them tightly together and flip them over so that the kugel can drop onto the plate. Remove the dish, place a large flat serving plate upside-down on the kugel, and while holding the kugel sandwiched between the plates, invert it onto the serving plate. Allow it to cool for another 30 minutes. Serve it lukewarm or at room temperature.

Matzo Fritters
Überzogene Mazes

I have two different but equally nice recipes for matzo fritters from my great-grandmother and her older sister. Riza néni's is the simpler recipe: it consists of pieces of matzo dipped into a matzo-meal batter and deep-fried. Lujza néni's recipe is slightly more involved because it calls for briefly soaking the pieces of matzo in wine, then coating them with a batter that is similar to what one would use for an almond-matzo sponge cake, and finally deep-frying them. Paradoxically, it takes a few minutes more to prepare the simpler recipe, but both recipes are quick and easy to make. I decided to include both recipes, so you can compare Riza néni's fritters, in which the pieces of matzo are clearly discernible inside the coating, with her sister's slightly softer and sweeter fritters, in which the matzo completely blends with the coating.

Riza Néni's Matzo Fritters

YIELD:	about 12 pieces
TOTAL TIME:	about 25 minutes
INGREDIENTS:	2 large eggs
	2–3 tablespoons white wine
	1 tablespoon sugar
	1 small pinch kosher salt
	¼ cup unsalted matzo meal
	2 sheets of unsalted matzo, each broken into 6 approximately 2" × 3½" rectangles
	3 cups canola oil
	2 tablespoons confectioners' sugar
	½ teaspoon ground cinnamon
SPECIAL EQUIPMENT:	deep fryer or an 8"-diameter and 3"–4"-deep pot
	deep-frying thermometer (unless your fryer has a thermostat)
	slotted spoon or skimmer

1. Preheat oven to 175°F. In a medium bowl, whisk together eggs, wine, sugar, and salt. Stir in the matzo meal, making sure that there are no lumps in the batter, and let it rest for about 10 minutes. The batter will thicken slightly. If necessary, add a little more wine by the teaspoonful (I had to add 3 teaspoons) to adjust the consistency, which should be similar to pancake batter.

2. Pour about 1" oil into a deep fryer or into a medium-sized pot or sauté pan and warm it over medium heat to 375°F. Clip a deep-frying thermometer to the side of your pot or fryer (if it is not thermostatically controlled) to measure the temperature of the oil. Make sure that the end of the thermometer is completely immersed and the tip doesn't touch the bottom. As soon as the oil reaches 370°F, adjust heat to medium-low, because the pot's residual heat will keep raising the tem-

perature of the oil for a few seconds. (If you don't have a thermometer, see page 308 for an alternate way of measuring the temperature.) Reheat the oil to 375°F between batches.

3. Dip a piece of matzo into the batter and lower it into the hot oil. Quickly, dip 2 more pieces and lower them in 1 layer into the oil. Don't fry more than 3 pieces at a time. Fry them about 15 seconds on each side, until their coating turns light golden brown. Remove them with a slotted spoon or skimmer and drain them on a wire rack set over paper towels. Continue coating and frying the pieces of matzo in batches of 3. Stir the batter before coating a new batch. I used a spoon to coat the last pieces of matzo because there wasn't enough batter left in the bowl to dip them. While you prepare a batch of fritters, keep the finished ones warm in the preheated oven on a wire rack placed over a baking sheet.

4. Arrange the pieces on a serving dish. Mix confectioners' sugar and cinnamon in a small bowl, pour the mixture into a small strainer and tap it over the pieces to generously dust them with sugar. Serve them as soon as possible, while they are still hot.

5. To reuse the oil, strain it through a paper towel and use it within two weeks, because it doesn't keep indefinitely. Discard the oil after the second use.

Lujza Néni's Matzo Fritters

YIELD:	about 12 pieces
TOTAL TIME:	about 15 minutes
INGREDIENTS:	1 cup fruity white wine
	2 tablespoons sugar
	⅓ cup raw almonds

3 tablespoons sugar
2 large egg yolks
3 tablespoons unsalted matzo meal
2 large egg whites
¼ teaspoon cream of tartar
2 sheets of unsalted matzo, each broken into 6 approximately 2" × 3½" rectangles
3 cups canola oil
2 tablespoons confectioners' sugar
½ teaspoon ground cinnamon

SPECIAL
EQUIPMENT: food processor
deep fryer or pot 8" in diameter and 3"–4" deep
deep–frying thermometer (unless your fryer has a thermostat)
slotted spoon or skimmer

1. Preheat oven to 175°F. Mix wine with 2 tablespoons sugar in a soup plate. Place almonds and 3 tablespoons sugar in the bowl of the food processor and process for about 20 seconds, until finely ground. Place egg yolks in a medium bowl, add matzo meal and ground almonds. Stir well to evenly moisten the dry ingredients and to break up lumps in the fairly dry mixture, which will resemble coarse cornmeal.

2. Whip egg whites and cream of tartar until they form firm peaks. Stir about ½ of the egg whites into the egg yolk mixture, then carefully fold in the rest of the whites.

3. Follow instructions in step 2 of the previous recipe for heating oil.

4. Briefly dip a piece of matzo into wine, then with a knife or spatula spread batter about ⅛" thick on one side of the matzo. Set it aside while you dip 2 more pieces into wine and spread batter on one side of them. With the batter side down, lower the 3 pieces of matzo into the hot oil in one layer. Fry them for about 15 seconds, until their coated side turns light golden brown. Remove them with a slotted spoon or skimmer and transfer them in one layer, batter side down, onto a wire rack to drain while you dip, coat, and fry the first side of the remaining

pieces of matzo in batches of three. Now, spread batter on the second side of the first 3 pieces and lower them with the freshly coated side down into the hot oil to fry for about 15 seconds, until this side turns light golden brown, too. Transfer them onto the wire rack to drain for a few minutes then to another wire rack set over a baking sheet in the preheated oven to keep warm while you fry the other pieces. Coat and fry the second side of the remaining pieces of matzo in batches of three.

5. Follow instructions in step 4 of the previous recipe for dusting the fritters with sugar and serving them. Should you wish to reuse the oil, follow instructions in step 5 of the previous recipe.

Jam-filled Potato-Matzo Dumplings
Húsvéti krumplis gombócz

Ever since the nineteenth century, plum- or jam-filled potato-dough dumplings have been one of the most popular desserts in Hungary, Austria, and Germany. Occasionally, people even ate them as the main course after a big bowl of hearty soup. There is something immensely satisfying in biting into the soft, warm dough and feeling the flavors of potato dough, jam, and the ground-walnut coating blend in your mouth. I believe even for those who didn't grow up with these dumplings, as I have, they will come to symbolize the comfort of good home cooking, the warmth and informality of a family meal.

Jews who didn't want to be without their favorite potato dumplings during Passover invented a special version in which they substituted matzo meal and pieces of matzo for flour. Contrary to the usual potato dumplings, this Passover version calls for separating the eggs and adding the whipped egg whites at the end, an idea borrowed from the Passover soup dumplings.

Lekvár, a kind of fruit butter that is so thick that one can cut it with a knife, is the ideal filling for these dumplings because it will not ooze out even if by chance a dumpling hasn't been perfectly sealed. Apricot and plum lekvár are quite widely available as Hungarian imports by Adro in our delicatessen stores and better supermarkets. Of the two, I prefer to use the slightly sweeter apricot lekvár for these dumplings. If you cannot locate lekvár, buy the thickest apricot jam you can find.

YIELD:	about 22 dumplings
TOTAL TIME:	about 2 hours 45 minutes (much of this is waiting time)
INGREDIENTS:	2 large or 3 medium russet (Idaho) potatoes (about 1¼ pounds)
	2½ sheets (6½" × 7") or 3 sheets (6" × 6") unsalted matzo, broken into 1" pieces
	3 large egg yolks
	¼ cup rendered chicken fat, softened
	¼ cup sugar
	1 pinch kosher salt
	⅔ cup unsalted matzo meal
	3 large egg whites
	¼ teaspoon cream of tartar
	½ cup apricot lekvár or very thick apricot jam
	⅓ cup walnut halves
	3 tablespoons sugar
	¼ cup rendered chicken fat (optional)
	½ cup sour cream (optional)
SPECIAL EQUIPMENT:	potato ricer
	electric mixer (optional)
	food processor
	slotted spoon or skimmer

1. Place scrubbed potatoes in their jackets in a medium saucepan, add water to cover by about 1", bring to a boil, lower heat, and simmer for 30–40 minutes, until tender when tested with a fork or the point of a paring knife. Don't allow the potatoes to burst. Drain them, hold the hot potatoes with a folded kitchen towel, and pull off their skin with a paring knife. Cut them into about 1" pieces and while they are still hot

put them through a potato ricer or a food mill set over a baking sheet. Spread the potatoes on the baking sheet and allow them to cool and dry for 1 hour.

2. Place the broken pieces of matzo in a medium bowl, add water to cover, let them soak for about 8 minutes, squeeze them out, and discard the water. Place about 4 quarts of water in a 10"-diameter pot and bring it to a boil. Preheat oven to 175°F.

3. Place egg yolks in a large bowl, add rendered fat, sugar, and salt. Whisk them well, add the soaked matzo, matzo meal, and potatoes, and stir until thoroughly blended. Let this mixture rest for 10 minutes.

4. Place walnuts and 3 tablespoons sugar in the food processor and process for about 10 seconds, until finely ground. Transfer them into a small bowl. Fill a medium bowl with cold water and place it near your work surface. Make 22 little balls of apricot lekvár, 1 level teaspoonful each, and place them also near your work surface.

5. Whip egg whites and cream of tartar until they form firm peaks. Stir ½ of the whipped egg whites into the matzo-potato mixture, then gently fold in the rest.

6. Dip your hands into cold water. Take 1 heaped (or 2 level) tablespoonful dough and flatten it in your palm into a disc about 2½" diameter and ¼" thick. Place a little ball of apricot lekvár in the middle, and make an approximately 1½"-diameter ball from the dough to completely enclose the filling. Roll it between you wet palms to seal it well and even out the shape. Repeat this with the rest of the dough. Frequently dip your hands into cold water to keep the dough from sticking. You should have about 22 dumplings.

7. One by one, drop half of the dumplings into the vigorously boiling water and move the dumplings a little with a wooden spoon to make sure they don't stick to the bottom. When the water has returned to a boil, partially cover, lower heat to a simmer and cook them for about 18 minutes. Remove 1 dumpling with a slotted spoon or skimmer and cut it open to check whether it has cooked all the way through. Trans-

fer the rest of the cooked dumplings with the slotted spoon in one layer onto a large plate and place them in the preheated oven to keep warm until you cook the second batch.

8. Roll the damp dumplings in ground walnuts to evenly coat them and serve them warm. Serve about 3 dumplings per person for dessert or 5 dumplings for a main course. Bring warm rendered chicken fat in a sauce cup to the table and ask your guests if they wish to spoon a little on their dumplings, as was suggested by the original recipe. The dumplings are also terrific with a little sour cream but, as you can imagine, this was not part of the original recipe.

Potato Flour Torte
Erdäpfelmehl Torte

Potato flour is made of cooked, dried, and ground potatoes. It is sold under the name of potato starch and can be found in the baking section of supermarkets. Its most common use is as a thickener, but it is sometimes also used in baking, where it lends an unusual tenderness and moist texture to cakes and biscuits. Jewish bakers took advantage of this and of the fact that unlike wheat flour it is allowed during Passover. A good example of such Passover desserts is Riza néni's torte, which is essentially a sponge cake made with potato flour instead of wheat flour.

She probably sprinkled this elegantly simple unfilled torte with powdered sugar and served it with coffee, fresh fruit, or compote. I decided to decorate my version of her torte with sliced almonds imbedded in its top, or one could say in its bottom, because the torte is baked upside down. The almond topping looks pretty, involves practically no extra work, and the crunch of the almonds offers pleasing contrast to the soft, moist sponge cake. Another variation could be adding a handful of golden raisins, or half teaspoon vanilla extract, or both, to the batter. As for the batter itself, my only change was to use one additional egg white for increased volume and an even lighter torte.

YIELD:	12 slices
TOTAL TIME:	about 45 minutes, plus cooling time
INGREDIENTS:	1 teaspoon canola oil or margarine
	⅓ cup sliced almonds (optional)
	4 large egg yolks
	⅓ cup sugar
	1 pinch kosher salt
	2 teaspoons grated lemon zest
	1½ tablespoons lemon juice
	7 tablespoons potato flour (potato starch)
	5 large egg whites
	½ teaspoon cream of tartar
	2 tablespoons sugar
SPECIAL EQUIPMENT:	9" spring form
	parchment paper
	electric stand mixer or electric hand mixer (optional)
	baking sheet

1. Center a rack in the oven and preheat the oven to 350°F. Grease the spring form with oil or margarine, line the bottom with parchment paper, and then flip the paper over so that its top surface is greased, too. Should you decide to use the optional sliced almonds, spread them evenly in one layer on the parchment paper.

2. Place egg yolks and sugar in a large mixing bowl and beat them with an electric mixer or by hand, until they turn very pale and become fluffy. Add salt, lemon zest, and lemon juice. Sprinkle potato starch over the yolk mixture and briefly mix it in.

3. Whip egg whites and cream of tartar until they form soft peaks. Sprinkle 2 tablespoons sugar over them and continue whipping until the whites become shiny and form firm peaks. Stir about ⅓ of the whipped whites into the egg yolk mixture, then gently fold in the remaining whites. Pour ⅓ of this batter into the spring form and tap lightly to get rid off air pockets. Pour in the rest of the batter; the form will be slightly less then half full. Place it on a baking sheet and bake it for 10 minutes on the middle rack of the preheated oven, propping the oven door slightly open with a wedged-in knife. Remove the knife, let the oven door close completely, and bake the torte for another 20 to 25 minutes, until the top turns light golden and springs back when lightly pressed in the middle with your finger and the side of the torte pulls away from the form.

4. Place a lightly greased cooling rack upside down on top of the hot form, hold them together and invert the form onto the rack. Let the torte cool covered by the form for about 1 hour. Invert the form again and run a paring knife around the torte to release it from the form. Unlatch and remove the side ring of the form. Place a large flat serving plate upside-down on the torte and invert the torte onto the serving plate. Remove the bottom of the form and peel off the parchment paper. Cut the torte with a long serrated knife and serve it with fresh fruit, compote, fruit syrup, lingonberries in sugar, or red currant preserves.

Macaroon Torte
Makronen Torte

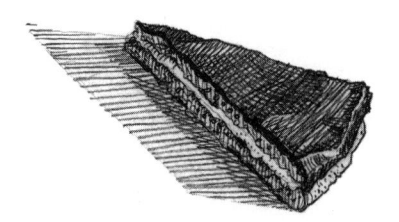

For centuries, macaroons have been part of the Passover tradition. The few exceptions to the rule notwithstanding, most macaroons are made without flour, making them appropriate for this holiday. In addition, they are made without any fat or dairy product, therefore they can be served after any meal. The many macaroon recipes in Riza néni's collection attest to her fondness for this type of dessert. Of all the different macaroons she prepared for Passover, her macaroon torte must have been the pièce de résistance.

Macaroon torte must have been popular in nineteenth-century Austria because I found versions of it in several cookbooks based on old handwritten recipe collections, including one that used to belong to Katharina Schratt, Emperor Franz Joseph's lady friend. However, Riza néni's recipe is considerably different from those versions, mainly because she adds slivered almonds to the commonly used ground almonds, making the texture of her macaroon torte layers more interesting. The basic idea of this Austrian dessert, especially of the common version made without slivered almonds, is not that far from the famous French *dacquoise*, a light, crisp sheet of meringue made with ground nuts. The main difference is that the layers of the macaroon torte are traditionally baked at a slightly higher temperature than the barely warm oven used for the dacquoise.

The original recipe for this torte included a small amount of bread crumbs, which she probably substituted with potato flour (potato starch) or matzo meal when she prepared it for Passover. Her recipe described only the dough and didn't spell out the type of filling and icing one should use. I decided to make it with whipped cream filling and a shiny chocolate glaze, making it a dairy version. Although it takes only about 15 minutes to make the chocolate glaze, omit it if you are pressed for time.

YIELD: 12 servings

TOTAL TIME: about 1 hour 10 minutes, plus setting time for the chocolate glaze

INGREDIENTS:
½ teaspoon unsalted butter, margarine, or oil (for greasing the flan rings)
4 large egg whites
½ teaspoon cream of tartar
¾ teaspoon vanilla extract
½ cup superfine sugar (or process granulated sugar into finer-grained sugar in the food processor)
¾ cup whole blanched almonds

½ cup confectioners' sugar
1 tablespoon potato starch
¾ cup slivered almonds
6 ounces bittersweet chocolate (for the chocolate glaze)
½ cup heavy cream (for the chocolate glaze)
½ cup heavy cream (for the filling)
1 tablespoon sugar

SPECIAL
EQUIPMENT: 2 baking sheets (12" x 18")
2 reusable nonstick silicone baking mats or parchment paper
food processor
2 flan rings, each 9½" diameter x ¾" high (optional)

1. Adjust oven racks to divide the oven into thirds; preheat oven to 300°F. Line the baking sheets with nonstick baking mats or parchment paper. Lightly grease the flan rings. If you are not using flan rings, draw a 9" circle on the back of each sheet of parchment paper. The circle should be visible through the paper.

2. Whip egg whites and cream of tartar until they form soft peaks; add vanilla and superfine sugar; continue whipping until the whites become glossy and form firm peaks.

3. Place almonds, confectioners' sugar, and potato starch in the food processor. Process for about 20 seconds until almonds are finely and uniformly ground. Transfer the mixture into a large bowl, add slivered almonds and stir to distribute them. Stir in ⅓ of the whipped egg whites, then gently fold in the rest. Evenly divide the macaroon mixture between the two flan rings and spread it with a rubber spatula to be smooth and level within the rings. If you don't have flan rings, use an offset spatula to evenly spread the mixture within the circles on the paper.

4. Bake the macaroon discs in the preheated oven for 30–35 minutes. Switch the baking sheets about halfway through the baking time to

ensure even baking. The macaroon discs should be a pale golden color when ready.

5. Run a paring knife around the discs and remove the flan rings. Run a long, wide spatula under each disc to release it from the paper or the baking mat and transfer the discs to a cooling rack. Be careful to support the warm and slightly soft discs during the transfer or they might break; they will firm up during cooling.

6. If you want to put off filling and glazing the torte, keep the completely cooled discs in a sealed plastic bag. When you are ready to prepare the glaze, select the disc with the smoothest bottom side (the side that was toward the baking sheet) and with the fewest air bubbles. Cut a cardboard circle about ½" smaller than the torte (or use a store-bought precut cake base), transfer the selected macaroon disc with the "good" side facing up onto the cardboard and place them on a small plate to elevate them over the work surface.

7. Cut chocolate into about 1" pieces, place them in the food processor, and process them into very small pieces. Pour the ground chocolate into a medium bowl. Bring ½ cup heavy cream to a boil in a small saucepan and pour it over the chocolate, then cover the bowl and wait for about 3 minutes until the chocolate melts. Stir the mixture with a small whisk until it becomes perfectly smooth, but be careful not to whip air into the mixture. Wait until the mixture has slightly thickened but is still quite liquid. Pour most of it over the middle of the macaroon disc and smooth it with the back and forth motion of a long metal spatula while the glaze is still liquid. Move the spatula across the whole top, don't try to "touch up" parts of the glaze. Take a small spatula or knife and quickly spread chocolate over the still bare parts of the side of the disc but don't touch the top anymore. Let it set for about 2 hours at room temperature.

8. Cut the chocolate-glazed top with a long serrated knife into 12 equal parts. Whip the remaining ½ cup well-chilled heavy cream in a chilled bowl until the cream forms soft peaks. Add 1 tablespoon sugar and continue whipping until stiff peaks form. Spread the whipped cream about ⅛" thick over the bottom layer of the torte, then one by one

carefully place the cut-up segments of the chocolate-glazed top over it. Use a long serrated knife guided by the top segments to cut the slices of the torte. The chocolate glaze will dull slightly when refrigerated.

Chocolate-Almond Cookies
Braune Mageron

Though Riza néni called these cookies macaroons, they don't belong to this group, because in addition to the egg whites typical of real macaroons, they also include egg yolks. Their dough reminds me of a chocolate-almond sponge cake. But categories become irrelevant when you taste these wonderful cookies, enjoy their intense spiced chocolate flavor, and admire their white meringue topping and cheerful colored sugar sprinkles glistening on top of the dark brown base.

Riza néni baked these cookies on little round edible wafers, which she bought in a local store; they are still available in Hungary, Austria, and Germany. Here they are obtainable in some ethnic stores specializing in imported foods, such as the German butcher and delicatessen store in New York City, where I bought them. These *Back-Oblaten* (edible baking wafers) are imported in different sizes and shapes from Germany. Buy the 70 mm. (2¾") diameter round wafers sold in packages of 100. The wafers are ideal for these cookies, but if you cannot buy them, line your baking sheet with a silicone nonstick mat instead. It works almost as well as the wafers; the cookies can be quite easily removed from it with a small spatula or knife. But the bottoms of a few cookies tend to remain a little sticky, which can take several hours to firm up, though much of this problem can be avoided if the whipped egg whites are thoroughly mixed into the chocolate-almond mixture. Parchment paper works fairly well as a last resort but the wafers or even the nonstick mats are a lot better for these cookies.

YIELD:	about 36 cookies
TOTAL TIME:	about 30 minutes, plus cooling time
INGREDIENTS:	1¼ cups raw almonds
	½ cup sugar
	2 ounces (2 squares) bittersweet chocolate, cut into ½" pieces
	½ teaspoon vanilla extract
	½ teaspoon ground cinnamon
	¼ teaspoon ground cloves
	1 tablespoon lemon juice
	2 teaspoons grated lemon zest
	2 large egg yolks
	3 large egg whites
	¼ teaspoon cream of tartar
	3 tablespoons sugar
	2 tablespoons multicolored coarse cake-decorating "confetti" sugar
SPECIAL EQUIPMENT:	food processor
	2 baking sheets (12" × 18")
	36 Back-Oblaten (edible baking wafers), 2¾" diameter each
	2 reusable nonstick baking mats, 11⅝" × 16½" each (if you cannot buy edible wafers)

1. Adjust oven racks to divide the oven into thirds and preheat the oven to 300°F. Place sugar and ½ cup of the almonds in the bowl of the food processor and process for about 15 seconds, until finely ground. Add chocolate and the remaining ¾ cup almonds, process for about 20 seconds, until the almonds are evenly but somewhat coarsely ground. Add vanilla, cinnamon, cloves, lemon juice and zest, and the egg yolks. Process for about 5 seconds, until the mixture sticks together and has

the consistency of damp sand. Transfer the mixture into a fairly large bowl.

2. Whip egg whites and cream of tartar until they form soft peaks, sprinkle 3 tablespoons sugar over them and continue whipping until they turn shiny and form firm peaks. Fold about ⅔ of the whipped egg whites into the chocolate mixture, reserve the rest (about 1 cup) for coating the cookies. Place the cake-decorating sugar in a small bowl near your work surface.

3. Place 18 wafers on each baking sheet. If you couldn't buy such wafers, line both baking sheets with nonstick mats. With a teaspoon, make about 1" × 1" high heaps of dough in the middle of each wafer. If you are using nonstick mats, keep at least 1½" space between the little heaps. It is important to make compact but high heaps that are spaced quite far apart, because the dough will spread during baking. I made 3 rows of 5 heaps on each sheet and 3 additional heaps about 2" from the rest. Use a knife or a small spatula to spread a thin and fairly even coating of whipped egg whites over the chocolate dough, being careful not to press down on the soft dough. Discard the remaining whipped egg whites. Sprinkle a little cake-decorating sugar over the egg white coating.

4. Bake them in the preheated oven for 15 to 18 minutes, switching the baking sheets halfway through to ensure even baking. The egg white coating of the cookies should remain mostly white with only faintest color at a few places. If you baked the cookies on wafers, place them on a cooling rack for about 30 minutes. If you used baking mats, transfer them with the cookies still on them to a cooling rack. After about 10 minutes use a small spatula or knife to remove the cookies from the mats and place them directly on the cooling rack for about 2 hours to finish firming up. Store them in a cookie tin at room temperature.

Hazelnut Macaroons
Haselnuss Konfekt

These macaroons are crunchy on the outside and slightly soft and chewy inside; they are also quick and easy to make and contain no fat or flour. If this isn't a winning combination, what is?

YIELD:	24 cookies
TOTAL TIME:	about 35 minutes, plus cooling time
INGREDIENTS:	1 cup blanched hazelnuts
	¼ cup sugar
	2 teaspoons grated lemon zest
	2 teaspoons lemon juice
	¾ teaspoon vanilla extract
	2 large egg whites
	¼ teaspoon lemon juice
	3 tablespoons sugar
	24 blanched whole hazelnuts
SPECIAL EQUIPMENT:	food processor
	2 baking sheets (12" × 18")
	parchment paper

1. Adjust racks to divide the oven into thirds and preheat the oven to 300°F. Line the baking sheets with parchment paper.

2. Place ½ cup of the hazelnuts and ¼ cup sugar in the food processor and process for about 10 seconds, until finely ground. Add the remaining hazelnuts and process for 5 seconds, until coarsely ground. Add lemon zest, lemon juice, and vanilla; pulse to blend.

3. Whip egg whites and ¼ teaspoon lemon juice to soft peaks, sprinkle 3 tablespoons sugar over the egg whites and continue whipping until they become shiny and form firm peaks. With a rubber spatula, fold ½ of the ground hazelnuts into the egg whites, then fold in the rest. The mixture will be soft, but shouldn't be runny.

4. Using a teaspoon, make 12 little heaps (3 rows of 4) each about 1¼" diameter on one of the parchment paper–lined baking sheets leaving at least 1½" space between the heaps. Try to make high heaps because the cookies will spread during baking. Repeat this on the second baking sheet. Place 1 blanched hazelnut on top of each heap.

5. Bake them in the preheated oven for 20 to 25 minutes, until they start to turn light golden at the edges. Switch the baking sheets after 10 minutes. Transfer the sheets of parchment with the cookies on them to cooling racks and allow the macaroons to cool and harden for 15 minutes. Peel off the parchment paper from the cookies. Serve them immediately or store them at room temperature in a cookie tin.

Meringue-Almond Clusters
Schaummandelhäufchen

The shiny almond slivers jut out of these cookies in all directions, making them look like spectacular mineral crystals. The crunch of the egg whites provides a most appealing contrast to the slightly chewy almonds. These are yet another kind of cookie made without flour or fat, and so they can be served during Pesach with any menu, be it meat or dairy.

YIELD:	about 30 cookies
TOTAL TIME:	about 40 minutes, plus cooling time
INGREDIENTS:	2 large egg whites
	¾ cup confectioners' sugar
	¾ teaspoon vanilla extract
	2 cups slivered almonds
SPECIAL EQUIPMENT:	double boiler (optional)
	2 baking sheets (12" × 18")
	parchment paper
	cooling rack

1. Adjust racks to divide the oven into thirds and preheat the oven to 275°F. Line baking sheets with parchment paper.

2. Away from the heat, place egg whites and sugar in a double boiler and whisk them well until the mixture becomes smooth. If you don't have a double boiler, use a medium-size heat-resistant glass or stainless steel bowl fitted into a saucepan.

3. Pour enough water into the lower part of the double boiler or into the saucepan so that the bottom of upper part barely touches the water. Bring it to a boil, lower heat to medium, and cook the egg whites, whisking them frequently but not continuously, for 6 to 8 minutes, until they becomes fluffy, thick, and sticky.

4. Remove the upper part; add vanilla and slivered almonds; use a teaspoon to thoroughly mix them with the egg whites. Let the mixture cool a minute or so to become less runny. Take a teaspoonful and with the help of a second teaspoon make a compact little cluster (about 1" wide and high) on the first baking sheet. Repeat this to make 15 cookies, keeping them about 1½" apart. Continue on the second baking sheet. You should have about 30 little clusters in total.

5. Bake them in the preheated oven for 20–22 minutes, until they start to turn light golden brown. Switch the baking sheets halfway through.

Transfer the sheets of parchment paper with the cookies on them onto a cooling rack for 15 minutes. Initially, the cookies will be slightly soft but will harden as they cool. Peel off the paper and place the cookies on the cooling rack to finish cooling and hardening for another 10 minutes. Serve them immediately or store them at room temperature in a cookie tin.

Almond-Chocolate Kisses
Chocolád Pusserln

These irresistible cookies are divine! Everything about them is great: they are pretty, with the blond almond glistening on top of the light brown cookie, their flavor is intense, and their texture offers the appealing contrast of firm exterior and moist, slightly soft interior. And last but not least, this is achieved with only about 10 minutes of work, not counting baking and cooling time. The food processor makes it even simpler and faster to make these cookies by allowing us to combine the previously separate steps of grinding the almonds and the chocolate. I prefer to whip such small quantities of egg whites by hand, because it is just as fast—or faster—than doing it with the electric mixer, and I believe it whips the eggs more uniformly. But it is a minor difference, so use the electric mixer if that is easier for you.

YIELD: about 28 cookies

TOTAL TIME: about 35 minutes, plus cooling time

INGREDIENTS:
- 1 cup raw almonds
- 1 ounce (1 square) bittersweet chocolate, cut into ½" pieces

¼ cup sugar
2 large egg whites
¼ teaspoon cream of tartar
3 tablespoons sugar
14 blanched almonds, split in half

SPECIAL
EQUIPMENT: 2 baking sheets (12" × 18")
parchment paper
food processor
cooling rack

1. Adjust racks to divide the oven into thirds and preheat the oven to 300°F. Line baking sheets with parchment paper.

2. Place almonds, chocolate, and ¼ cup sugar in the bowl of the food processor. Process for about 35 seconds; carefully reach into the bowl, avoiding the sharp blades, to see if the almonds are finely and evenly ground, and process a few seconds longer, if necessary.

3. In a large bowl, whip egg whites and cream of tartar with a balloon whisk by hand or with an electric mixer until the whites form soft peaks; sprinkle 3 tablespoons sugar over them and continue whipping until they become shiny and form firm peaks. Use a rubber spatula to fold about ½ of the ground almond mixture into the egg whites, then fold in the rest of the mixture.

4. Take heaped teaspoonfuls of batter and with the help of a second teaspoon make 14 compact little heaps, each about 1¼" diameter and at least 1" high, on the first baking sheet. Leave at least 1½" space between the cookies to allow room for the cookies to spread during baking. Place a split almond on top of each heap. Repeat this on the second baking sheet; you should have about 28 cookies in total.

5. Bake them in the preheated oven for 20–22 minutes, until somewhat firm to the touch. Switch the baking sheets halfway through baking. Transfer the sheets of parchment paper with the cookies on them to the cooling rack. After about 10 minutes, peel off the paper from the cookies. Place the cookies back on the cooling rack to finish cooling

and firming up for 10 more minutes. Serve them immediately or store them in a cookie tin with parchment or wax paper between the layers.

Walnut Meringue Kisses
Nussenpusserl

The contrast between the earthy and chewy chopped walnuts and the ethereally light and crisp meringue makes these kisses most appealing. In adapting the recipe, I adjusted the amount of sugar to the usual egg-sugar ratio of meringues. It is best to make these cookies on days of low humidity.

YIELD:	about 24 cookies
TOTAL TIME:	about 1 hour 30 minutes
INGREDIENTS:	1 cup walnuts, chopped into about ¼" pieces
	2 large egg whites
	¼ teaspoon cream of tartar
	½ cup superfine sugar or regular granulated sugar processed in the food processor into finer-grained sugar
SPECIAL EQUIPMENT:	electric mixer (optional)
	baking sheet
	parchment paper

1. Center a rack in the oven and preheat the oven to 200°F. Line the baking sheet with parchment paper. Coarsely chop walnuts with a knife.

2. Whip egg whites and cream of tartar with a balloon whisk by hand or with an electric mixer until egg whites form fairly stiff peaks. With the whisk or with the mixer running, gradually stir in about ⅔ of the sugar, until the whites become stiff and shiny. Don't stir the egg whites more than necessary for the even distribution of sugar, because the more you mix them, the tougher the meringues will be. Using a rubber spatula, gently fold in first the remaining sugar then the chopped walnuts.

3. I followed Riza néni's suggestion to use heaped teaspoonfuls of this mixture to make free-form cookies and made 26 little heaps, each about 1¼" in diameter and 1" high, on the baking sheet leaving about 1" of space between them. If you prefer more regularly shaped cookies, pipe the meringue from a pastry bag. Don't use a tip on the pastry bag because the walnuts could get stuck in it.

4. Bake the meringues in the preheated oven for about 1 hour 15 minutes. They should remain white or turn only the slightest beige. You should be able to easily lift the dry and crisp cookies off the paper. Store them in an airtight container, where they will keep for weeks.

PART THREE

Last Years in Budapest

1926–1938

The End of Riza Néni's World

MOTHER'S DESCRIPTION of Riza néni's life and household captured a world on the verge of disappearing. When my mother lived in Moson, Riza néni's way of living was still a nineteenth-century existence. By that time, however, the whole lifestyle in this house, where the lack of running water or bathroom seemed perfectly consistent with a comfortable middle-class existence, became more and more anachronistic. It is not surprising that it ended. What is surprising is that it survived as long as it did.

The events that finally brought Riza néni's world to a close happened in rather quick succession. The first major change was the death of her husband Bernhard in 1926. He was born in 1838, was much older than she, and had been in declining health for years. But even with the onset of senility he, even more than his wife, had been the guardian of tradition in both religion and everyday life. He presided over the Seder and strictly observed the other holidays. He no longer participated in the family business, which for many years had been run by Frigyes, his oldest son.

Easygoing, jovial Frigyes was already forty-eight years old but perfectly happy with his bachelor existence at home and with his longstanding Catholic lady friend, Ilka Decker. Like Paula, she was a German-speaking "Swabian." Her husband died when she was very young and left her with two little daughters, Fritzi and Gusti. "She was wonderful," my mother remembered, "and we all adored her. I wish she had been Jewish, then uncle Frigyes would certainly have married her. He would have been so much better off with her than with Erzsi, whom he finally married.

Unfortunately, marrying Ilka néni was out of question because my grandparents would have never approved of it."

I believe all of Riza néni's granddaughters were a little bit in love with their stylish uncle, who loved kids, understood them and was always ready to take them to the Danube for a swim or to a pastry shop in the next town. As my mother tellingly described him, "He didn't look Jewish at all. He was tall; he was the tallest man in the family. He had magnificent blue eyes; he was a very beautiful man. He was elegant and a gentleman from head to toe." I find the unmistakable echo of childhood infatuation just as interesting as her equation of not looking Jewish with being a "beautiful" man. I recognize traces of my mother's ambiguous feelings toward her Jewishness in this comment. As I recall, this was a fairly typical comment not only by her but also by relatives and other Jewish friends of her generation. I understand this as a reaction to the period of antisemitism and persecution, when "looking Jewish" could have been an added burden to being Jewish, but I must say I never had much patience for such comments and their underlying self-hatred.

Although Frigyes ate pork and didn't attend synagogue regularly, he respected and loved his father. Unless he was out of town, he showed up every day exactly at noon for lunch at the family table. He participated in the Seder and other holidays with his parents even if he poked gentle fun at the rituals. He probably wouldn't have married had his parents not nudged him to do so. As my mother described it: "He was not eager to get married; he had to be talked into marrying. He finally married Erzsi Frankl, a niece of Mrs. Wertheimer, one of our Jewish neighbors in Moson. Erzsi was an unpleasant woman, a conceited offspring of a rich family." After their wedding in Budapest, Frigyes and his new wife moved to the house in Moson and converted the old living room, what used to be called the szalon, into their apartment.

Following the death of Riza néni's husband, the next step in the gradual dissolution of her world was the departure of Paula, their servant, in 1926. After so many decades with the family, Paula had become as much part of them as any real family member. She was well into her forties, and after taking a good look at Frigyes' newly acquired wife she decided this was more change than she was willing to put up with. She had had various romantic attachments in the past, but had always decided that life at Riza néni's was preferable to married life. But this time she accepted an offer and got married.

The following year there were dramatic changes in the other side of the family house: First Sándor bácsi died in February 1927, then five months later his wife Lujza followed him. This had been a symmetrical household of two brothers who were business partners and two sisters who were their wives. Now Riza néni was the only one left from this original setup. Although she frequently had quarreled with her sister about the jointly used attic or the shared garden, they had spent their entire lives together. Since nobody from Lujza néni's side of the family lived in Moson, her daughter decided to sell their half of the house, and Riza néni had to get used to strangers living on the other side of her courtyard.

But the most traumatic and completely unexpected blow came last. In 1932 Frigyes, her son, developed a bad sinus infection that, in those days before antibiotics, required surgery. Everybody thought it would be a routine operation; his wife didn't even go to Vienna with him for the surgery. The operation went well, but a few days later he got blood poisoning, supposedly because he couldn't resist smoking one of his beloved cigars, and died. At the time of her son's operation and death Riza néni herself was lying in bed gravely ill in Moson. For a while they didn't even dare to tell her that her son had died. They thought she wouldn't recover anyway from her illness and didn't want to torture her with such dreadful news. Although she did recover later, without Frigyes there was nobody to carry on the family business. Therefore, her daughter, my grandmother, convinced her to move to Budapest to live with them.

With Riza néni the last original inhabitant left the house, and only Frigyes' widow remained there. She sold most of her share of the house, keeping only a small apartment for herself and a new store she opened from the street for income. In 1944, she was taken to the town ghetto and from there to Auschwitz, where she perished.

My grandparents lived under very modest circumstances in a crowded Budapest apartment, which they shared with not only three of their four grown children, but also with two roomers, whose rent complemented my grandfather's small pension. The apartment behind the impressive street façade was miserable: three of the six rooms faced a dark interior courtyard and the only window of another room was to a closet-sized air shaft. All my grandparents could offer to Riza néni was one of the tiny dark rooms facing the courtyard.

Living in Budapest was a huge change for Riza néni, testing her adaptability and flexibility. She was surrounded by her adoring daughter and grandchildren, but had to adjust to life in a largely secular household. In addition, she had to coexist somehow with a neurotic, clinically depressed son-in-law, who couldn't stand her.

My impression is that of these two difficult areas of adjustment, the first one was easier for her. Of course Riza néni knew that her daughter didn't keep the dietary rules, but she was a very practical, down-to-earth woman. When she moved to Budapest she told her daughter: "Was du mir gibst, das ist kosher; ich frage nicht und du sag es nicht." (Whatever you give me is kosher; I won't ask and you shouldn't tell.) Although my grandmother didn't mix sour cream into the meat sauce and she used, as much as possible, goose fat instead of lard, occasionally she cooked pork, and she didn't keep the dairy things separate from the meat stuff. This didn't bother my great-grandmother who seemed to feel: "Now I am at their place and will eat like the rest of them."

Unfortunately, my grandfather didn't get along with Riza néni. Just seeing her already irritated him. Grandfather was a very tidy, rather pedantic person. Great-grandmother was, on the other hand, not always so tidy. At times her nose dripped slightly. My God, she was old. And occasionally she would wipe her nose in her napkin. Grandfather couldn't stand this. It is also true, she had some bladder problems. When she got up from a chair, sometimes she left a damp spot on the seat. At times she had a slight smell. This disturbed my grandfather no end. The way she ate, the way she sat, the way she did anything: it was all unacceptable to him. Grandfather had no reason to be embarrassed by her; she was an educated, well-read woman. And she was an easygoing, adaptable person, something one couldn't say about my grandfather.

When Riza néni died in 1938 and my grandfather wanted to go to the funeral, my grandmother forbade him to go. Grandmother was a very mild-mannered person who always tried to accommodate him and hardly ever contradicted him, but this time she couldn't forget how badly my grandfather had behaved towards my great-grandmother.

So Riza néni's life came to an end, but the world she loved and cherished so much had already ended years earlier. Her world was centered in that strangely impractical but wonderfully accommodating old house in Moson. Near the geometric center of that house was the elegantly shaped pink marble catch basin of the well in the middle of the huge square courtyard. After the death of Frigyes, her son, she decided to move this marble catch basin to the Moson Jewish cemetery and use it as a planter on his grave. This was probably one of the last things she did before moving to Budapest. Regardless of whether she was conscious of its symbolism, she made a stunningly appropriate choice. The marble basin, which was the center of a lively household, became a memorial to the demise of Riza néni's world.

After the war there were only five Jews left in Moson. Most of the more than seven hundred Jews who lived there before 1939 were killed; the rest moved away. The old Jewish cemetery became overgrown with weeds; the mortuary building was in terrible shape. Finally, in 1990, a group of Moson expatriates got together and contributed money to restore the cemetery. They also arranged for it to be officially declared a place of reverence, which removed the very real danger of destruction that frequently threatens cemeteries no longer active. The cemetery restora-

She decided to use the basin of the well as a planter on her son's grave.

tion committee organized a gathering to celebrate the renovation and printed an invitation to this gathering. I was happy and a little surprised to see that they used a picture of the pink marble planter from Frigyes' grave on the cover of the invitation. They must have liked the shape of it, but I am quite sure none of them realized that they had elected to represent the former Jewish community with the gravestone of a bacon- and sausage-loving Jew.

Throughout Riza néni's life she tried hard to reconcile frequently conflicting requirements of the traditions of her grandparents with those of the rapidly changing world around her. When she was young she wanted to be both a daughter of her ancestral culture and an integral part of the surrounding non-Jewish society. After her marriage, she maintained an occasionally idiosyncratic version of a traditional Jewish household. Later, she felt it was equally important to remain close and understanding to her children and grandchildren who were no longer religious. Although I am sure she never thought of it this way, she was by nature an inclusive person, never dogmatic, always eager to mediate. Some people would say she was too eager to compromise, but from her whole life it is this inclusiveness that speaks to me the most. Both my traditionally religious and secular ancestors are equally close to me. I embrace them all and don't want to choose between them. This is my tradition.

APPENDIX A

Family Tree of People Mentioned in This Book

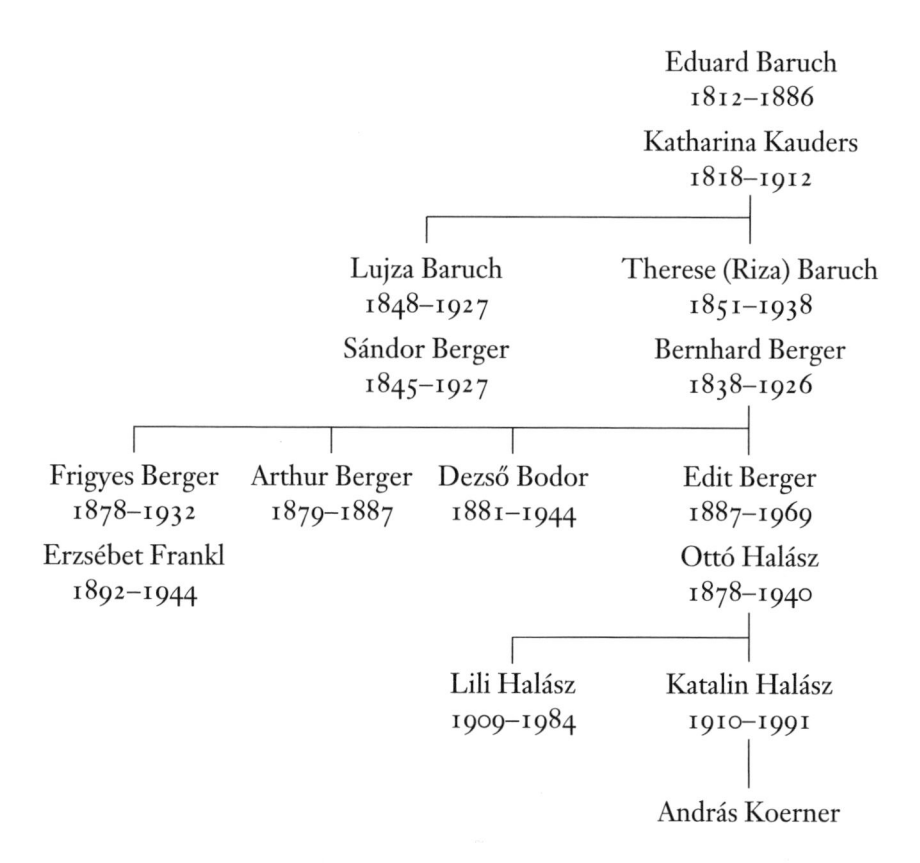

Eduard Baruch
1812–1886

Katharina Kauders
1818–1912

Lujza Baruch
1848–1927

Sándor Berger
1845–1927

Therese (Riza) Baruch
1851–1938

Bernhard Berger
1838–1926

Frigyes Berger
1878–1932

Erzsébet Frankl
1892–1944

Arthur Berger
1879–1887

Dezső Bodor
1881–1944

Edit Berger
1887–1969

Ottó Halász
1878–1940

Lili Halász
1909–1984

Katalin Halász
1910–1991

András Koerner

Note:

Although this book is about members of my family, it is not intended to be a family history, but rather a depiction of daily life and cooking in the late nineteenth and early twentieth century. I tried to keep the number of family members mentioned in the book to the minimum and excluded all unmentioned members, siblings, and spouses from this chart.

APPENDIX B

Recipes in Riza Néni's Collection

Instead of simply translating Riza néni's not always very informative titles, I tried to describe the recipes as well as a brief name allows it, but left her antiquated, idiosyncratic German titles, including her frequently strange and inconsistent spelling, unaltered. The titles in *parentheses* are the original German or Hungarian titles.

Updated versions of the *underlined* recipes are included in the text of this book. Riza néni gave the recipes marked with an *asterisk* to her daughter, sister, or other family members; and these recipes were handed down to me with their collections. I reconstructed three recipes based on my mother's recollections.

Soups and Soup Garnishes

Beef-vegetable soup*
Ginger-flavored soup biscuits (Semmelfanzeln für Suppe)
Green pea soup with egg dumplings (Grüne Erbsen Suppe)
Liver dumplings for soup (Leberknedel für Suppe)
Matzo balls (Osterknedel)

Appetizers

Anchovy eggs (Sardellen Eier)
Chopped calves' liver (Leberpastete)
Chopped smoked beef in scrambled eggs (Schinken-fleckeln)
Diced pickle and carrot sausage (Fleischwurst zu Assiet)
Pickled herring (Angemachte Häringe)

Main Courses

Almond-studded meatballs in sweet-and-sour sauce (Fleischherzl oder Zunge)
Boiled beef*
Braised beef with vegetable sauce (Gedünstetes Fleisch)

Braised chicken with game sauce (Hühner wild bereitet)
Braised veal cutlets in onion-lemon sauce (Kalbschnitzel braun gedünstet)
Braised veal tongue "Bohemian" style (Böhmische Zunge)
Chicken or squab stuffed under the skin (Gefüllte Hühner oder Tauben)
Cholent (Bohnen Scholet)
Fish with walnut-vegetable sauce (Diós hal)*
Noodles with toasted farina (Grízes metélt)*
Pike in sour aspic (Gesulzte Fische)
Poached carp in vinegary broth with horseradish (Heiszgesottener Karpfen)

Sauces

Gooseberry sauce for boiled beef (Agras Sauce)
Sauce made of hard-cooked eggs (Eiersoss für 8 Personen)

Side Dishes

Apple-matzo kugel (Osterkugel)
Bread dumplings (Semmelknödel)
Bread kugel with raisins and diced apples (Semmelkugel)
Cabbage dumplings (Káposztás gombóc)*
Cholent dumpling (Ganef)*
Farina-potato dumplings (Gries Knödel)
Green beans (Grüne Fisolen)
Green pea purée (Erbsen Pirée)
Green peas (Grüne Erbsen)
Green peas with rice (Erbsen mit Reis)
Kohlrabi (Kohlrüben Gemüse)
Matzo kugel (Laska kugli)*
Potato dumplings (Erdäpfel Knödel)
Stuffed goose neck (Halsli)*

Pickled Fruits and Vegetables

Fermented dill pickles (Wasser-Gurken)
Pickled green walnuts (Grüne Nüsse)
Sour cherries (or prune plums) preserved in spiced vinegar (Weichsel in Essig)

Breads, Biscuits, and Biscotti

Almond-lemon biscotti (Spanische Wind)
Anise biscotti (Reichenauer Zwieback)
Biscotti in memory of the late Crown Prince Rudolf (Weiland Kronprinz Rudolf Theebäckerei)
Butter challah (Barches)*
Farmer cheese biscuits (Pogatscheln aus süssem Topfen für 6 Personen)
Flatbread for snack (Lángos)*
Tea biscuits (plain flat cookies) made with goose fat or butter (Caces)
Tea biscuits a different way (Irma Caces)

Desserts Served Warm

Almond-meringue noodles (Nudel mit Souffle)
Almond soufflé (Mandelkoch)
Baked apricot foam (Schaumkoch)
Candied apple fritters (Kandierte Äpfel)
Crêpes (Palatschinten)
Farina dessert dumplings (Griesknödel)
Fried potato-yeast dough crescents (Erdäpfel Kipfel)
Jam-filled potato-matzo dumplings (Húsvéti krumplis gombócz)*
Steamed lemon or orange pudding (Citronen Auflauf)
Matzo fritters (Überzogene Mazes)
Napkin dessert dumpling with vanilla sauce (Servietten Knedel)
Pastry fritters (Fritteln)
Plum-filled bread dumplings (Semmelknödeln mit Zwetschken gefüllt)
Potato dessert dumplings (Erdäpfel Knödel)
Potato noodles with poppy seed*
White bread soufflé (Semmelkoch)
Yeast crêpes (Gerbenpalatschinken)

Home-style Desserts

Almond-chocolate "saddle of venison" cake (Rehschlegel)
Almond slices (Hamburger Schnitt)
Apple-filled noodle dough "wheels" (Apfelräder)

Apple kugel (Apfelkugel)
Bread pudding in noodle dough (Semmel Scheiterhaufen)
Cheese turnovers made with noodle dough (Topfendelkel geknetet)
Chocolate gugelhupf (Chokolade Kugelhopf)
Chocolate cream (Chokolade Crème ohne Gelatine)
Corn cake (Prósza)*
Cream puffs (Magnaten Krapfen)
*Fládni**
Fládni a different way (Fledel-Fächer)
Fruit cake (Catalaner Brot)
Hazelnut slices (Haselnuss Schnitt)
Jam or almond turnovers (Gleichgewicht und Schnellgebäck)
Jelly roll (Rolade)
*Kindli**
Linzer slices (Linzer)
Non-dairy coffee cream (Caffée Crème ohne Obers)
Nut hoop (Nussenbeigel)
Poppy seed squares (Mohnbitter)
Puff pastry filled with cheese or almonds (Butterteig)
Puff pastry layers made with beef marrow and filled with preserves, nuts, or summer squash (Marchdorten)
Rice and apple pudding with wine sauce (Eine kalte Schüssel von Reis)
Rich gugelhupf (Englischer Kugelhopf)
Sour cherry cake (Weichselkuchen)
Spice strudel (Gewürtz Strudel)
Walnut cake (Nusskuchen)
Walnut-hazelnut slices (Nuss Schnitten)
Walnut squares (Diós lepény)
Wine cake (Weinkuchen)

Tortes

Apple torte (Apfeltorte)
Apricot torte (Marillen Torte)
Cheese-filled linzer torte (Topfen Torte)
Chestnut torte (Kastanien Torte)
Chocolate-almond torte (Chokoladdorte)
Dobos torte (Dobos torta)

Layers of wafer filled with chocolate-butter cream (Pischinger Torte)
Lemon-almond torte (Citrom torta)*
Linzer torte (Linzertorte)
Linzer torte with meringue and slivered almond topping (Linzer)
Macaroon torte (Makronen Torte)
Meringue torte with almond cookie dough base (Eistorte)
Poppy seed flourless torte (Mohntorte)
Potato flour torte (Erdäpfelmehl Torte)
Potato torte (Erdäpfel Torte)
Sacher torte (Sacher Torte)
Short dough torte with poppy seed filling (Mürbe Torte)
Spice cake or torte (Gewürzkuchen oder Torte)
Sponge torte (Piskoten Dorte)
Walnut-chocolate torte (Nussdorte)

Cookies, Small Pastries, and Small Cakes

Almond-chocolate kisses (Chocolád Pusserln)
Almond-chocolate pretzels (Mandelbretzel)
Almond macaroons (Weisse Mageron)
Almond sticks, bows, and pretzels (Pariser Stangel, Mandel Bogen, und Mandel Bretzel)
Almond-topped noodle dough strips (Kleine Linzer)
Chocolate-almond cookies (Braune Mageron)
Coconut kisses (Kokus Pusserl)
Cookies as in Brno (Brünner Küchel)
Cookies made with beef marrow (Kleine Marchbäckerei)
Evening flowers (Pletzl)
Hazelnut macaroons (Haselnuss Konfekt)
Honey cookies (Honigpusserl)
Jam-filled walnut or hazelnut slices (Nuss oder Haselnuss Confeckt)
Meringue-Almond Clusters (Schaummandelhäufchen)
Meringue-coated almond sandwich cookies (Tortlette)
Sponge dough discs (Pletzel)
Sugar-almond pretzels (Zuckerbretzeln)
Sugar pretzels (Zuckerbretzeln)
Walnut clusters (Nusspusserln)
Walnut meringue kisses (Nussenpusserl)

Preserved Fruits and Vegetables

Apricot jelly (Marillensulz)
Apricot jam (Marillen Marmelade)
Apricots in sugar syrup (Marillen in Zucker)
Cornel cherries in sugar syrup (Derndl in Zucker)
Cornel cherry jelly (Derndl Sulz)
Preserved summer squash (Eingesottene Kürbis)
Quince paste (Quittenkäse)
Quince preserves (Quitten zum Verehren)
Quince preserves another way (Quitten auf eine andere Art zum Verehren)

Glossary

afikoman—A piece of the matzo put aside at the beginning of the Seder, and eaten at the end of the meal.

Ashkenazi (pl.: Ashkenazim)—German or Western, Central, or Eastern European Jew(s), as contrasted with Sephardi Jews.

Austro-Hungarian—Pertaining to the Dual Monarchy of Austria and Hungary (1867–1918), loosely also to things common to the cultural heritage of Austria and Hungary.

bácsi—Hungarian for "older man."

barches (also *berches*; in Hungary: *barhesz*)—Braided loaves of bread made for the Sabbath and other holidays; a term used in Austria, Germany, Hungary, and some other countries for challah.

besamim—Hebrew for "spices." Spices used in the Jerusalem Temple for incense offering, also the spices sniffed during the *havdalah* ceremony on Saturday night.

Biedermeier—A style of paintings and applied arts popular in Austria, Germany, and Hungary between 1820 and 1850.

broche (pl.: *broches*)—Yiddish for "blessing."

cantor—*Hazzan* in Hebrew. A person who leads the congregation in prayers and religious songs.

challah—Hebrew for "dough." In ancient times it meant the tithe taken from dough before baking and given to a priest; in modern times it means a small portion of the dough separated off and burnt in the oven. In modern times it also came to mean a loaf of yeast-leavened white bread, usually made with eggs and braided, traditionally eaten by Jews on the Sabbath and other festivals.

chametz—Hebrew for "leaven." Leavened bread and food, as well as dishes and cooking utensils touched by them. It is forbidden to use chametz during the festival of Pesach (Passover).

Chanukah—Hebrew for "dedication." An eight-day festival beginning on the twenty-fifth of the Jewish month of Kislev, usually in mid-December. It celebrates the victory of the Maccabees in 165 B.C.E.

over the Sleucid rulers of Palestine and the rededication of the Temple.

cholent (also *shalet, schalet*; in Hungary: *sólet*)—Stew, usually made with beans, meat, and other ingredients, prepared by the Ashkenazim on Friday for the Sabbath, allowed to slowly cook overnight, and eaten at the midday meal on Saturday.

derma—From the Yiddish *derme* meaning "intestines," the plural of *darm*. Beef casing stuffed with a seasoned mixture of matzo meal or flour, onion, and suet, prepared by boiling, then roasting. It is similar to *kishke*.

dreidl—From the Yiddish *dreyen*, to turn. Four-sided top, spun by the children in a game of chance during the festival of Chanukah.

Exodus—The miraculous departure of the Israelites, led by Moses, from slavery in Egypt.

fiáker—Hungarian from the German *Fiaker*. Viennese-style two-horse carriage for hire.

fladen (also *fluden*; in Hungary: *flódni* or *fládni*)—From medieval Latin *flado*, flat cake. Filled pastry squares in which one or more kinds of filling are sandwiched between sheets of dough.

fleischig (also *flayshig*)—Yiddish for "meaty, fleshy." Meats, poultry, or foods prepared with animal fats.

Franz Joseph I—(1830–1916), Emperor of Austria (1848–1916) and King of Hungary (1867–1916).

Galicia—Historical region of southeast Poland and the western part of the Ukraine, from 1846 a province of the Austrian Empire and from 1867 of the Austro-Hungarian Empire.

ganef (also *gonif, gonef, gonov*)—Yiddish for "thief," from Hebrew *ganav*. An Ashkenazi dumpling baked with the cholent in the same pot.

gefilte fish—Yiddish for "stuffed fish." Ashkenazi Jewish delicacy.

Genesis (or the book of Genesis)—The first part of the Pentateuch, the beginning of the Hebrew Bible, which recounts the creation of the world, the early history of humanity, and the history of the patriarchs to the death of Joseph.

griebenes (also *gribenes*)—Yiddish for "cracklings." An Ashkenazi appetizer made by rendering fat out of small pieces of poultry skin.

gugelhupf (also *gugelhopf, kugelhupf,* and *kugelhopf*)—Light yeast cake (a few versions are prepared without yeast) made in a special fluted tube form, supposedly patterned after a Turkish turban. It is popular

GLOSSARY

in Hungary (where it is called *kuglóf*), Austria, Germany, and in the Alsatian region of France.

haggadah (pl.: haggadoth)—Hebrew for "narration." The text read at the Pesach Seder.

halsli (also *helzel*)—From Yiddish. Filled skin of goose neck, frequently baked by Ashkenazi Jews in the same pot with the cholent.

hamantaschen—From Yiddish-German "pockets of Haman." Ashkenazi triangular filled cookies, made for the holiday of Purim. They are made of yeast or pastry dough and filled with poppy seeds or prune butter.

haroset—A paste made of wine, nuts, and other ingredients; it is one of the symbolic foods used at the Seder.

hatan (pl.: *hatanim*)—Hebrew for "bridegroom." *Hatan torah* (bridegroom of the law) and *hatan bereshit* (bridegroom of Genesis) are the titles of the two honorary functionaries at the synagogue service on Simchat Torah.

havdalah—Hebrew for "differentiation" or "separation." Prayer recited at the conclusion of Sabbaths and festivals to indicate the distinction between the sacred day and weekday.

húsvét—Hungarian for Easter.

inarsz (also *inars, inneres*)—Yiddish. Chilled and thinly sliced garlic-flavored and paprika-coated goose fat eaten by Ashkenazi Jews as a cold cut.

kashrut—From Hebrew *kosher*, meaning "fit" or "proper." Jewish dietary laws.

kiddush—Hebrew for "sanctification." A prayer recited over a cup of wine, immediately before a meal to proclaim the holiness of Sabbath or a festival.

kishke (also *kishka*)—From Yiddish-Russian "intestines," "entrails." A sausage-like Ashkenazi Jewish delicacy made by stuffing a mixture of onion, chicken fat, flour, and sometimes meat into beef intestine and baking it.

knaydl (also *knaidl*; pl.: *knaydlach* or *knaidlach*)—Yiddish for "dumpling."

kohen (pl.: *kohanim*)—Male descendants of Aaron from the tribe of Levi who were endowed with responsibilities and privileges of the priestly office.

kol nidre (also *kol nidrei*)—Aramaic for "all vows." A declaration recited at the beginning of the evening service that starts the Day of Atonement

(Yom Kippur) set to a melody, which is perhaps the best-known example of Jewish liturgical music.

korzó—Hungarian for "promenade," from the Italian "*corso*."

kosher (adjective)—Hebrew for "fit." Food that is permitted to be eaten according to the Jewish dietary laws.

kosher (verb)—To bring something in compliance with the dietary laws, for example the koshering (salting) of meat, the broiling of liver, or the cleansing of pots with boiling water.

kreplach (also *kreplech*; singular: *krepl*)—Triangular (sometimes also square) boiled dumplings made by the Ashkenazim of noodle dough and filled with chopped meat or cheese. Traditional for Yom Kippur, Hoshanah Rabbah (the seventh day of Sukkot), and Purim.

kreuzer—German. From the also German *Kreuz* (cross), because there was a double cross on one side of the coin. Small coins of low value used in the Austro-Hungarian Monarchy until 1892.

kugel—From the German-Yiddish word for "ball." Ashkenazi baked pudding traditionally served at the midday meal on Saturday.

kugelhupf or *kugelhopf*—See gugelhupf.

lekvár—Hungarian. A very thick fruit spread, also called fruit butter, usually made of Italian plums, prunes, or apricots cooked with or sometimes without sugar.

leviathan—Biblical gigantic sea monster.

lokshen kugel (also *lukshen kugel*)—Ashkenazi noodle pudding served at the midday meal on Saturday; it is usually sweet but there are also a few savory versions of it.

mah nishtanah—Hebrew for "Why is this different?" the opening words of the Four Questions recited during the Seder.

manna—The food miraculously provided, according to the Hebrew Bible, for the Israelites in the wilderness during their flight from Egypt.

matzo (also matzah; pl.: matzoth or matzot)—Hebrew for "unleavened bread." Because it doesn't require time-consuming fermentation of the dough it became the bread of the Exodus, the miraculous departure from Egypt. The "bread of affliction," that is, the bread of the poor and the slaves. It is the only kind of bread permitted during Pesach (Passover).

menorah—Hebrew for "candelabrum." A seven-branched candelabrum fuelled by olive oil burned at all times in the Jerusalem Temple; an eight-branched menorah is lit during the festival of Chanukah to celebrate the rededication of the Temple candelabrum in the second century B.C.E.

meshuggeh (also *meshugge*)—Yiddish from Hebrew for "crazy."

Messiah—From Hebrew *mashiach*, meaning "anointed." The anointed king of the House of David who will be sent by God to inaugurate the final redemption in the end of days.

messianic—Pertaining to the Messiah.

milchig (also *milchedig* or *milchik*)—Milk or milk products and the dishes made of them; also dishes and utensils that came in contact with dairy foods.

Millennium—The 1896 celebration of the thousandth anniversary of the arrival of the Magyar tribes from the east to the present-day Hungary.

miltz—Yiddish for milt, the sperm and seminal fluid of the male fish.

mishlo'ah manot—Hebrew for "sending of portions." Gifts sent by a messenger on Purim, one of the five commandments (*mitzvot*) associated with the celebration of Purim.

Mishnah—The earliest codification of the Jewish oral law, completed in the third century.

mitzvah (pl.: *mitzvot*)—Hebrew for "commandment." Originally it meant a divine command, but eventually it came to mean any good deed.

Monarchy—Abbreviated, informal term for the Austro-Hungarian Monarchy (1867–1918).

néni—Hungarian for "older woman."

neológ **Judaism**—Hungarian Jewish movement begun in the nineteenth century, which sought to reconcile religious traditions with reforms, such as establishing modern institutions for training rabbis, using Hungarian in Jewish education, allowing weddings and organ music in the synagogues, and the like.

Orthodox Judaism—Jewish traditionalists who reject all or most of the religious reforms of the eighteenth and nineteenth century.

Oster—German for "Easter."

pareve (also *parev*, *parve*, or *parveh*)—Yiddish for "neutral." Food that is neither meat nor dairy according to the Jewish dietary laws, for example, fish, eggs, or vegetables.

Passover—See Pesach.

pénecl (also *pénec*)—From Yiddish "slice." The name of deep-fried bread in Hungarian Jewish usage.

Pesach—Hebrew for "Passover." An eight-day (seven in Israel) festival beginning on the fifteenth of the Jewish month of Nisan, in March or April. It commemorates the Exodus from Egypt.

prophet—From the Greek *prophetes*, describing a person who is a messenger of Divine message. The Hebrew bible describes several prophets, but in this book this word refers to only one of them, Elijah.

Purim—Festival commemorating the delivery of Jews in Persia; celebrated on the fourteenth (in Jerusalem on the fifteenth) of the Jewish month of Adar, in February or March.

Rosh Hashanah—Jewish New Year festival observed for two days starting on the first of the Jewish month of Tishrei, in September or October.

Sabbath (Shabbat)—From the Hebrew *shabbat*; the Jewish Sabbath lasts from Friday evening to Saturday night.

schmaltz—Yiddish for "fat." Rendered poultry fat.

Seder—Hebrew for "order." The traditional home ceremony of Pesach (Passover).

Sephardi (pl.: Sephardim)—Spanish and Portuguese Jews and their descendants. Loosely used term for Jews from Oriental countries; as contrasted with the Ashkenazim.

shammas (also *shammes*)—Hebrew for "servant." Synagogue beadle, his duties include keeping the synagogue clean, putting the prayer books in order, preparing the Torah scrolls, and other support to the rabbi and the cantor.

Shavuot—Hebrew for "Pentecost," literally "weeks." One of the three pilgrim or harvest festivals celebrated one day in Israel and two days elsewhere starting on the sixth of the Jewish month of Sivan, in May or June.

sheitel—Yiddish for "wig." Used by married woman who are forbidden to expose their hair to anyone but their husbands.

shochet—Yiddish from the Hebrew *shechitah* meaning "slaughter." A trained slaughterer who must be an adult male Jew accredited by rabbinic authority to perform the ritual killing of animals and birds as prescribed by the Jewish dietary laws.

Simchat Torah—Hebrew for "rejoicing of the Torah." It describes the ceremonies associated with the conclusion of the annual Torah reading, which take place on the ninth (in Israel on the eighth) day of Sukkot.

status quo ante—Latin for "pre-existing condition." It is the name of a movement in Hungarian Judism that rejected the structural reforms of the 1868/69 Hungarian Jewish Congress, did not wish to join the Orthodox organizations founded in 1871, but wanted to preserve the conditions that existed prior to the Congress.

sukkah—Hebrew for "tabernacle." A makeshift hut where the Jews eat and some of them live during the festival of Sukkot. It is meant to remind them of the huts in which their ancestors dwelt when they wandered in the wilderness during the Exodus.

Sukkot (also Sukkoth)—Hebrew for "tabernacles." One of the three harvest festivals, it is a seven-day festival beginning on the fifteenth of the Jewish month of Tishri, in late September or early October.

Swabian—English translation of the Hungarian *sváb* and ultimately of the German *Schwabe*. It is the name of all German minorities in Hungary, regardless whether their ancestors came from Swabia, a region in southwest Germany.

szaletli—Old-fashioned Hungarian word for a garden pavilion or gazebo, from the German *Salettel*, which in turn comes from Italian.

synagogue—From Greek for "a place of gathering." A building or place of meeting for Jewish worship and religious instruction.

szalon—Hungarian for "drawing room" or "sitting room." A kind of formal living room.

tallith—A four-cornered prayer shawl, frequently with bands of black or blue, and with knotted fringes (*tzitziyot*) hanging from each corner, worn by Orthodox and Conservative Jewish men, especially at prayer.

Talmud—Hebrew for "study." Compendium of commentaries on the Mishnah, completed in the sixth century C.E.

tefillin—Hebrew for "prayer objects" or Aramaic for "ornaments." The two leather boxes containing four biblical passages and attached by leather straps to the left arm and upper forehead. Tefillin are worn by adult males during the weekday morning service or morning prayer at home.

Temple—The central building of Jewish sacrificial cult, situated in ancient Jerusalem and looked after by the priests and Levites. The first Temple was built by Solomon and destroyed by Babylonians. Ezra rebuilt it but the Romans destroyed this second Temple in 70 C.E.

temple—An informal synonym for synagogue.

Torah—Hebrew for "teaching." The term may refer to a scroll or scrolls of parchment containing the Jewish teaching of the Pentateuch (the five books of Moses) and used in the synagogue during services, or to the Hebrew bible, or in its widest sense to the whole of the Jewish tradition.

treyf (also *trayf* or *tref*)—From Yiddish *treyf* and Hebrew *terefah* meaning "torn." An animal not slaughtered according to the ritual laws and any food that is not kosher.

ushpizin—Aramaic for "guests." Seven biblical characters who come as guests to the sukkah on the festival of Sukkot. The word also came to mean the Aramaic invitation of these guests to the sukkah.

varenikes (pl.)—Ashkenazi Jewish boiled noodle dough pockets filled with fruit or meat. They are similar to *kreplach*, but while kreplach are usually triangular and not made with fruit filling, varenikes are usually round and can be filled with fruit.

yeshiva (also yeshivah; pl.: yeshivas or yeshivot)—Hebrew for "sitting." A Jewish institute of learning where students study the Talmud. An elementary or secondary school with a curriculum that includes Jewish religion and culture as well as general education.

Yiddish—A Judeo-German language rooted in medieval German with many words borrowed from Hebrew, Aramaic, and Slavic that is written in Hebrew characters and spoken chiefly as a vernacular in Eastern European Jewish communities and emigrants from these countries.

Yom Kippur—Hebrew for the "day of atonement." The holiest and most solemn Jewish holiday, on which fasting and prayer for the atonement of sins are proscribed. It is celebrated on the tenth day of Tishri, in September or October.

Bibliography

Adler, Aladárné (Giti néni): *A zsidó háziasszony könyve* (The Jewish housewife's book), Kecskemét, Hungary, 1935.
Ausubel, Nathan: *A Treasury of Jewish Humor*, Galahad Books, 1993, 1951.
Beard, James: *Beard on Bread*, Knopf, 1987.
———: *Theory and Practice of Good Cooking*, Knopf, 1979.
Bittman, Mark: *Fish*, Macmillan, 1994.
Champe, Gertrud (ed.): *To Set Before the King; Katharina Schratt's Favorite Recipes*, University of Iowa Press, 1996.
Child, Julia and Dorie Greenspan: *Baking with Julia*, Knopf, 1996.
Christensen, Lillian Langseth: *Gourmet's Old Vienna Cookbook*, Gourmet Books, 1959.
Cohn, Sarah: *Israelitisches Kochbuch* (Jewish cookbook), Pressburg (Bratislava) and Frankfurt am Main, 1880 and 1900.
Cooper, John: *Eat and Be Satisfied; A Social History of Jewish Food*, Jason Aronson, 1993.
Czifray, István: *Magyar nemzeti szakácskönyv* (Hungarian national cookbook), Sixth enlarged edition, Pest, 1840 (first edition: 1816).
De Pomiane, Edouard: *The Jews of Poland; Recollections and Recipes*, Pholiota Press, 1985 (Original French edition: 1929).
Derecskey, Susan: *The Hungarian Cookbook*, Harper & Row, 1972.
Deutsch, Róbert and others: *Halljad Izrael* (Hear, O Israel), Budapest, 1988.
Die wirtschaftliche israelitische Köchin (The economical Jewish cook), Verlag Jakob Schön, Fünfkirchen (Pécs), Hungary, 1873.
Dobos, József C.: *Magyar–francia szakácskönyv* (Hungarian–French cookbook), Budapest, 1881.
Engle, Fannie and Gertrude Blair: *The Jewish Festival Cookbook*, Dover, 1988.
Escoffier, Auguste: *The Escoffier Cookbook*, Crown Publishers, Inc., 1989.
Feiertags Küchenkalender für die jüdische Hausfrau (Holiday kitchen calendar for Jewish housewives), Heim des jüdischen Frauenbundes, Neu-Isenburg, Germany, ca. 1910.
Féner, Tamás and Sándor Scheiber: *And You Shall Tell Your Son*, Budapest, 1984.
Ferenczi, Imre: *Purimi népszokások* (Purim folk customs), in: *A hagyományok kötelékében* (In the bonds of tradition), Budapest, 1990.

Fischer, Leah Loeb: *Mama Leah's Jewish Kitchen*, Macmillan, 1994.
Fischman, Priscilla: *Minor and Modern Festivals*, Keter Books, Jerusalem, 1973.
Flesch, Carl: *The Memoirs of Carl Flesch*, Da Capo Press, 1979.
Friedland, Susan R.: *Shabbat Shalom*, Little, Brown & Co., 1999.
Frojimovics, Kinga and others: *Jewish Budapest*, C.E.U. Press, Budapest, 1999.
Gálosi, Soma: *Mosoni emlékek* (Recollections of Moson), Magyaróvár, Hungary, 1923.
Ganzfried, Shlomo: *Kitzur Shulchon Oruch* (Translated and annotated by Rabbi Eliyahu Touger), Moznaim Publishing, 1991.
Gazda, Anikó and others: *Magyarországi zsinagógák* (Hungarian synagogues), Budapest, 1989.
Glazer, Nahum N.: *The Passover Haggadah*, Schocken Books, 1979.
Gööck, Roland: *Das Neue Grosse Kochbuch* (The new big cookbook), Mosaik Verlag, 1975.
Greene, Gloria Kaufer: *The New Jewish Holiday Cookbook*, Random House, 1999.
Grunauer, Peter and Andreas Kisler: *Viennese Cuisine*, Doubleday, 1987.
Gumprich, Joseph, Witwe: *Vollständiges Prakitsches Kochbuch für die jüdische Küche* (Complete practical cookbook for the Jewish kitchen), Verlag von Kaufmann & Co., Trier, Germany, 1888.
Gundel, Károly: *Gundel's Hungarian Cookbook*, Corvina, Budapest, 1986.
Hahn, István: *Zsidó ünnepek és népszokások* (Jewish holidays and folk customs), Budapest, 1940.
Hazelton, Nika Standen: *The Cooking of Germany*, Time-Life, 1969.
Hegyesi, József: *Házi cukrászat kézikönyve* (The handbook of home patisserie), Budapest, 1893.
Heine, Heinrich: *Werke* (Works), Aufbau Verlag, 1976.
Herbst, Sharon Tyler: *Food Lover's Companion*, Barron's, 1995.
Herbst-Krausz, Zorica: *Old Jewish Dishes*, Corvina, Budapest, 1988.
Hercz, Rafael Rezsőné: *Szakácskönyv vallásos izraeliták háztartása számára* (Cookbook for the household of religious Jews), Budapest, 1899.
Hess: *Wiener Küche* (Viennese cooking), Franz Deuticke, Wien, 1963.
Hyman, Paula E.: *Gender and Assimilation in Modern Jewish History*, University of Washington Press, 1995.
Jólesz, Károly: *Zsidó hitéleti kislexikon* (Lexicon of Jewish religious life), Budapest, 1987.
Kauders, Witwe Marie: *Vollständiges israelitisches Kochbuch* (Complete Jewish cookbook), Verlag von Jakob B. Brandeis, Prague, 1885.
Kemény, József: *Vázlatok a győri zsidóság történetéből* (Sketches from the history of the Győr Jewish community), Győr, Hungary, 1930.
Klein, Mordell: *Passover*, Keter Books, Jerusalem, 1973.

Kohlbach, Bertalan: *Sütemények a zsidó szertartásban* (Pastries in Jewish religious ceremonies), in: *IMIT Évkönyve* (The almanac of IMIT), 1914.
Kovi, Paul: *Transylvanian Cuisine*, Crown, 1985.
Kugler, Géza: *A legújabb és legteljesebb budapesti szakácskönyv* (The latest and most complete cookbook of Budapest), Budapest, 1897.
———: *Házi cukrászat* (Home patisserie), Budapest, 1904.
Kushner, Harold S.: *To Life!*, Warner Books, Inc., 1994.
Lang, George: *The Cuisine of Hungary*, Atheneum, 1971.
Lang, Jenifer Harvey (ed.): *Larousse Gastronomique*, Crown, 1988.
Lejtényi-Waldhauser: *Nagyanyáink Sütötték* (Baked by our grandmothers), Népszava, Budapest, 1985.
Leonard, Leah H.: *Jewish Cooking*, Crown, 1949.
Lukacs, John: *Budapest 1900*, Weidenfeld & Nicolson, 1988.
Magyar, Elek: *The Gourmet's Cookbook*, Corvina, Budapest, 1989.
Malgieri, Nick: *How to Bake*, HarperCollins, 1995
Marks, Gil: *The World of Jewish Cooking*, Simon & Schuster, 1996.
McCagg, Jr., William O.: *A History of Habsburg Jews*, Indiana University Press, 1989.
Morton, Marcia Colman: *The Art of Viennese Cooking*, Doubleday, 1963.
———: *The Art of Viennese Pastry*, Doubleday, 1969.
Nathan, Joan: *Jewish Cooking in America*, Random House, 1998.
———: *The Jewish Holiday Baker*, Schocken Books, 1997.
Patai, Raphael: *The Jews of Hungary*, Wayne State University Press, 1996.
Pépin, Jacques: *Jacques Pépin's Table*, KQED Books, 1995.
Peterson, James: *Fish & Shellfish*, William Morrow and Co., 1996.
Philpot, Rose: *Viennese Cookery*, Hodder and Stoughton, London, 1965.
Rékai, Miklós: *A munkácsi zsidók "terített asztala"* (The "prepared table" of the Munkács Jews), Osiris, Budapest, 1997.
———: *Keserű gyökér* (Bitter herbs; literally: Bitter roots), Budapest, 1995.
Ranki, Vera: *The Politics of Inclusion and Exclusion*, Holmes & Meier, 1999
Reich, Lilly Joss: *The Viennese Pastry Cookbook*, Macmillan, 1970.
Rhode, Irma: *The Viennese Cookery Book*, John Lehmann, London, 1952.
Roden, Claudia: *The Book of Jewish Food*, Knopf, 1996.
Root, Waverly: *Food*, Simon & Schuster, 1980.
Rosenfeld, Mártonné: *A zsidó nő szakácskönyve* (The Jewish woman's cookbook), Subotica, 1927.
Rosten, Leo: *The Joys of Yiddish*, McGraw-Hill, 1968.
Saint Hilaire, Jozéfa: *Képes pesti szakácskönyv* (Illustrated cookbook of Pest), Budapest, 1870.
Scharfenberg, Horst: *The Cuisines of Germany*, Poseidon Press, 1989.

Schauss, Hayyim: *The Jewish Festivals*, Schocken Books, 1996.
Scheibenpflug, Lotte: *Specialties of Austrian Cooking*, Pinguin Verlag, 1969.
Scheiber, Sándor: *Folklór és tárgytörténet* (Folklore and history of objects), Budapest, 1977–1984.
Sheraton, Mimi: *From my Mother's Kitchen*, HarperCollins, 1979, 1991.
———: *The German Cookbook*, Random House, 1965.
Sokolov, Raymond and Susan R. Friedland: *The Jewish American Kitchen*, Wings Books, 1993.
Sternberg, Robert: *Yiddish Cuisine*, Jason Aronson, 1993.
Szántó, András: *Eleink Ételei* (Foods of our ancestors), Mezőgazdasági Kiadó, Budapest, 1986.
Száraz, György: *Egy Előitélet Nyomában* (Tracing a prejudice), Magvető, Budapest, 1976.
Szathmáry, Louis: *The Chef's Secret Cook Book*, Quadrangle Books, 1971.
Toussaint-Samat, Maguelonne: *A History of Food*, Blackwell, 1992.
Újvári, Péter: *Magyar Zsidó Lexikon* (Hungarian Jewish Lexicon), Budapest, 1929.
Ullmann, Jenny: *A zsidó konyha művészete* (The art of the Jewish kitchen), Arad, 1933.
Unterman, Alan: *Dictionary of Jewish Lore and Legend*, Thames and Hudson, 1991.
Venesz, József: *Hungarian Cuisine*, Corvina, Budapest, 1963.
Venetianer, Lajos: *A Magyar Zsidóság Története* (The history of the Jews in Hungary), Budapest, 1922.
Vízváry, Mariska: *Treasure-trove of Hungarian Cookery*, Corvina, Budapest, 1981.
Wechsberg, Joseph: *The Cooking of Vienna's Empire*, Time-Life, 1968.
Werblowsky, R. J. Zwi and G. Wigoder (eds.): *The Encyclopedia of the Jewish Religion*, Holt, Rinehart and Winston, 1966.
William, Susan: *Savory Suppers; Dining in Victorian America*, Pantheon Books, 1985.
Wolf, Rebekka: *Kochbuch für israelitsche Frauen* (Cookbook for Jewish women), Adolf Kohn Verlag, Berlin, 1875.
Wolff, Flora: *Koch und Wirtschaftsbuch für jüdische Hausfrauen* (Cookbook and home economy book for Jewish housewives), Verlag von Siegfried Kronbach, Berlin, 1888.
Yerushalmi, Yosef Hayim: *Haggadah and History*, The Jewish Publication Society of America, Philadelphia, 1975.
Zilahy, Ágnes: *Valódi Magyar Szakács Könyv* (Authentic Hungarian cookbook), Budapest, 1892.

Acknowledgments

The recollections of Árpád Buzási, Clara Eros, Mrs. László Geréb, and Miklós Löwin complemented my mother's reminiscences of my great-grandmother's household and the Jewish community of Moson. In addition to these recollections, my great-grandmother's letters, recipes, and personal belongings were the main sources of this book. They survived due to the devotion of my grandmother, who saved them after her mother's death, protected them throughout the horrors of the war and brought them with her when she immigrated to the United States in 1946. She brought few things of value; the truth was she hardly had any. But all those old photos, manuscripts, century-old bed linens that wouldn't fit modern beds, her mother's nineteenth-century haggadah and prayer book, and stacks of other family mementos were clearly more precious to her than anything else. She even brought her mother's old hand-knitted, monogrammed socks. She must have instinctively felt that she could draw strength from these tangible connections to her roots, strength she needed to cope with the stress of adjusting to a new country and learning a new language in old age. Her love of family and traditions has been constant inspiration in my work.

My son-in-law, Leonard Imas, was the person who first suggested that I should write a book using old family recipes. Kati, my elder daughter, gave me the idea to frame the book with journeys to the houses where my great-grandmother had lived. Nancy Wallace most generously helped me with editorial advice and encouragement. She kept telling me, the novice writer, so many times that I could do it, that at the end I almost believed her. Rick Hibberd, one of my oldest friends and a wonderful graphic designer, spent many days helping me to develop ideas for the design of this book. Joan Nathan, George Lang, Sylvia Fuks Fried, and Ezra Mendelsohn took time from their busy schedules to wade through my lengthy manuscript and generously shared their insights with me. Phyllis Deutsch, my editor, enthusiastically supported my project and helped in shaping the book and sharpening its focus.

In Hungary, my sister Zsuzsa Körner Fábri spent endless hours with research, and without her assistance I wouldn't have been able to complete this project. Eszter Kisbán, the best-known expert in ethnological food research in Hungary, gave crucial advice and warm encouragement. Additional advice came from Miklós Rékai, a researcher of Jewish folklore and eating habits.

Unfortunately, it doesn't make for lively reading to describe in detail the help I received from a great number of other people, but at least I would like to list their names and express my gratitude to them. In Hungary, Irén Bak, Dezső Jakabovits, Sándor Kovács, Gábor Körner, Tamás Körner, Miklós Löwin, Magda Szántó, Zsuzsa Tátrai, István Thullner, and Ilona Vágvölgyi selflessly assisted me with research and advice. In the United States, I would like to thank Susan Braunstein, Molly Finn, János Gát, Judith Jones, Réka Koerner, David Krasnow, Paul Makowsky, and Vicki Steinhardt.

A.K.

Subject Index

Antisemitism. *See* Hungary; Moson
Ashkenazi Jews, 56, 216, 240, 247, 285; culture of, 315
Askenazi Jewish cooking. *See* in Index of Recipes and Foods
Assicurazione Generali, 39
Assimilation, Jewish, 5
Auschwitz, 37, 381
Austria, 136, 139, 155, 163, 172, 182, 309, 321, 343, 357, 366; antisemitism in, 19
Austrian cuisine. *See* in the Index of Recipes and Foods
Austro-Hungarian Monarchy, 39, 126, 130, 187, 321

Baruch, Eduard, as president of the Győr Jewish community, 10; charity work of, 21; founding the family store, 7; haberdashery of, 7, 8; household of, 12; preferring to speak German, 8, 9; recalling his life in a speech, 8; religiosity of, 9
Baruch, Katharina (Kati), monogrammed china of, 148, 149; participating in the family business, 8, 17; religiosity of, 8; warning Riza not to visit balls given by Christians, 25; wearing a hairpiece instead of a wig, 193, 194
Baruch (later: Berger), Lujza, 21, 39, 40, 44, 59, 69, 75, 145, 206, 344, 347, 353, 355; as president of the Hebrew Ladies' Society in Moson, 191; death of, 381; erecting a *sukkah*, 297
Baruch (later: Berger), Therese (Riza): accepting the secular lifestyle of her children and grandchildren, 3, 76, 382, 385; carrying money under her skirt, 52; charity work of, 20, 21; conflicts with her sister Lujza, 42, 69, 381; conflicts with parents concerning assimilation, 25; cultural ambitions of, 14; death of, 382; education of, 14, 16; engagement of, 28; Gentile friends of, 23, 24, 25; haggadah of, 4, 339–341; helping in the family business, 17, 50; her drafts of letters, 4, 12, 13, 30; house cleaning on Saturdays, 239; keeping bread in a granary during Pesach for secular relatives, 336; keeping kosher, 76; pursuing letter writing as a creative outlet, 15; matzo bag of, 337; moving to the Berger house, 39; moving to Budapest, 381; moving to Moson, 28; national identity of, 18; not trusting her servant with baking, 77, 149; opinion of intermarriage and conversion, 26, 27; opinion of women pursuing a profession, 17, 18; preference for German language, 18, 25, 51; religiosity of, 24; restricting pork sausages and bacon to a granary, 76; social life of, 21, 22, 148–150, 207; switching to Hungarian as the primary language, 176; wedding of, 28; willingness to eat non-kosher food, 76, 382
Beethoven, Ludwig van, 241
Berger, Arthur, 341
Berger, Bernhard: at the *havdalah* ceremony, 269–270; blessing the bread at lunch 79; death of, 379; engagement and wedding of, 28; entering partnership with his brother, 39; going to the synagogue on Fridays, 214; morning prayer of, 48; on being old, 49; on Saturday mornings, 238; presiding over

Berger, Bernhard *(continued)*
    the Seder, 337–339; religiosity of, 47; Saturday afternoons in the synagogue, 268; searching for leaven, 335
Berger, Frigyes, 78, 79, 206, 279, 335; death in Vienna, 381; grave in the Moson Jewish cemetery, 382–384; his relationship with a Catholic widow, 210, 313, 379; lax observance of religion, 214; fondness for pork sausages and bacon, 60, 380, 384; playing billiards during the Sabbath, 268; working in the family business, 49, 72, 379
Berger house in Moson: attic of, 191, 335; courtyard of, 40, 44; floor plans of, 32, 33; formal dining room in, 336; garden of, 40, 41, 56, 60; granaries in, 40, 59, 190; kitchen in, 72–75; lack of bathrooms in, 43, 44; lack of running water in, 44; laundry room in, 44; pantry closet *(Handspeiz)* in, 71, 335; pantry room in, 71; *szaletli* (gazebo) of, 41, 77, 296; *szalon* in, 149; well of, 42, 43, 382, 383, 384
Berger insurance business in Moson, 39, 47, 49, 72, 379, 381
Berger, Sándor (Alexander), 47, 206; death of, 381; founding the family business in Moson, 39
Bible, 239, 285
Biedermeier style, 72, 148
Bizsu (the Bergers' dog), 195, 206
Blood libel trial of Jews (Tiszaeszlár, 1882), 24
Bodor (previously: Berger), Dezső, 335, 343
Bohemia, 18
Bókay (lawyer in Moson), 191
Börne, Ludwig, 240
Brighton Beach (New York City), 225
Britain, 116
Brno, 330
Budapest: assimilated Jews of, 303; author's grandparents' apartment in, 381; beginnings of industrialization in, 7; ghetto of (1944), 20
Budapest-Vienna highway, 36, 191

Canada, 201
Capitalism, Jews in, 8; rise of, 7
Catalonia, 166
Charity, Jewish, 21, 25, 191, 313
Chernin, Kim, 56
Christian Hungary, symbols of, 20
Citarella (New York City), 105, 225
Communist revolution in 1919 (in Hungary), 24
Conversion: from Christianity to Judaism, 26; from Judaism to Christianity, 27
Cookbooks: American Jewish, 315; Austrian, 87, 139, 163, 255, 261, 285, 309; German, 330; Jewish, 96, 251; 19th-century German Jewish, 321, 325, 343; 19th-century Hungarian, 102, 139, 185; 19th-century Hungarian Jewish, 56, 80, 212, 242, 321, 325, 343; 19th-century Hungarian Yiddish, 321; 16th-century Hungarian, 98; 20th-century Hungarian, 87, 116, 117, 139, 163, 185, 221, 255, 258, 261, 274, 285, 309; 20th-century Hungarian Jewish, 80, 320, 321, 326, 343
Cooper, John, 56, 215, 216, 240, 251, 321, 347
Cotillion(s), 21, 192
Czech Republic, 330

Danube, 148
Danube Street (Duna utca). *See* Moson
Decker, Ilka (Ilka néni), 210, 313, 379
Deutsch (family in Moson), 37
Dezső bácsi. *See* Bodor, Dezső
Domesticity, cult of, 17
Diaspora, 240
Divine guidance (for educational choices of women), 17, 18
Duna utca. *See* Moson

Education, Jewish: of women, 16; of men, 16
Education, public secondary and university: acquisition by women, 16, 17
Education, private secular: of women at home, 12, 16
Egypt, 296, 338
Elijah (Prophet), 337, 343

Emancipation. *See* Hungarian Jews, emancipation of
England, 172
Escoffier, Auguste, 116, 251
Exodus, 215

Fairway (New York City), 116, 121
Farkas, Pista (Gypsy band leader), 313
Fenákel, Lajos (cantor in Moson), 284
Fleischmann, Charles, 216
Flesch, Carl (violinist), 38, 87, 191
Flesch, Zsigmond, (baker in Moson), 62
Fő utca (Main Street). *See* Moson
France, 179, 233, 285, 300
Frankl (later: Berger), Erzsébet (Erzsi), 379, 380; deportation to Auschwitz, 381
Franz Joseph, Emperor, 20, 108, 110, 204, 363
Frigyes bácsi. *See* Berger, Frigyes
Friedmann (family in Moson), 38

Genesis, 299
Georgia, 315
German-speaking Jews in Hungary. *See* Hungarian Jews
German occupation of Hungary, xi, xii
Germany, 130, 136, 172, 211, 248, 251, 321, 343, 357, 366
Gróf, Árpád, 220
Győr: assimilation in the Jewish community of, 12; author's trip to, 3–7; *Casino* of, 16, 20, 21; Hotel Lamm in, 21; Jewish community of, 5, 7, 10–12; *neológ* synagogue of, 10–12, 28; percentage of Jews in, 7; population in 1869, 7; present population of, 6; its occupation by Napoleon's army, 7; relationship in the 1870s between Jews and Gentiles in, 23
Győrsziget: Híd utca (Bridge Street) 6; Jewish cemetery of, 12; Jewish community of, 10, 11; old synagogue of, 10; percentage of Jews in, 7

Halász, Lili, 72, 82, 148, 210
Heatter, Maida, 309
Heatter, Saidie, 309

Hebrew Ladies' Society (of Moson). *See* Moson
Heine, Heinrich, 240, 241, 248
Hellmesberger, Joseph H., Jr., (Pepi), (violinist), 191
Herbst-Krausz, Zorica, 104, 198, 315
Herz, Imre, 190
Híd utca. *See* Győrsziget
Hirsch, Ludwig, 18
Holland, 201
Holocaust, xi
Horváth, Teréz, 56, 69
Hungarian, cuisine. *See* in Index of Recipes and Foods
Hungarian identity, of Jews, 18
Hungarian Jewish Congress (1868–1869), 7, 8
Hungarian Jewish community: *neológ* movement in, 7; Orthodox Judaism in, 8; *status quo ante* movement in, 8; structural disunity in, 8
Hungarian Jewish cuisine. *See* in the Index of Recipes and Foods
Hungarian Jews: assimilationist social contract, 18; emancipation of, 7, 23; German-speaking, 9, 176; patriotism of, 176; role in the rise of capitalism, 8; Sephardim a tiny minority among, 56; urban concentration of, 7; Yiddish-speaking, 9
Hungarian language, replacing German in schools, 16; embraced by Hungarian Jews, 18, 176
Hungarian nationalism, in the 19th century, 18; of Jews, 18–20
Hungarian revolution of 1956. *See* Hungary
Hungary: antisemitism in, 18, 19, 35; civil marriages in, 26; German occupation of, xi, xii; Hungarians as a minority in, 18; Millenium of, 19; minorities in, 18; 1956 revolution in, 5; 1919 Communist revolution in, 24; percentage of Jews in, 7; population of, 18; rise of capitalism in, 7, 8

Iceland, 201
Ilka (Lujza néni's servant), 54, 69, 206

Ilka néni. *See* Decker, Ilka
Iran, 315
Ibn Ezra, Abraham, 318
Isaac Ben Moses (rabbi, 13th-century Vienna), 240
Israel, 215
Isserlein, Israel Ben Pethahiah (rabbi, 15th-century Austria), 240
Italy, 179, 233

Jerusalem, 215, 306
Jewish, Congress. *See* Hungarian Jewish Congress
Jewish cuisine. *See* in the Index of Foods and Recipes
Jewish observance and religious customs: blessing over bread, 79; *kapparot* ceremony, 282; morning prayer, 48; restoring a *treyf* knife, 76; ritual hand washing, 79
Jewish self-hatred, 380
Jews. *See* Ashkenazi Jews; Hungarian Jewish community; Sephardi Jews
Jobs, women discouraged from taking, 17
Judah Maccabeus, 306

Kashrut, rules of, 4, 143, 343
Kauders, Abraham, 296
Kauders, Jacob, 296
Kirchan (17th-century rabbi), 216
Koppi, Pál, 210
Koshering, of poultry, 57, 58, 212
Körmend, 296
Korzó. *See* Moson
Kreuzer, xiii, 271, 292, 313
Kushner, Rabbi Harold, 215

Lang, George, 123, 169, 170, 241, 242, 244, 315, 407
Lasner, Karl (cellist), 191
Lenin Street (Moson), 36
Levél (village near Moson), 47
Letter writing, role in women's life, 12–16
Leviathan, 220
Lithuania, 248
Louvre, 225
Löwin, Miklós, 36, 46, 407
Löwin, Miksa, 335, 336
Lujza néni. *See* Baruch, Lujza

Machzor Vitry, 285
Main Street (Fő utca). *See* Moson
Manna, 215
Mendelsohn, Ezra, 407
Messiah, 220, 343
Millenium. *See* Hungary
Mishnah, 220, 240
Mocca coffeehouse. *See* Moson
Monarchy. *See* Austro-Hungarian Monarchy
Moravia, 330
Mormon Church, Family History Center of, 4
Moses, 299
Moson, (since 1939 part of Mosonmagyaróvár): antisemitism in, xi; author's mother reminiscing of, 3; author's visit to, xi, 35–46; Catholic cemetery in, 208; deportation of Jews in, 37; Duna utca (Danube Street) in, 57, 69, 280; Fő utca (Main Street) in, 36, 57, 191, 208, 210, 335; ghetto (in 1944) xi, 37, 381; grain trade in, 28; Hebrew Ladies' Society of, 38, 191, 313; Jewish cemetery in, 36, 46, 382–384; Jewish community of, xi, 28, 29, 36–38; Jewish population of, 28; *korzó* in, 36, 210; kosher butchers in, 57, 76, 199; market in, 49, 53, 211, 220; middle class of, 148; Mocca coffeehouse in, 210, 268; night watchman in, 207–210; Ostermayer Street in, 36, 62; relationship between Jews and Gentiles, xi, 28, 29, 38; *shochet*'s cabin in, 57; synagogue in, 37, 57, 214, 238, 268, 283, 284, 298, 299; Vilmos Rév Street in, 57; White Horse (Weisses Rössl) Inn in, 191, 313
Mosoni Duna (a branch of the River Danube), 36, 56, 148; beach on, 148, 195; *tashlikh* ceremony at, 280
Mukachevo (Munkács), 321

Napoleon, 7
Nathan, Joan, 407
National identity, 18
Nationalism. *See* Hungarian nationalism
Neológ movement. *See* Hungarian Jewish community

Neu-Isenburg, 326
Nikisch, Arthur (conductor and pianist), 191
Norway, 201
Novák, Károly (Riza's Catholic friend), 15, 16, 21; as organist in the Győr synagogue, 25, 26; his desire to become a Jew, 26; marriage to a Jewish woman, 26, 27

Oetker, Dr. August, 152
Orthodox Judaism. *See* Hungarian Jewish community
Ördögh (butcher in Moson), 76
Ostermayer Street. *See* Moson

Paula (Riza néni's servant): bathing in the laundry room, 73, 74; cooking at Riza néni's, 55, 77; cooking plum butter, 69; familiarity with Jewish customs and dietary laws, 47, 341; force-feeding geese, 54; koshering poultry, 57, 212; leaving Riza néni, 380; making bread, 60–62; making noodles and strudel dough, 82, 83; plucking geese, 57; setting fire in the stove, 72; sleeping in the kitchen, 73; teaching the grandchildren how to cook, 80
Pépin, Jacques, 196
Peru, 56
Poland, 212, 225, 248
Pollák, Julia, 16, 26, 27, 216
Pollák, Mina, intermarriage and conversion of, 26, 27
Pollák, Ludwig, 27, 28
Population: Jewish of Moson in 1880, 28; Magyar of Hungary in 1867, 18; of Győr at the present, 6; of Győr in 1869, 7; of Hungary in 1867, 18
Prague, 321

Rába (river), 6
Rabl (neighbor in Moson), 53
Ránki, Vera, 18
Rappach (Riza's Jewish friend), 25
Riza néni. *See* Baruch, Therese
Roden, Claudia, 221, 251
Russia, 56, 212

Sacher, 133
Sándor bácsi. *See* Berger, Sándor
Saphir, Moritz G., 248
Schiller, Friedrich, 241
Schlesinger (kosher butcher in Moson), 57
Schmidt (Riza's friend), 24, 25
Schratt, Katharina, 204, 363
Schwarmeier (entertainer in Győr), 27
Scotland, 201
Sephardi, Jewish cooking. *See* in the Index of Recipes and Foods
Sephardi Jews, 180, 216, 240, 315; in Hungary, 56
Serkes, Rabbi Joel Ben Samuel, 321
Sheitel, 193, 194
Sheraton, Mimi, 225
Sommer, Frida, 207
Spain, 166
Stadler (family in Moson), 38, 207, 333
Status quo ante movement of Hungarian Jews. *See* Hungarian Jewish community
Swabian(s) (German minority in Hungary), 47, 54, 191, 210, 379
Szathmáry, Louis, 226

Talmud, 220, 322
Temple, the Second (Jerusalem), desecration of, 306; destruction of, 215
Teutsch, Reinhold (Holdi), 210
The Jewish Museum (New York City), 337
Toklas, Alice B., 116
Torah, 297, 299
Tóth, Antal, pub of (Moson), 38, 313
Turkey, 315
Turks: Turkish occupation of Hungary (1541–1686), 170, 172, 274; Turkish siege of Vienna (1683), 288

Union Square green market (New York City), 121
Ukraine, 212, 321

Venesz, József, 123
Vienna, 3, 36, 46, 108, 191, 242, 288, 339
Vilmos Rév Street. *See* Moson

Wagner, Richard, 208
Wertheimer (family in Moson), 38, 380

White Horse (Weisses Rössl) Inn. *See* Moson
Wieselburg (the German name of Moson).
   See Moson
World War I, 76

World War II, 24, 274, 284

Yeshiva, 16
Yiddish language, in Hungary, 9

Index of Recipes and Foods

Page numbers of recipes included in the book appear in boldface.

Almonds
    almond-chocolate kisses, **372**
    almond macaroons, **179**
    almond-meringue noodles, **126**
    almond-studded meatballs in sweet-and-sour sauce, **96**
    chocolate-almond cookies, **366**
    jam or almond turnovers (or crescents), **159**
    lemon-almond torte, **261**
    meringue-almond clusters, **370**
    meringue-coated almond sandwich cookies, **187**
    meringue torte with almond cookie dough base, **257**
Anchovy eggs: *see* Appetizers
Appetizers and light luncheon dishes (in Hungary, light supper dishes)
    anchovy eggs, **204**
    chopped calves' liver, **198**
    chopped smoked beef in scrambled eggs, **195**
    diced pickle and carrot sausage, **196**
    flatbread for snack, **62**
    pickled herring, **200**
Apples
    apple-filled noodle dough "wheels," **163**
    apple kugel, **251**
    apple-matzo kugel, **347**
    applesauce-filled yeast crêpes, **142**
    apple torte, **255**
    bread kugel with raisins and diced apples, 247

    candied apple fritters, **309**
    rice and apple pudding with wine sauce, **145**
    sliced apple filling for yeast crêpes, **142**
Apricots
    preserves, 144
    jam or *lekvár*, 357, 358
    apricot-filled potato dessert dumplings, **130**
    apricot jam-filled crêpes, **142**
    baked apricot foam, **143**
Arugula, 110
Ashkenazi Jewish cooking
    braided oval-shaped challah in, 216
    braised meat dishes in, 99
    cholent tradition in, 240
    differences in, 315
    fondness for sweet-and-sour flavors in, 96, 98
    helzel and cholent dumplings in, 244
    honey cakes in, 285
    in general, 155
    in Hungary, 56
    kugels in, 247
    mixing of sweet and savory flavors in, 350
    poppy seed desserts in, 172
Aspic
    pike in sour aspic, **225**
Austrian cuisine
    as major influence on Riza néni's cooking, 212
    reflection of social classes in, 109
    tomatoes in, 56

INDEX OF RECIPES AND FOODS

Bacon
  as eaten by assimilated Jews, 60
  paprika bacon, 196
Back-Oblaten (edible baking wafers), 366
Baked apricot foam, **143**
Baking powder
  introduction in Austria and Hungary, 152, 309
Barches: *see* Challah
Beans (dried)
  cholent, **239**
Beans (fresh): *see* Green beans
Beef
  almond-studded meatballs in sweet-and-sour sauce, **96**
  beef-vegetable soup, 79, **88**
  boiled beef, **86**
  braised beef with vegetable sauce, **99**
  cholent, **239**
  chopped smoked beef in scrambled eggs, 195
  koshering of, 100
  liver dumplings for soup, **91**
  ritual slaughter of cows, 99
Beets: *see* borscht at Soups
Bing cherries, 170
Biscuits
  farmer cheese biscuits, **152**
  ginger-flavored soup biscuits, **89**
Boiled beef, **86**
Borscht: *see* Soups
Braising
  braised beef with vegetable sauce, **99**
  braised chicken with game sauce, **93**
  braised veal cutlets in onion-lemon sauce, **101**
  braised veal tongue "Bohemian" style, **104**
Bread
  bread crumbs, as use for stale bread, 156
  bread dumplings (savory), 81
  bread kugel with raisins and diced apples, **247**
  bread making at Riza néni's, 60
  bread pudding in noodle dough, **155**
  butter challah, **215**
  flatbread for snack, 62
  plum-filled bread dumplings (dessert), **133**
  starter for dough, 60
  taking it to the baker in Moson, 62

Cabbage
  cabbage dumplings, 108
  cabbage flatbread (cabbage *lángos*), **66**
  layered, 81
  stuffed, 81, 299
Cakes
  chocolate gugelhupf, **291**
  corn cake, **67**
  fruit cake, **166**
  nut hoop, **333**
  rich gugelhupf, **288**
  sour cherry cake, **169**
  wine cake, **299**
  see also Pastries; Tortes
Candied apple fritters, **309**
Carp
  about, 220
  buying, 221
  carp (or pike) with walnut-vegetable sauce, **315**
  poached carp in vinegary broth with horseradish, **220**
Carrots
  diced pickle and carrot sausage, **196**
  eating during Rosh Hashanah, 280
Challah
  butter challah, **215**
  making challah at Riza néni's, 211
Cheese
  cottage cheese filling for yeast crêpes, **143**
  farmer cheese biscuits, **152**
  farmer cheese soufflé filling for yeast crêpes, **143**
Cherries: *see* Bing cherries; Sour cherries
Chestnuts
  about, 232
  chestnut torte, **232**
Chicken
  braised chicken with game sauce, **93**
  chicken or squab stuffed under the skin, **229**

INDEX OF RECIPES AND FOODS 417

chicken soup, 282, 341
cleaning, 57
cracklings (*griebenes*), 66, **111**
koshering, 58, 59
ritual slaughter of, 57
Chocolate
  almond-chocolate kisses, **372**
  chocolate glaze (for spice torte and macaroon torte), **273**, **365**
  chocolate gugelhupf, **291**
  chocolate-almond cookies, **366**
Cholent, **239**
Cholent *knaydl* (cholent dumpling): see *Ganef*
Chopped liver
  chopped calves' liver, **198**
  why Riza néni didn't make it from chicken liver, 199
  see also Liver
Coarse semolina: *see* Semolina
Cocoa-filled yeast crêpes, **142**
Coffee with matzo, 343
Corn cake (prósza), **67**
Cone sugar, 71
Cookies
  almond macaroons, **179**
  almond-chocolate kisses, **372**
  chocolate-almond cookies, **366**
  cookies as in Brno, **330**
  evening flowers, **184**
  hazelnut macaroons, **369**
  hazelnut slices, **185**
  meringue-almond clusters, **370**
  meringue-coated almond sandwich cookies, **187**
  sponge dough discs, **182**
  walnut meringue kisses, **374**
Cracklings (chicken)
  in flatbread, **66**
  with cabbage dumplings, **111**
Cranberries, 170, 180, 181
Crêpes
  yeast crêpes, **139**
    fillings for (apricot jam, prune butter and ground walnuts, ground walnuts alone, cocoa, cooked walnut paste, poppy seed paste, apple sauce, cooked sliced apples, cottage cheese, farmer cheese soufflé, or vanilla sauce), **142–143**
Cucumbers
  fermented dill pickles, **123**

Dacquoise, 363
Dairy menus
  for Fridays 212
  for Shavuot, 216
Derelye (jam-filled noodle dough squares), 81
Derma, 244
Desserts
  baked apricot foam, **143**
  rice and apple pudding with wine sauce, **145**
  see also Cakes; Cookies; Crêpes; Dessert dumplings; Fritters; Hot noodle desserts; Pastries; Strudels; Tortes
Diced pickle and carrot sausage, **196**
Dill
  fermented dill pickles, **123**
  sweet-and-sour summer squash with dill, 81
Dumplings
  dessert
    farina dessert dumplings, **128**
    jam-filled potato-matzo dumplings, **357**
    napkin dessert dumpling with vanilla sauce, **136**
    plum-filled bread dumplings, **133**
    potato dessert dumplings, 82, **130**
  savory
    bread dumplings, 81
    cabbage dumplings, 81, **108**
    cholent dumpling (*ganef*), **244**
    egg dumplings for green pea soup, **83**
    farina-potato dumplings, 81, **111**
    liver dumplings for soup, **91**
    matzo balls, **344**
    napkin dumplings, 81
    potato dumplings, 81, **113**

Eggs
  anchovy eggs, **204**

Eggs *(continued)*
  chopped smoked beef in scrambled eggs, 195
Evening flowers, **184**

Fächer Torte, 325
Farina
  compared to semolina, 107
  farina dessert dumplings, **128**
  farina-potato dumplings, 81, **111**
  noodles with toasted farina, 82, **107**
Farmer cheese biscuits, **152**
Fermented dill pickles, **123**
Filo (phyllo), 274
Fish
  as part of the Sabbath tradition, 220
  Ashkenazi Jewish tradition of eating freshwater fish, 220
  fish with walnut-vegetable sauce, **315**
  see also Carp; Herring; Pike; Whitefish
Fládni (also *flódni*), 172, **325**
Flatbread for snack
  baked 60, **62**
  fried, **66**
  made with cabbage, **66**
  made with dill, **66**
  made with cracklings, **66**
  rubbed with garlic, **66**
  with sour cream, **66**
Focaccia, 63
Fritters
  candied apple fritters, **309**
  Lujza néni's matzo fritters, **355**
  pastry fritters, **305**
  Riza néni's matzo fritters, **354**
Fruit cake, **166**
Frying oil, ways to measure its temperature, 308

Ganef (cholent dumpling), **244**, 247
Gefilte fish
  absence in Riza néni's cooking, 211, 212
  pike in, 225
Gelatin
  about kosher pareve gelatin, 261
Ginger (powdered dried)
  dried compared to fresh, 89
  ginger-flavored soup biscuits, **89**

past popularity in Hungary, 55
Goose
  buying, 54
  corn mush for feed, 55
  force-feeding, 54, 55
  fricassee of goose
    with chestnut sauce, 280
    with horseradish sauce or applesauce, 341
  goose cracklings, 195
  goose liver, 55, 199, 244
  inarsz (goose "bacon"), 196
  plucking, 57
  rendered goose fat (*schmaltz*), 71, 84, 258, 330
  roast goose, 87, 214, 341
  stuffed goose neck (*halsli*), **244**
Gooseberry sauce for boiled beef, 86, **98**
Green beans
  flat beans or Italian romano beans, 120
  green beans (in spiced vinegar sauce), **120**
  snap beans or string beans, 120
  wax beans, 121
Green peas
  frozen compared to fresh, 83, 84
  green pea purée, 81, **119**
  green pea soup with egg dumplings, **83**
  peas with rice (*risibisi*), 81
Green peppers, stuffed, 81
Griebenes: *see* cracklings
Gugelhupfs, 53
  chocolate gugelhupf, **291**
  custom of eating it at the end of the fast on Yom Kippur, 284
  rich gugelhupf, **288**

Halsli: *see* Stuffed goose neck
Hamantaschen, 172, 318
Handwritten recipe collections, as part of family traditions, 133
Haroset, 337
Hazelnuts
  hazelnut macaroons, **369**
  hazelnut slices, **185**
Herring
  about cured herring, 200
  in Ashkenazi Jewish cuisine, 201

milt herring, 202
pickled herring, 200
Honey
  association with Rosh Hashanah, 285
  honey cookies, 285
  past use in Jewish education, 285
Horseradish, with poached carp in vinegary broth, 220
Hot noodle desserts
  in Austria and Hungary, 126
  almond-meringue noodles, 126
  derelye (jam-filled raviolis), 81
  potato noodles with poppy seeds, 318
Hungarian cuisine
  beginnings of tomato's popularity in, 56
  paprika becoming the predominant seasoning in, 55, 121
  popular seasonings before the nineteenth century in, 55
  preference for long-cooked vegetables in, 77
  reflection of social classes in, 109
Hungarian Jewish cuisine
  dominance of Ashkenazi influence in, 56
  exceptions in, 104
  marginality of chopped liver in, 198, 315
  marginality of gefilte fish in, 212, 225
  novelty of tomatoes in, 56
  rare Sephardi influence in, 315
  rarity of borscht in, 79, 80
  versions of cholent in, 241, 242

Inarsz (goose "bacon"), 196
Indianerkrapfen, 167

Jam or almond turnovers, 159
Jewish cuisine
  boiled noodle desserts in, 155
  foods loosely associated with holidays, 104
  foods specific to a holiday, 104
  long-cooked vegetables in, 77
  macaroons in, 180
  sponge dough in, 182
  see also Ashkenazi Jewish cooking; Hungarian Jewish cusine; Sephardi Jewish cooking

Kindli, 172, 320
Kishke, 244
Kohlrabi
  braised, 116
  soup, 81
  stuffed, 81
Kugels (baked Sabbath puddings)
  apple kugel, 247, 248, 251
  apple-matzo kugel, 347
  bread kugel with raisins and diced apples, 247
  cholent kugel or *Schalet Kugel* (cholent dumpling), 244, 247
  lokshen kugel, 126, 155, 248
  matzo kugel, 350
  potato kugel, 248
Kreplach (filled noodle dough dumplings), 155, 282, 299, 315
Kvass, 123

Lángos: see Flatbread for snack
Lekvár
  about, 128
  see also Apricots; Plum or prune butter
Lemons
  lemon-almond torte, 261
  onion-lemon sauce (for veal cutlets), 101
Liver, calves'
  chopped calves' liver, 198
  compared to beef liver, 91
  koshering of, 92
  liver dumplings for soup, 79, 91
Lokshen kugel: see *Kugels*

Macaroons
  almond macaroons, 179
  hazelnut macaroons, 369
  macaroon torte, 362
  their history, 179
  their popularity among Jews, 180
Matzo
  apple-matzo kugel, 347
  baking it in Moson, 335, 336
  chocolate-matzo torte, 342
  coffee with matzo, 343
  jam-filled potato-matzo dumplings, 357
  layered matzo, 342
  matzo balls, 344

Matzo *(continued)*
  matzo fritters (two versions of), **353**
  matzo kugel, **350**
Meringues
  meringue torte with almond cookie dough base, **257**
  meringue-almond clusters, **370**
  meringue-coated almond sandwich cookies, **187**
Milk soup, 212
Mohntaschen, 318
Mohr im Hemd, 167

Napkin dessert dumplings with vanilla sauce, **136**
Non plus ultra: see Meringue-coated almond sandwich cookies
Noodles
  almond-meringue noodles, **126**
  making noodles at Riza néni's, 82
  noodles with toasted farina, 81, **107**
Noodle dough
  apple kugel, **251**
  apple-filled noodle dough "wheels," **163**
  bread pudding in noodle dough, **155**
  derelye, 81
  Riza néni's use in baked desserts, 155
Nut hoop, **333**

Onions
  onion-lemon sauce for braised veal cutlets, **101**

Palacsinta (also *Palatschinken*): *see* Crêpes
Paprika, beginnings of popularity in Hungary, 55
Passover, foods for
  almond-chocolate kisses, **372**
  chocolate-almond cookies, **366**
  hazelnut macaroons, **369**
  macaroon torte, **362**
  meringue-almond clusters, **370**
  potato flour torte, **360**
  walnut meringue kisses, **374**
  see also Matzo
Pastries
  apple-filled noodle dough "wheels," **163**
  fládni, **325**
  jam or almond turnovers, **159**
  kindli, **320**
  poppy seed squares, **172**
  walnut squares, **176**
Pastry fritters, **305**
Peas: *see* Green peas
Pénecl (fried bread), 60
Phyllo (filo), 274
Pickles
  diced pickle and carrot sausage, **196**
  fermented dill pickles, **123**
  pickled green walnuts, **123**
Pickled herring, **200**
Pike
  about, 225
  buying, 225
  pike (or carp) with walnut-vegetable sauce, **315**
  pike in sour aspic, **225**
Pizza, 63
Plum or prune butter (plum or prune *lekvár*)
  about buying, 128
  filling for *derelye,* 81, 113
  filling for potato dessert dumplings, **130**
  making it at Riza néni's, 69
Plums (Italian or prune)
  plum-filled bread dumplings, 133
  plum-filled potato dessert dumplings, **130**
  plums preserved in spiced vinegar, 70
Poached carp in vinegary broth with horseradish, **220**
Pogácsa: see Farmer cheese biscuits
Poppy seeds
  about buying, grinding, and storing, 173
  poppy seed filling for yeast crêpes, **142**
  poppy seed squares, **172**
  potato noodles with poppy seed, 81, **318**
Pork sausages, as eaten by assimilated Jews, 60, 76
Pörkölt (paprika-seasoned meat stew), 55
Potatoes
  farina-potato dumplings, **111**
  potato dough (for savory and dessert dumplings, short noodles), **113**
  potato kugel, 248
  potato torte, **265**

INDEX OF RECIPES AND FOODS 421

Potato dough
   derelye, 81
   potato dessert dumplings, 82, 113, **130**
   potato dumplings (savory), **111**
   potato noodles, 81, 114, **318**
Potato flour torte, **360**
Poultry
   koshering of, 57, 58
   ritual slaughter of, 57
   see also Chicken; Goose; Squab
Prósza: see Corn cake
Prune butter or *lekvár*: *see* Plum or prune butter

Quince paste, 69

Raspberry syrup, 68
Rice
   rice and apple pudding with wine sauce, **145**
   rice and peas (*risibisi*), 81
Rich gugelhupf, **288**
Rigó Jancsi, 167
Rum baba, 300

Sacher torte, 133
Salzburger Nockerl (Salzburg soufflé)
   almond-meringue noodles, **128**
Sauces
   dessert
      vanilla sauce, **136**
      wine sauce, **145**
   savory
      game sauce (for braised chicken), **93**
      gooseberry sauce for boiled beef, **98**
      onion-lemon sauce (for veal cutlets), **101**
      walnut-vegetable sauce (for fish), **315**
Sausages
   diced pickle and carrot sausage, **196**
Savarin, 300
Schmaltz
   about, 71
   container for, 71
Schnapps, 284
Semolina (coarse), compared to farina, 107
Sephardi Jewish cooking
   fish with walnut sauce in, **315**

   its minimal influence in Hungary, 56
   macaroons in, 180
   round Sabbath loaves in, 216
   Sabbath stew in, 240
   tomatoes in, 56
Soups
   beef-vegetable soup, **88**, 89
   borscht, 79
   caraway seed soup, 79
   chicken soup, 282, 341
   green pea soup with egg dumplings, **83**
   kohlrabi soup, 81
   milk soup, 212
Soup garnishes
   ginger-flavored soup biscuits, 79, **89**
   liver dumplings for soup, 79, **91**
   potato dumplings (small) for soup, **113**
Sour cherries
   about, 170
   buying fresh compared to canned imported, 170
   sour cherries preserved in spiced vinegar, 70
   sour cherry cake, **169**
Sour cream
   flatbread with sour cream, **66**
Sponge dough
   about, 182
   method of baking and cooling, 261
   popularity among Jews, 182
   sponge dough discs, **182**
Sponge fingers (ladyfingers), in baked apricot foam, **145**
Spice torte, **270**
Spice strudel, **274**
Squab (or chicken) stuffed under the skin, **229**
Squash
   sweet-and-sour summer squash with dill, 81
Strudels
   buying strudel leaves, 275
   spice strudel, **274**
   stretching the dough at Riza néni's, 83
   their introduction in Hungary by the Turks, 274
Stuffed goose neck (*halsli*) and cholent dumpling (*ganef*), **244**

Tomatoes
- avoidance during Rosh Hashanah, 280
- in 19th-century Hungarian cooking, 56
- introduction in Hungary, 56
- taboo of, 56

Tortes
- apple torte, **255**
- chestnut torte, **232**
- lemon-almond torte, **261**
- macaroon torte, **362**
- meringue torte with almond cookie dough base, **257**
- potato flour torte, **360**
- potato torte, **265**
- spice torte, **270**
- sponge torte, 261

Turkey, drumstick skin (as substitution for goose neck skin), **244**

Turnovers: *see* Jam or almond turnovers

Vanilla
- napkin dessert dumpling with vanilla sauce, **136**
- vanilla sauce filling for yeast crêpes, **143**

Varenikes (filled dumplings), 155

Veal
- braised veal cutlets in onion-lemon sauce, **101**
- braised veal tongue "Bohemian" style, 81, **104**
- calf lung, 81
- calves' liver dumplings, **91**

Vinegar
- pike in sour aspic, 225
- poached carp in vinegary broth with horseradish, 220
- prune plums or sour cherries preserved in spiced vinegar, 70

Riza's home-made, 222
strength of, 222

Walnuts
- as fertility symbol, 299
- chopped walnut and prune butter filling for yeast crêpes, **142**
- fish with walnut-vegetable sauce, **315**
- ground walnut filling for yeast crêpes, **142**
- nut hoop, **333**
- *papír dió* (paper walnuts), 191
- potato noodles with ground walnut, 81
- tossing them from the synagogue window, 299
- walnut meringue kisses, **374**
- walnut paste filling for yeast crêpes, **142**
- walnut squares, **176**

Whitefish (as substitution for pike)
- pike in sour aspic, **225**

Wine
- at kiddush, 214
- at the *havdalah* ceremony, 270
- at the Seder, 337, 342, 343
- ordering Passover wine, 335
- rice and apple pudding with wine sauce, **145**
- wine cake, **299**

Yeast
- Charles Fleischmann and the beginnings of commercial yeast manufacturing, 216
- Hungarian method of manufacturing, 216
- use before the introduction of baking powder, 152
- yeast crêpes, **139**
- yeast-leavened corn cake, 67

A Note on the Book Ornaments and Typeface

The decorative initials and other book ornaments in this book are based on a sampler Riza néni helped her young daughter prepare in 1896.

The text of this book was set—most appropriately—in a typeface called Kis Classico or Janson Text, which was designed in 1685 by the Hungarian engraver and printer Miklós (Nicholas) Kis. One of the most significant book designers of his age, Kis was born in 1650 in Alsómisztótfalu and died in 1702 in Kolozsvár (today, Cluj), Transylvanian towns that then belonged to Hungary but are now part of Romania. Between 1683 and 1690, Kis lived in Amsterdam, where he studied printing, designed his famous typeface, and used it to publish a bible in Hungarian. He included a Hebrew alphabet in the sample sheet he printed to show various applications of his typeface. Among the books he published when he returned to Transylvania was the first Hungarian cookbook, which Kis dedicated to "honest kitchens . . . without a cook," meaning that it was not intended for the chefs of aristocrats.